RENT-A-GIRLFRIEND

VOLUME 5

REIJI MIYAJIMA

CONTENTS

A Kodansha Comics Trade Paperback Original
Rent-A-Girlfriend 5 copyright © 2018 Reiji Miyajima
English translation copyright © 2021 Reiji Miyajima

Published in the United States by Kodansha Comics, an imprint of Kodansha USA Publishing, LLC, New York.

Publication rights for this English edition arranged through Kodansha Ltd., Tokyo.

First published in Japan in 2018 by Kodansha Ltd., Tokyo as *Kanojo, okarishimasu*, volume 5.

ISBN 978-1-64651-089-4

Original cover design by Kohei Nawata Design Office

Printed in the United States of America.

www.kodanshacomics.com

9 8 7 6 5 4 3 2 1
Translation: Kevin Gifford
Lettering: Paige Pumphrey
Editing: Jordan Blanco
Kodansha Comics edition cover design by Phil Balsman

Publisher: Kiichiro Sugawara

Director of publishing services: Ben Applegate
Associate director of operations: Stephen Pakula
Publishing services managing editor: Noelle Webster
Assistant production manager: Emi Lotto, Angela Zurlo
Logo and character art ©Kodansha USA Publishing, LLC

Young characters and steampunk setting, like *Howl's Moving Castle* and *Battle Angel Alita*

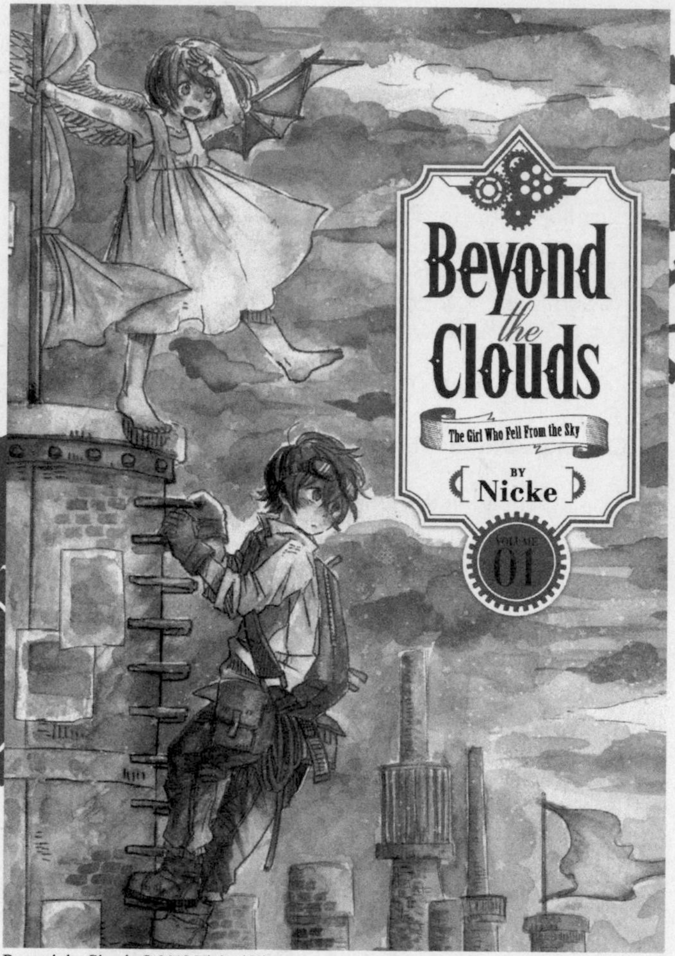
Beyond the Clouds
The Girl Who Fell From the Sky
BY Nicke
VOLUME 01
Beyond the Clouds © 2018 Nicke / Ki-oon

A boy with a talent for machines and a mysterious girl whose wings he's fixed will take you beyond the clouds! In the tradition of the high-flying, resonant adventure stories of Studio Ghibli comes a gorgeous tale about the longing of young hearts for adventure and friendship!

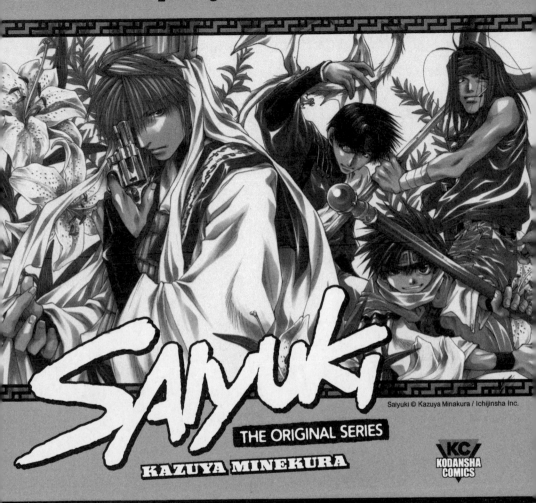

A SMART, NEW ROMANTIC COMEDY FOR FANS OF *SHORTCAKE CAKE* AND *TERRACE HOUSE*!

A romance manga starring high school girl Meeko, who learns to live on her own in a boarding house whose living room is home to the odd (but handsome) Matsunaga-san. She begins to adjust to her new life away from her parents, but Meeko soon learns that no matter how far away from home she is, she's still a young girl at heart — especially when she finds herself falling for Matsunaga-san.

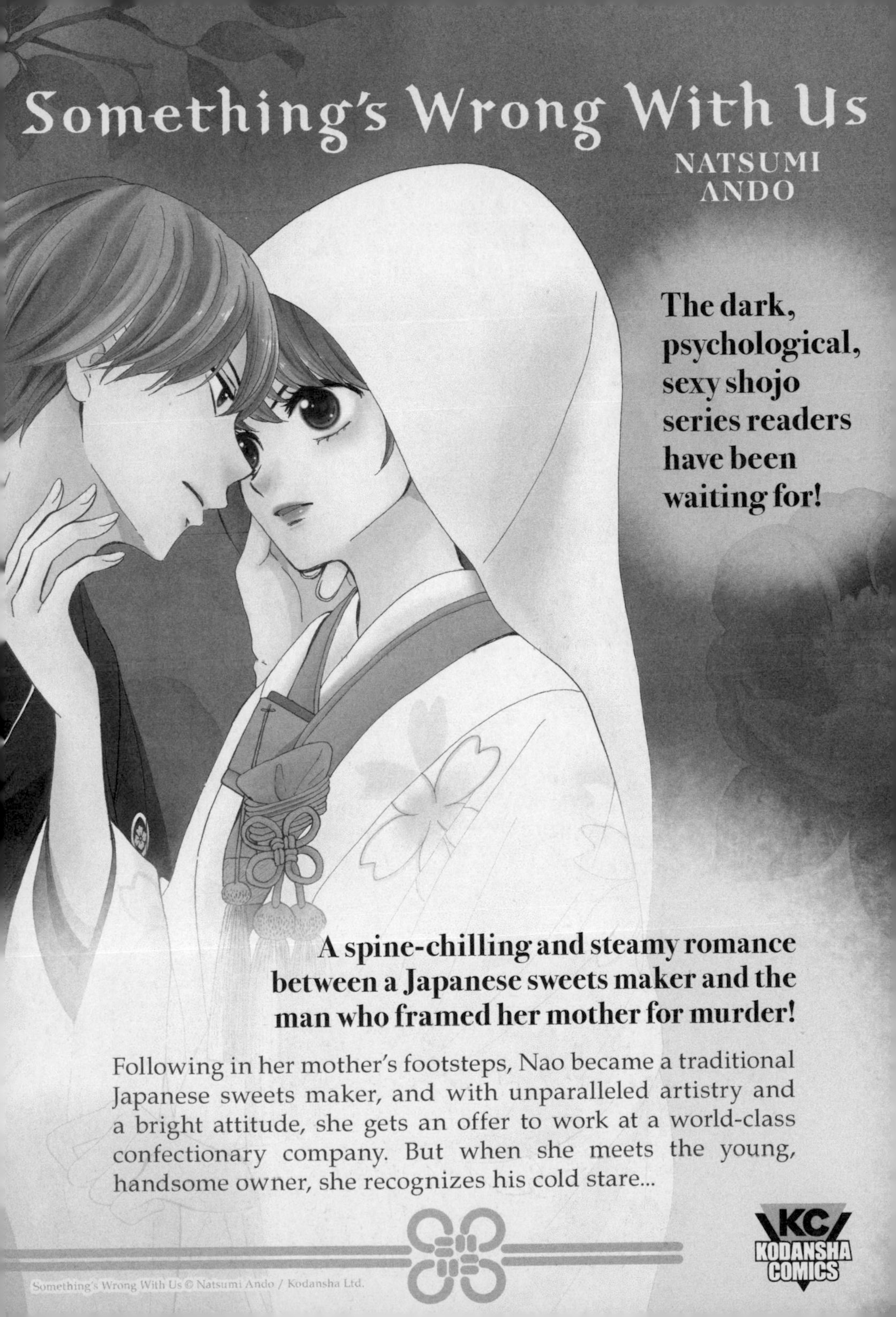
Something's Wrong With Us
NATSUMI ANDO
The dark, psychological, sexy shojo series readers have been waiting for!
A spine-chilling and steamy romance between a Japanese sweets maker and the man who framed her mother for murder!
Following in her mother's footsteps, Nao became a traditional Japanese sweets maker, and with unparalleled artistry and a bright attitude, she gets an offer to work at a world-class confectionary company. But when she meets the young, handsome owner, she recognizes his cold stare...
KC KODANSHA COMICS
Something's Wrong With Us © Natsumi Ando / Kodansha Ltd.

Knight of the ICE

Yayoi Ogawa

Knight of the Ice ©Yayoi Ogawa/Kodansha Ltd.

SKATING THRILLS AND ICY CHILLS WITH THIS NEW TINGLY ROMANCE SERIES!

A rom-com on ice, perfect for fans of *Princess Jellyfish* and *Wotakoi*. Kokoro is the talk of the figure-skating world, winning trophies and hearts. But little do they know... he's actually a huge nerd! From the beloved creator of *You're My Pet* (*Tramps Like Us*).

Chitose is a serious young woman, working for the health magazine *SASSO*. Or at least, she would be, if she wasn't constantly getting distracted by her childhood friend, international figure skating star Kokoro Kijinami! In the public eye and on the ice, Kokoro is a gallant, flawless knight, but behind his glittery costumes and breathtaking spins lies a secret: He's actually a hopelessly romantic otaku, who can only land his quad jumps when Chitose is on hand to recite a spell from his favorite magical girl anime!

KC KODANSHA COMICS

PERFECT WORLD

Rie Aruga

A TOUCHING NEW SERIES ABOUT LOVE AND COPING WITH DISABILITY

An office party reunites Tsugumi with her high school crush Itsuki. He's realized his dream of becoming an architect, but along the way, he experienced a spinal injury that put him in a wheelchair. Now Tsugumi's rekindled feelings will butt up against prejudices she never considered — and Itsuki will have to decide if he's ready to let someone into his heart...

"Depicts with great delicacy and courage the difficulties some with disabilities experience getting involved in romantic relationships... Rie Aruga refuses to romanticize, pushing her heroine to face the reality of disability. She invites her readers to the same tasks of empathy, knowledge and recognition."
—Slate.fr

"An important entry [in manga romance]... The emotional core of both plot and characters indicates thoughtfulness... [Aruga's] research is readily apparent in the text and artwork, making this feel like a real story."
—Anime News Network

SAINT ☆ YOUNG MEN

A LONG AWAITED ARRIVAL IN PREMIUM 2-IN-1 HARDCOVER

After centuries of hard work, Jesus and Buddha take a break from their heavenly duties to relax among the people of Japan, and their adventures in this lighthearted buddy comedy are sure to bring mirth and merriment to all!

"Brilliant...the physical comedy and facial expressions will make you literally LOL."
—Sam Humphries (host of *DC Daily*; writer, *Green Lanterns, Legendary Star-Lord*)

THE SWEET SCENT OF LOVE IS IN THE AIR! FOR FANS OF OFFBEAT ROMANCES LIKE *WOTAKOI*

Sweat and Soap © Kintetsu Yamada / Kodansha Ltd.

In an office romance, there's a fine line between sexy and awkward... and that line is where Asako — a woman who sweats copiously — meets Koutarou — a perfume developer who can't get enough of Asako's, er, scent. Don't miss a romcom manga like no other!

xxxHOLiC © CLAMP-ShigatsuTsuitachi CO.,LTD./Kodansha Ltd.
xxxHOLiC Rei © CLAMP-ShigatsuTsuitachi CO.,LTD./Kodansha Ltd.

Kimihiro Watanuki is haunted by visions of ghosts and spirits. He seeks help from a mysterious woman named Yuko, who claims she can help. However, Watanuki must work for Yuko in order to pay for her aid. Soon Watanuki finds himself employed in Yuko's shop, where he sees things and meets customers that are stranger than anything he could have ever imagined.

The beloved characters from *Cardcaptor Sakura* return in a brand new, reimagined fantasy adventure!

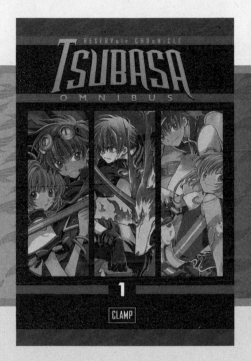

"[*Tsubasa*] takes readers on a fantastic ride that only gets more exhilarating with each successive chapter." —Anime News Network

In the Kingdom of Clow, an archaeological dig unleashes an incredible power, causing Princess Sakura to lose her memories. To save her, her childhood friend Syaoran must follow the orders of the Dimension Witch and travel alongside Kurogane, an unrivaled warrior; Fai, a powerful magician; and Mokona, a curiously strange creature, to retrieve Sakura's dispersed memories!

The art-deco cyberpunk classic from the creators of *xxxHOLiC* and *Cardcaptor Sakura!*

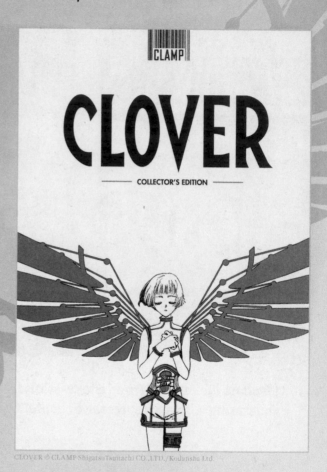

CLOVER © CLAMP-ShigatsuTsuitachi CO.,LTD./Kodansha Ltd

Su was born into a bleak future, where the government keeps tight control over children with magical powers—codenamed "Clovers." With Su being the only "four-leaf" Clover in the world, she has been kept isolated nearly her whole life. Can ex-military agent Kazuhiko deliver her to the happiness she seeks? Experience the complete series in this hardcover edition, which also includes over twenty pages of ravishing color art!

KC
KODANSHA
COMICS

MAGIC KNIGHT RAYEARTH
25TH ANNIVERSARY EDITION
CLAMP

A BELOVED CLASSIC MAKES ITS STUNNING RETURN IN THIS GORGEOUS, LIMITED EDITION BOX SET!

This tale of three Tokyo teenagers who cross through a magical portal and become the champions of another world is a modern manga classic. The box set includes three volumes of manga covering the entire first series of *Magic Knight Rayearth*, plus the series's super-rare full-color art book companion, all printed at a larger size than ever before on premium paper, featuring a newly-revised translation and lettering, and exquisite foil-stamped covers.

A strictly limited edition, this will be gone in a flash!

One of CLAMP's biggest hits returns in this definitive, premium, hardcover 20th anniversary collector's edition!

CLAMP

Chobits

20TH ANNIVERSARY EDITION

Poor college student Hideki is down on his luck. All he wants is a good job, a girlfriend, and his very own "persocom"—the latest and greatest in humanoid computer technology. Hideki's luck changes one night when he finds Chi—a persocom thrown out in a pile of trash. But Hideki soon discovers that there's much more to his cute new persocom than meets the eye.

KC KODANSHA COMICS

THE WORLD OF CLAMP!

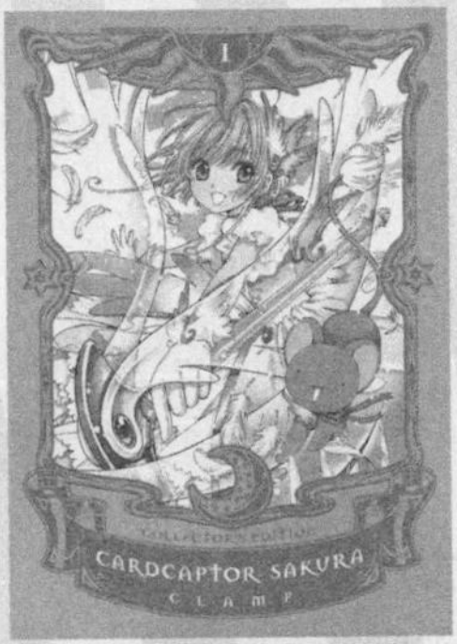
1
CARDCAPTOR SAKURA
CLAMP

Cardcaptor Sakura Collector's Edition

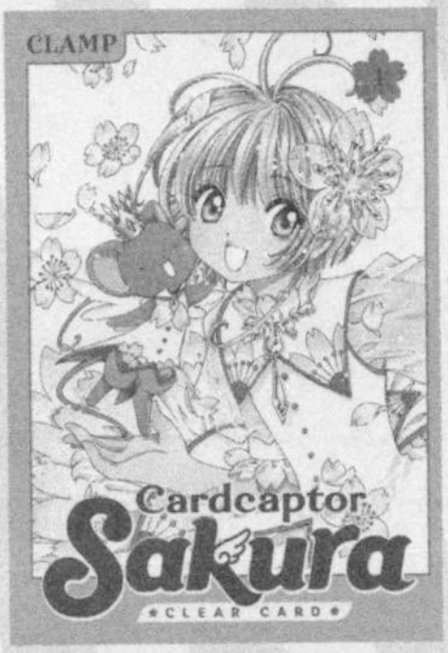
CLAMP
Cardcaptor
Sakura
CLEAR CARD

Cardcaptor Sakura: Clear Card

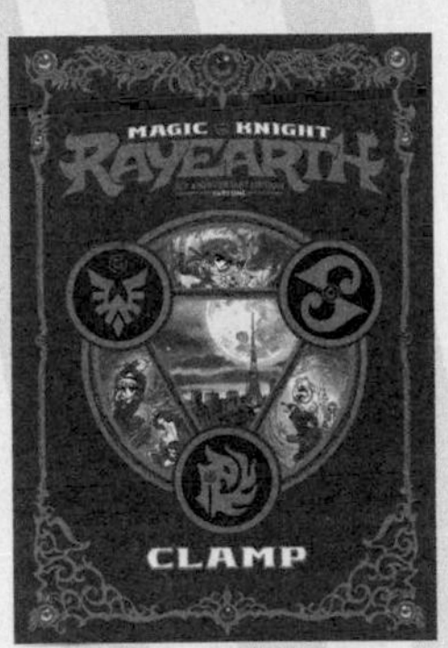
MAGIC KNIGHT
RAYEARTH
CLAMP

Magic Knight Rayearth 25th Anniversary Box Set

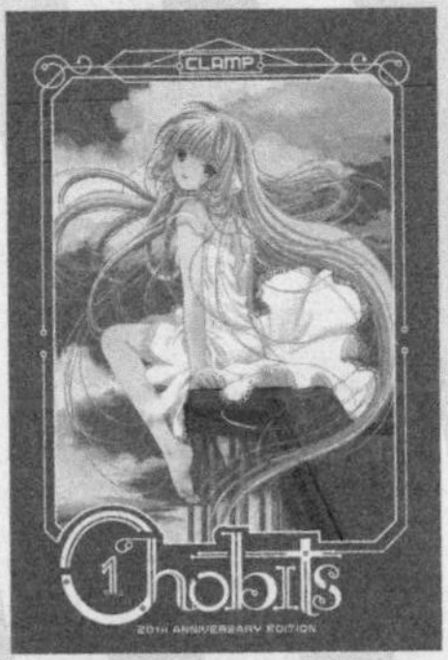
CLAMP
1
Chobits
20th ANNIVERSARY EDITION

Chobits

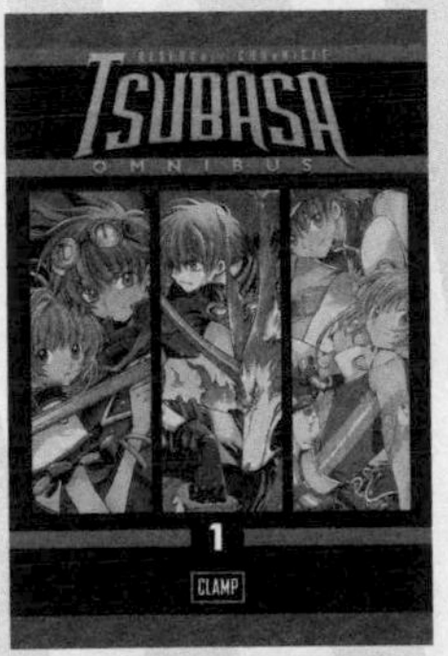
TSUBASA
OMNIBUS
1
CLAMP

TSUBASA Omnibus

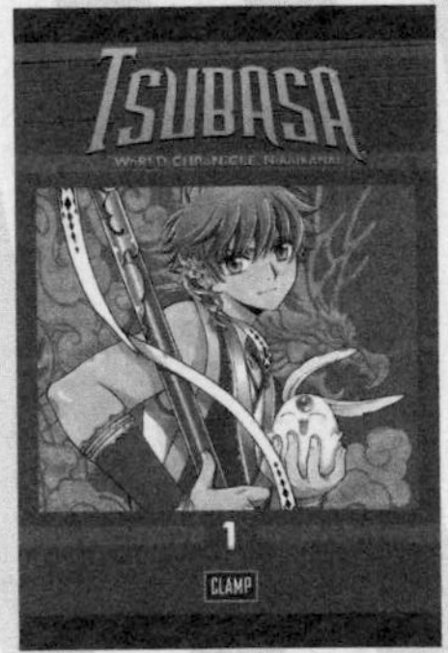
TSUBASA
1
CLAMP

TSUBASA WoRLD CHRoNiCLE

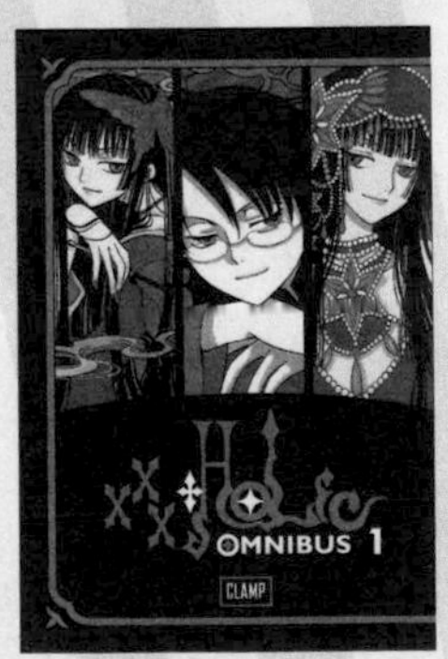
xxxHOLiC
OMNIBUS 1
CLAMP

xxxHOLiC Omnibus

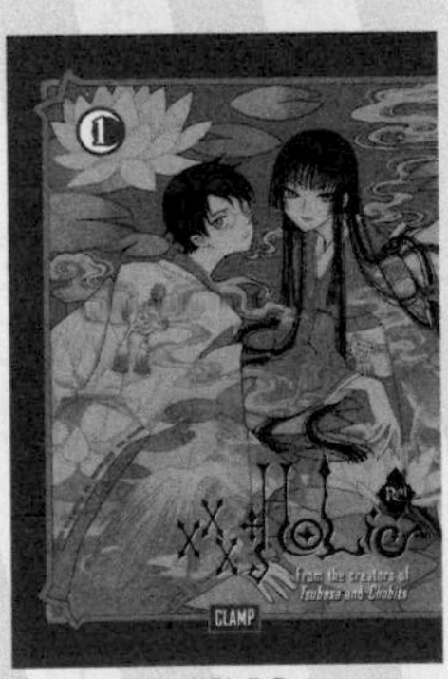
1
xxxHOLiC
From the creators of Tsubasa and Chobits
CLAMP

xxxHOLiC Rei

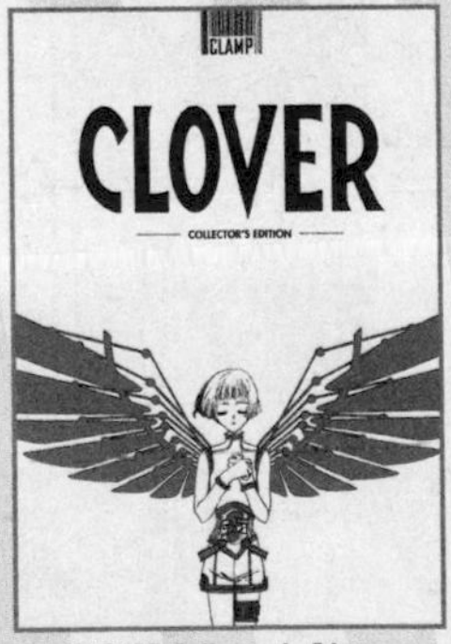
CLAMP
CLOVER
COLLECTOR'S EDITION

CLOVER Collector's Edition

KC KODANSHA COMICS

Kodansha Comics welcomes you to explore the expansive world of CLAMP, the all-female artist collective that has produced some of the most acclaimed manga of the century. Our growing catalog includes icons like *Cardcaptor Sakura* and *Magic Knight Rayearth*, each crafted with CLAMP's one-of-a-kind style and characters!

RENT-A-GIRLFRIEND STAFF: A, IROHKI, TEMAENO, KUSUMI, MITSUKI

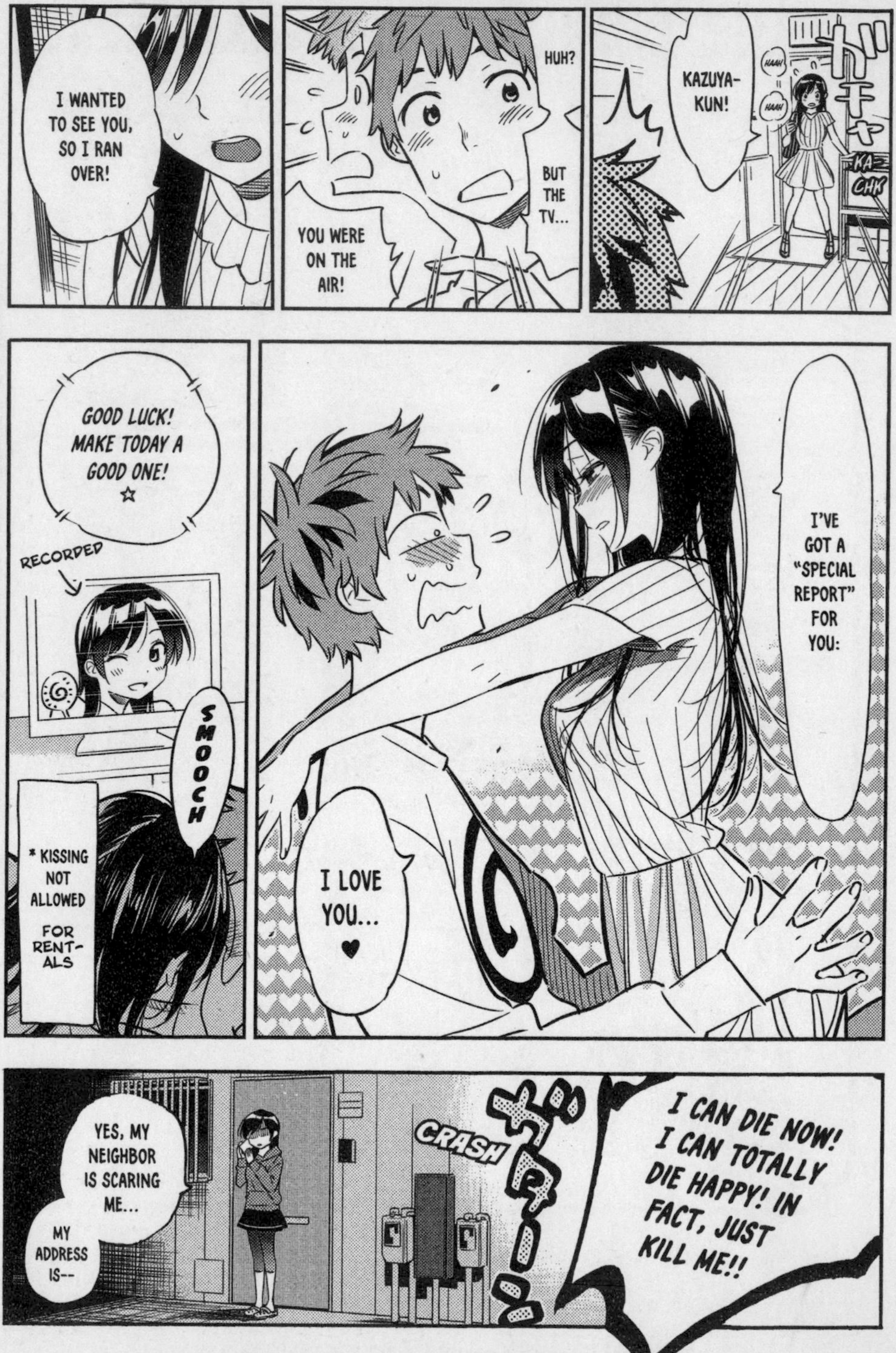
KAZUYA-KUN!
HAAH
HAAH
KA-CHK
HUH?
BUT THE TV...
YOU WERE ON THE AIR!
I WANTED TO SEE YOU, SO I RAN OVER!
I'VE GOT A "SPECIAL REPORT" FOR YOU:
I LOVE YOU... ♥
GOOD LUCK! MAKE TODAY A GOOD ONE! ☆
RECORDED
SMOOCH
* KISSING NOT ALLOWED FOR RENTALS
I CAN DIE NOW! I CAN TOTALLY DIE HAPPY! IN FACT, JUST KILL ME!!
CRASH
YES, MY NEIGHBOR IS SCARING ME...
MY ADDRESS IS--

EDITORS: HIRAOKA-SAN, HIRATSUKA-SAN, CHOKAI-SAN THANKS TO EVERYONE ELSE WHO PICKED THIS UP!

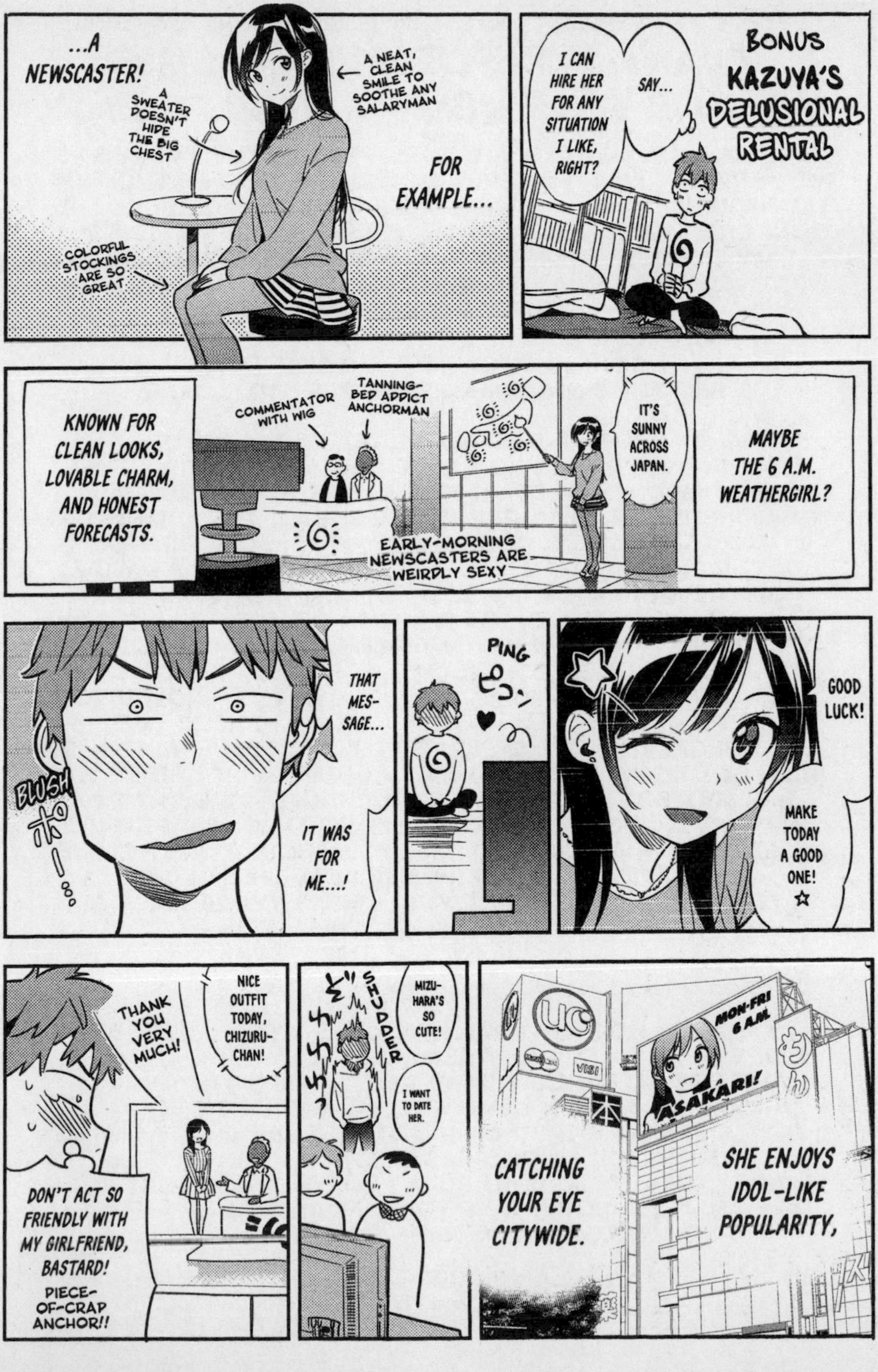
BONUS KAZUYA'S DELUSIONAL RENTAL
SAY...
I CAN HIRE HER FOR ANY SITUATION I LIKE, RIGHT?
FOR EXAMPLE...
...A NEWSCASTER!
A NEAT, CLEAN SMILE TO SOOTHE ANY SALARYMAN
A SWEATER DOESN'T HIDE THE BIG CHEST
COLORFUL STOCKINGS ARE SO GREAT
MAYBE THE 6 A.M. WEATHERGIRL?
IT'S SUNNY ACROSS JAPAN.
TANNING-BED ADDICT ANCHORMAN
COMMENTATOR WITH WIG
EARLY-MORNING NEWSCASTERS ARE WEIRDLY SEXY
KNOWN FOR CLEAN LOOKS, LOVABLE CHARM, AND HONEST FORECASTS.
GOOD LUCK!
MAKE TODAY A GOOD ONE! ☆
PING
ピコン
THAT MES-SAGE...
IT WAS FOR ME...!
BLUSH
ポー
SHE ENJOYS IDOL-LIKE POPULARITY,
MON-FRI 6 A.M.
ASAKARI!
CATCHING YOUR EYE CITYWIDE.
MIZU-HARA'S SO CUTE!
I WANT TO DATE HER.
SHUDDER
NICE OUTFIT TODAY, CHIZURU-CHAN!
THANK YOU VERY MUCH!
DON'T ACT SO FRIENDLY WITH MY GIRLFRIEND, BASTARD!
PIECE-OF-CRAP ANCHOR!!

A BONUS WRITTEN MOSTLY TO ESCAPE REALITY DURING PAGE WORK.

THANK YOU FOR PURCHASING VOLUME 5 OF RENT-A-GIRLFRIEND!

THERE HAS NEVER BEEN A BONUS PAGE IN THE TRADES FOR THIS SERIES, A WILD EXAMPLE OF FALLING BEHIND THE TIMES (ALTHOUGH I'D LIKE TO THINK WE REALLY PACKED IN THE CONTENT IN THE REST OF THE VOLUMES), AND I ALMOST LOST MY CHANCE AT ONE IN THIS VOLUME'S STRICTURE TOO, SO I WENT SO FAR AS TO REMOVE THE PREVIEW PAGE TO STUFF THIS IN HERE.

(LOOKING BACK, IT'S A GOOD THING I PUT THE BONUS MANGA UNDER THE COVER...)

SO I THOUGHT I COULD REVEAL SOME SECRETS BEHIND THE PRODUCTION OF THIS MANGA, BUT THERE'S NOT MUCH SECRET TO IT-I HEARD ABOUT RENTAL GIRLFRIENDS, IT SOUNDED REALLY NEAT, AND I THOUGHT I COULD MAKE A MANGA OUT OF IT...SO I DID! FOR CHIZURU MIZUHARA, ALL I'M DOING IS DRAWING MY IDEA OF THE IDEAL WOMAN-SEXY, STRONG, GENTLE, SEXY (AGAIN), AND TRYING TO LIVE WITH REALITY. BASICALLY, I LIKE SEXY GIRLS WHO HAVE IDEALIST TRAITS AND LET THEIR EMOTIONS GET THE BEST OF THEM. ALSO, GIRLS WHO GET ANGRY. THIS IS IMPORTANT; IT'LL SHOW UP ON THE TEST. AS YOU ALL KNOW, THE MAIN HERO (ME) IS AN INDECISIVE PIECE OF TRASH (I.E. ME), AN EXAMPLE OF HOW SOMEONE CAN BE SPOILED IN EVERY POSSIBLE WAY (I.E. ME). BUT SEEING EVEN TRASH (ME) LIKE THAT BE SUPPORTED, NOT ABANDONED-ISN'T THAT WONDERFUL?! REALLY, WITH AN OAF LIKE ME, YOU SHOULD JUST SMILE, SAY "OH, RIGHT, HEH HEH" AND LEAVE-BUT LOOK AT CHIZURU. SHE YELLS AT YOU, LIKE: "YOU'RE WRONG! YOU CAN'T DO THIS!

I WANTED TO DRAW HER

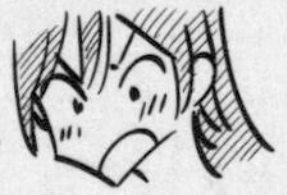

IF THAT'S NOT NATURAL KINDNESS, THEN WHAT IS?! MODERN SOCIETY HAS BEEN DILUTED BY SOCIAL MEDIA AND THE INTERNET, BUT HERE'S HOPING THAT RENT-A-GIRLFRIEND CAN LEND A HAND AND SHOW YOU ALL THE COURAGE, AND THE IMPORTANCE, BEHIND BUILDING REAL, HUMAN RELATIONSHIPS!! ...OH, I'M ALMOST OUT OF SPACE. STILL, I THINK KAZUYA WILL SLOWLY GROW OVER TIME AS WELL. HOPEFULLY YOU'LL WANT TO SPEND A BIT MORE TIME WITH THEM TOO.

VOLUME 6 IS ON SALE NOW!
SHREWDLY THROWING THAT IN,
REIJI MIYAJIMA

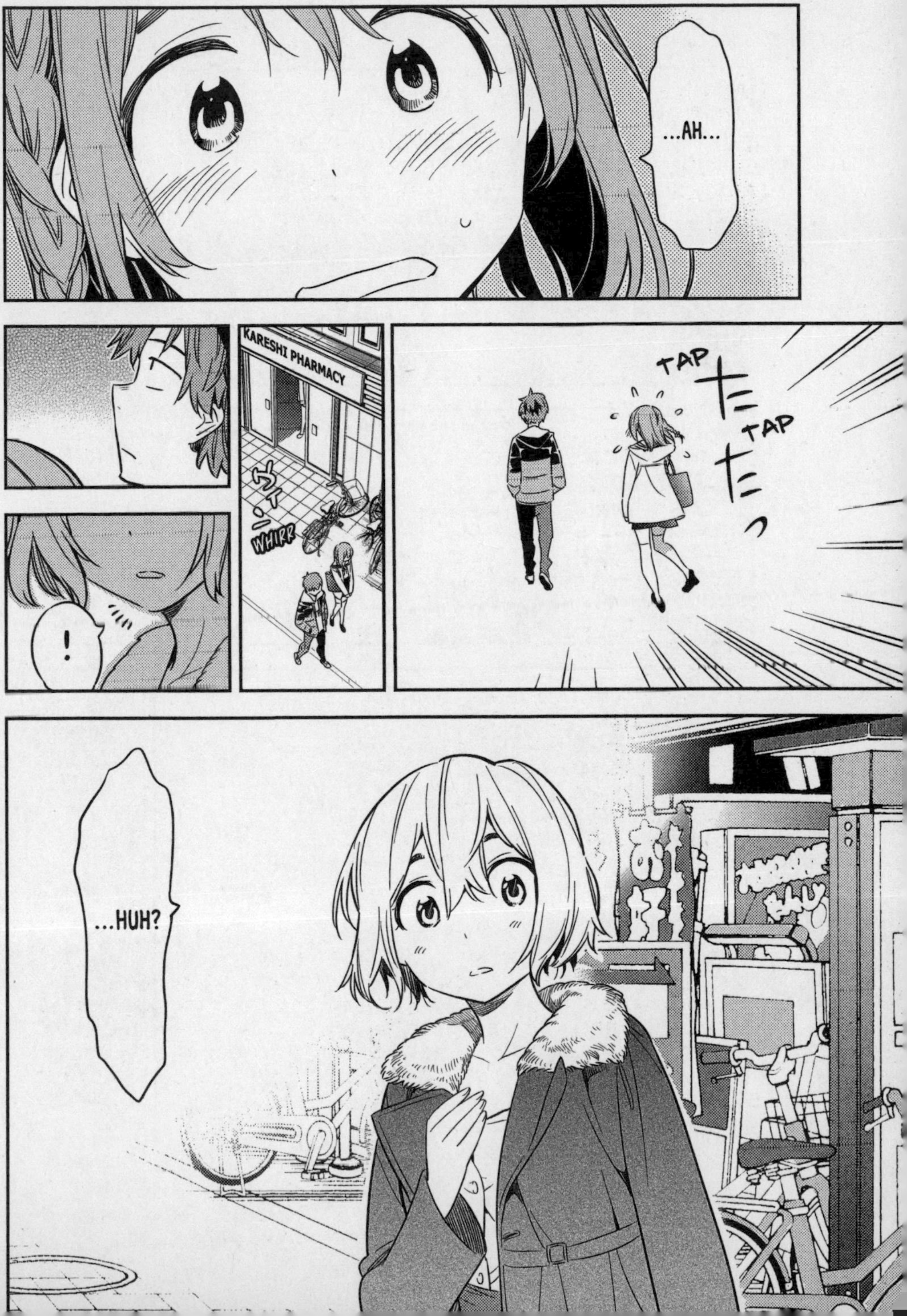

...AH...
TAP
TAP
KARESHI PHARMACY
WHIRR
!
...HUH?

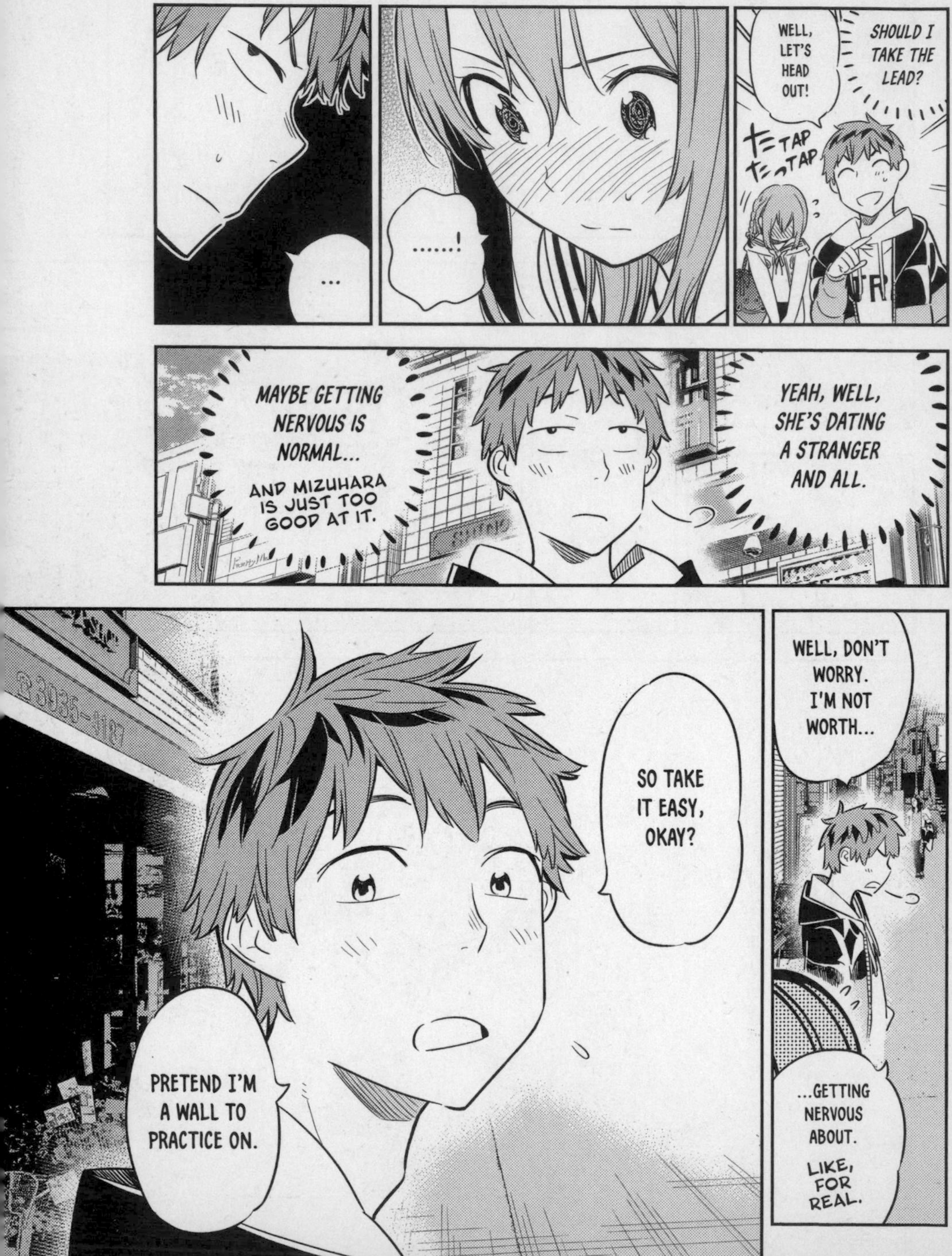
SHOULD I TAKE THE LEAD?
WELL, LET'S HEAD OUT!
TAP TAP
......!
...
YEAH, WELL, SHE'S DATING A STRANGER AND ALL.
MAYBE GETTING NERVOUS IS NORMAL...
AND MIZUHARA IS JUST TOO GOOD AT IT.
WELL, DON'T WORRY. I'M NOT WORTH...
...GETTING NERVOUS ABOUT.
LIKE, FOR REAL.
SO TAKE IT EASY, OKAY?
PRETEND I'M A WALL TO PRACTICE ON.

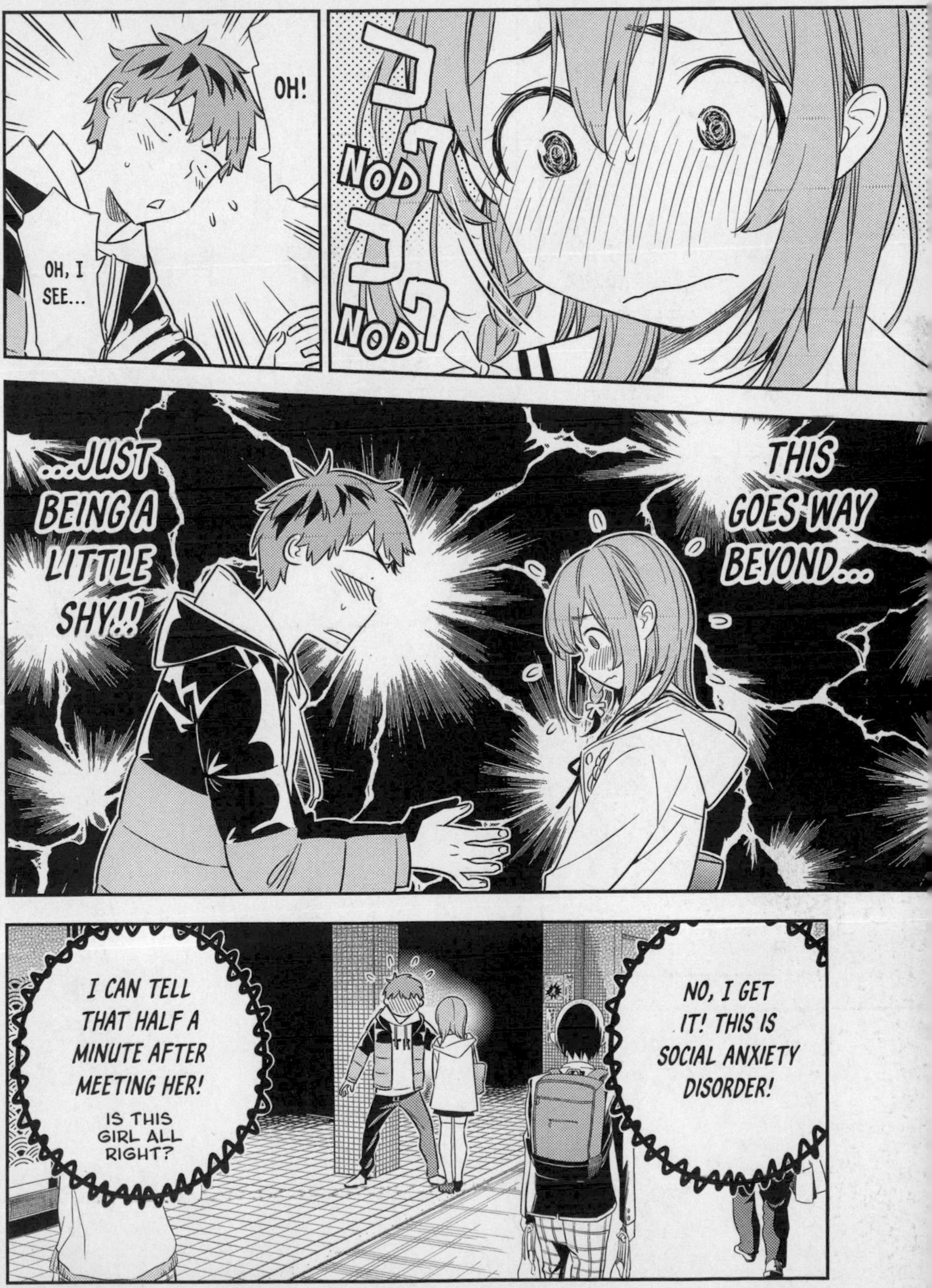
コク
NOD
コク
NOD
OH!
OH, I SEE...
THIS GOES WAY BEYOND...
...JUST BEING A LITTLE SHY!!
NO, I GET IT! THIS IS SOCIAL ANXIETY DISORDER!
I CAN TELL THAT HALF A MINUTE AFTER MEETING HER!
IS THIS GIRL ALL RIGHT?

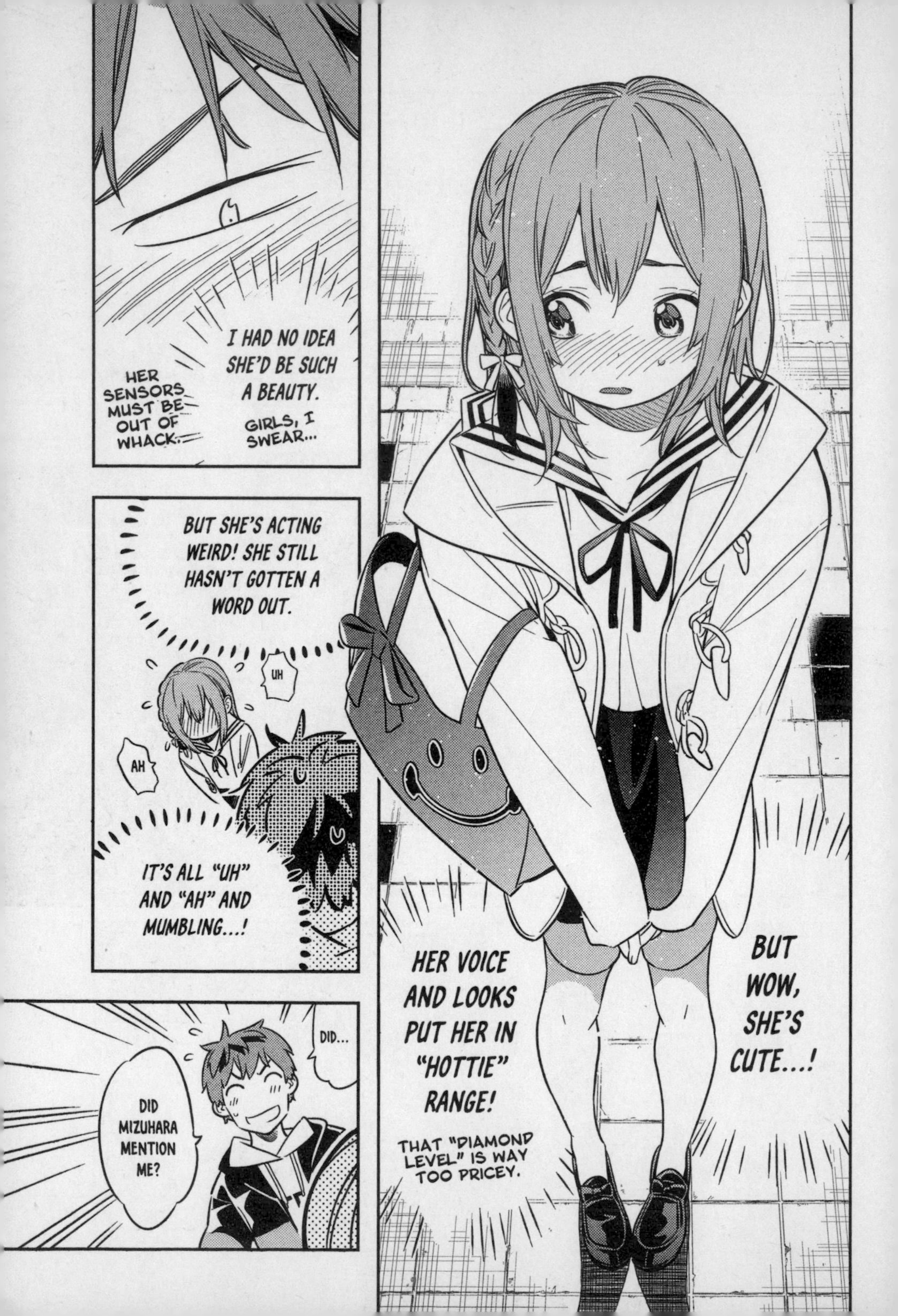
BUT WOW, SHE'S CUTE...!
HER VOICE AND LOOKS PUT HER IN "HOTTIE" RANGE!
THAT "DIAMOND LEVEL" IS WAY TOO PRICEY.
I HAD NO IDEA SHE'D BE SUCH A BEAUTY.
GIRLS, I SWEAR...
HER SENSORS MUST BE OUT OF WHACK.
BUT SHE'S ACTING WEIRD! SHE STILL HASN'T GOTTEN A WORD OUT.
UH
AH
IT'S ALL "UH" AND "AH" AND MUMBLING...!
DID...
DID MIZUHARA MENTION ME?

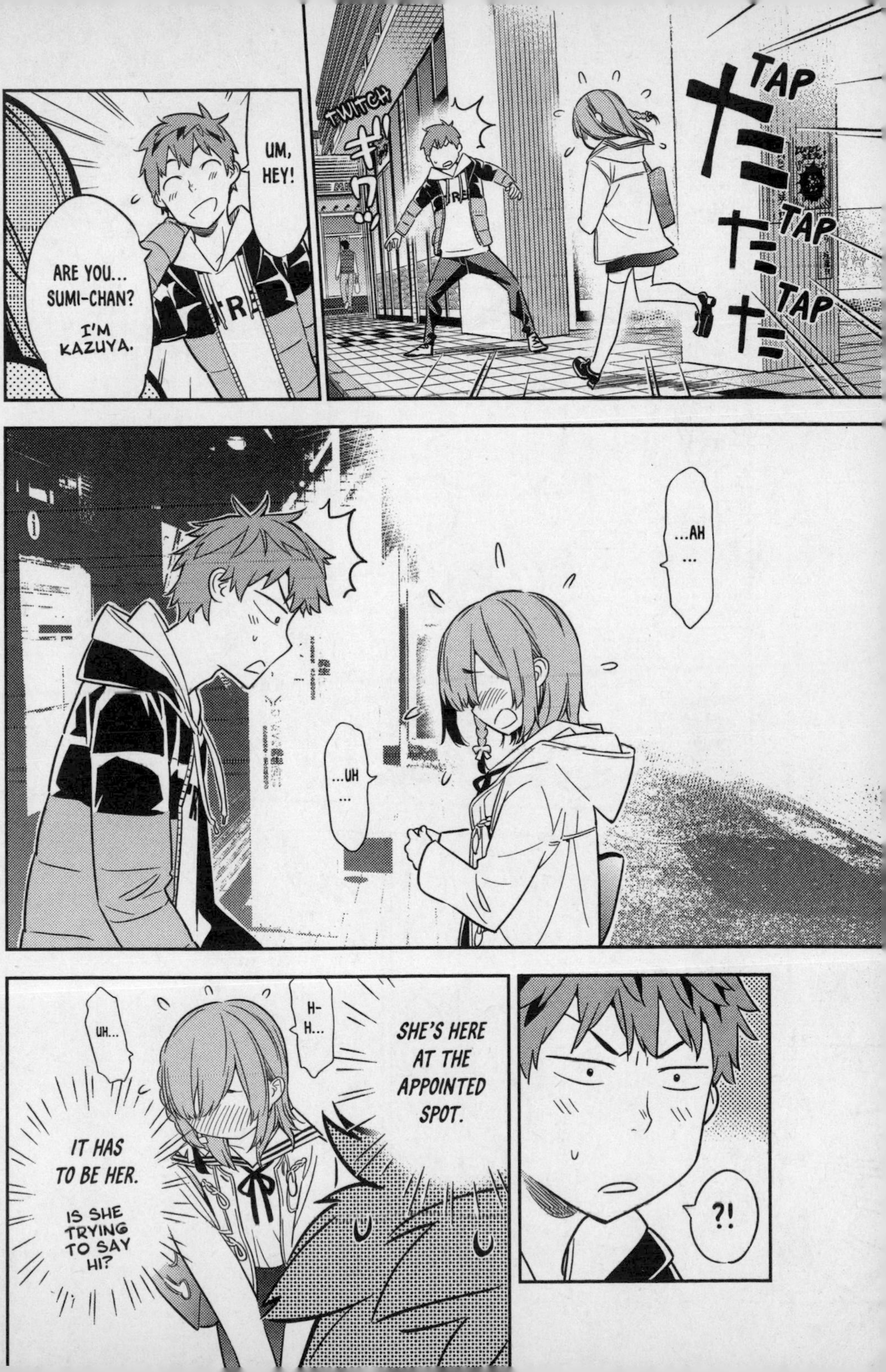
TAP
TAP
TAP
TWITCH
UM, HEY!
ARE YOU... SUMI-CHAN?
I'M KAZUYA.
...AH ...
...UH ...
?!
H- H...
UH...
SHE'S HERE AT THE APPOINTED SPOT.
IT HAS TO BE HER.
IS SHE TRYING TO SAY HI?

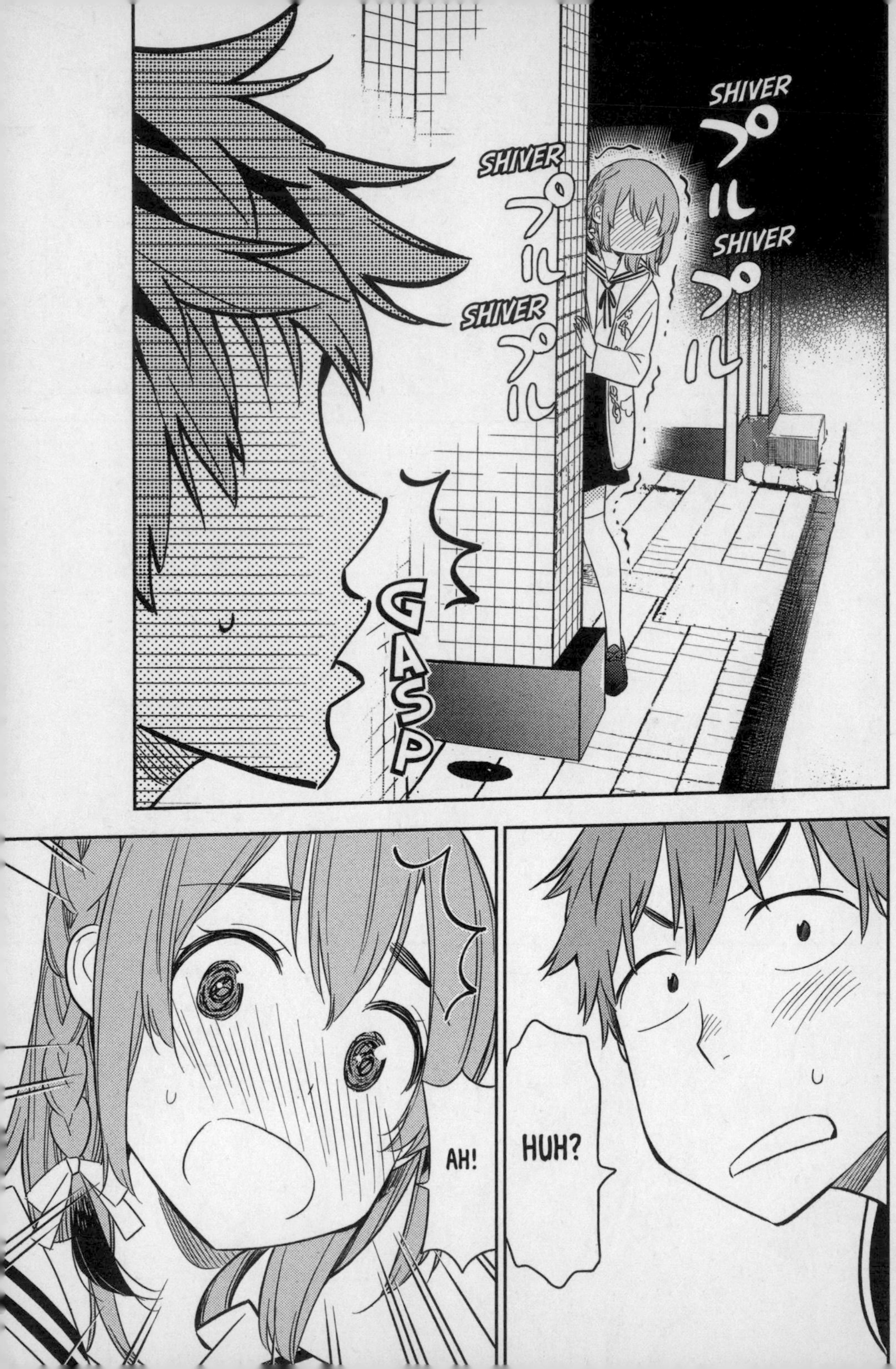
SHIVER
プル
SHIVER
プル
SHIVER
プル
SHIVER
プル
GASP
HUH?
AH!

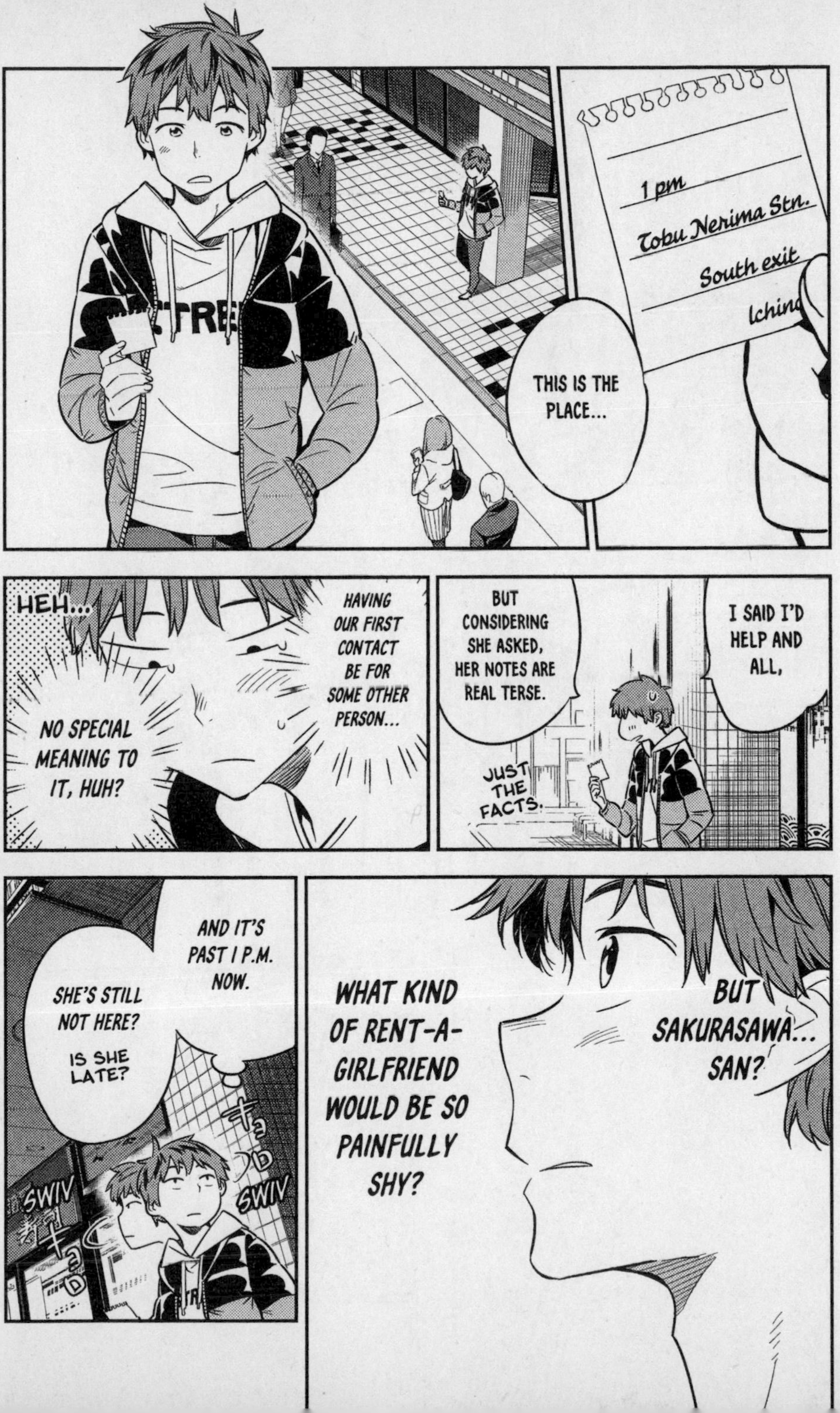
1 pm
Tobu Nerima Stn.
South exit
Ichin
THIS IS THE PLACE...
I SAID I'D HELP AND ALL,
BUT CONSIDERING SHE ASKED, HER NOTES ARE REAL TERSE.
JUST THE FACTS.
HAVING OUR FIRST CONTACT BE FOR SOME OTHER PERSON...
HEH...
NO SPECIAL MEANING TO IT, HUH?
BUT SAKURASAWA... SAN?
WHAT KIND OF RENT-A-GIRLFRIEND WOULD BE SO PAINFULLY SHY?
AND IT'S PAST 1 P.M. NOW.
SHE'S STILL NOT HERE?
IS SHE LATE?
キョロ
SWIV
キョロ
SWIV

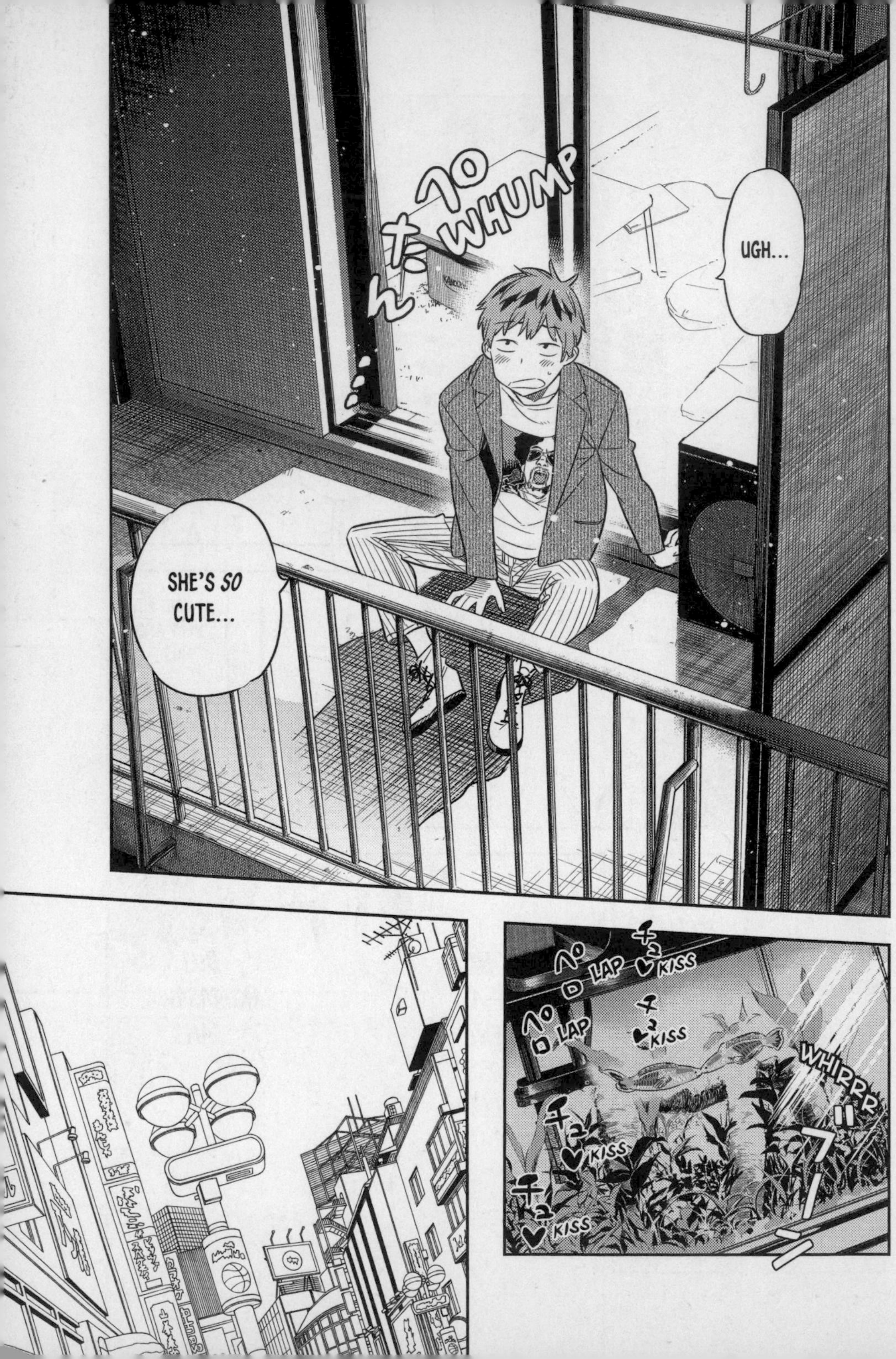
UGH...
WHUMP
SHE'S *SO* CUTE...
LAP
KISS
LAP
KISS
WHIRRR
KISS
KISS

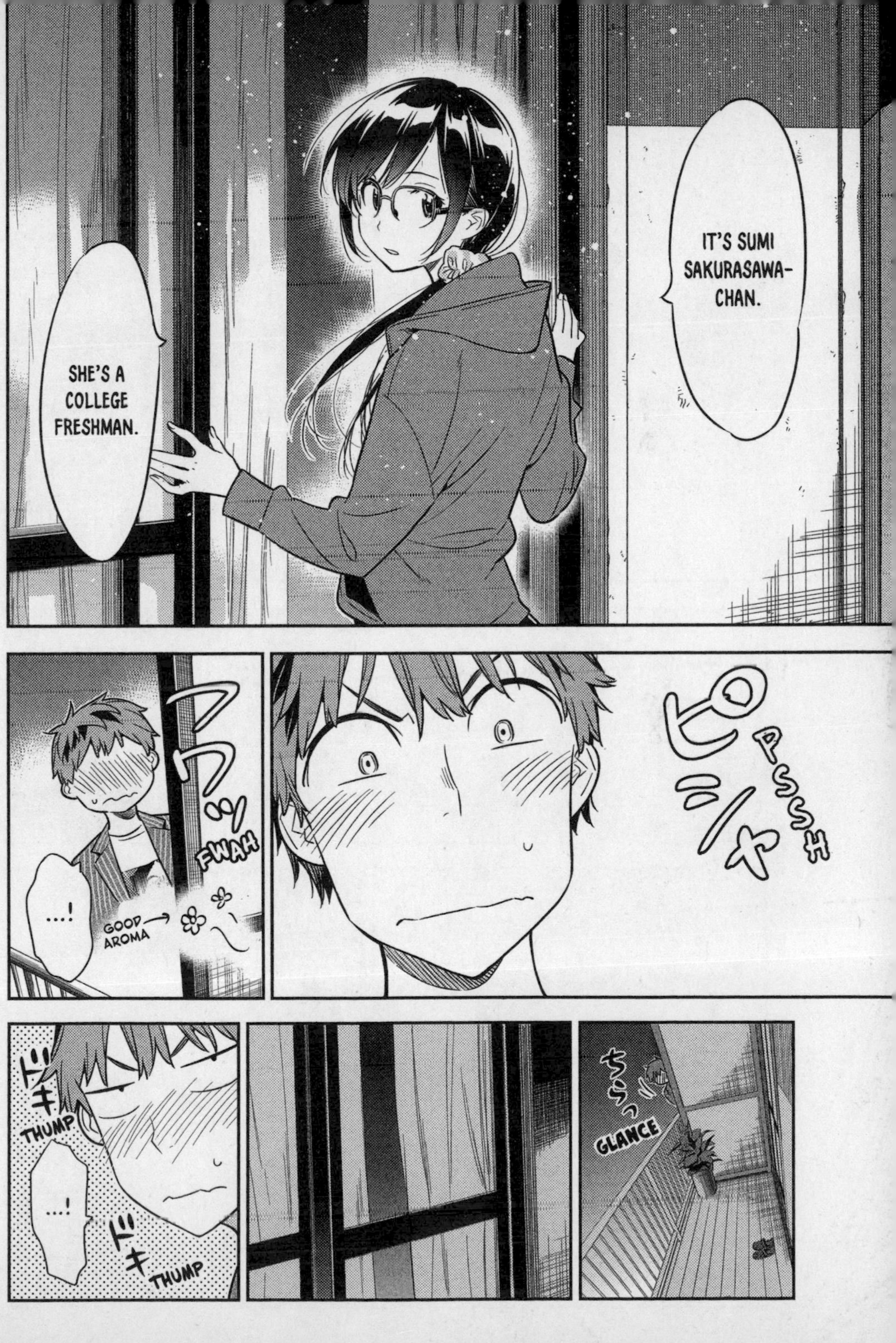
IT'S SUMI SAKURASAWA-CHAN.
SHE'S A COLLEGE FRESHMAN.
ピシャ
PSSH
フワッ
FWAH
GOOD AROMA
...!
ちらっ
GLANCE
ドキ
THUMP
...!
ドキ
THUMP

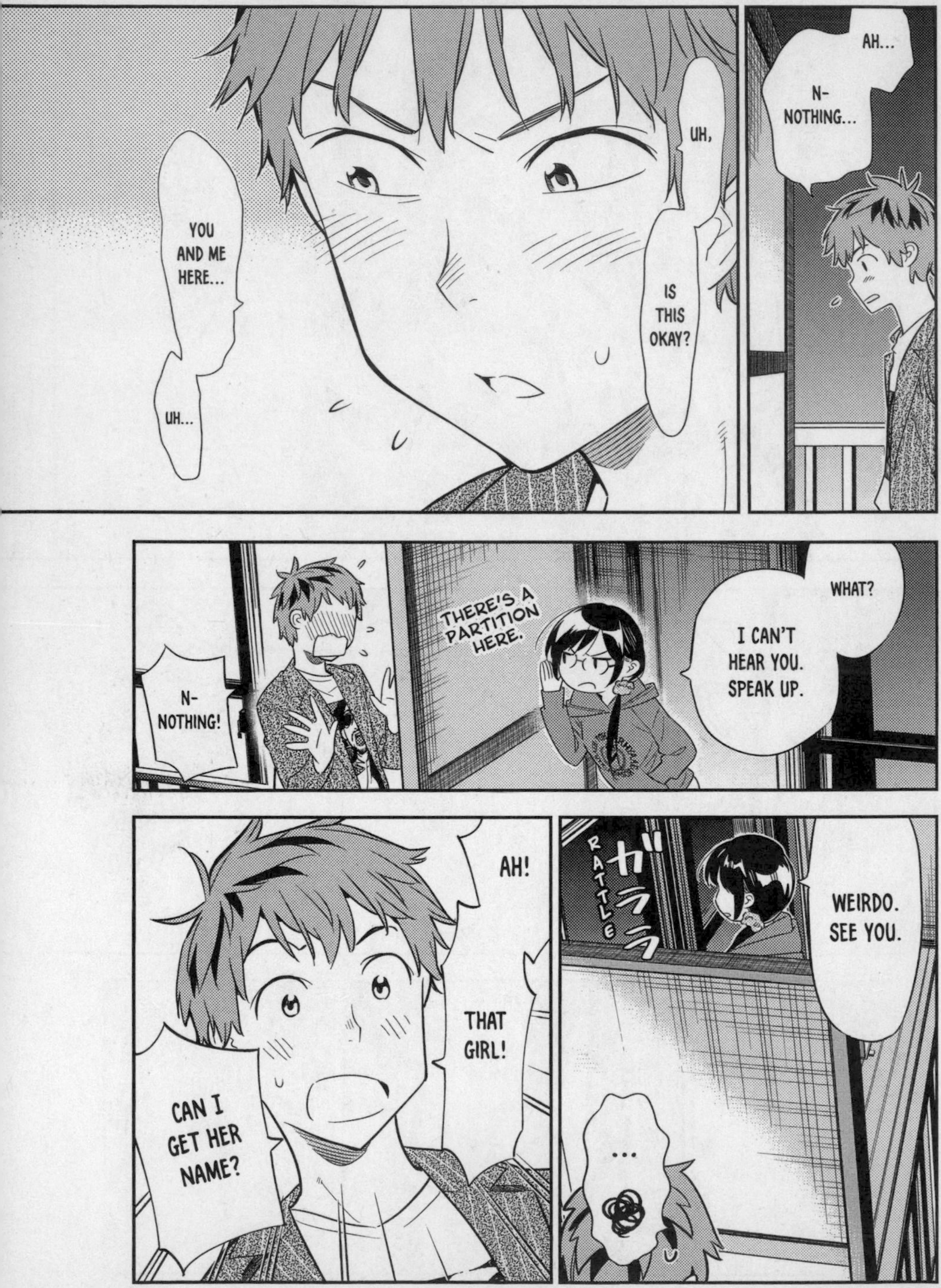
AH...
N-NOTHING...
UH,
IS THIS OKAY?
YOU AND ME HERE...
UH...
WHAT?
I CAN'T HEAR YOU. SPEAK UP.
THERE'S A PARTITION HERE.
N-NOTHING!
WEIRDO. SEE YOU.
ガララ
RATTLE
...
AH!
THAT GIRL!
CAN I GET HER NAME?

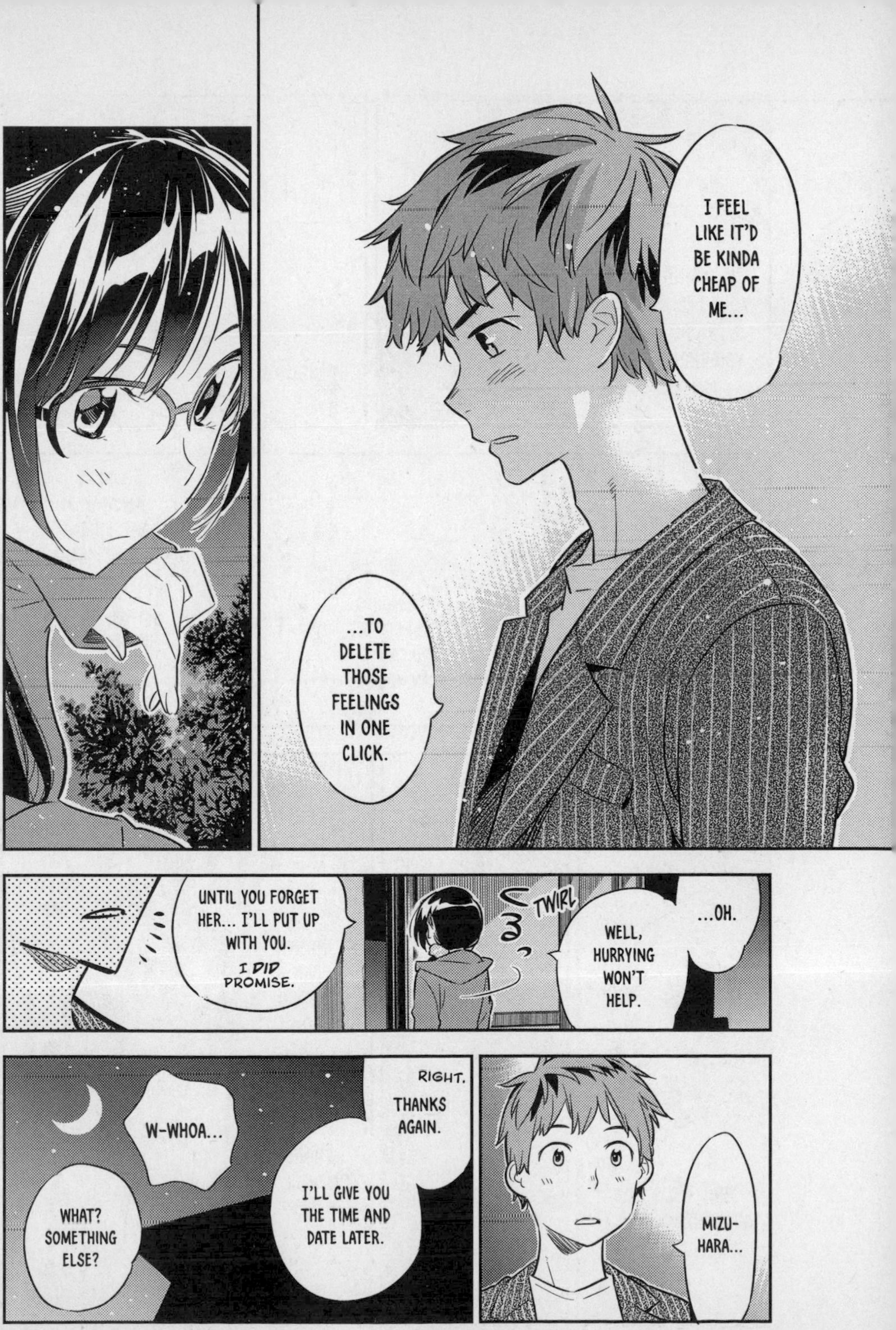
I FEEL LIKE IT'D BE KINDA CHEAP OF ME...
...TO DELETE THOSE FEELINGS IN ONE CLICK.
...OH.
WELL, HURRYING WON'T HELP.
TWIRL
UNTIL YOU FORGET HER... I'LL PUT UP WITH YOU.
I DID PROMISE.
MIZU-HARA...
RIGHT.
THANKS AGAIN.
W-WHOA...
I'LL GIVE YOU THE TIME AND DATE LATER.
WHAT? SOMETHING ELSE?

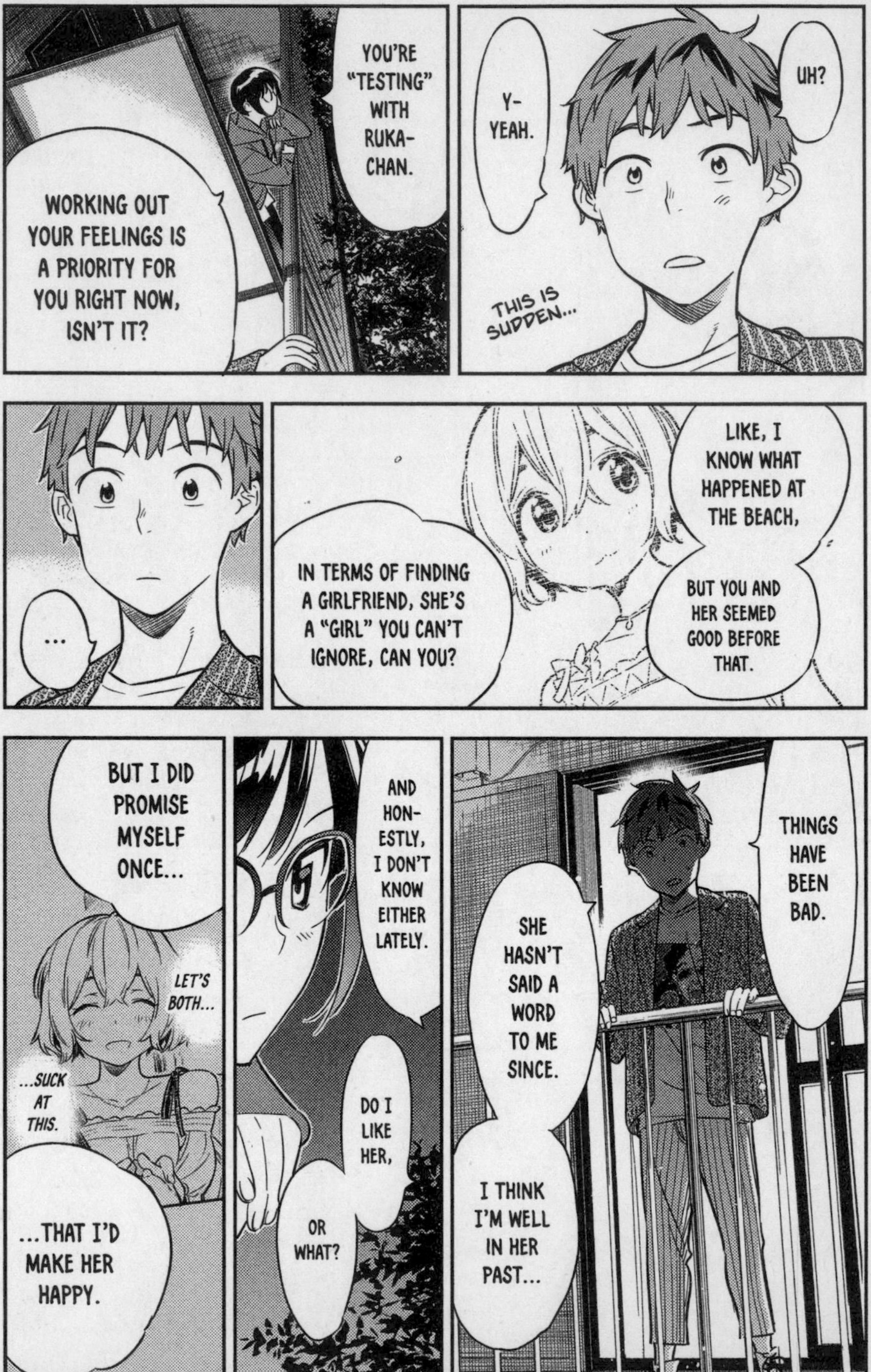
UH?
Y-YEAH.
THIS IS SUDDEN...
YOU'RE "TESTING" WITH RUKA-CHAN.
WORKING OUT YOUR FEELINGS IS A PRIORITY FOR YOU RIGHT NOW, ISN'T IT?
LIKE, I KNOW WHAT HAPPENED AT THE BEACH,
BUT YOU AND HER SEEMED GOOD BEFORE THAT.
IN TERMS OF FINDING A GIRLFRIEND, SHE'S A "GIRL" YOU CAN'T IGNORE, CAN YOU?
...
THINGS HAVE BEEN BAD.
SHE HASN'T SAID A WORD TO ME SINCE.
I THINK I'M WELL IN HER PAST...
AND HONESTLY, I DON'T KNOW EITHER LATELY.
DO I LIKE HER,
OR WHAT?
BUT I DID PROMISE MYSELF ONCE...
LET'S BOTH...
...SUCK AT THIS.
...THAT I'D MAKE HER HAPPY.

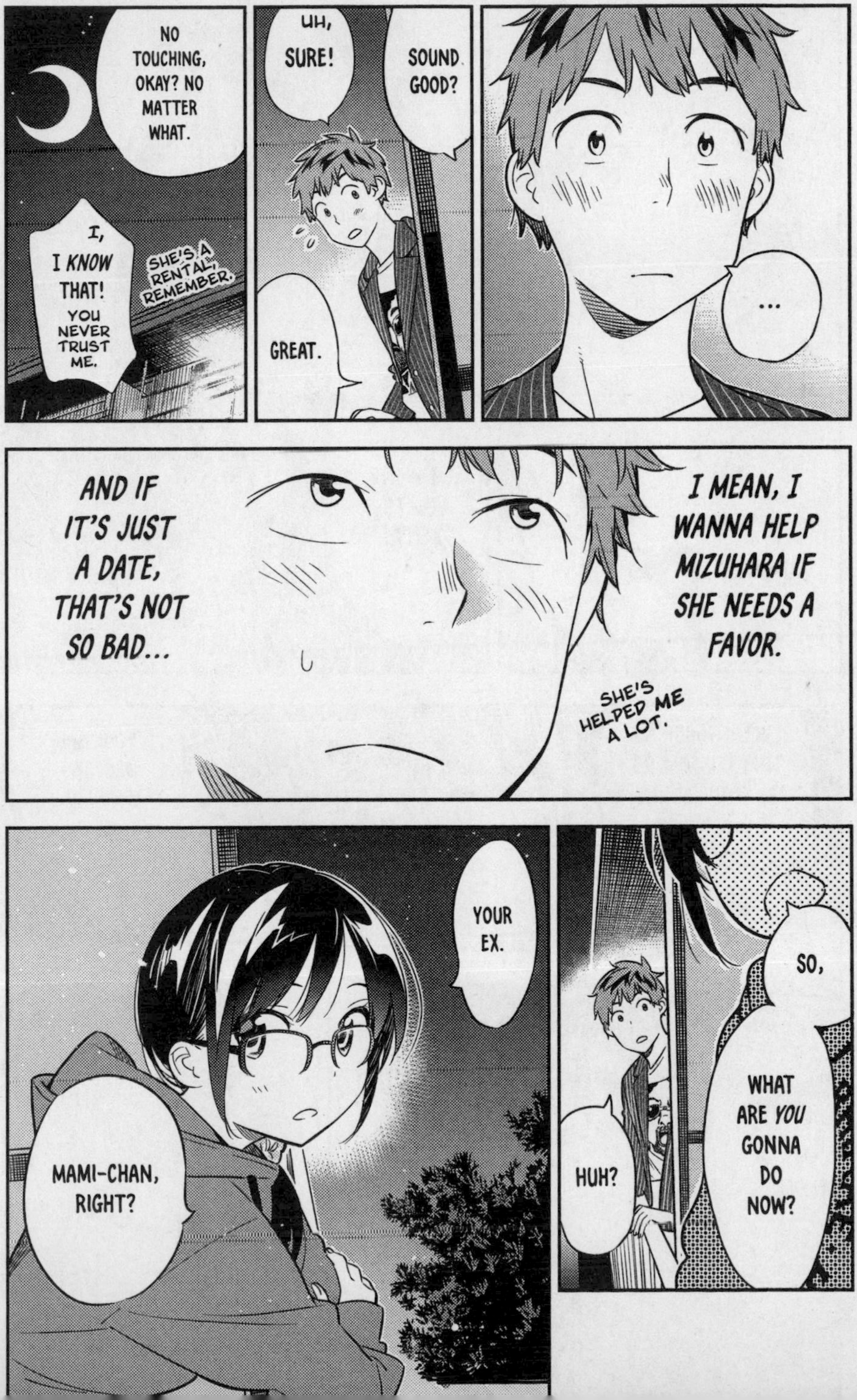
...
SOUND GOOD?
UH, SURE!
GREAT.
NO TOUCHING, OKAY? NO MATTER WHAT.
I, I KNOW THAT! YOU NEVER TRUST ME.
SHE'S A RENTAL, REMEMBER.
I MEAN, I WANNA HELP MIZUHARA IF SHE NEEDS A FAVOR.
SHE'S HELPED ME A LOT.
AND IF IT'S JUST A DATE, THAT'S NOT SO BAD...
SO,
WHAT ARE *YOU* GONNA DO NOW?
HUH?
YOUR EX.
MAMI-CHAN, RIGHT?

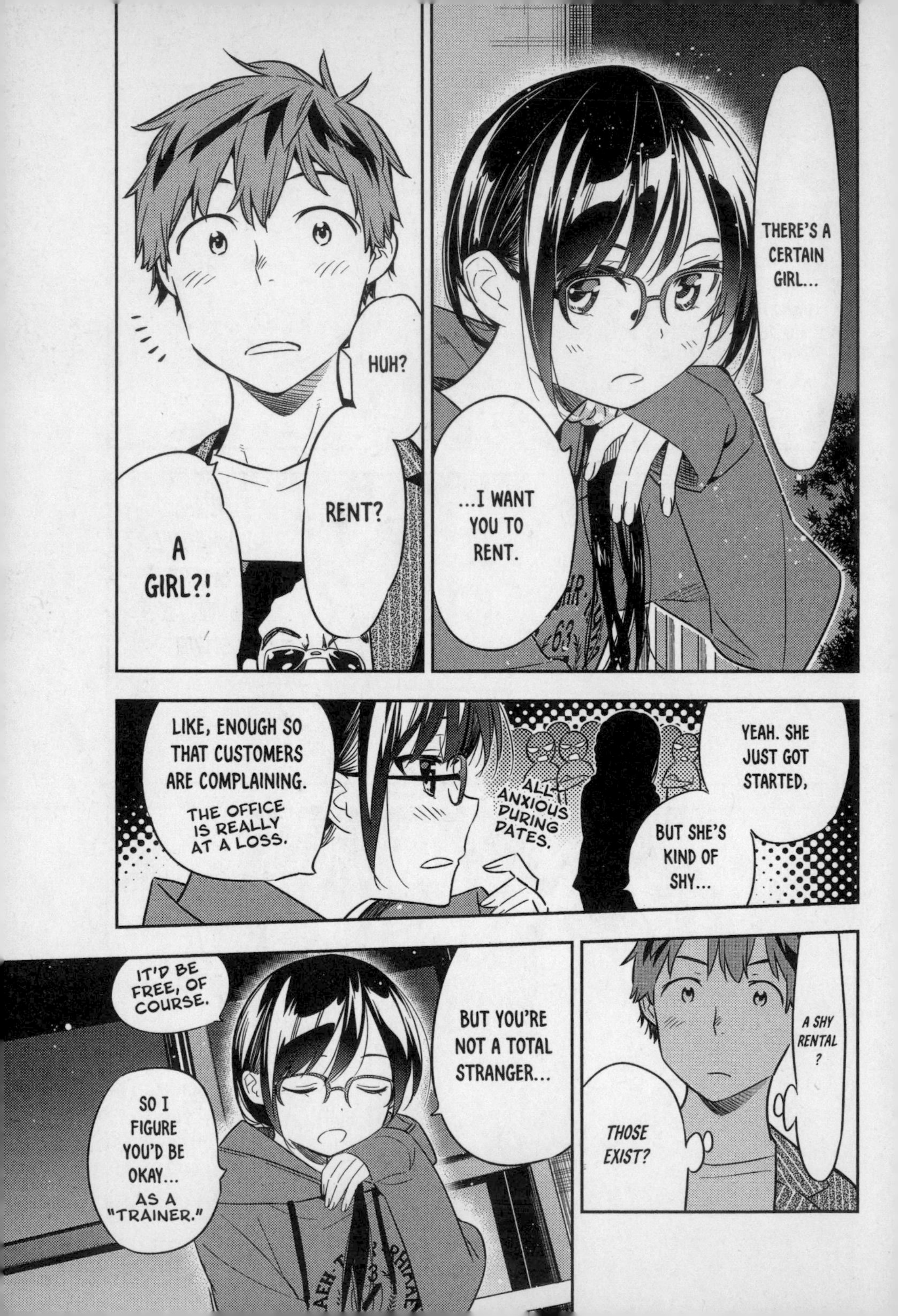
THERE'S A CERTAIN GIRL...
...I WANT YOU TO RENT.
HUH?
RENT?
A GIRL?!
YEAH. SHE JUST GOT STARTED,
BUT SHE'S KIND OF SHY...
ALL ANXIOUS DURING DATES.
LIKE, ENOUGH SO THAT CUSTOMERS ARE COMPLAINING.
THE OFFICE IS REALLY AT A LOSS.
A SHY RENTAL?
THOSE EXIST?
BUT YOU'RE NOT A TOTAL STRANGER...
IT'D BE FREE, OF COURSE.
SO I FIGURE YOU'D BE OKAY... AS A "TRAINER."

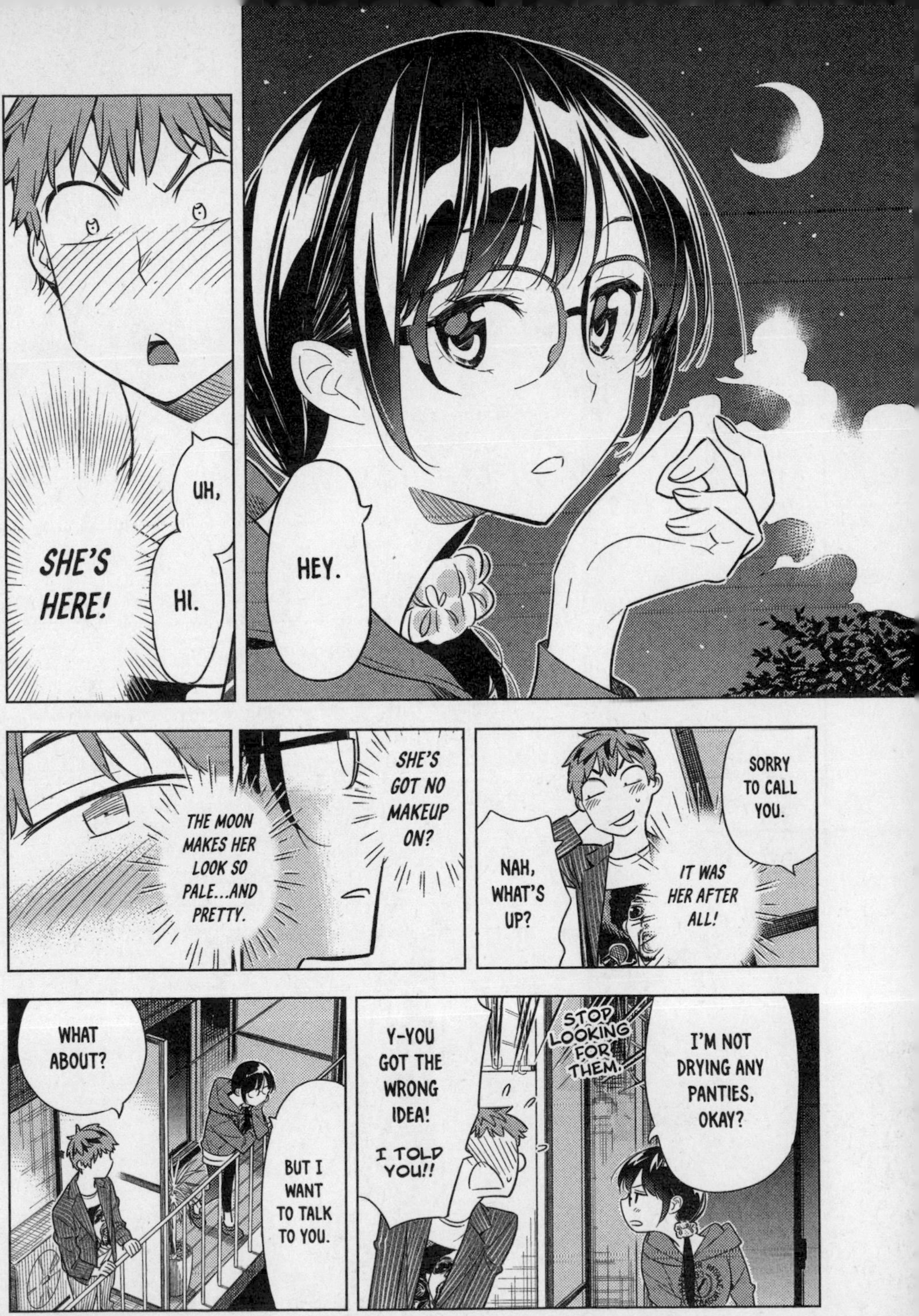
HEY.
UH,
HI.
SHE'S HERE!
SORRY TO CALL YOU.
IT WAS HER AFTER ALL!
NAH, WHAT'S UP?
SHE'S GOT NO MAKEUP ON?
THE MOON MAKES HER LOOK SO PALE...AND PRETTY.
I'M NOT DRYING ANY PANTIES, OKAY?
STOP LOOKING FOR THEM.
Y-YOU GOT THE WRONG IDEA!
I TOLD YOU!!
BUT I WANT TO TALK TO YOU.
WHAT ABOUT?

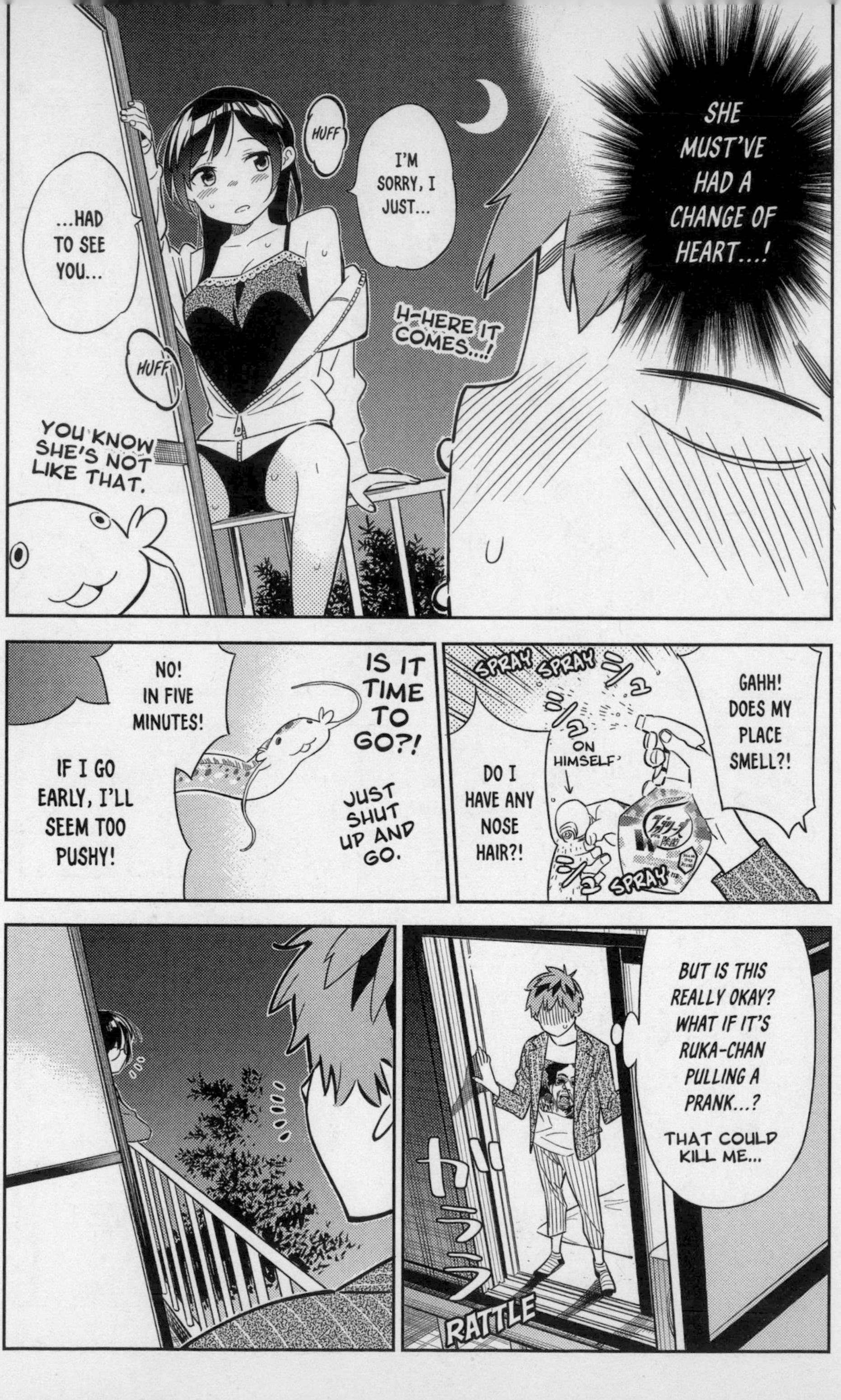
SHE MUST'VE HAD A CHANGE OF HEART...!
H-HERE IT COMES...!
I'M SORRY, I JUST...
HUFF
...HAD TO SEE YOU...
HUFF
YOU KNOW SHE'S NOT LIKE THAT.
SPRAY
SPRAY
GAHH! DOES MY PLACE SMELL?!
DO I HAVE ANY NOSE HAIR?!
ON HIMSELF
SPRAY
IS IT TIME TO GO?!
NO! IN FIVE MINUTES!
IF I GO EARLY, I'LL SEEM TOO PUSHY!
JUST SHUT UP AND GO.
BUT IS THIS REALLY OKAY? WHAT IF IT'S RUKA-CHAN PULLING A PRANK...?
THAT COULD KILL ME...
RATTLE

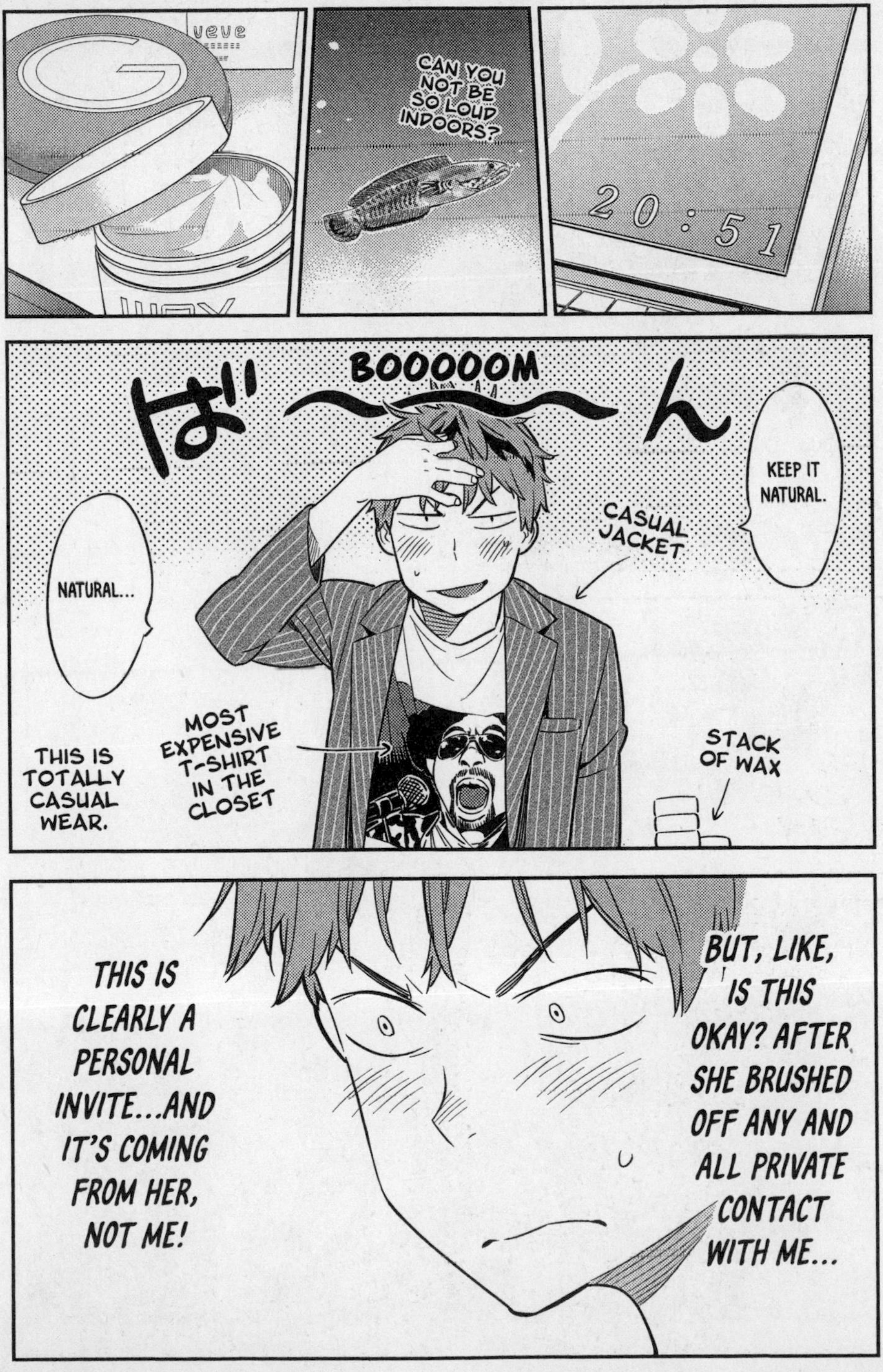
20:51
CAN YOU NOT BE SO LOUD INDOORS?
veve
BOOOOOM
ば〜〜〜ん
KEEP IT NATURAL.
CASUAL JACKET
NATURAL...
STACK OF WAX
MOST EXPENSIVE T-SHIRT IN THE CLOSET
THIS IS TOTALLY CASUAL WEAR.
BUT, LIKE, IS THIS OKAY? AFTER SHE BRUSHED OFF ANY AND ALL PRIVATE CONTACT WITH ME...
THIS IS CLEARLY A PERSONAL INVITE...AND IT'S COMING FROM HER, NOT ME!

RATING 41

MY GIRLFRIEND AND THE PROMISE ON THE BALCONY (1)

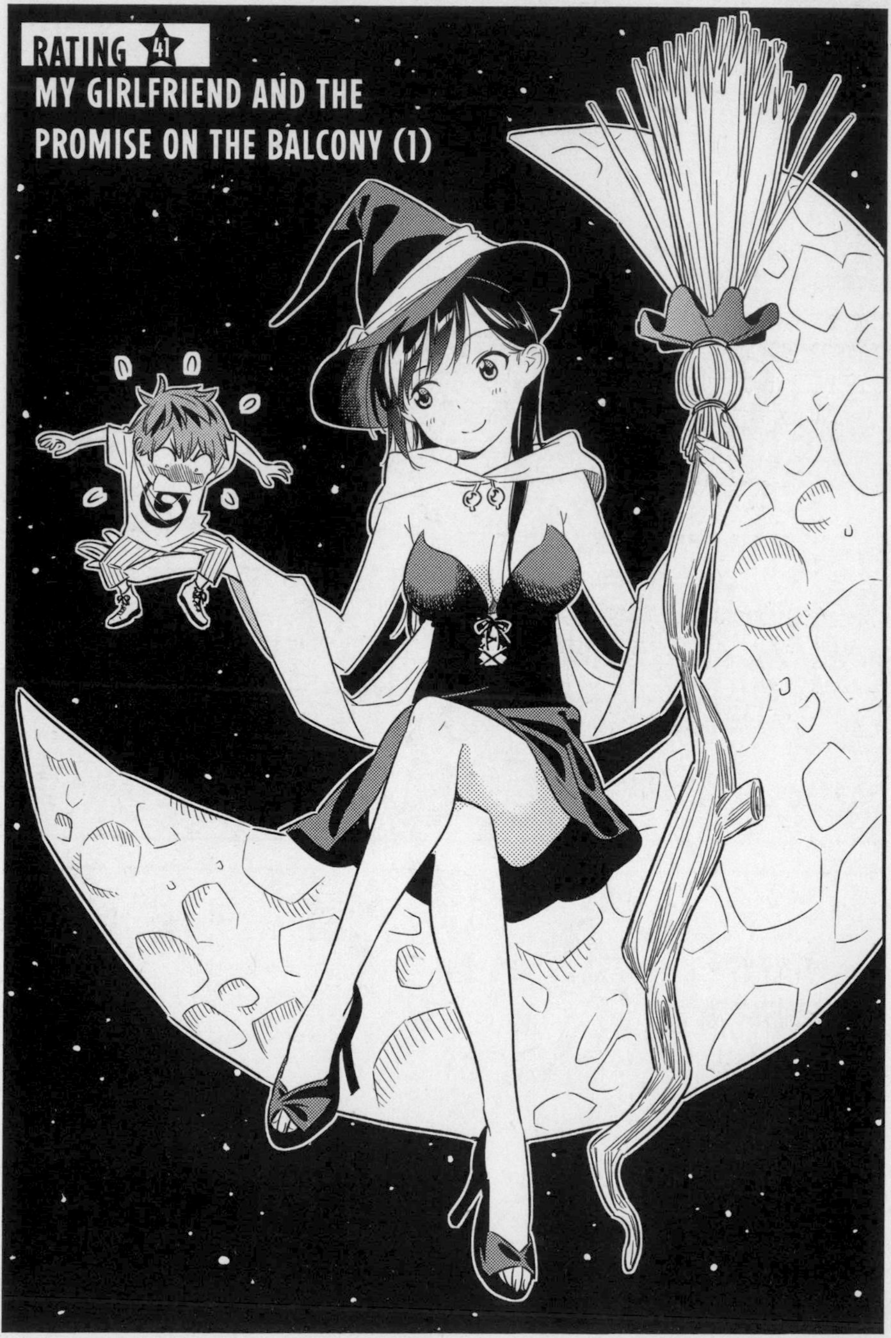

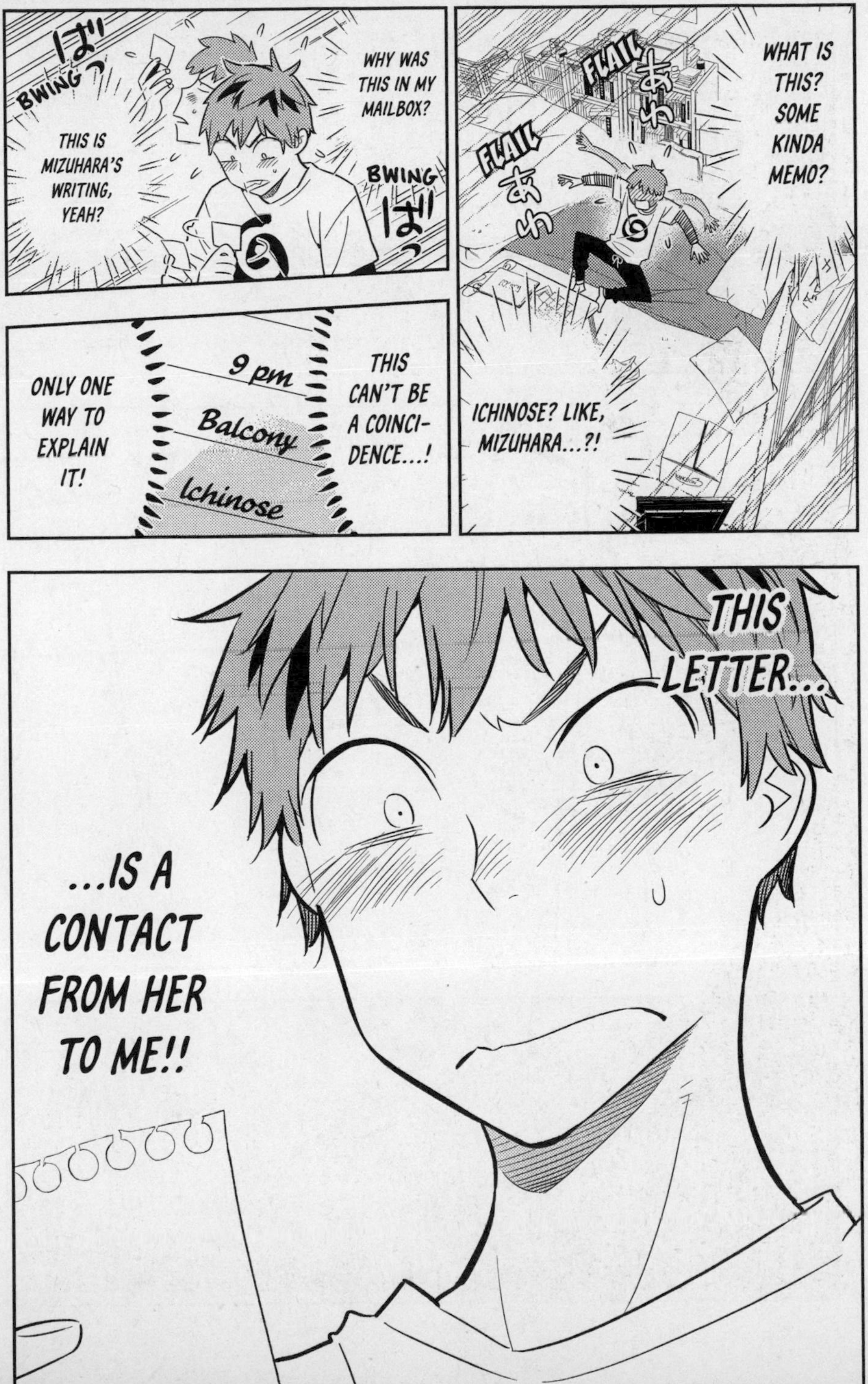
FLAIL
あわ
WHAT IS THIS? SOME KINDA MEMO?
FLAIL
あわ
ICHINOSE? LIKE, MIZUHARA...?!
ぱっ
BWING
WHY WAS THIS IN MY MAILBOX?
THIS IS MIZUHARA'S WRITING, YEAH?
BWING
ぱっ
THIS CAN'T BE A COINCIDENCE...!
9 pm
Balcony
Ichinose
ONLY ONE WAY TO EXPLAIN IT!
THIS LETTER...
...IS A CONTACT FROM HER TO ME!!

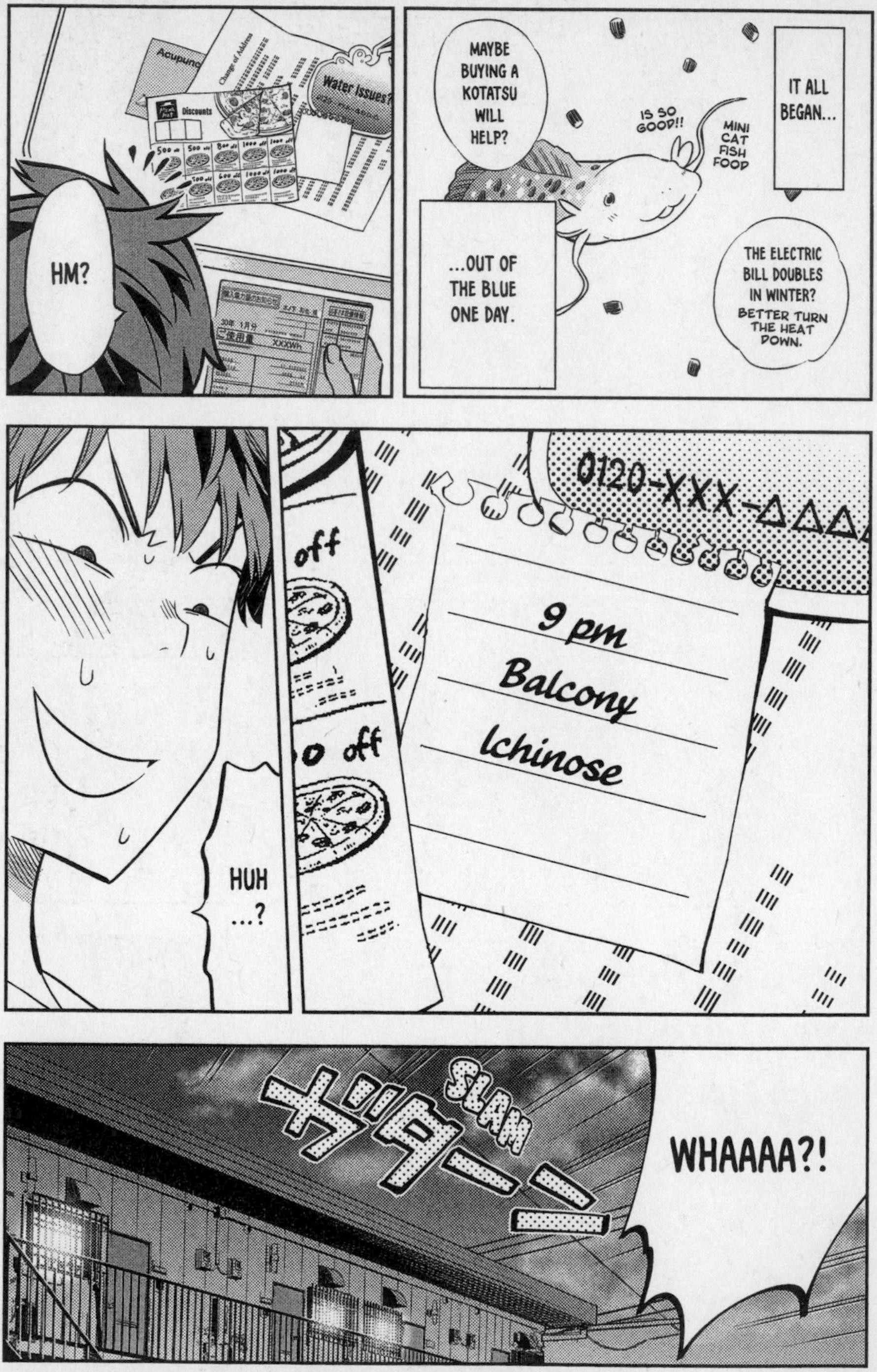
IT ALL BEGAN...
MINI CAT FISH FOOD
IS SO GOOD!!
MAYBE BUYING A KOTATSU WILL HELP?
THE ELECTRIC BILL DOUBLES IN WINTER? BETTER TURN THE HEAT DOWN.
...OUT OF THE BLUE ONE DAY.
Water Issues?
Change of Address
Discounts
HM?
0120-XXX-△△△
9 pm
Balcony
Ichinose
off
off
HUH ...?
SLAM
WHAAAA?!

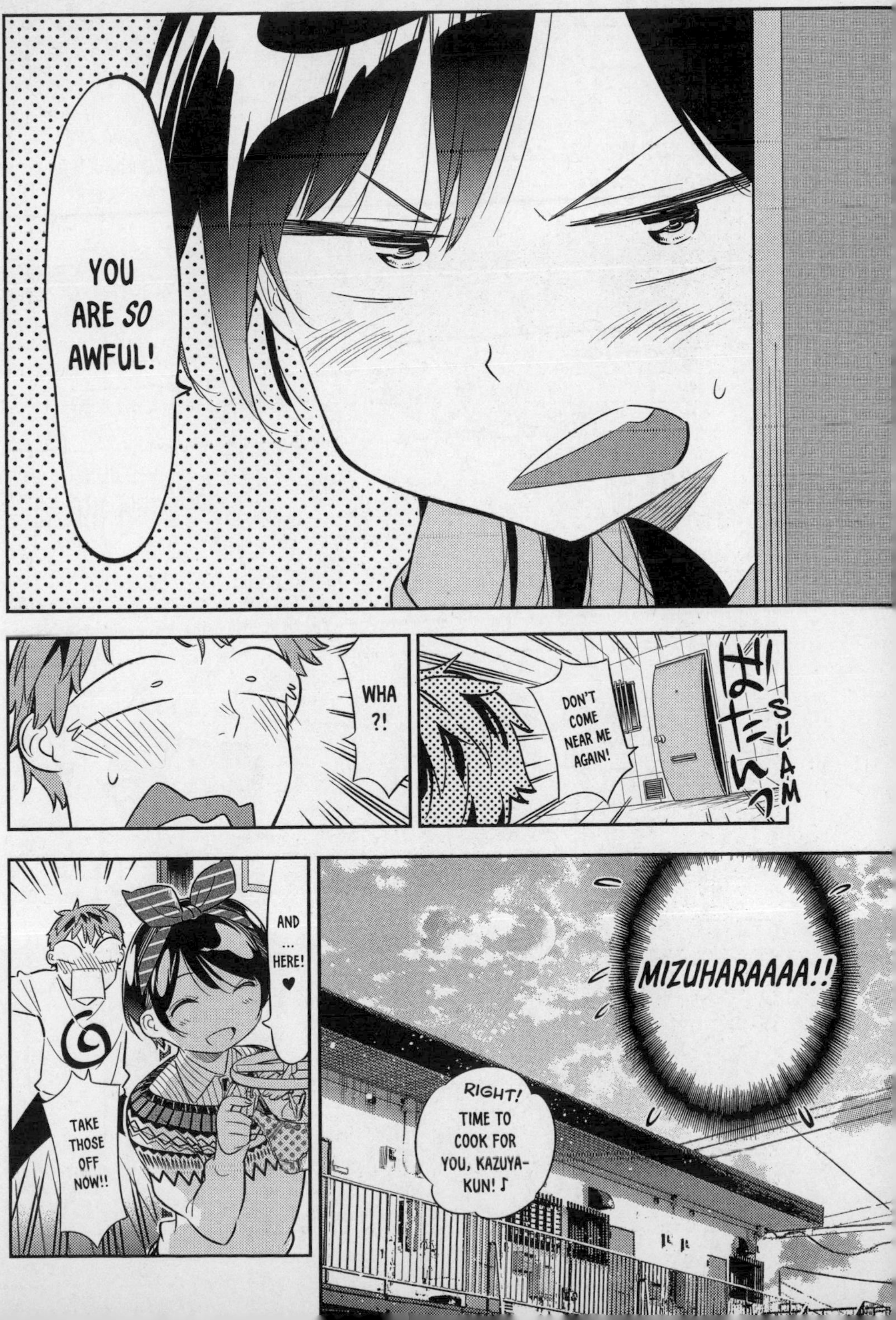
YOU ARE SO AWFUL!
DON'T COME NEAR ME AGAIN!
ぱたんっ
SLAM
WHA ?!
MIZUHARAAAA!!
RIGHT! TIME TO COOK FOR YOU, KAZUYA-KUN! ♪
AND ... HERE! ♥
TAKE THOSE OFF NOW!!

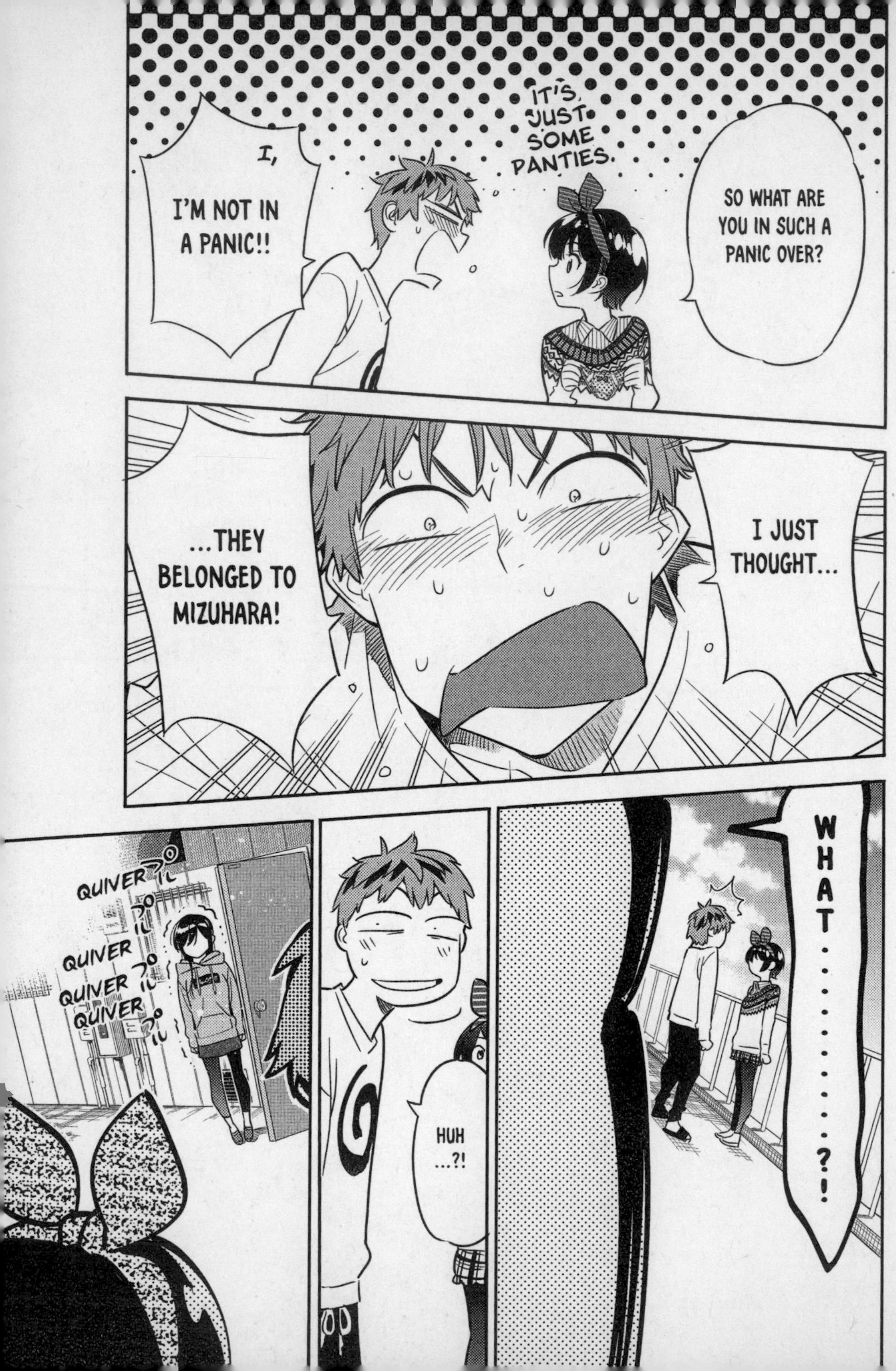
SO WHAT ARE YOU IN SUCH A PANIC OVER?
IT'S JUST SOME PANTIES.
I, I'M NOT IN A PANIC!!
I JUST THOUGHT...
...THEY BELONGED TO MIZUHARA!
WHAT.........?!
HUH ...?!
QUIVER
QUIVER
QUIVER
QUIVER

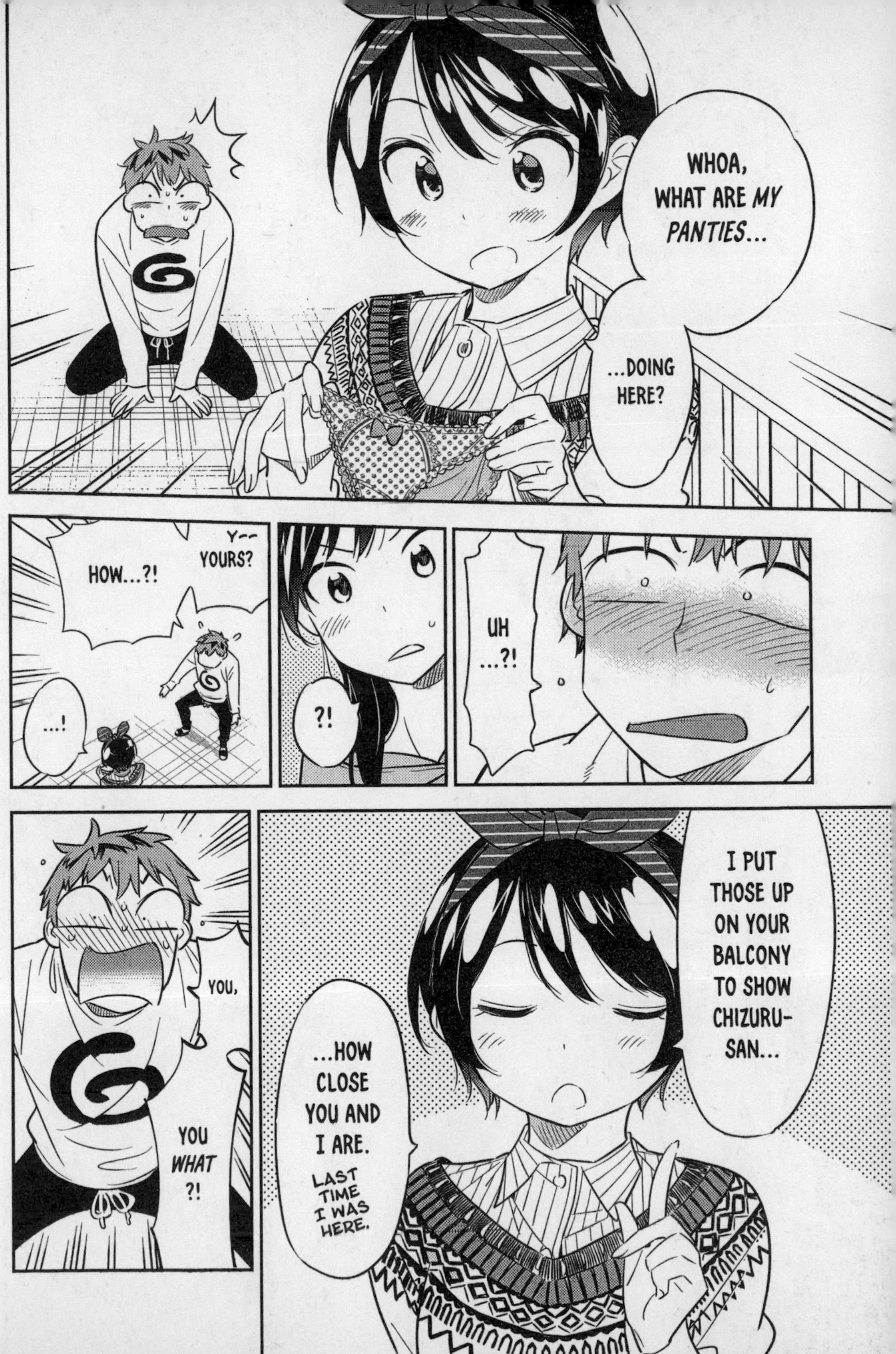
WHOA, WHAT ARE *MY* PANTIES...
...DOING HERE?
UH ...?!
?!
Y-- YOURS?
HOW...?!
...!
I PUT THOSE UP ON YOUR BALCONY TO SHOW CHIZURU-SAN...
...HOW CLOSE YOU AND I ARE.
LAST TIME I WAS HERE.
YOU,
YOU *WHAT* ?!

FLITTER

LAUNDRY ...?

WHAT'S THIS...?

ZWIP

...!!

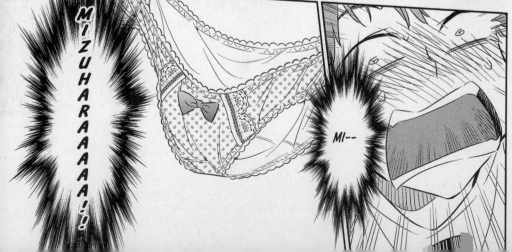

MIZUHARAAAAA!!

MI--

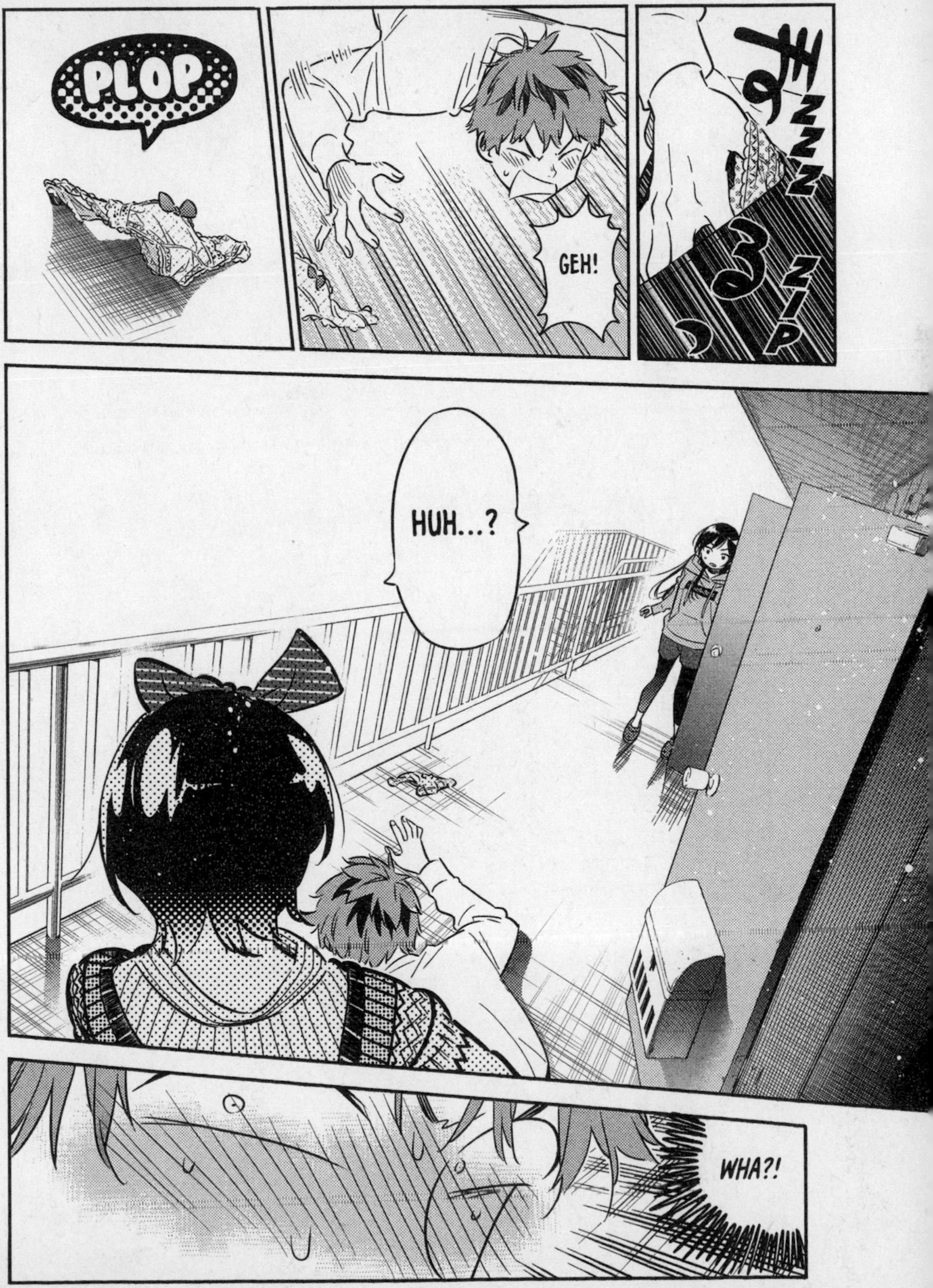
ZZZZ
ZIP
GEH!
PLOP
HUH...?
WHA?!

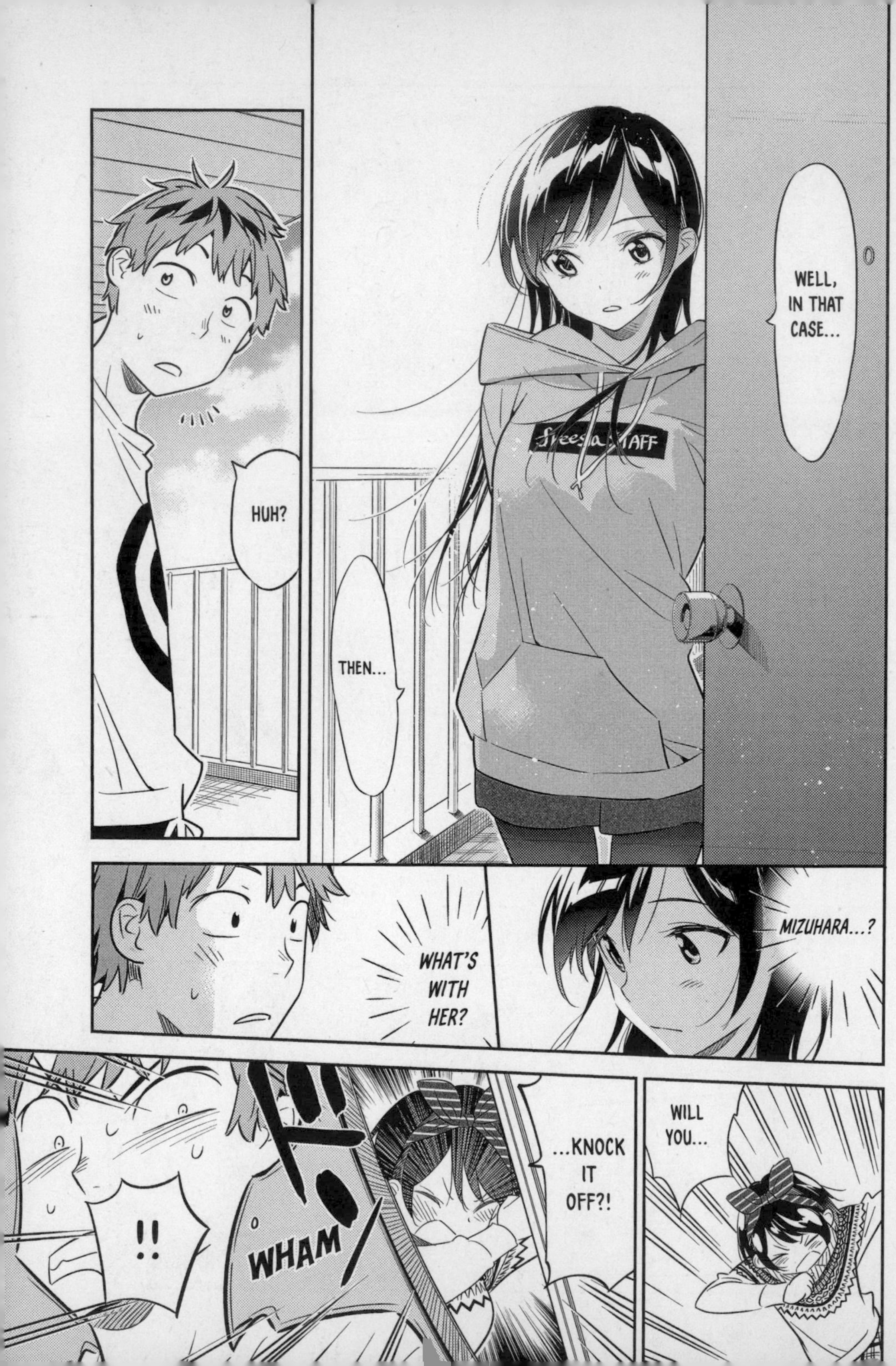
WELL, IN THAT CASE...
THEN...
HUH?
MIZUHARA...?
WHAT'S WITH HER?
WILL YOU...
...KNOCK IT OFF?!
WHAM
!!

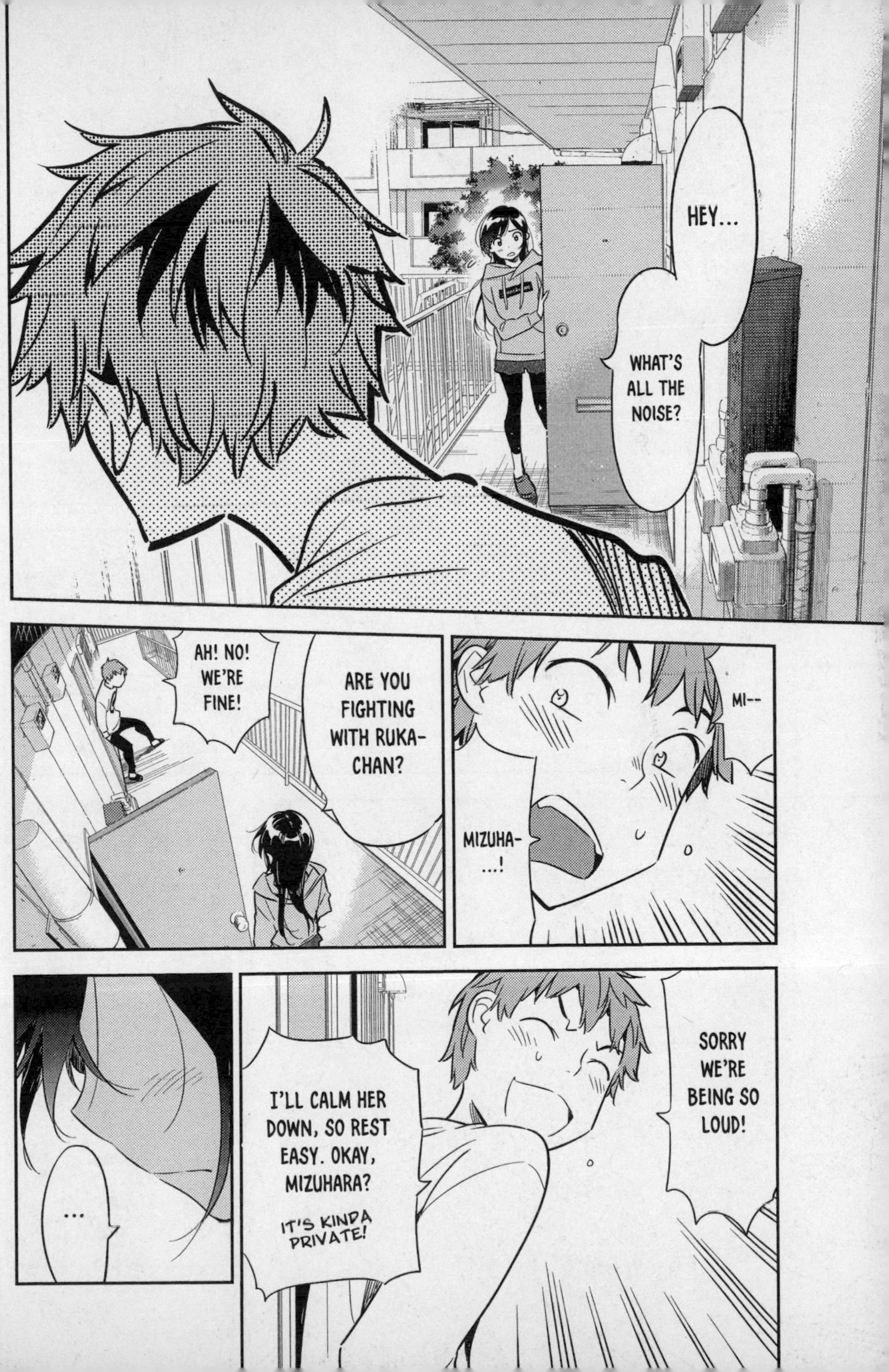
HEY...
WHAT'S ALL THE NOISE?
MI--
MIZUHA-...!
ARE YOU FIGHTING WITH RUKA-CHAN?
AH! NO! WE'RE FINE!
SORRY WE'RE BEING SO LOUD!
I'LL CALM HER DOWN, SO REST EASY. OKAY, MIZUHARA?
IT'S KINDA PRIVATE!
...

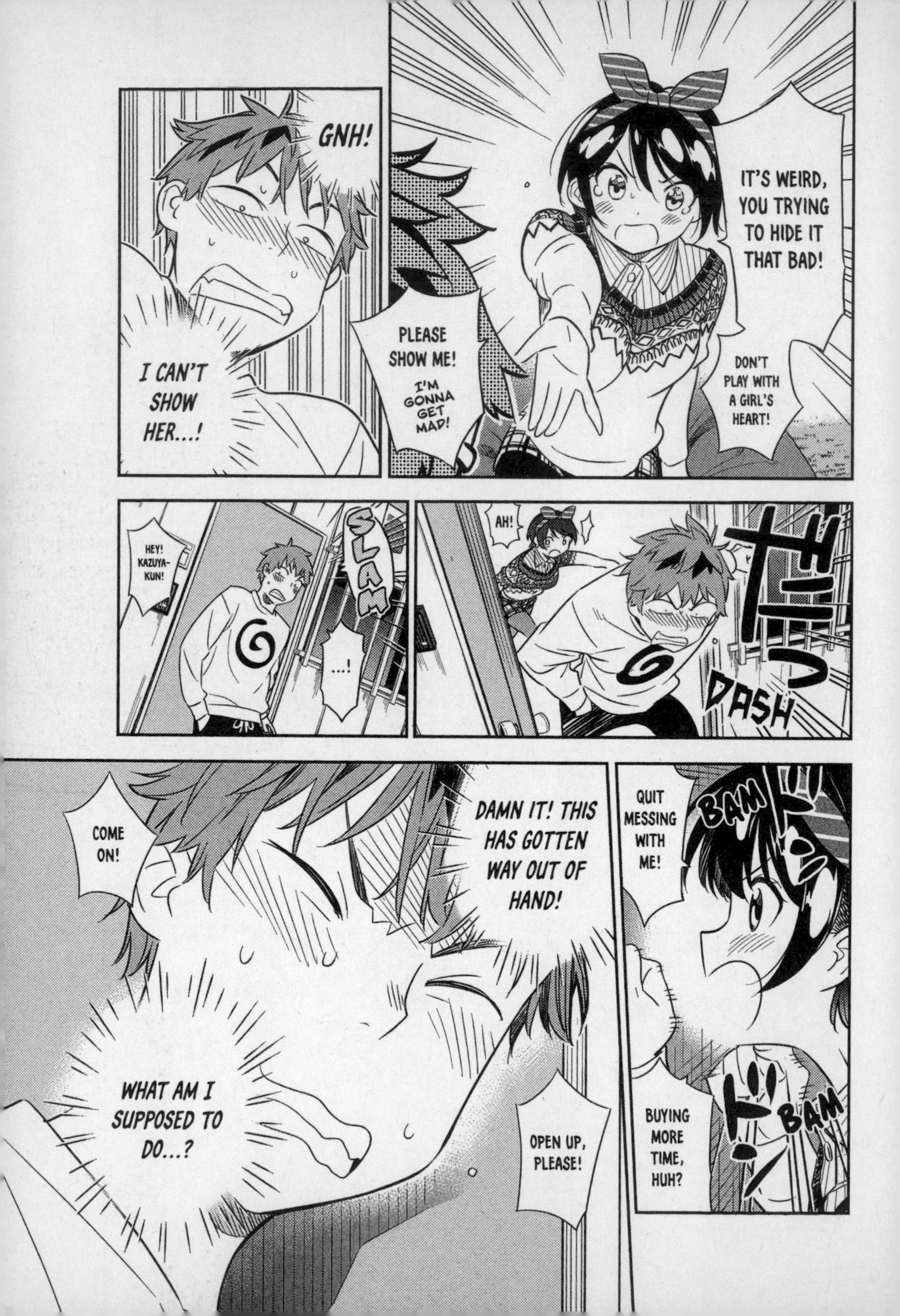
IT'S WEIRD, YOU TRYING TO HIDE IT THAT BAD!
DON'T PLAY WITH A GIRL'S HEART!
PLEASE SHOW ME!
I'M GONNA GET MAD!
GNH!
I CAN'T SHOW HER...!
AH!
DASH
SLAM
HEY! KAZUYA-KUN!
...!
BAM
QUIT MESSING WITH ME!
BAM
BUYING MORE TIME, HUH?
DAMN IT! THIS HAS GOTTEN WAY OUT OF HAND!
COME ON!
OPEN UP, PLEASE!
WHAT AM I SUPPOSED TO DO...?

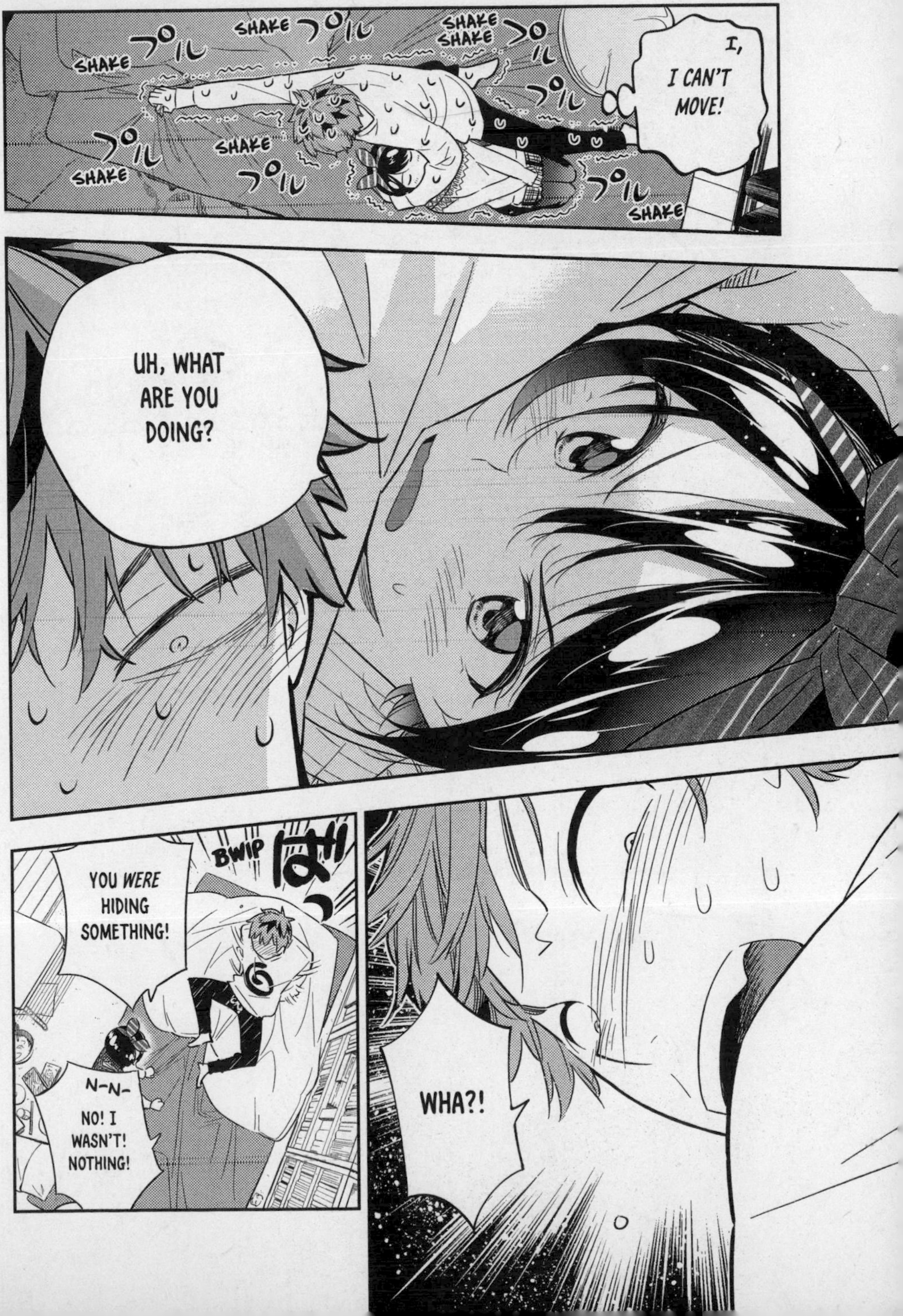
I, I CAN'T MOVE!
SHAKE SHAKE プル
SHAKE プル
SHAKE プル
SHAKE プル
SHAKE プル
SHAKE プル
UH, WHAT ARE YOU DOING?
WHA?!
BWIP ばっ
YOU *WERE* HIDING SOMETHING!
N-N-
NO! I WASN'T! NOTHING!

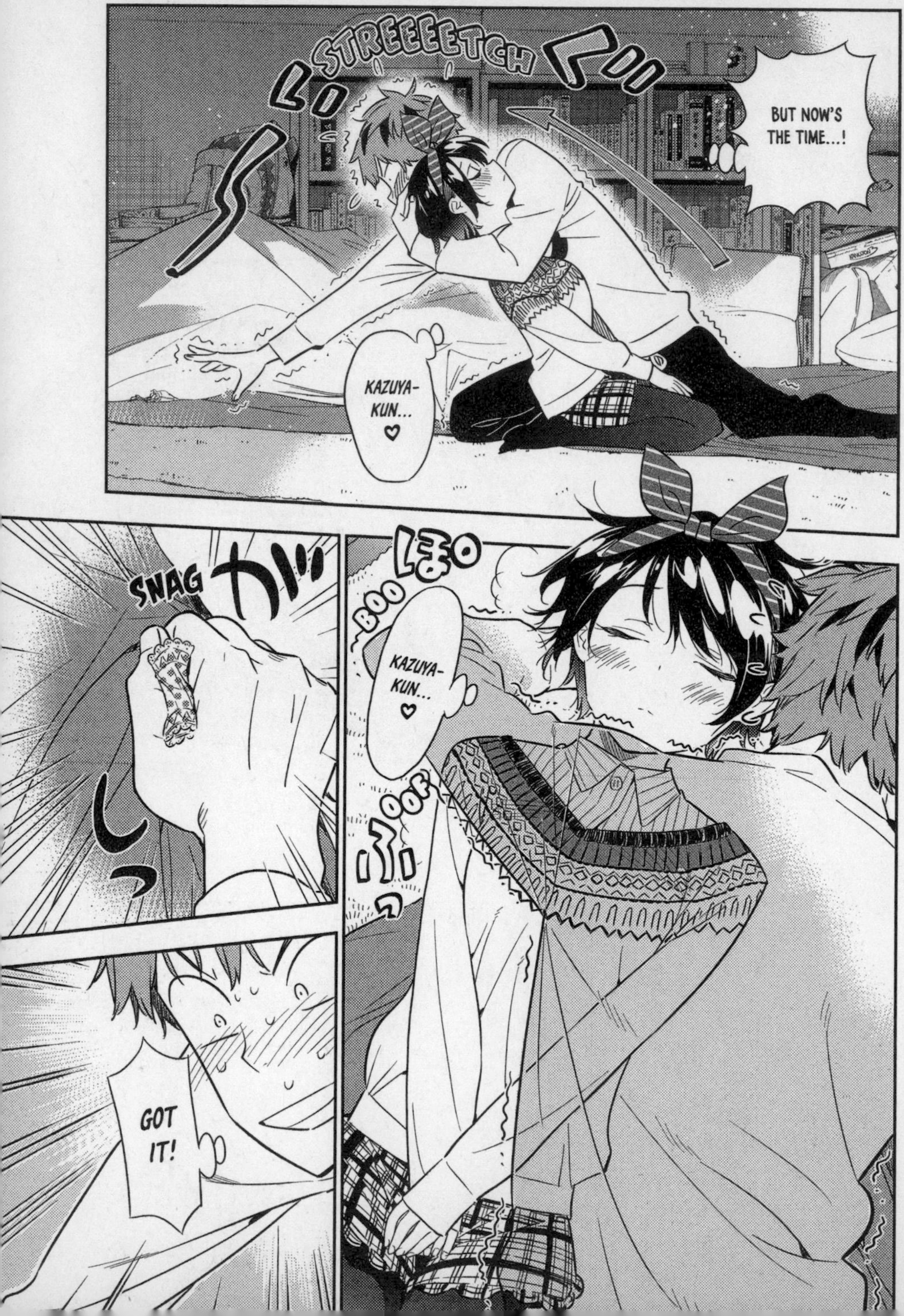
BUT NOW'S THE TIME...!
STREEEEETCH
KAZUYA-KUN... ♡
BOO
KAZUYA-KUN... ♡
OOF
SNAG
GOT IT!

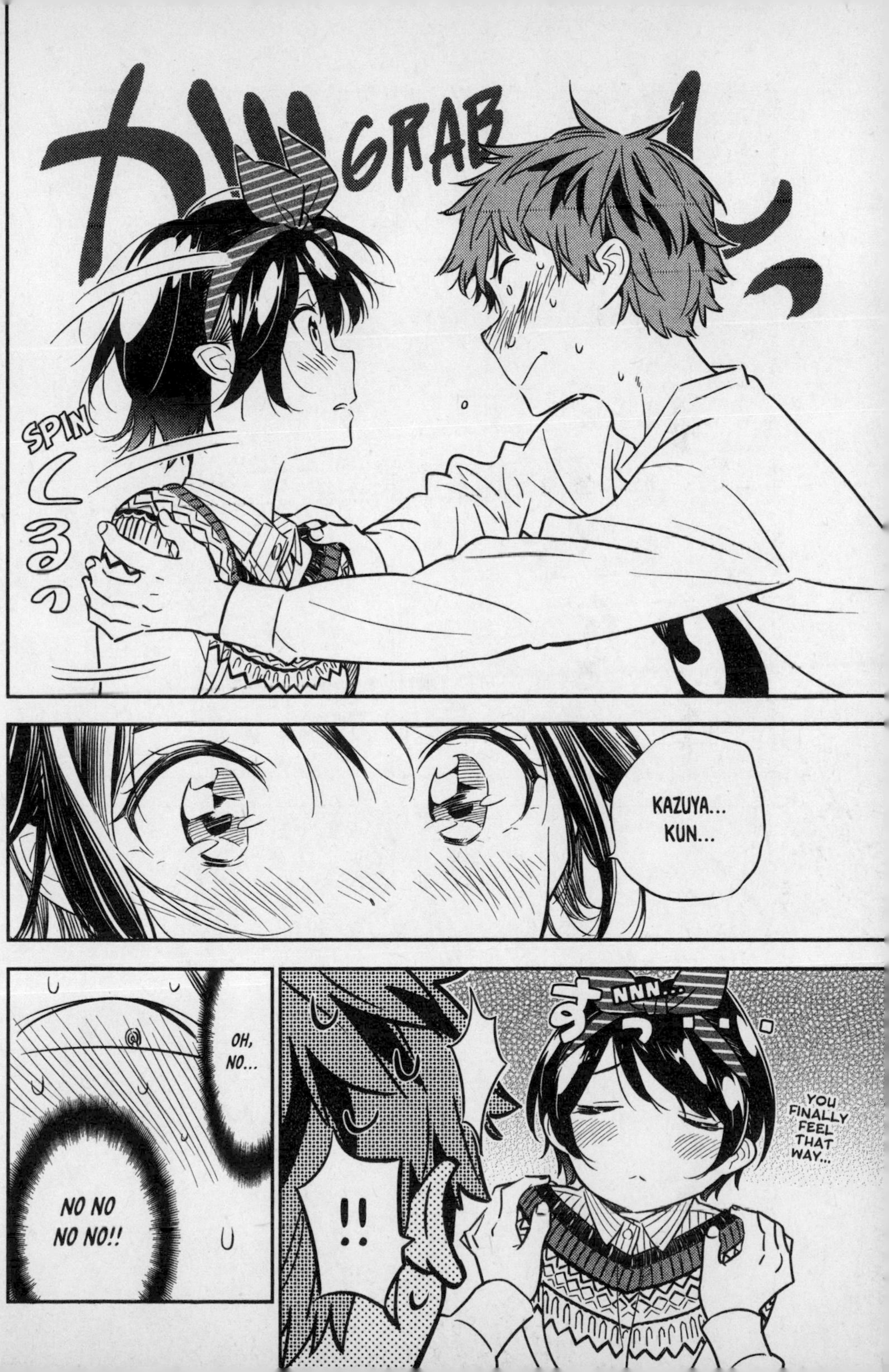
GRAB
SPIN
くるっ
KAZUYA... KUN...
すっ
NNN...
YOU FINALLY FEEL THAT WAY...
!!
OH, NO...
NO NO NO NO!!

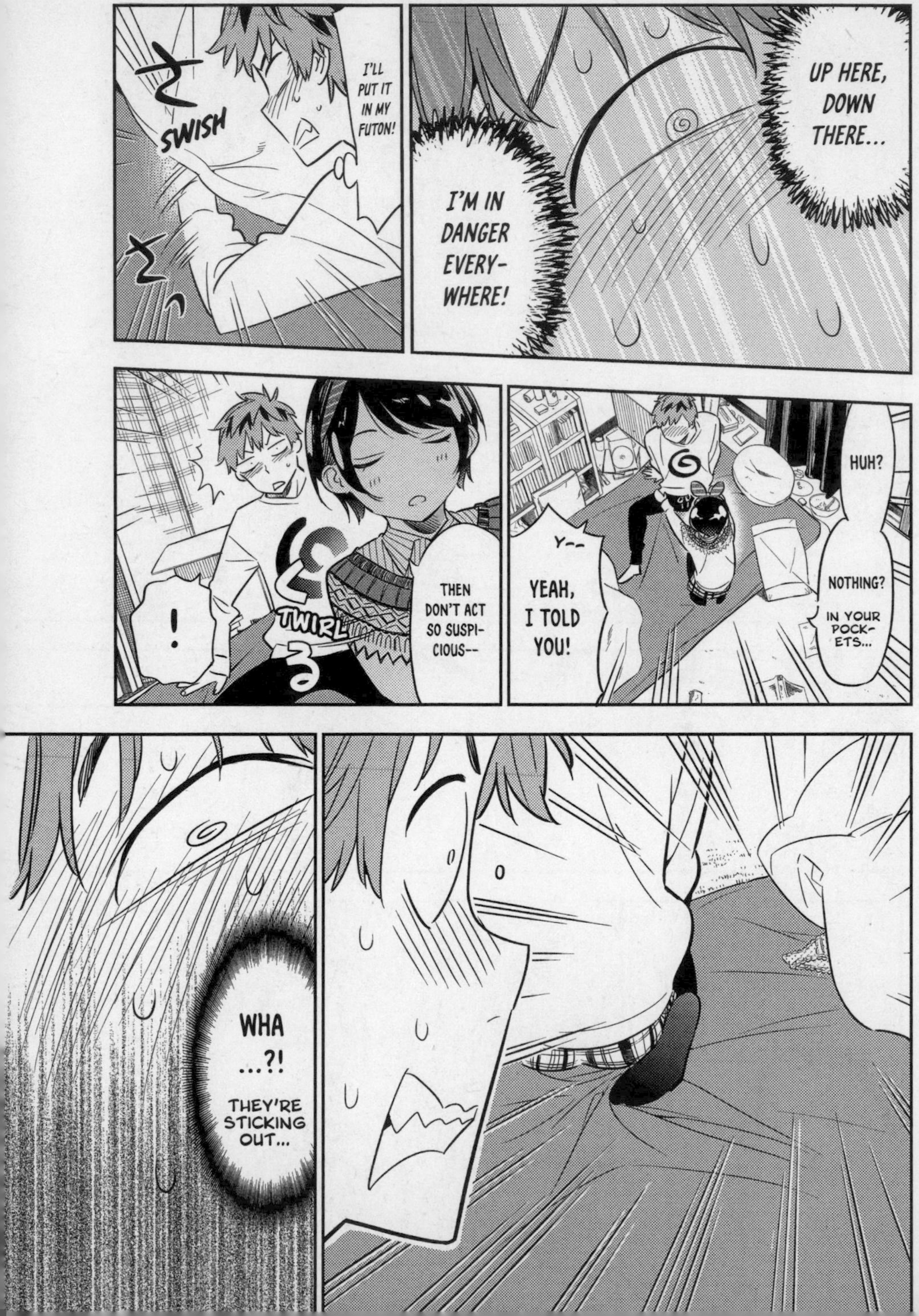
UP HERE, DOWN THERE...
I'M IN DANGER EVERYWHERE!
I'LL PUT IT IN MY FUTON!
SWISH
HUH?
NOTHING? IN YOUR POCKETS...
Y--
YEAH, I TOLD YOU!
THEN DON'T ACT SO SUSPICIOUS--
TWIRL
!
WHA...?!
THEY'RE STICKING OUT...

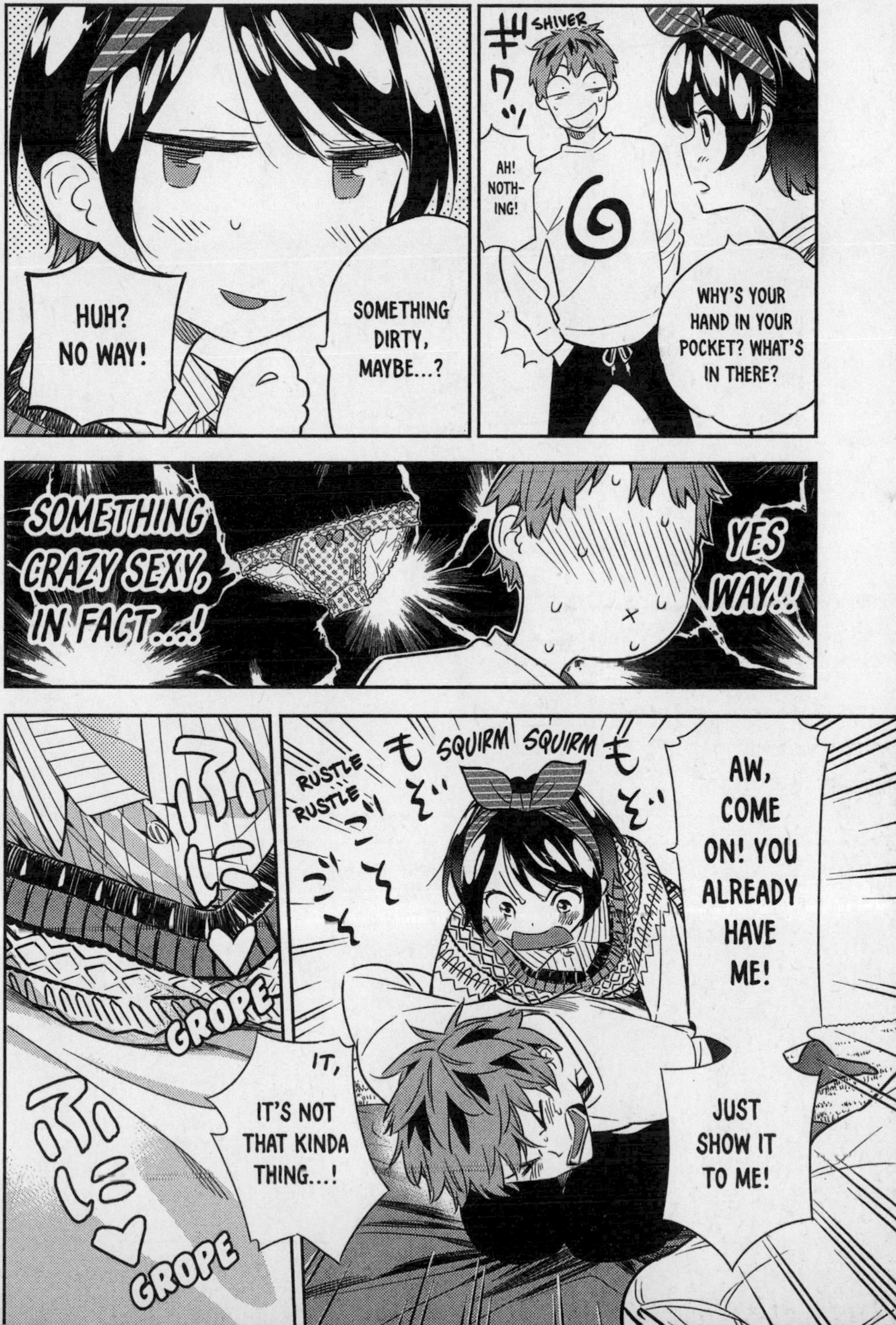
SHIVER
WHY'S YOUR HAND IN YOUR POCKET? WHAT'S IN THERE?
AH! NOTH-ING!
SOMETHING DIRTY, MAYBE...?
HUH? NO WAY!
YES WAY!!
SOMETHING CRAZY SEXY, IN FACT...!
AW, COME ON! YOU ALREADY HAVE ME!
SQUIRM SQUIRM
RUSTLE RUSTLE
JUST SHOW IT TO ME!
IT, IT'S NOT THAT KINDA THING...!
GROPE
GROPE

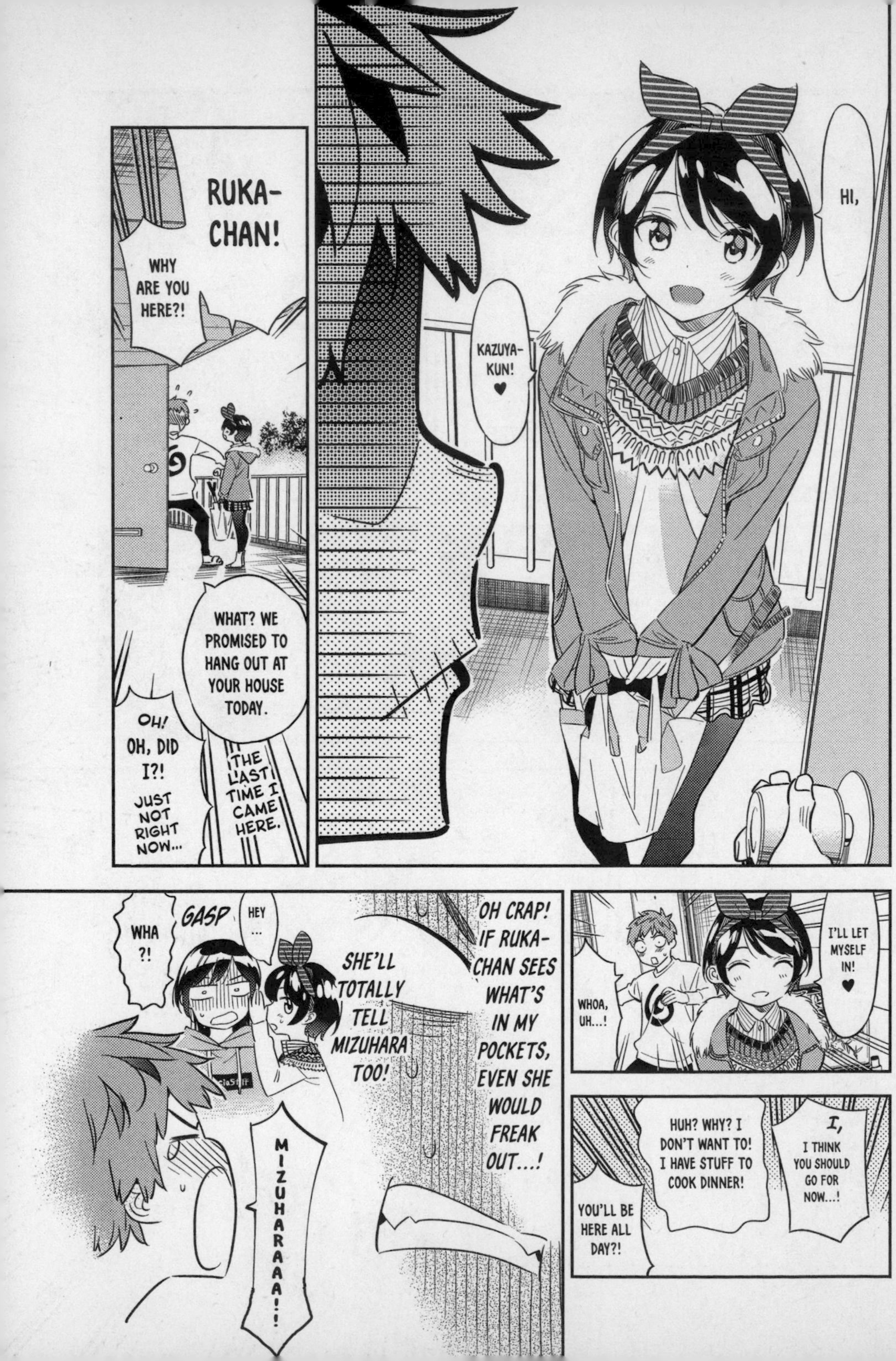
HI,
KAZUYA-KUN! ♥
RUKA-CHAN!
WHY ARE YOU HERE?!
WHAT? WE PROMISED TO HANG OUT AT YOUR HOUSE TODAY.
THE LAST TIME I CAME HERE.
OH! OH, DID I?!
JUST NOT RIGHT NOW...
I'LL LET MYSELF IN! ♥
WHOA, UH...!
I, I THINK YOU SHOULD GO FOR NOW...!
HUH? WHY? I DON'T WANT TO! I HAVE STUFF TO COOK DINNER!
YOU'LL BE HERE ALL DAY?!
OH CRAP! IF RUKA-CHAN SEES WHAT'S IN MY POCKETS, EVEN SHE WOULD FREAK OUT...!
SHE'LL TOTALLY TELL MIZUHARA TOO!
HEY ...
GASP
WHA ?!
MIZUHARARAAA!!

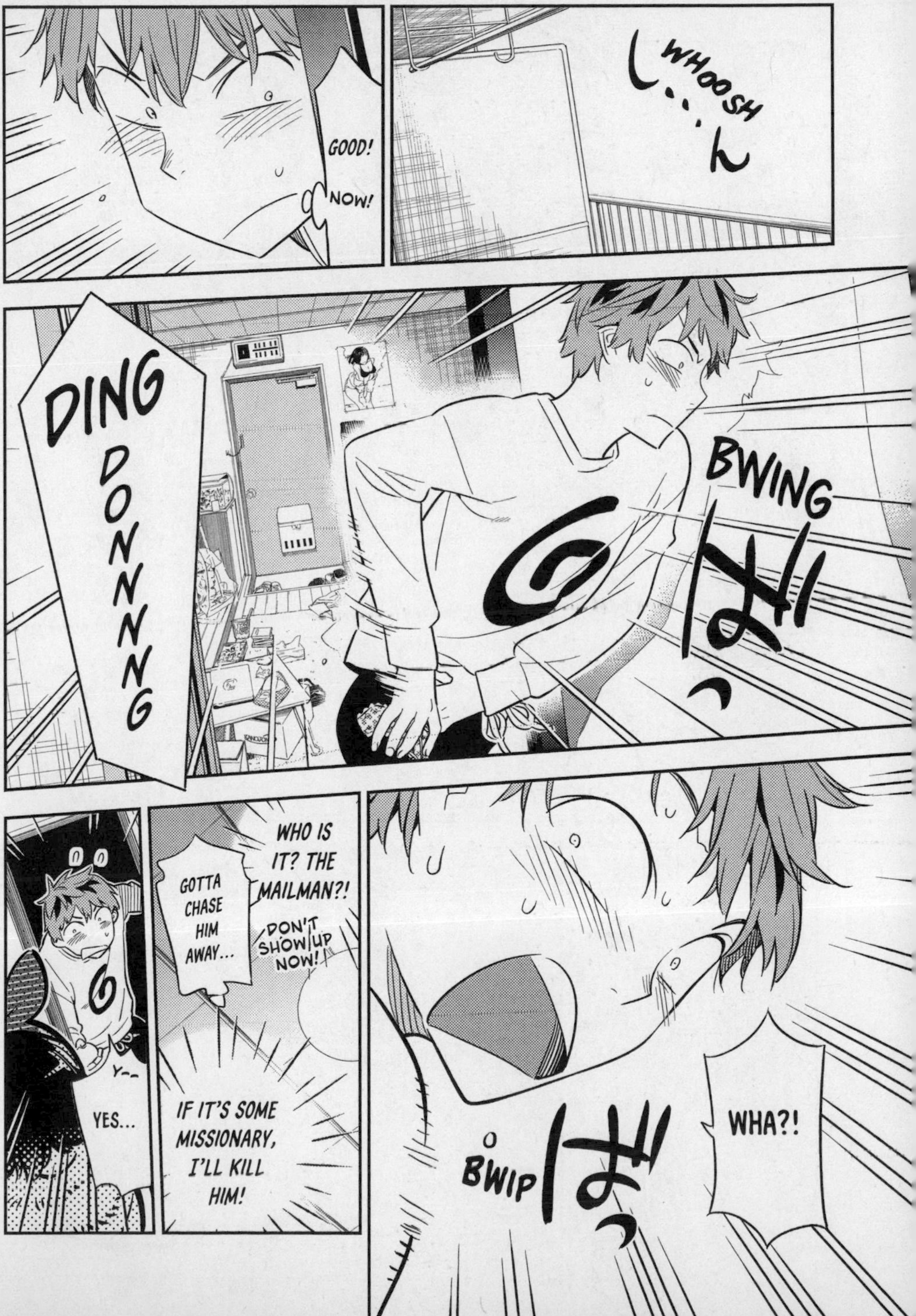
WHOOSH
GOOD!
NOW!
BWING
DING DONNNNG
WHA?!
BWIP
WHO IS IT? THE MAILMAN?!
DON'T SHOW UP NOW!
GOTTA CHASE HIM AWAY...
IF IT'S SOME MISSIONARY, I'LL KILL HIM!
Y--
YES...

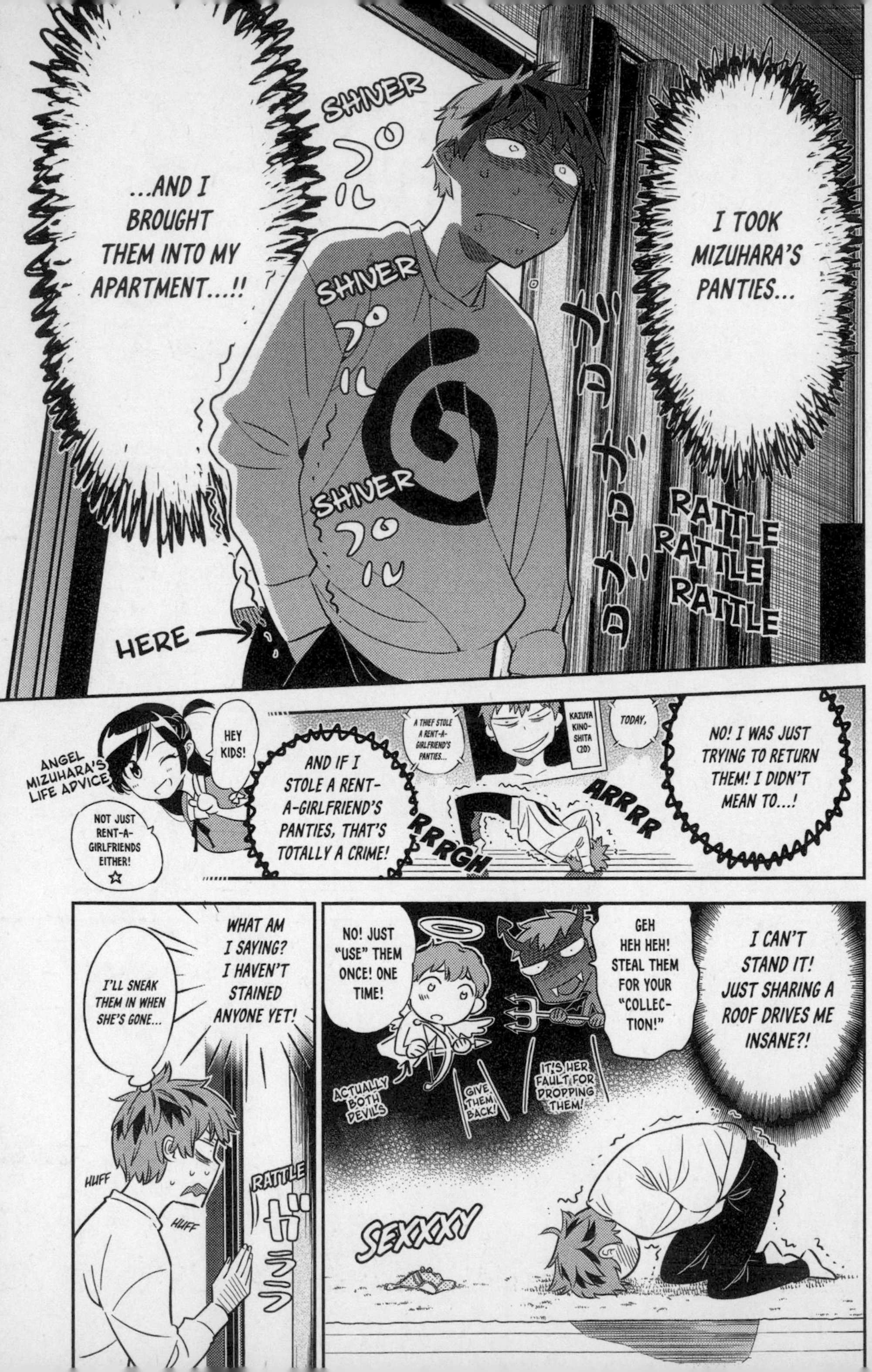
I TOOK MIZUHARA'S PANTIES...
...AND I BROUGHT THEM INTO MY APARTMENT...!!
SHIVER
SHIVER
SHIVER
RATTLE RATTLE RATTLE
HERE
NO! I WAS JUST TRYING TO RETURN THEM! I DIDN'T MEAN TO...!
TODAY,
KAZUYA KINOSHITA (20)
A THIEF STOLE A RENT-A-GIRLFRIEND'S PANTIES...
ARRRR
RRRGH
AND IF I STOLE A RENT-A-GIRLFRIEND'S PANTIES, THAT'S TOTALLY A CRIME!
HEY KIDS!
ANGEL MIZUHARA'S LIFE ADVICE
NOT JUST RENT-A-GIRLFRIENDS EITHER! ☆
I CAN'T STAND IT! JUST SHARING A ROOF DRIVES ME INSANE?!
GEH HEH HEH! STEAL THEM FOR YOUR "COLLECTION!"
NO! JUST "USE" THEM ONCE! ONE TIME!
IT'S HER FAULT FOR DROPPING THEM!
GIVE THEM BACK!
ACTUALLY BOTH DEVILS
SEXXXY
WHAT AM I SAYING? I HAVEN'T STAINED ANYONE YET!
I'LL SNEAK THEM IN WHEN SHE'S GONE...
HUFF
HUFF
RATTLE

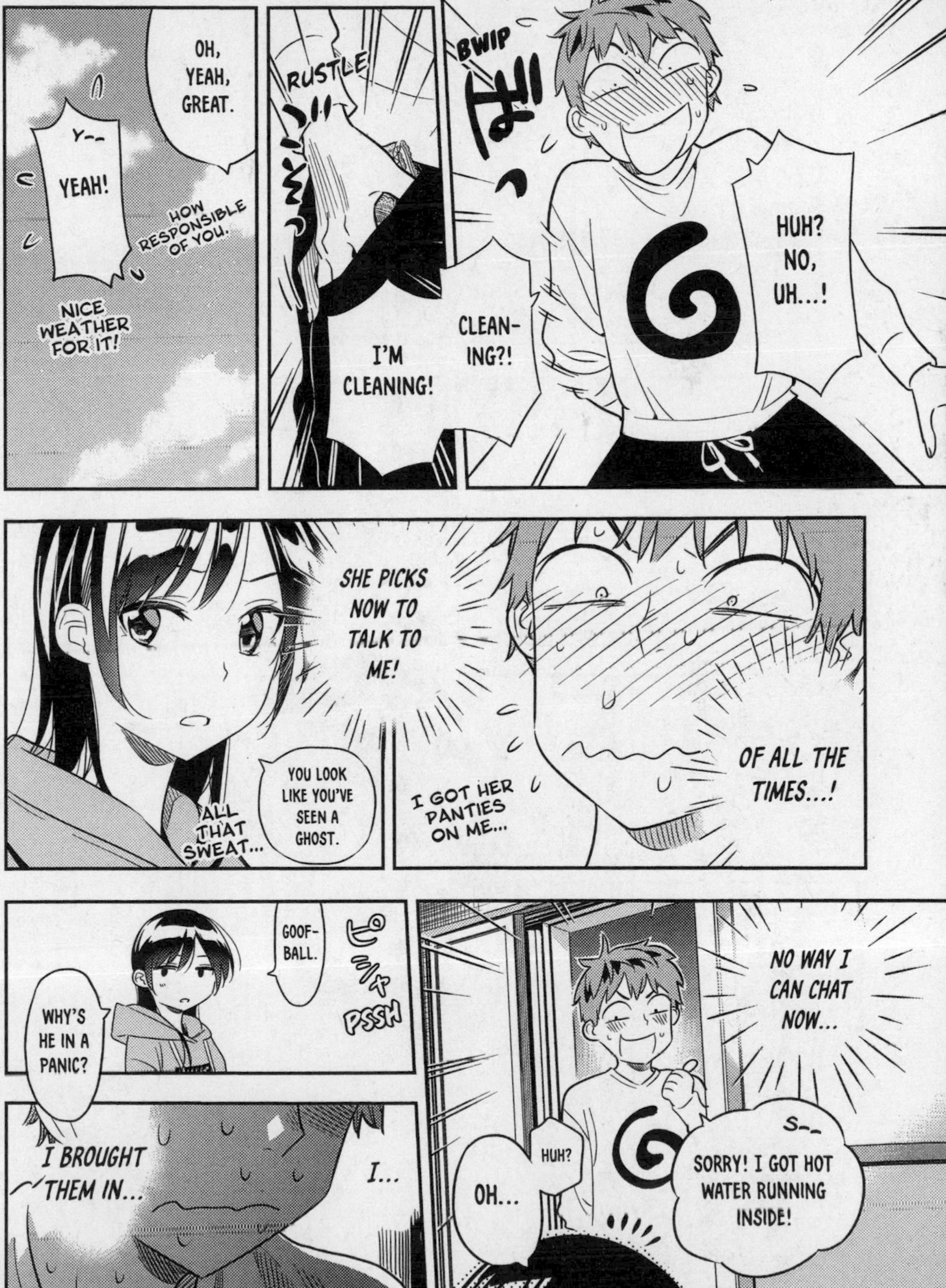
BWIP
HUH? NO, UH...!
RUSTLE
CLEANING?!
I'M CLEANING!
OH, YEAH, GREAT.
Y-- YEAH!
HOW RESPONSIBLE OF YOU.
NICE WEATHER FOR IT!
OF ALL THE TIMES...!
I GOT HER PANTIES ON ME...
SHE PICKS NOW TO TALK TO ME!
YOU LOOK LIKE YOU'VE SEEN A GHOST.
ALL THAT SWEAT...
NO WAY I CAN CHAT NOW...
S-- SORRY! I GOT HOT WATER RUNNING INSIDE!
HUH?
OH...
PSSH
GOOF-BALL.
WHY'S HE IN A PANIC?
I...
I BROUGHT THEM IN...

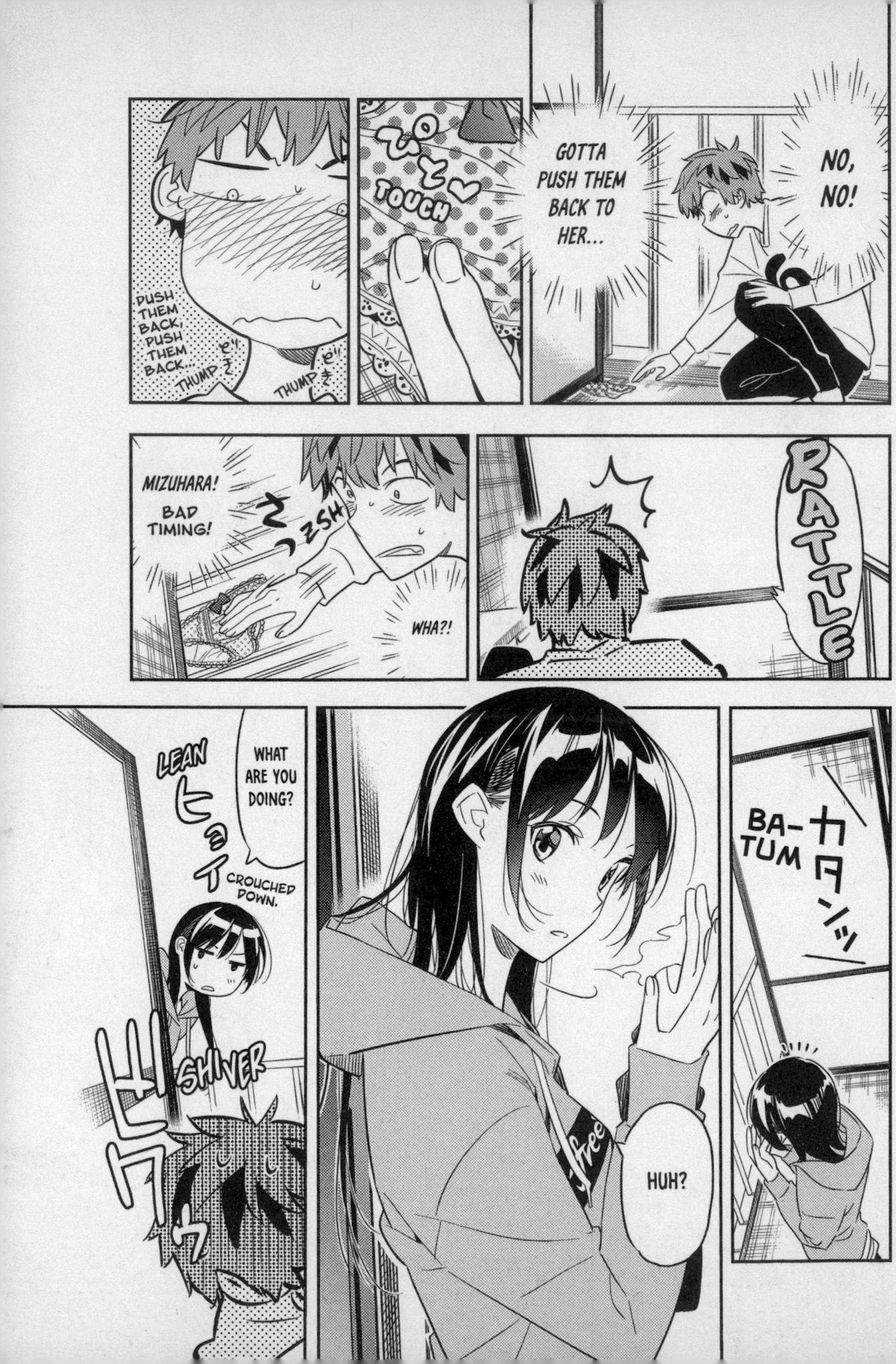
NO, NO!
GOTTA PUSH THEM BACK TO HER...
ぴと TOUCH
THUMP
PUSH THEM BACK, PUSH THEM BACK...
THUMP
RATTLE
MIZUHARA! BAD TIMING!
ZSH
WHA?!
BA-TUM カタンッ
HUH?
WHAT ARE YOU DOING?
LEAN ヒョイ
CROUCHED DOWN.
SHIVER

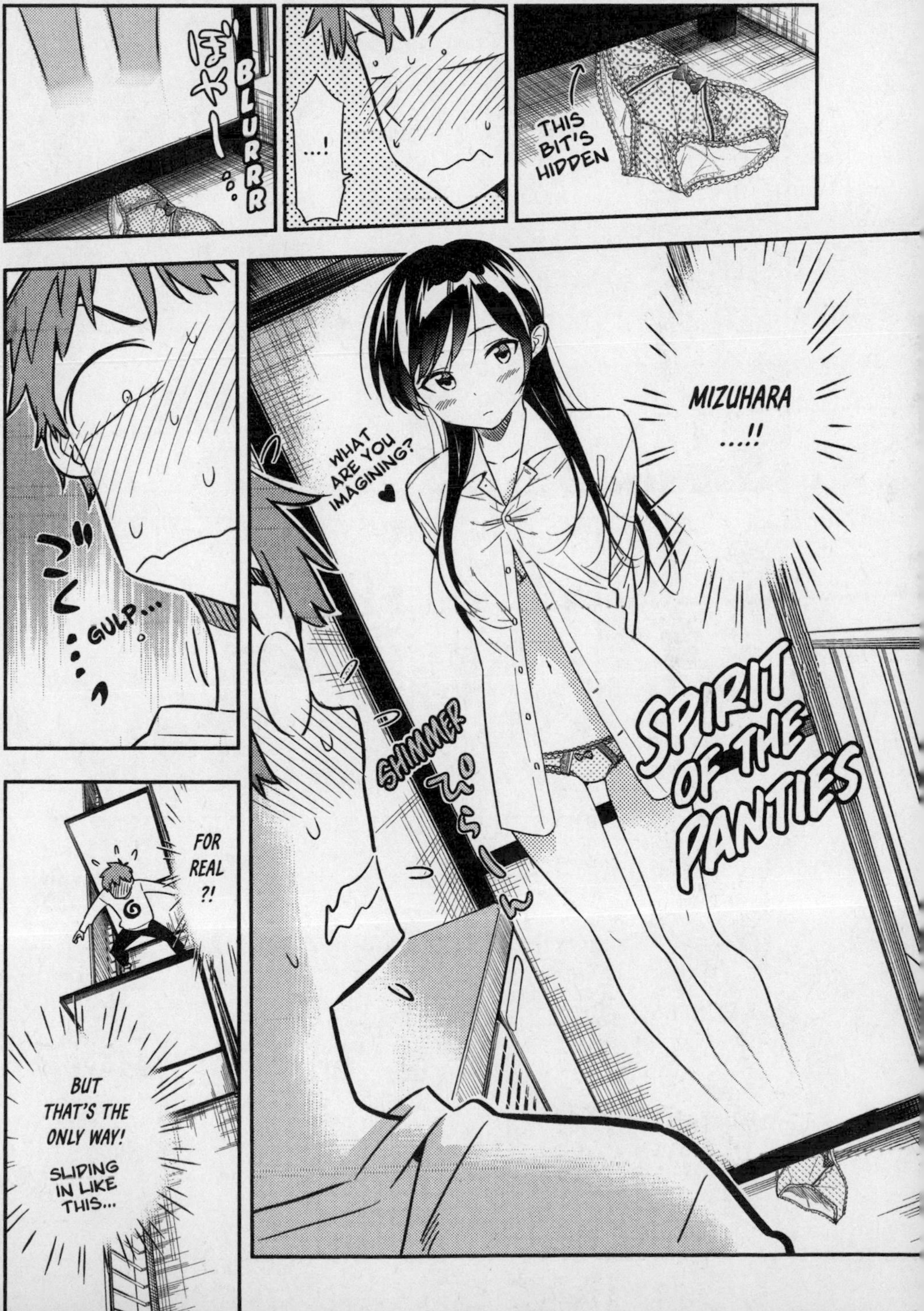
THIS BIT'S HIDDEN
...!
BLURRR
MIZUHARA ...!!
WHAT ARE YOU IMAGINING? ♥
SPIRIT OF THE PANTIES
SHIMMER
GULP...
FOR REAL ?!
BUT THAT'S THE ONLY WAY!
SLIDING IN LIKE THIS...

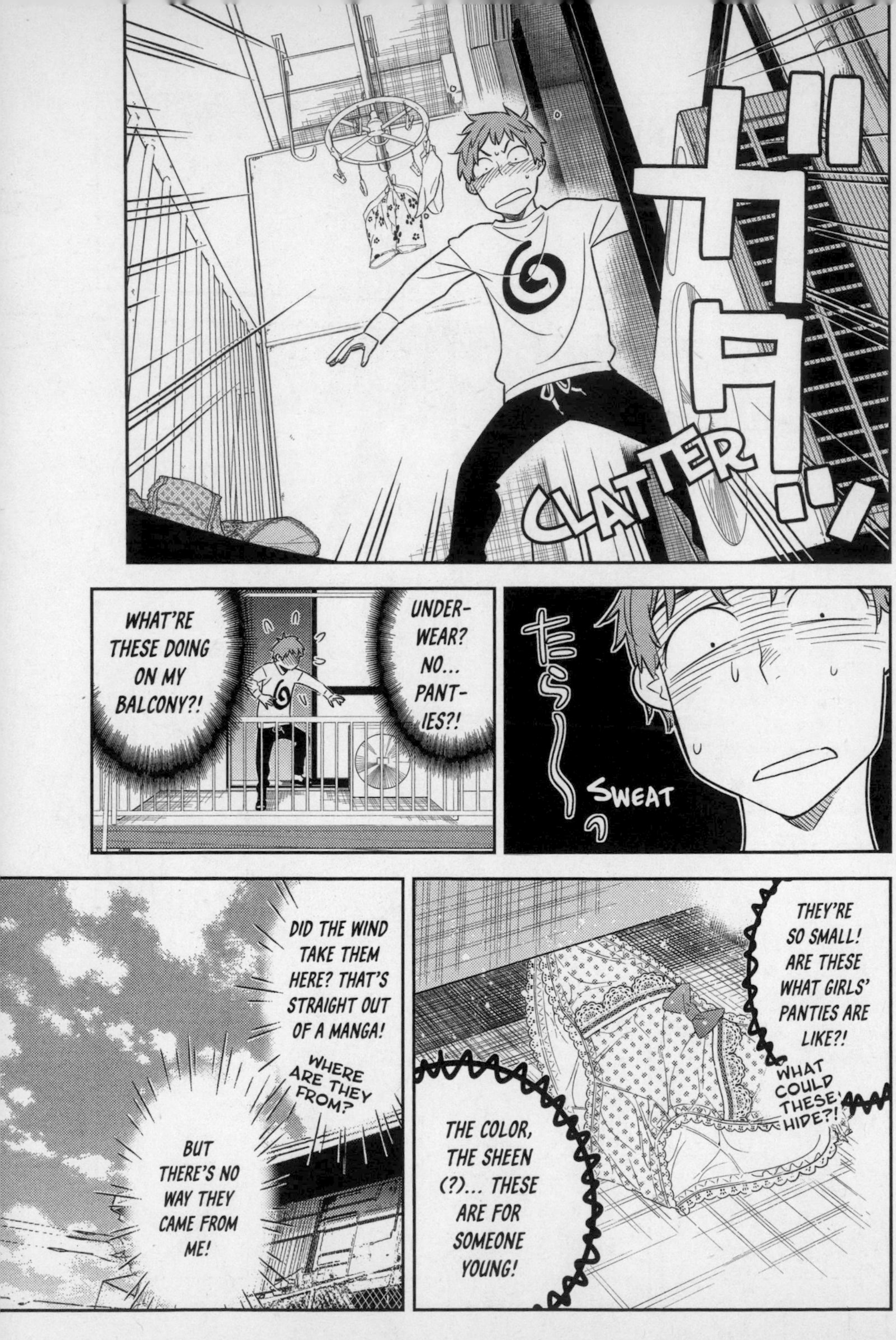
ガタッ
CLATTER
SWEAT
WHAT'RE THESE DOING ON MY BALCONY?!
UNDER-WEAR? NO... PANT-IES?!
THEY'RE SO SMALL! ARE THESE WHAT GIRLS' PANTIES ARE LIKE?!
WHAT COULD THESE HIDE?!
THE COLOR, THE SHEEN (?)... THESE ARE FOR SOMEONE YOUNG!
DID THE WIND TAKE THEM HERE? THAT'S STRAIGHT OUT OF A MANGA!
WHERE ARE THEY FROM?
BUT THERE'S NO WAY THEY CAME FROM ME!

RATING 40

MY GIRLFRIEND AND THE PAIR OF PANTIES

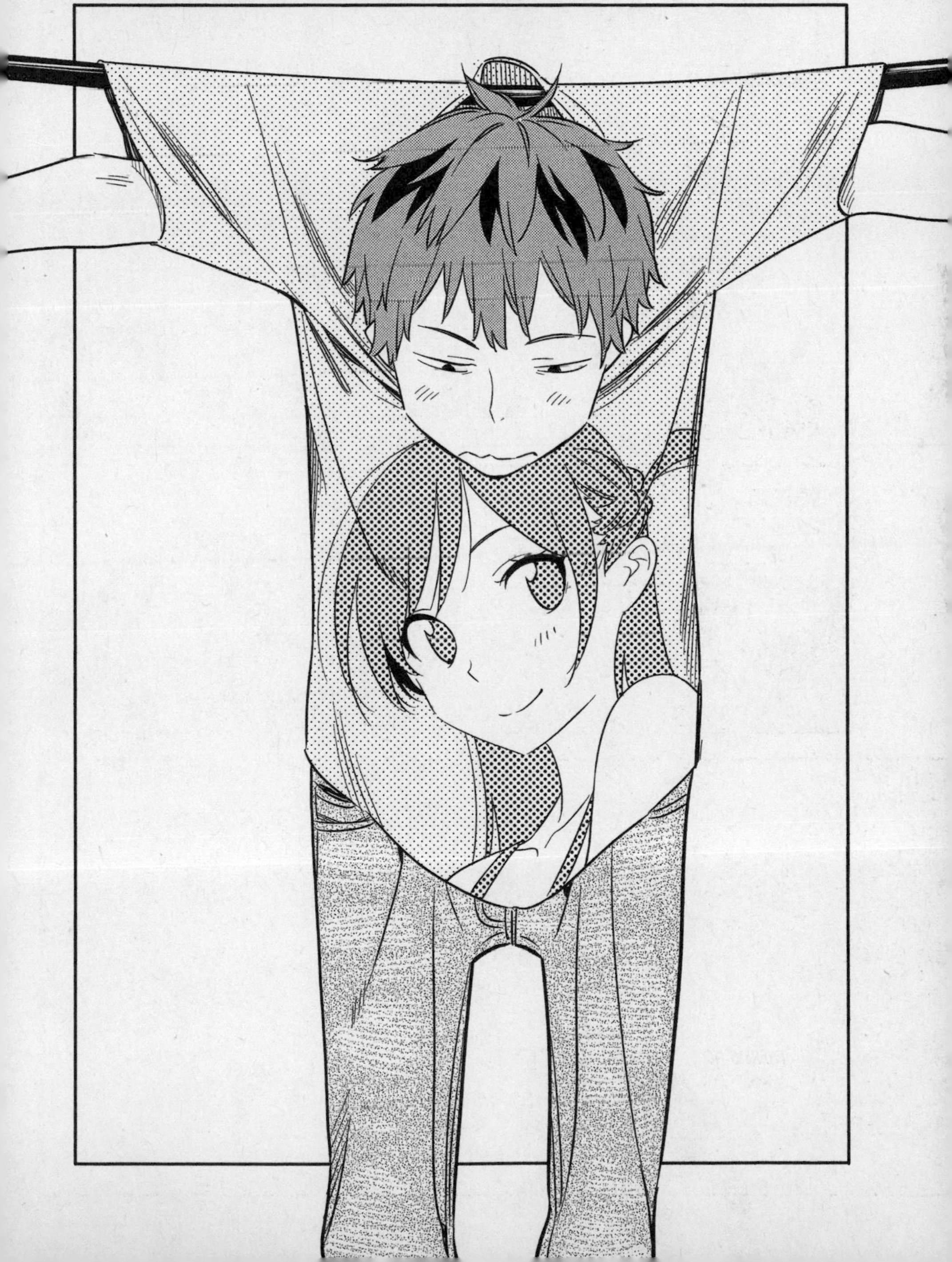

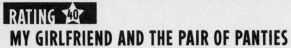

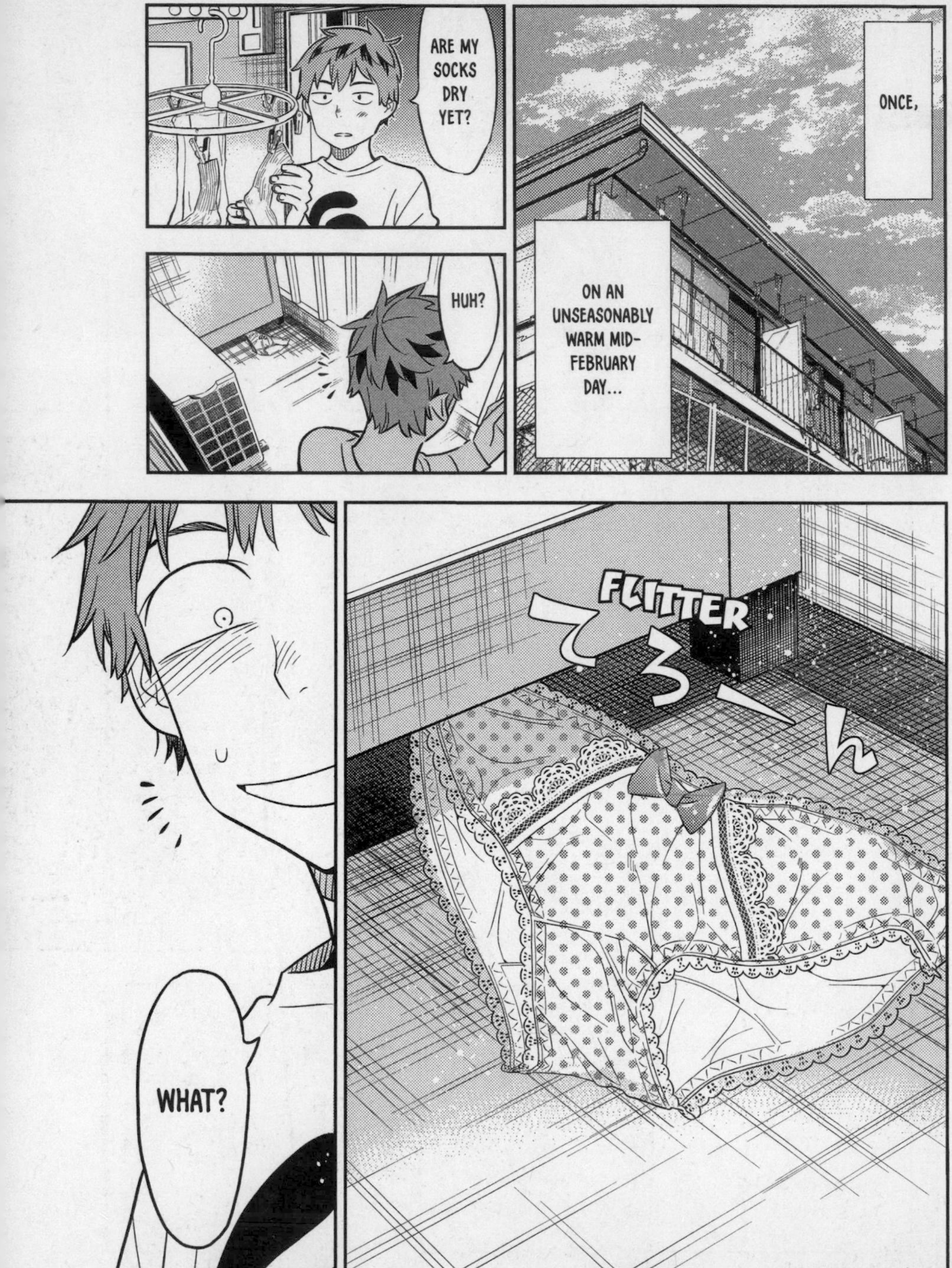
ONCE,
ON AN UNSEASONABLY WARM MID-FEBRUARY DAY...
ARE MY SOCKS DRY YET?
HUH?
FLITTER
てろーん
WHAT?

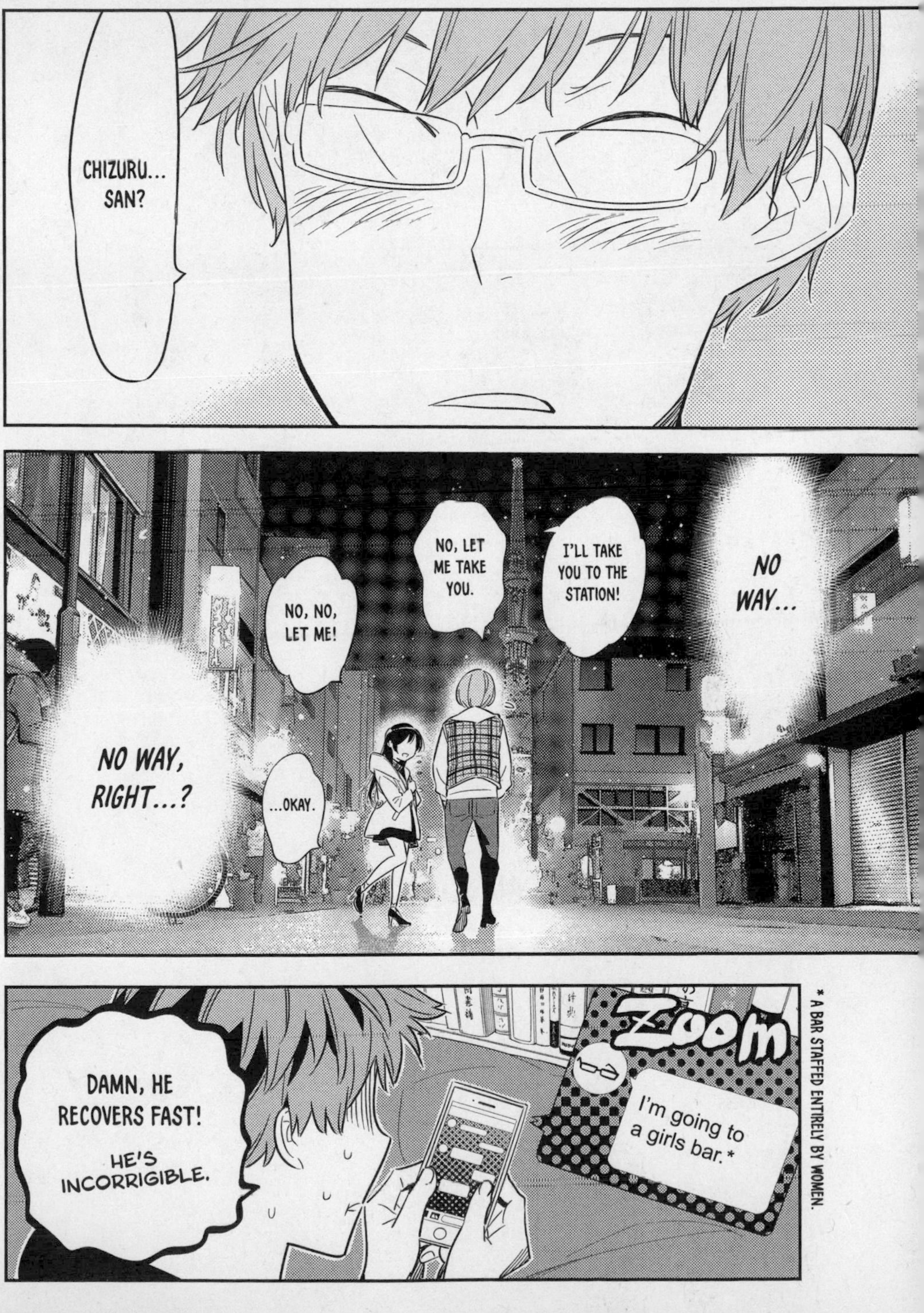
CHIZURU... SAN?
NO WAY...
I'LL TAKE YOU TO THE STATION!
NO, LET ME TAKE YOU.
NO, NO, LET ME!
...OKAY.
NO WAY, RIGHT...?
ZOOM
I'm going to a girls bar.*
DAMN, HE RECOVERS FAST!
HE'S INCORRIGIBLE.

* A BAR STAFFED ENTIRELY BY WOMEN.

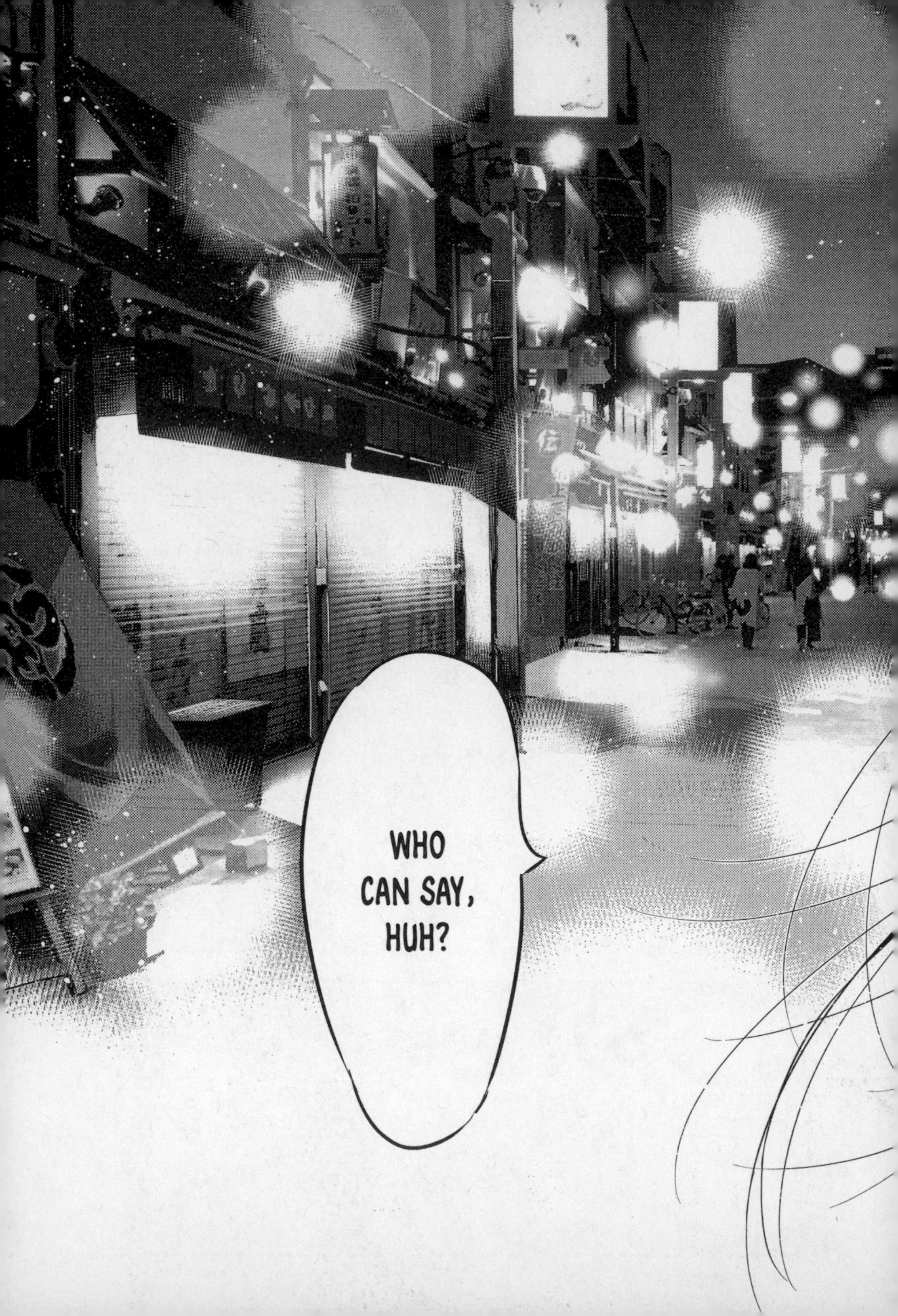
WHO CAN SAY, HUH?

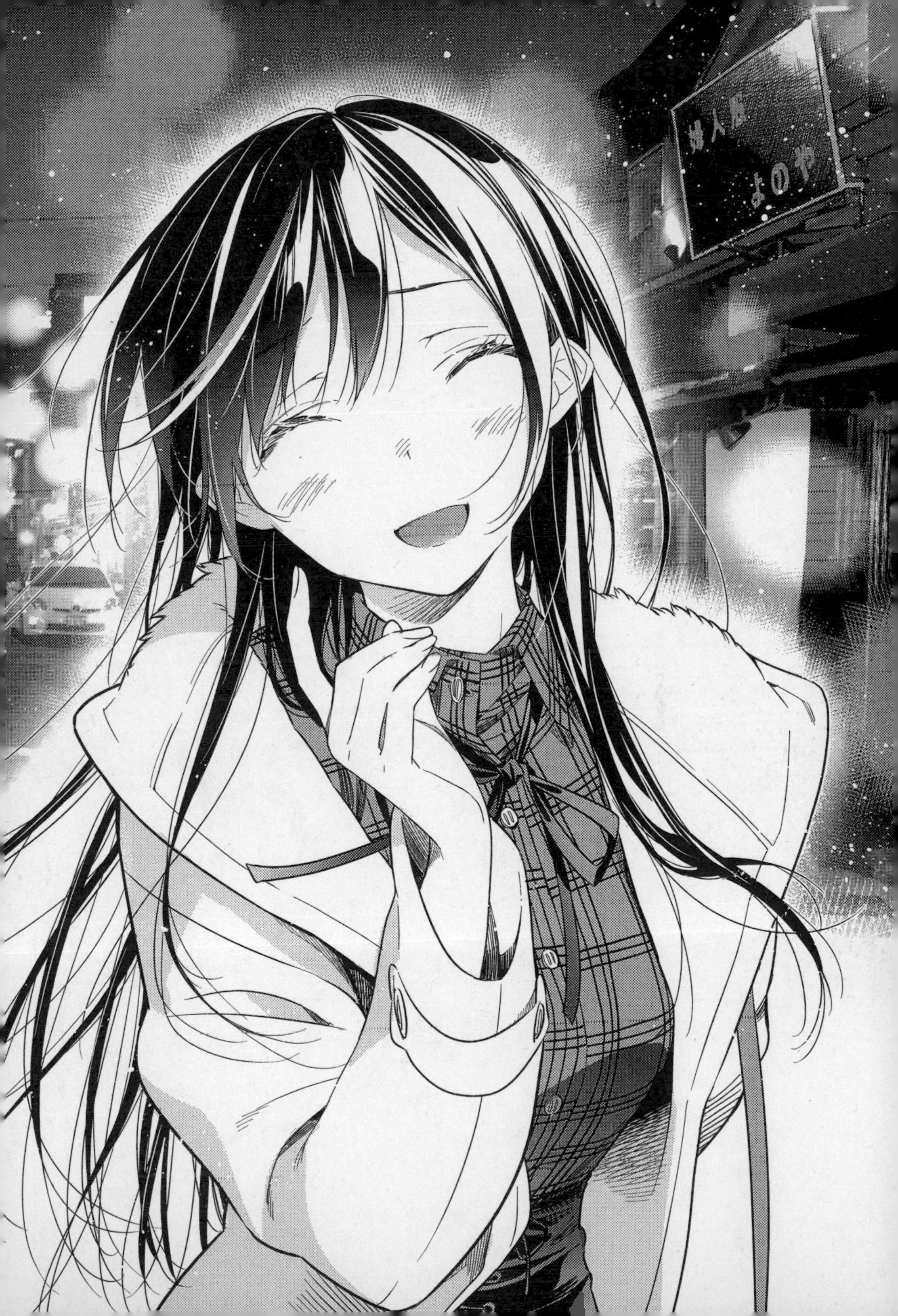
婦人服
よのや

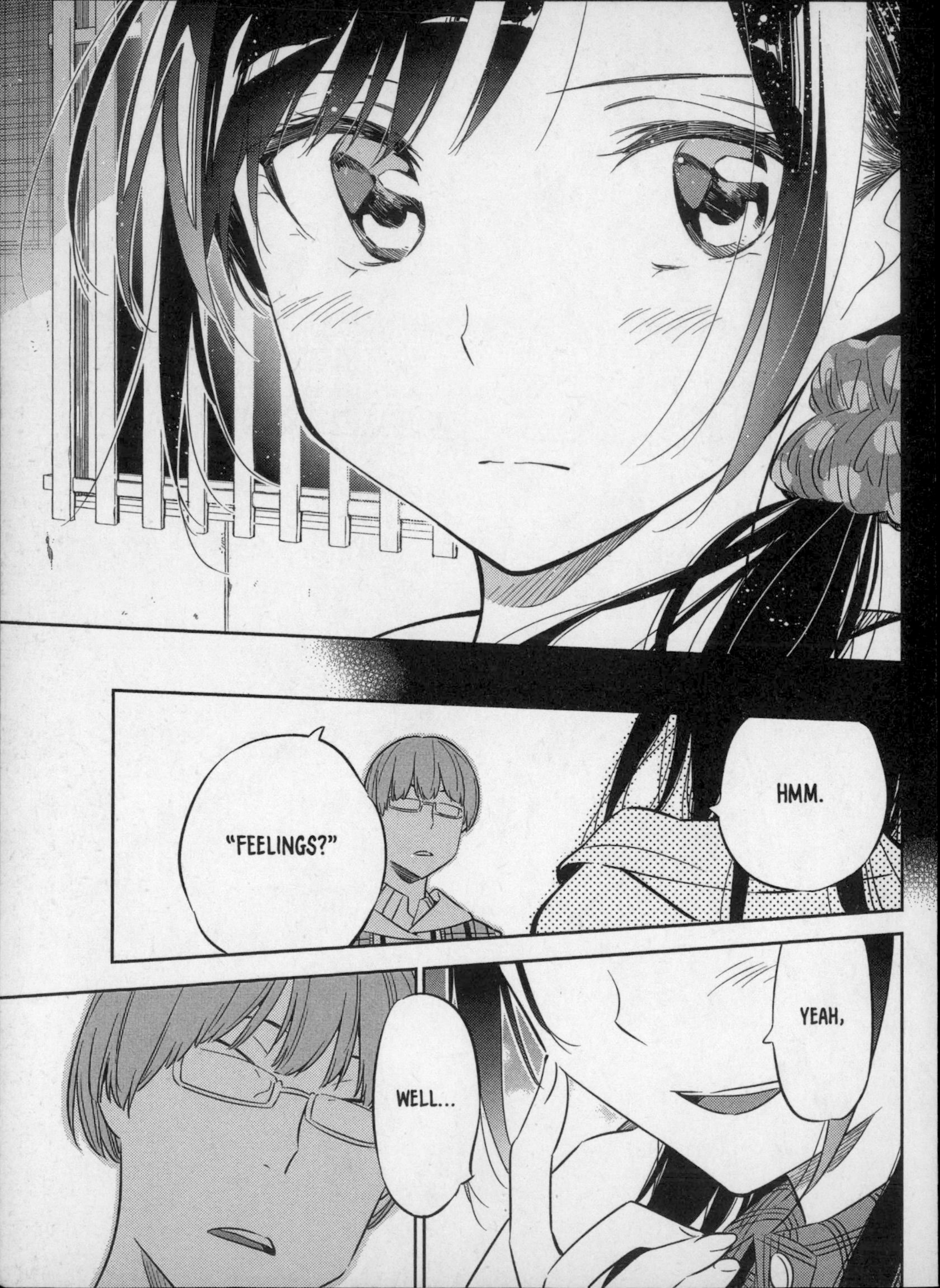
HMM.
"FEELINGS?"
YEAH,
WELL...

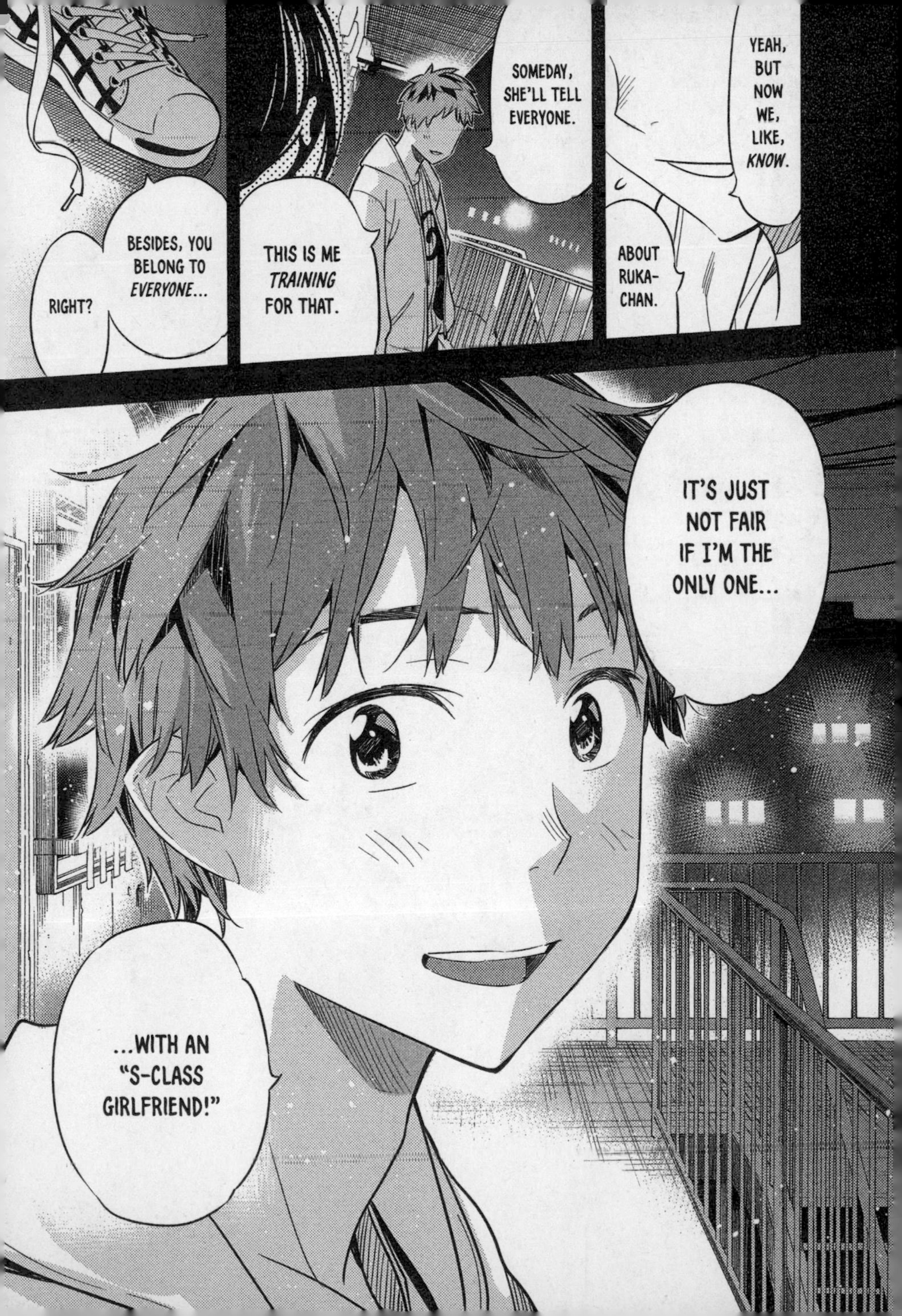
YEAH, BUT NOW WE, LIKE, *KNOW*.
ABOUT RUKA-CHAN.
SOMEDAY, SHE'LL TELL EVERYONE.
THIS IS ME *TRAINING* FOR THAT.
BESIDES, YOU BELONG TO *EVERYONE*...
RIGHT?
IT'S JUST NOT FAIR IF I'M THE ONLY ONE...
...WITH AN "S-CLASS GIRLFRIEND!"

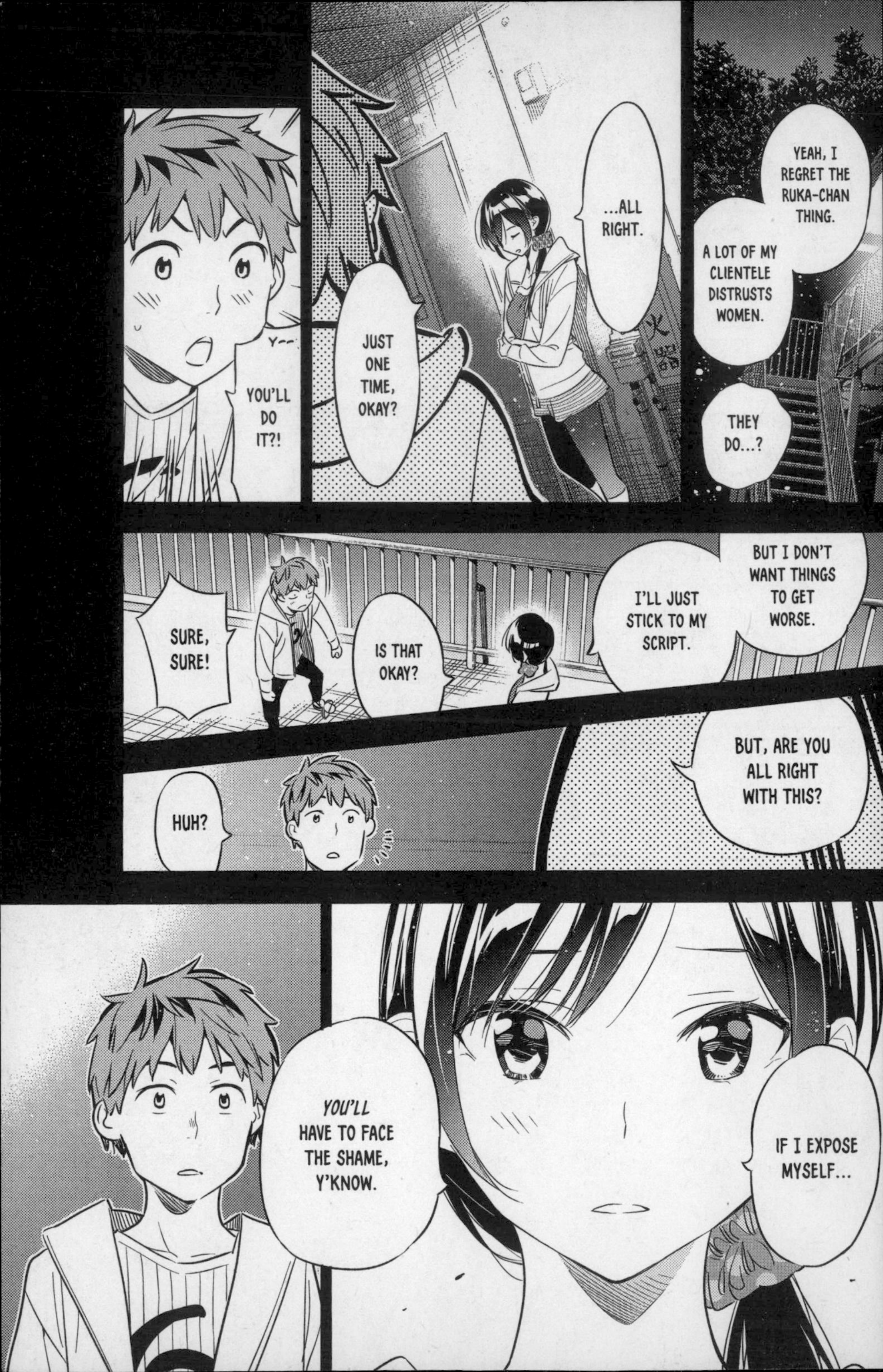

YEAH, I REGRET THE RUKA-CHAN THING.
A LOT OF MY CLIENTELE DISTRUSTS WOMEN.
THEY DO...?
...ALL RIGHT.
JUST ONE TIME, OKAY?
Y--
YOU'LL DO IT?!
BUT I DON'T WANT THINGS TO GET WORSE.
I'LL JUST STICK TO MY SCRIPT.
IS THAT OKAY?
SURE, SURE!
BUT, ARE YOU ALL RIGHT WITH THIS?
HUH?
IF I EXPOSE MYSELF...
YOU'LL HAVE TO FACE THE SHAME, Y'KNOW.

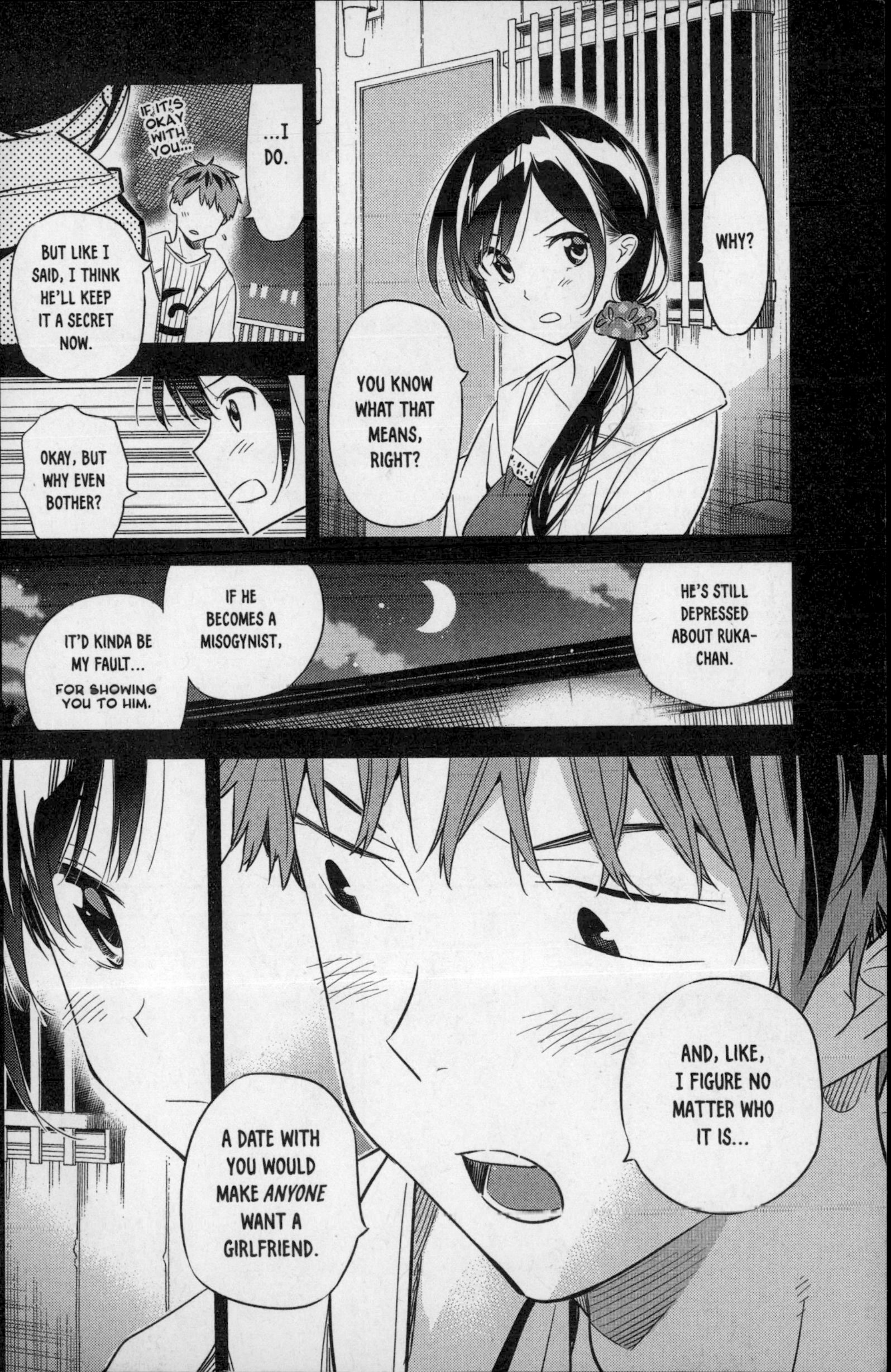
WHY?
YOU KNOW WHAT THAT MEANS, RIGHT?
...I DO.
IF IT'S OKAY WITH YOU...
BUT LIKE I SAID, I THINK HE'LL KEEP IT A SECRET NOW.
OKAY, BUT WHY EVEN BOTHER?
HE'S STILL DEPRESSED ABOUT RUKA-CHAN.
IF HE BECOMES A MISOGYNIST,
IT'D KINDA BE MY FAULT...
FOR SHOWING YOU TO HIM.
AND, LIKE, I FIGURE NO MATTER WHO IT IS...
A DATE WITH YOU WOULD MAKE *ANYONE* WANT A GIRLFRIEND.

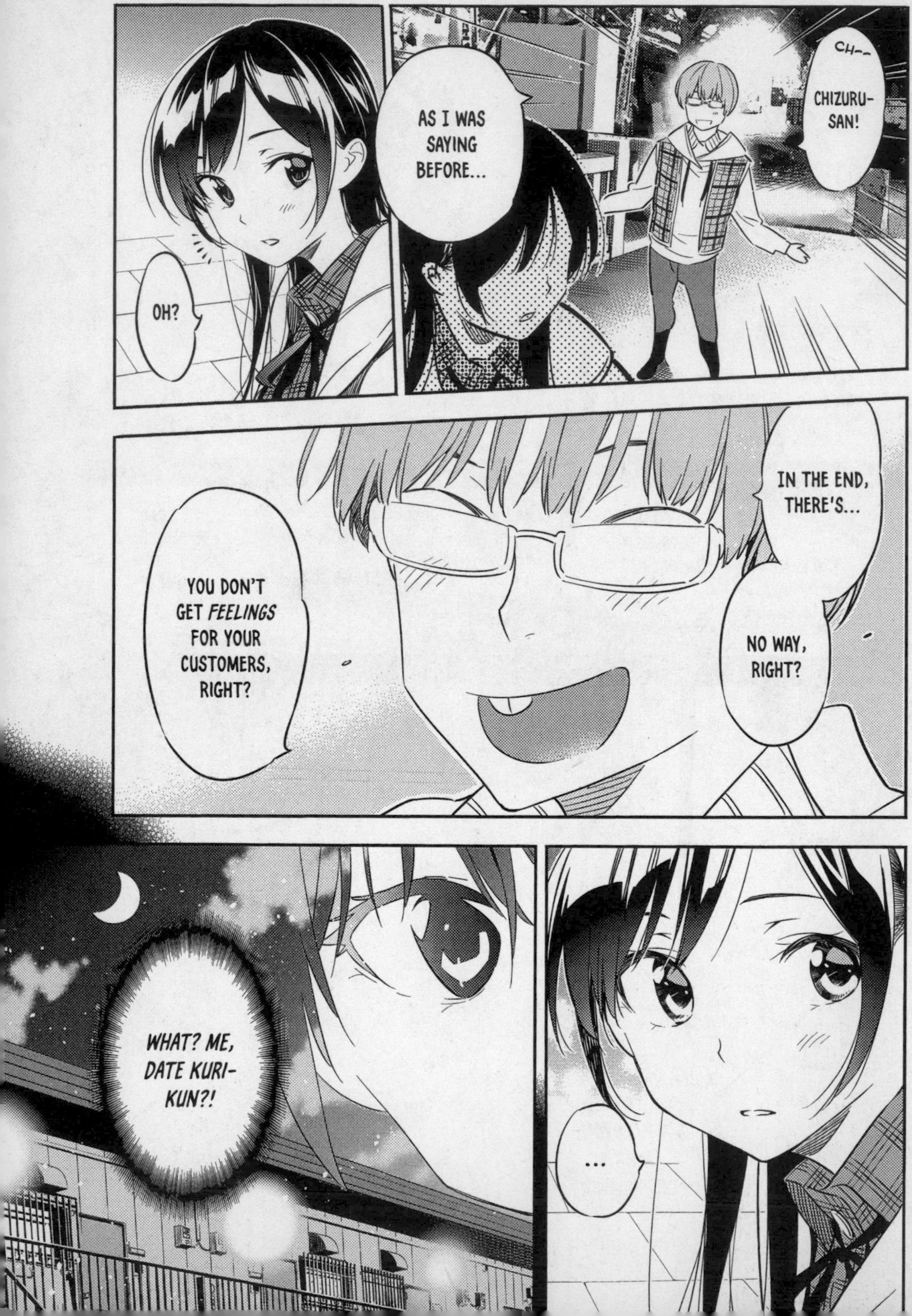
CH--
CHIZURU-SAN!
AS I WAS SAYING BEFORE...
OH?
IN THE END, THERE'S...
NO WAY, RIGHT?
YOU DON'T GET *FEELINGS* FOR YOUR CUSTOMERS, RIGHT?
...
WHAT? ME, DATE KURI-KUN?!

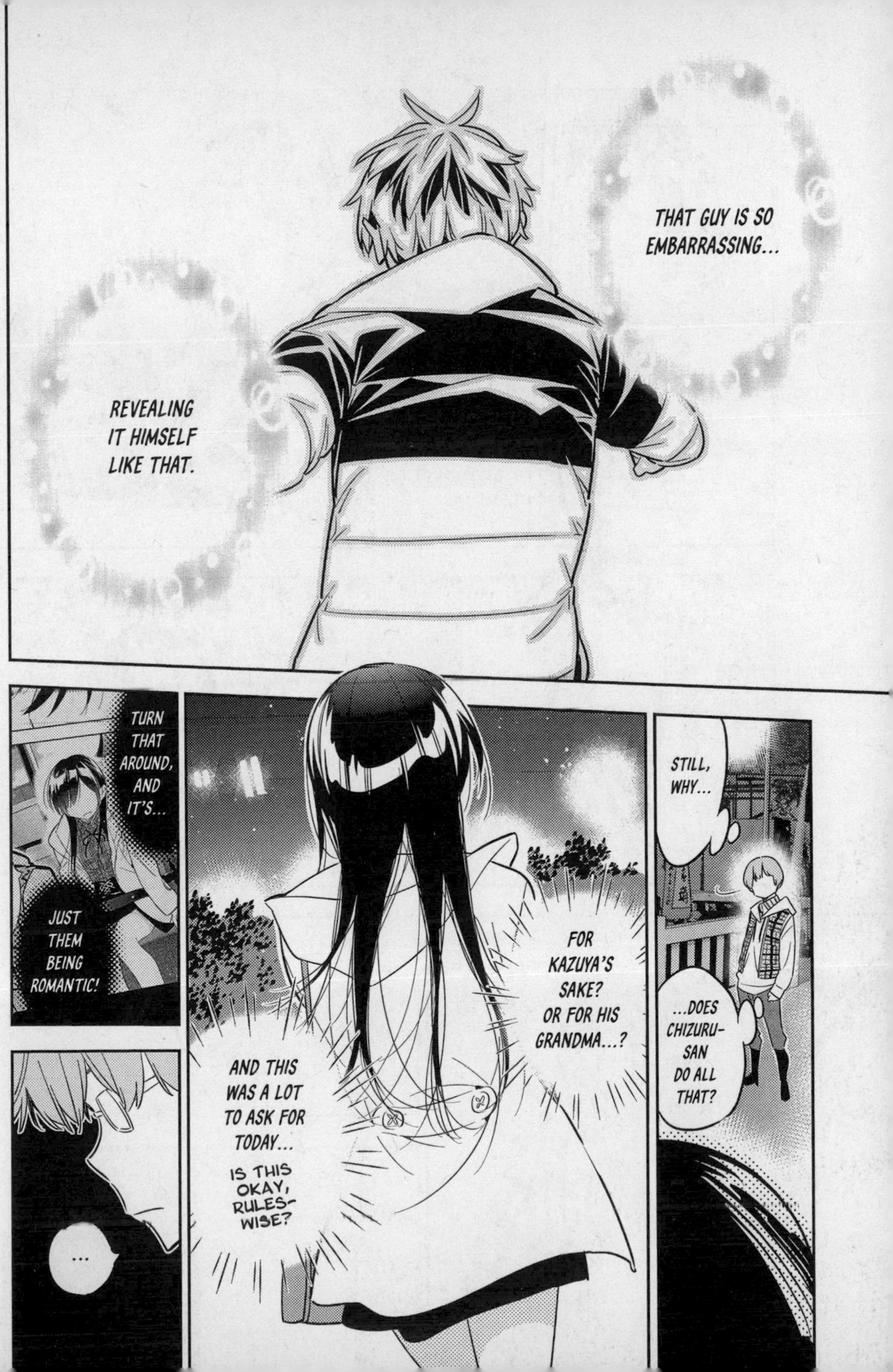
THAT GUY IS SO EMBARRASSING...
REVEALING IT HIMSELF LIKE THAT.
STILL, WHY...
...DOES CHIZURU-SAN DO ALL THAT?
FOR KAZUYA'S SAKE? OR FOR HIS GRANDMA...?
AND THIS WAS A LOT TO ASK FOR TODAY...
IS THIS OKAY, RULES-WISE?
TURN THAT AROUND, AND IT'S...
JUST THEM BEING ROMANTIC!
...

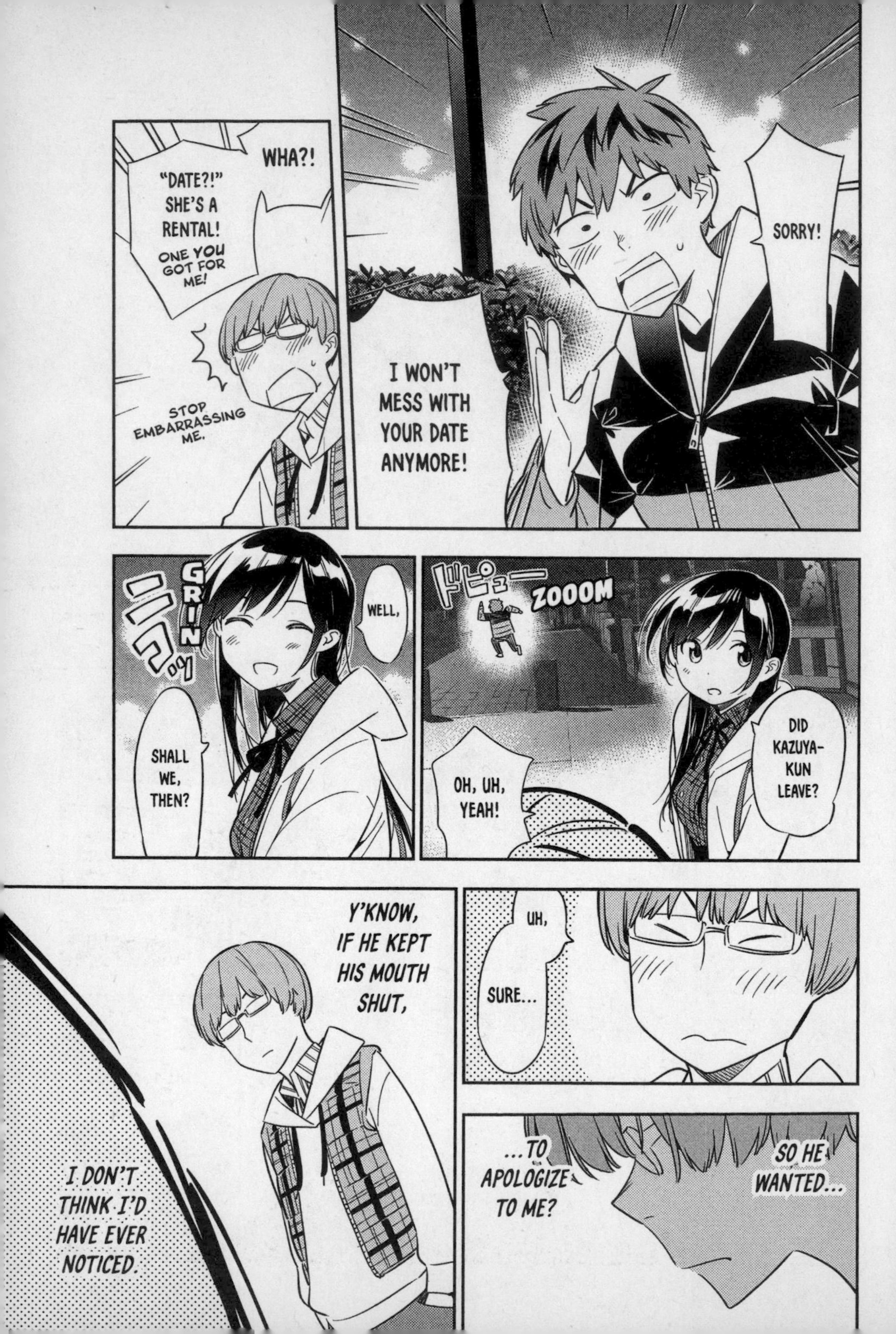
SORRY!
I WON'T MESS WITH YOUR DATE ANYMORE!
WHA?!
"DATE?!" SHE'S A RENTAL!
ONE YOU GOT FOR ME!
STOP EMBARRASSING ME.
ドピュー
ZOOOM
DID KAZUYA-KUN LEAVE?
OH, UH, YEAH!
ニコッ
GRIN
WELL,
SHALL WE, THEN?
UH,
SURE...
SO HE WANTED...
...TO APOLOGIZE TO ME?
Y'KNOW, IF HE KEPT HIS MOUTH SHUT,
I DON'T THINK I'D HAVE EVER NOTICED.

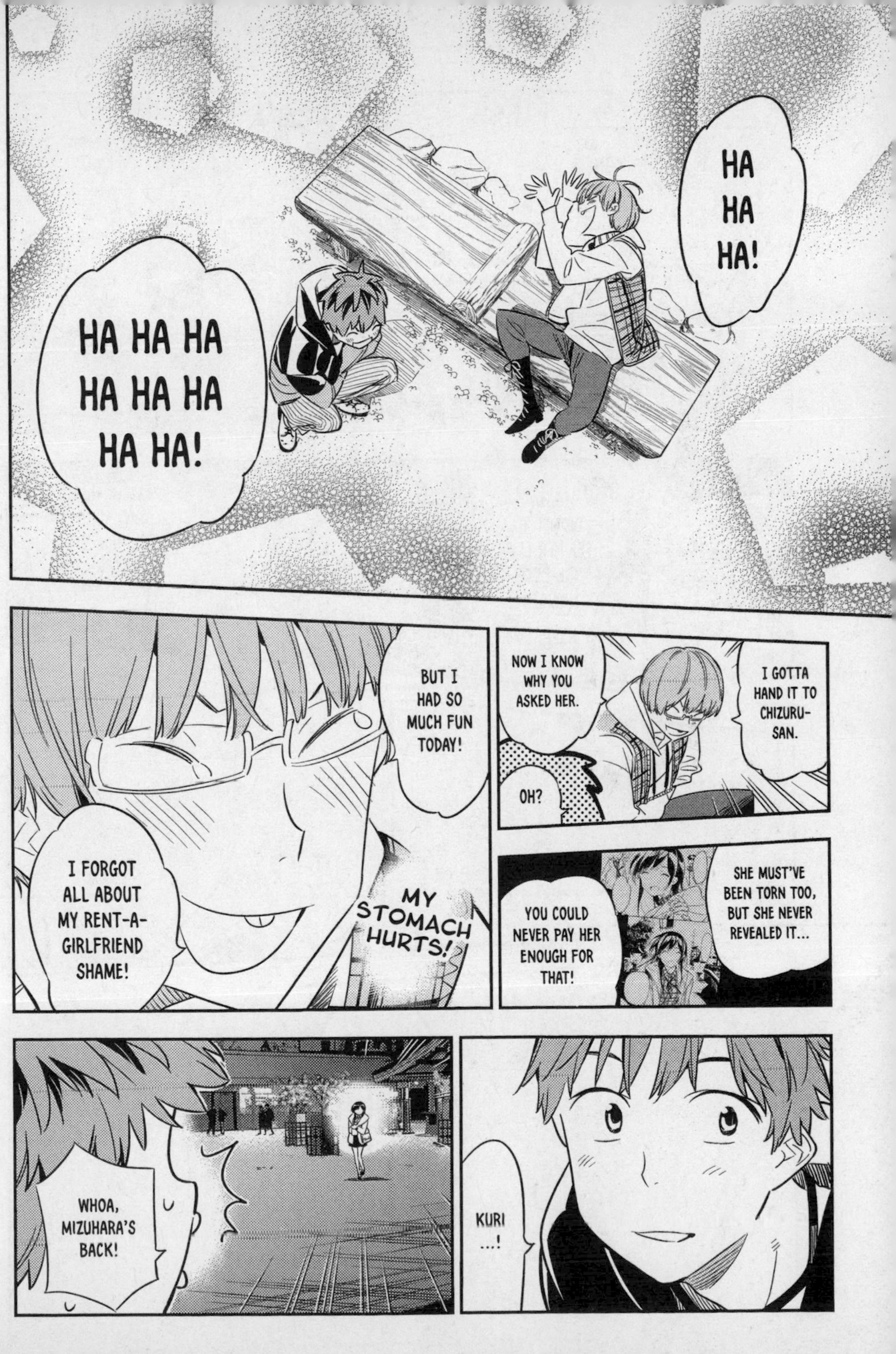
HA HA HA!
HA HA HA HA HA HA HA HA!
I GOTTA HAND IT TO CHIZURU-SAN.
NOW I KNOW WHY YOU ASKED HER.
OH?
SHE MUST'VE BEEN TORN TOO, BUT SHE NEVER REVEALED IT...
YOU COULD NEVER PAY HER ENOUGH FOR THAT!
BUT I HAD SO MUCH FUN TODAY!
MY STOMACH HURTS!
I FORGOT ALL ABOUT MY RENT-A-GIRLFRIEND SHAME!
KURI ...!
WHOA, MIZUHARA'S BACK!

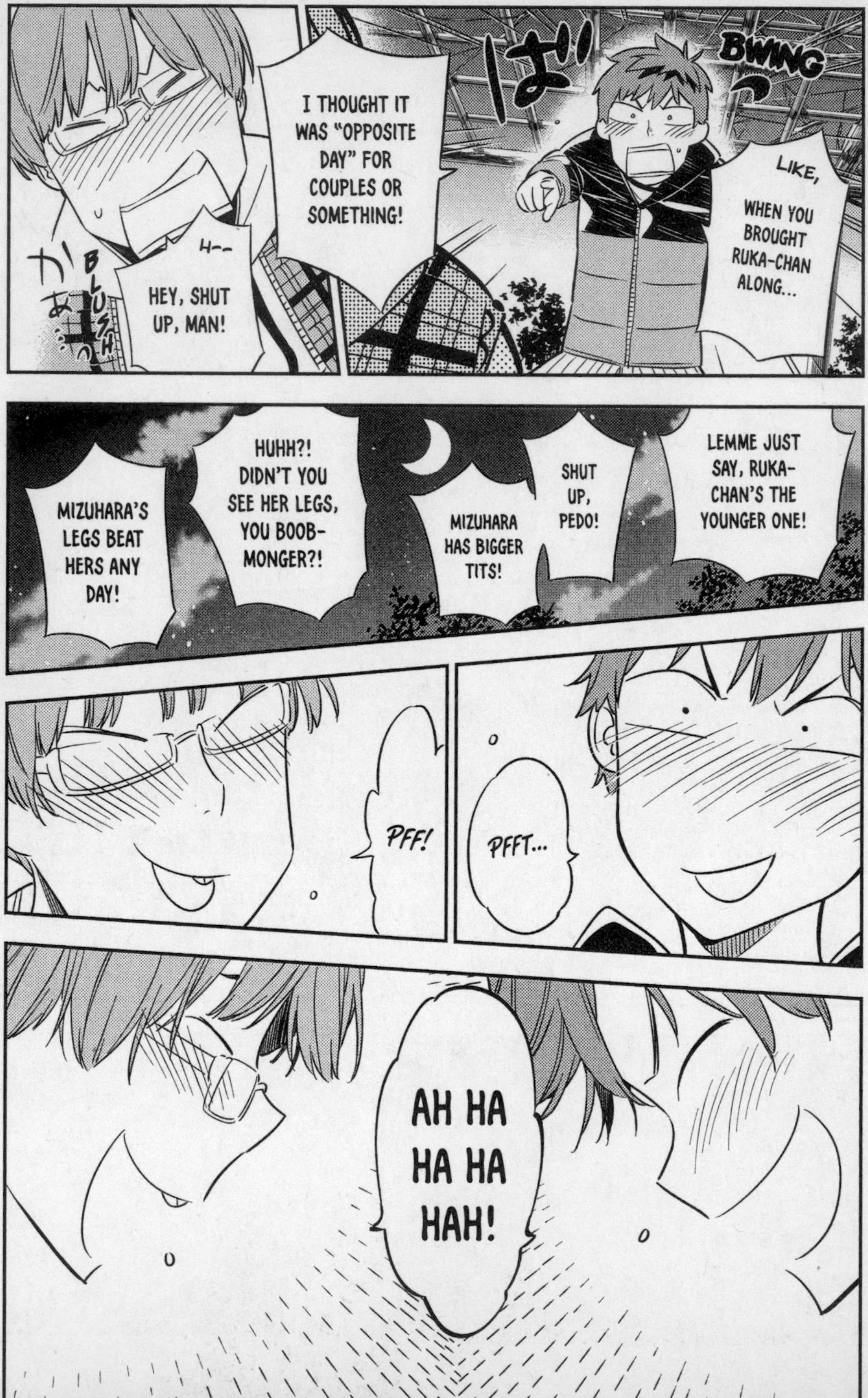
BWING
ぱっ
LIKE, WHEN YOU BROUGHT RUKA-CHAN ALONG...
I THOUGHT IT WAS "OPPOSITE DAY" FOR COUPLES OR SOMETHING!
H--
HEY, SHUT UP, MAN!
かぁっ
BLUSH
LEMME JUST SAY, RUKA-CHAN'S THE YOUNGER ONE!
SHUT UP, PEDO!
MIZUHARA HAS BIGGER TITS!
HUHH?! DIDN'T YOU SEE HER LEGS, YOU BOOB-MONGER?!
MIZUHARA'S LEGS BEAT HERS ANY DAY!
PFFT...
PFF!
AH HA HA HA HAH!

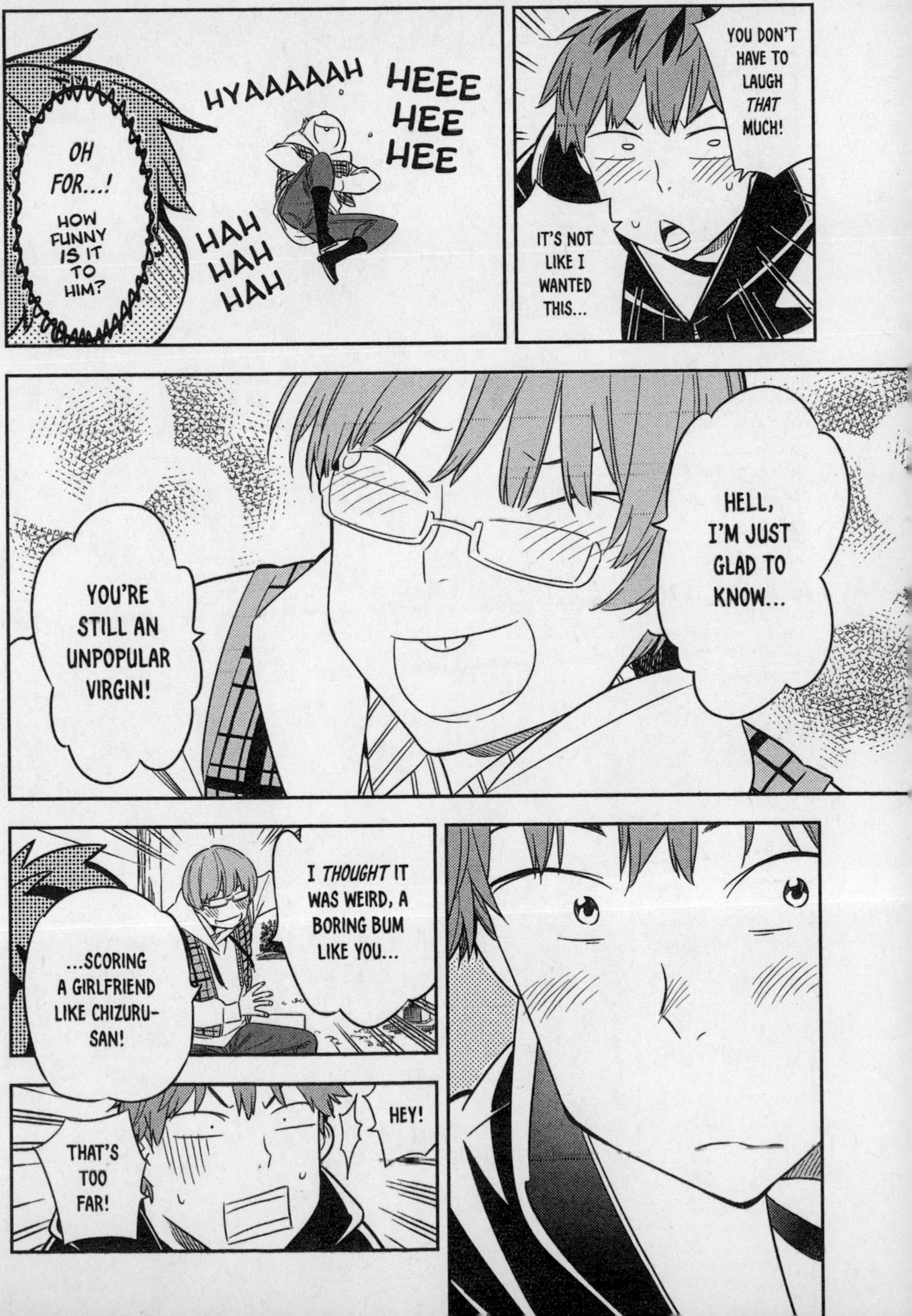
YOU DON'T HAVE TO LAUGH *THAT* MUCH!
IT'S NOT LIKE I WANTED THIS...
HEEE HEE HEE
HYAAAAAH
OH FOR...!
HOW FUNNY IS IT TO HIM?
HAH HAH HAH
HELL, I'M JUST GLAD TO KNOW...
YOU'RE STILL AN UNPOPULAR VIRGIN!
I *THOUGHT* IT WAS WEIRD, A BORING BUM LIKE YOU...
...SCORING A GIRLFRIEND LIKE CHIZURU-SAN!
HEY!
THAT'S TOO FAR!

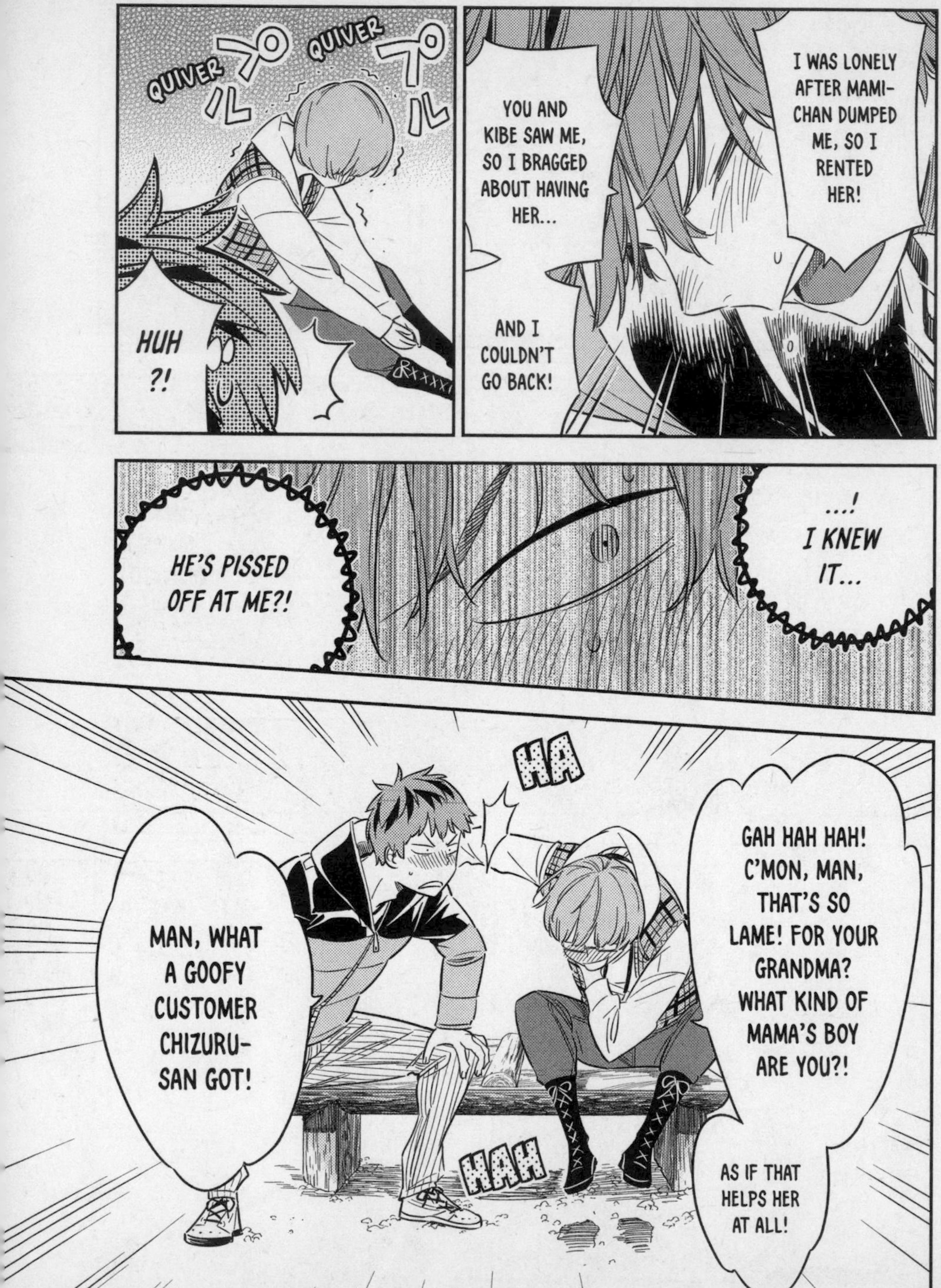
I WAS LONELY AFTER MAMI-CHAN DUMPED ME, SO I RENTED HER!
YOU AND KIBE SAW ME, SO I BRAGGED ABOUT HAVING HER...
AND I COULDN'T GO BACK!
QUIVER
プル
QUIVER
プル
HUH ?!
...! I KNEW IT...
HE'S PISSED OFF AT ME?!
HA
GAH HAH HAH! C'MON, MAN, THAT'S SO LAME! FOR YOUR GRANDMA? WHAT KIND OF MAMA'S BOY ARE YOU?!
AS IF THAT HELPS HER AT ALL!
HAH
MAN, WHAT A GOOFY CUSTOMER CHIZURU-SAN GOT!

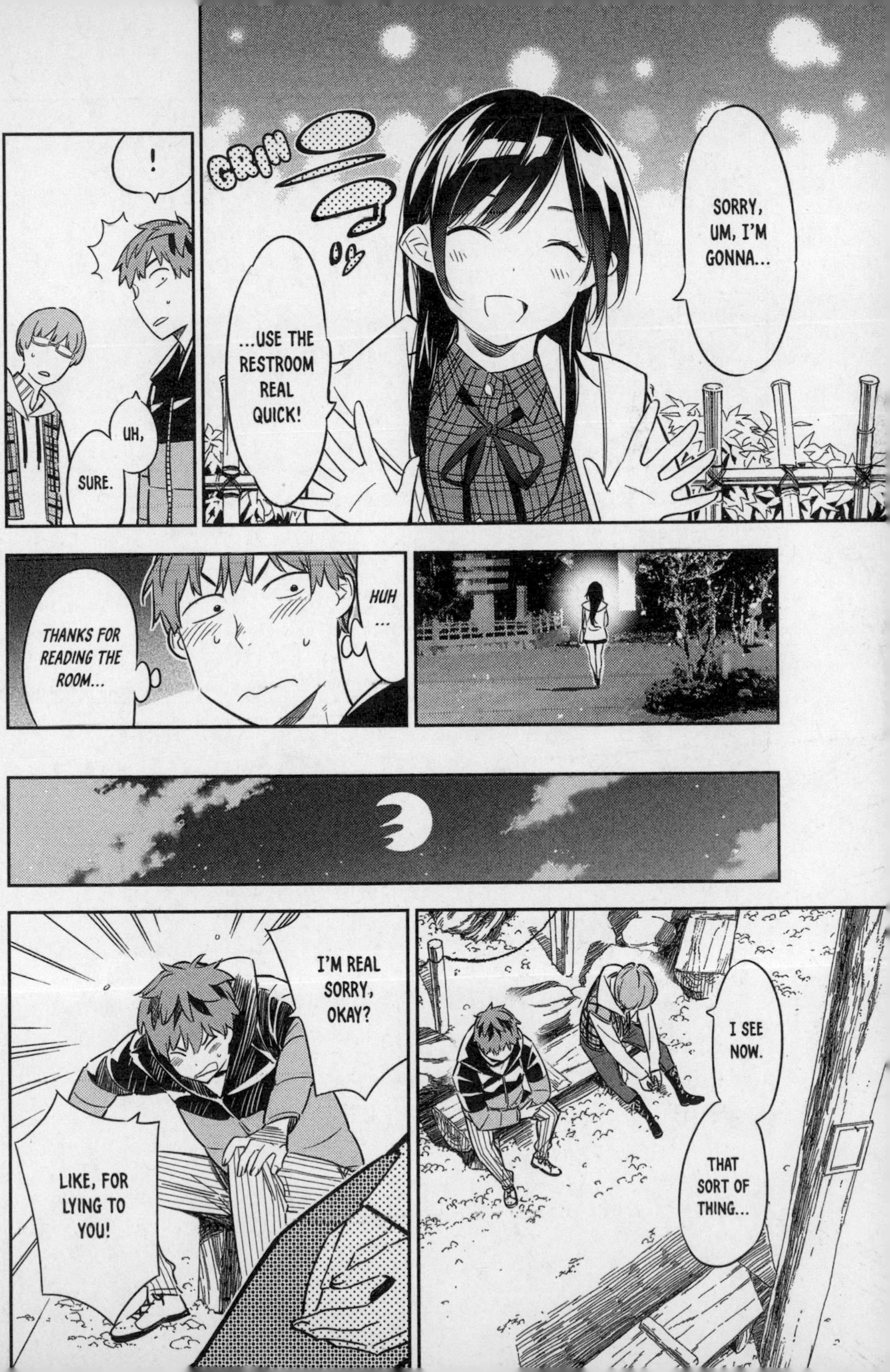
GRIN
SORRY, UM, I'M GONNA...
...USE THE RESTROOM REAL QUICK!
!
UH, SURE.
HUH ...
THANKS FOR READING THE ROOM...
I SEE NOW.
THAT SORT OF THING...
I'M REAL SORRY, OKAY?
LIKE, FOR LYING TO YOU!

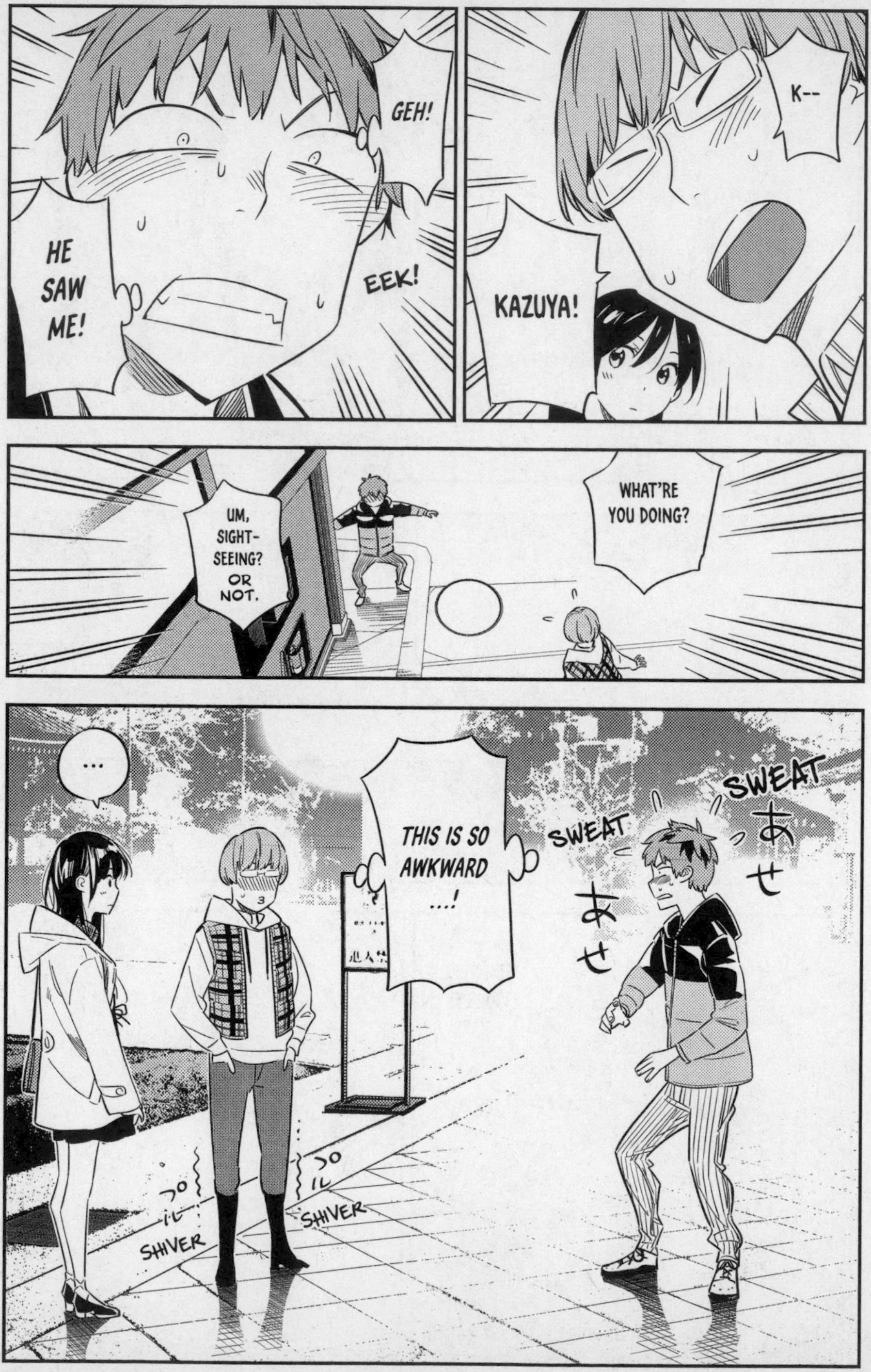
K--
KAZUYA!
GEH!
EEK!
HE SAW ME!
WHAT'RE YOU DOING?
UM, SIGHT-SEEING? OR NOT.
SWEAT
あせ
SWEAT
あせ
THIS IS SO AWKWARD ...!
...
SHIVER
SHIVER

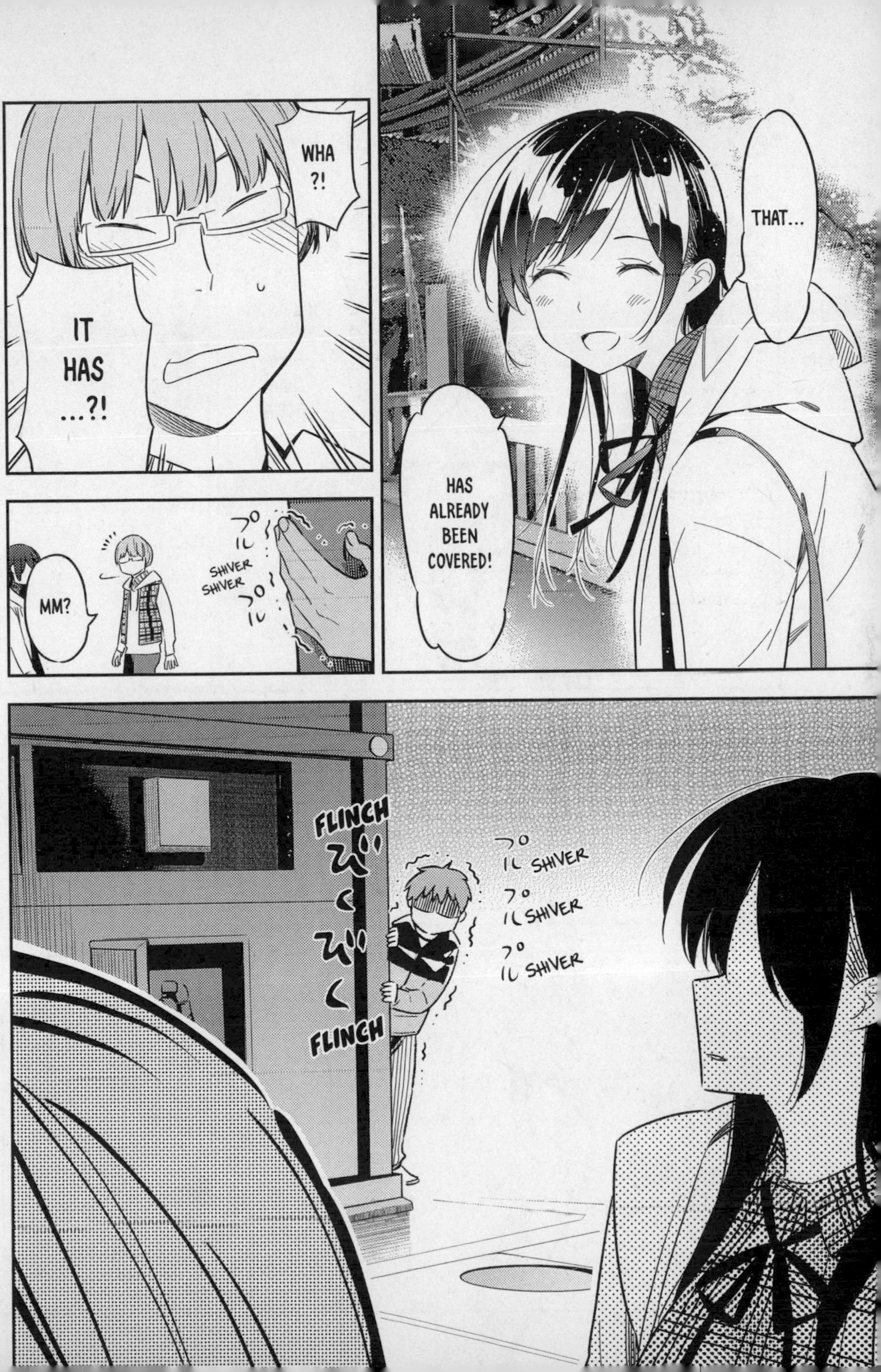

THAT...
HAS ALREADY BEEN COVERED!
WHA ?!
IT HAS ...?!
SHIVER SHIVER
MM?
FLINCH
FLINCH
SHIVER
SHIVER
SHIVER

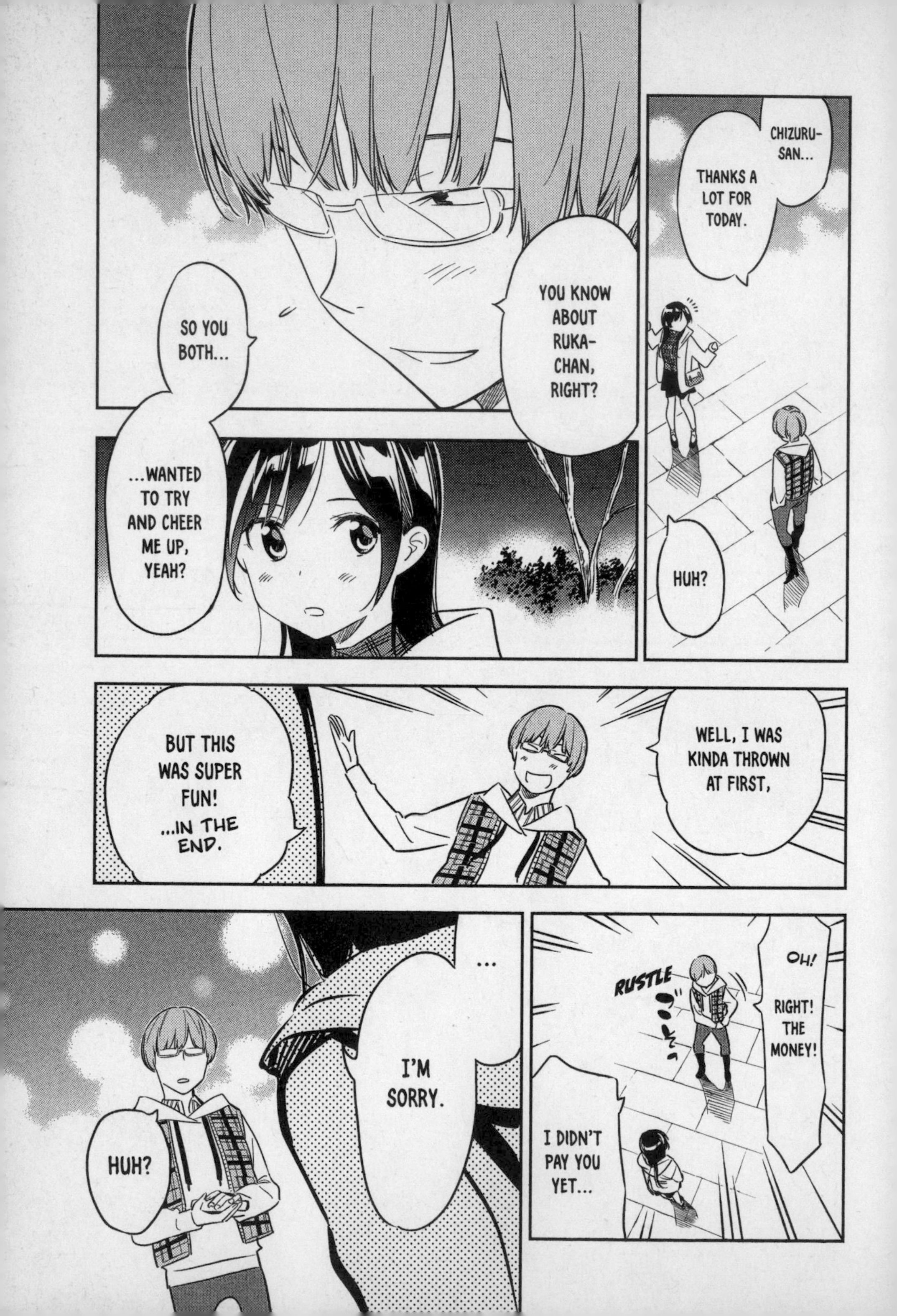
CHIZURU-SAN...
THANKS A LOT FOR TODAY.
HUH?
YOU KNOW ABOUT RUKA-CHAN, RIGHT?
SO YOU BOTH...
...WANTED TO TRY AND CHEER ME UP, YEAH?
WELL, I WAS KINDA THROWN AT FIRST,
BUT THIS WAS SUPER FUN! ...IN THE END.
OH!
RIGHT! THE MONEY!
RUSTLE
I DIDN'T PAY YOU YET...
...
I'M SORRY.
HUH?

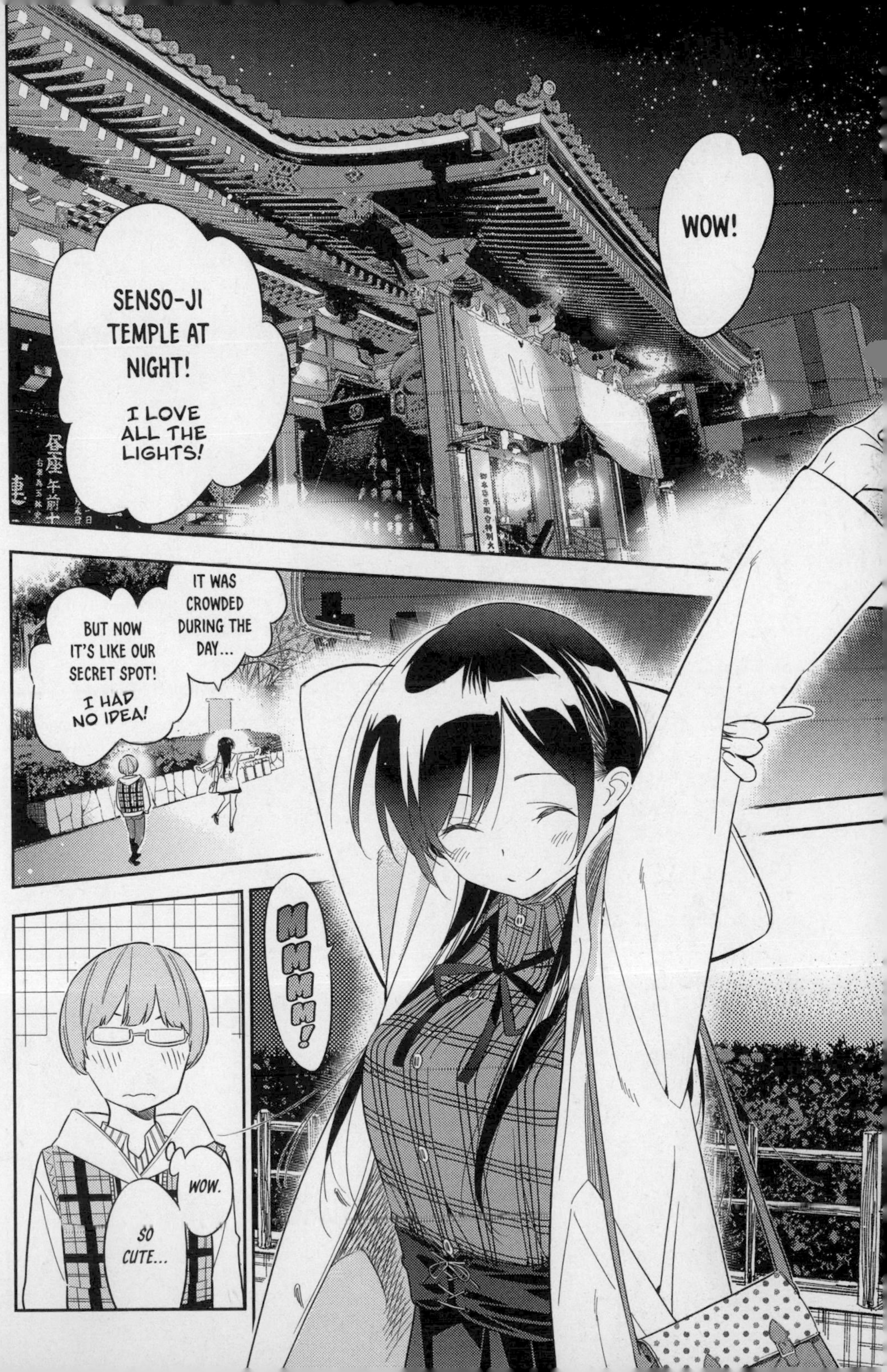
WOW!
SENSO-JI TEMPLE AT NIGHT!
I LOVE ALL THE LIGHTS!
MMMMM!
IT WAS CROWDED DURING THE DAY...
BUT NOW IT'S LIKE OUR SECRET SPOT!
I HAD NO IDEA!
WOW.
SO CUTE...

RATING 39
MY GIRLFRIEND AND THE CHICKEN (3)

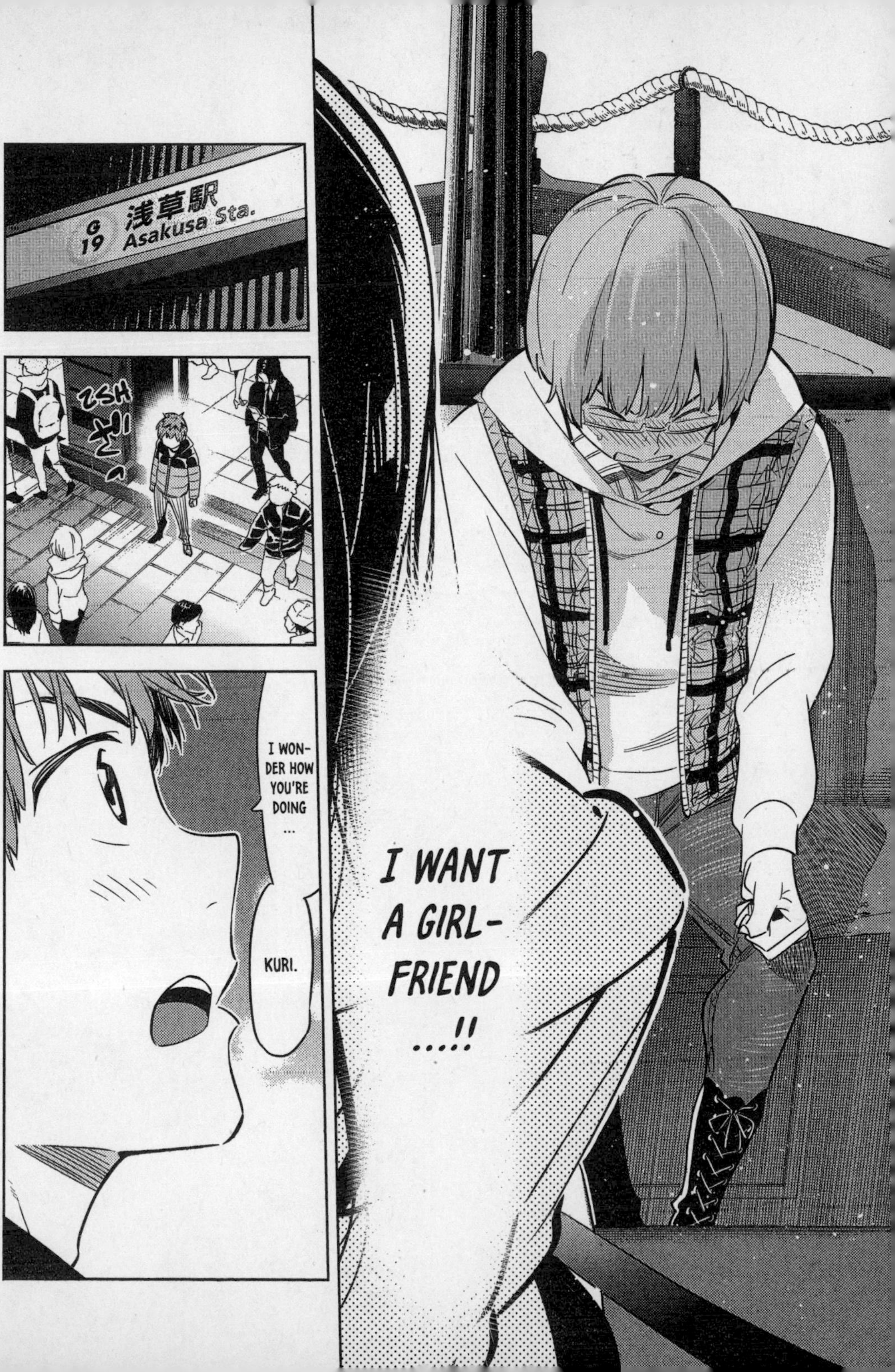
I WANT A GIRL-FRIEND ...!!
浅草駅
G 19
Asakusa Sta.
ZSH
I WON-DER HOW YOU'RE DOING ...
KURI.

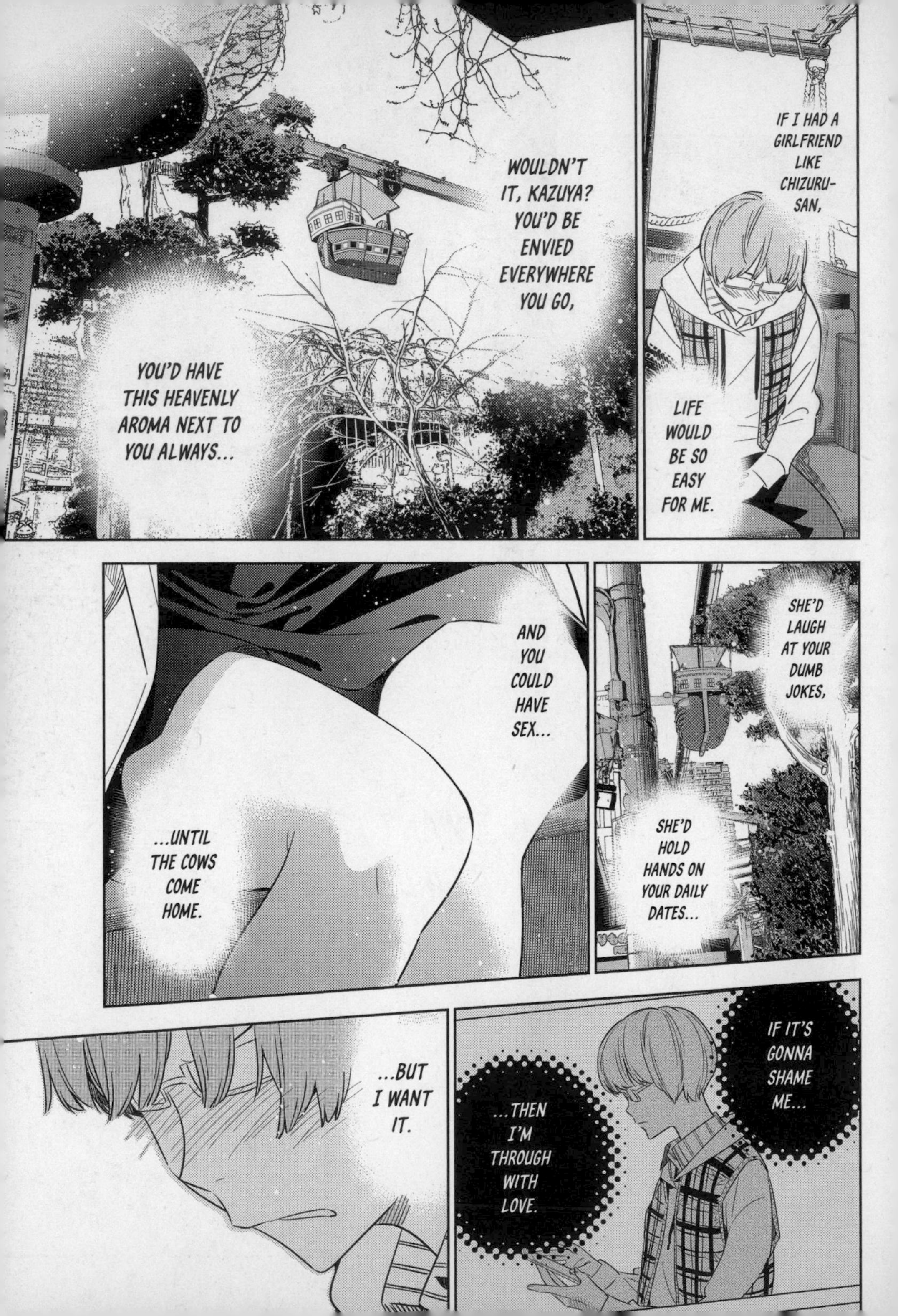
IF I HAD A GIRLFRIEND LIKE CHIZURU-SAN,
LIFE WOULD BE SO EASY FOR ME.
WOULDN'T IT, KAZUYA? YOU'D BE ENVIED EVERYWHERE YOU GO,
YOU'D HAVE THIS HEAVENLY AROMA NEXT TO YOU ALWAYS...
SHE'D LAUGH AT YOUR DUMB JOKES,
SHE'D HOLD HANDS ON YOUR DAILY DATES...
AND YOU COULD HAVE SEX...
...UNTIL THE COWS COME HOME.
IF IT'S GONNA SHAME ME...
...THEN I'M THROUGH WITH LOVE.
...BUT I WANT IT.

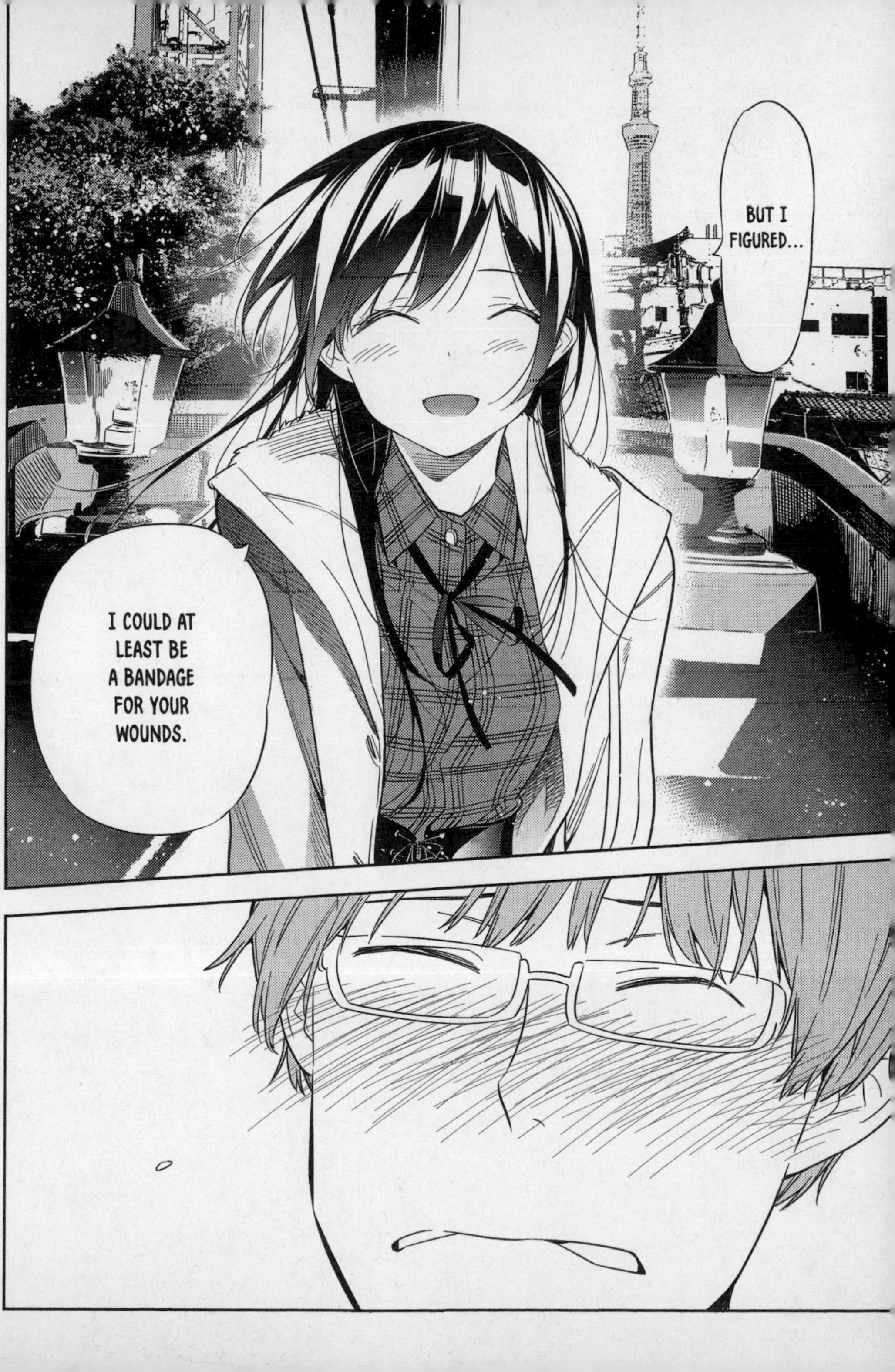
BUT I FIGURED...
I COULD AT LEAST BE A BANDAGE FOR YOUR WOUNDS.

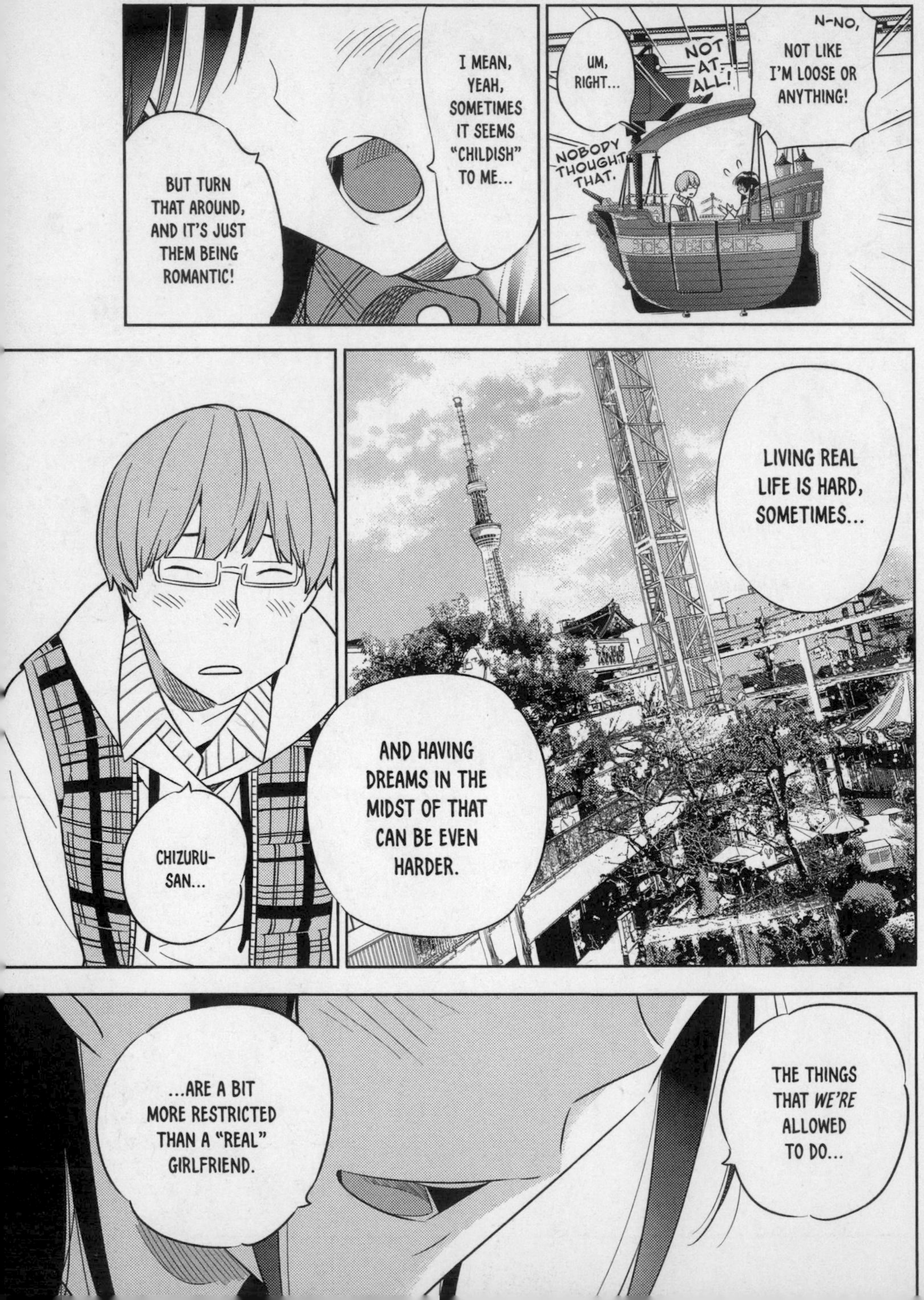
N-NO, NOT LIKE I'M LOOSE OR ANYTHING!
NOT AT ALL!
UM, RIGHT...
NOBODY THOUGHT THAT.
I MEAN, YEAH, SOMETIMES IT SEEMS "CHILDISH" TO ME...
BUT TURN THAT AROUND, AND IT'S JUST THEM BEING ROMANTIC!
LIVING REAL LIFE IS HARD, SOMETIMES...
AND HAVING DREAMS IN THE MIDST OF THAT CAN BE EVEN HARDER.
CHIZURU-SAN...
THE THINGS THAT *WE'RE* ALLOWED TO DO...
...ARE A BIT MORE RESTRICTED THAN A "REAL" GIRLFRIEND.

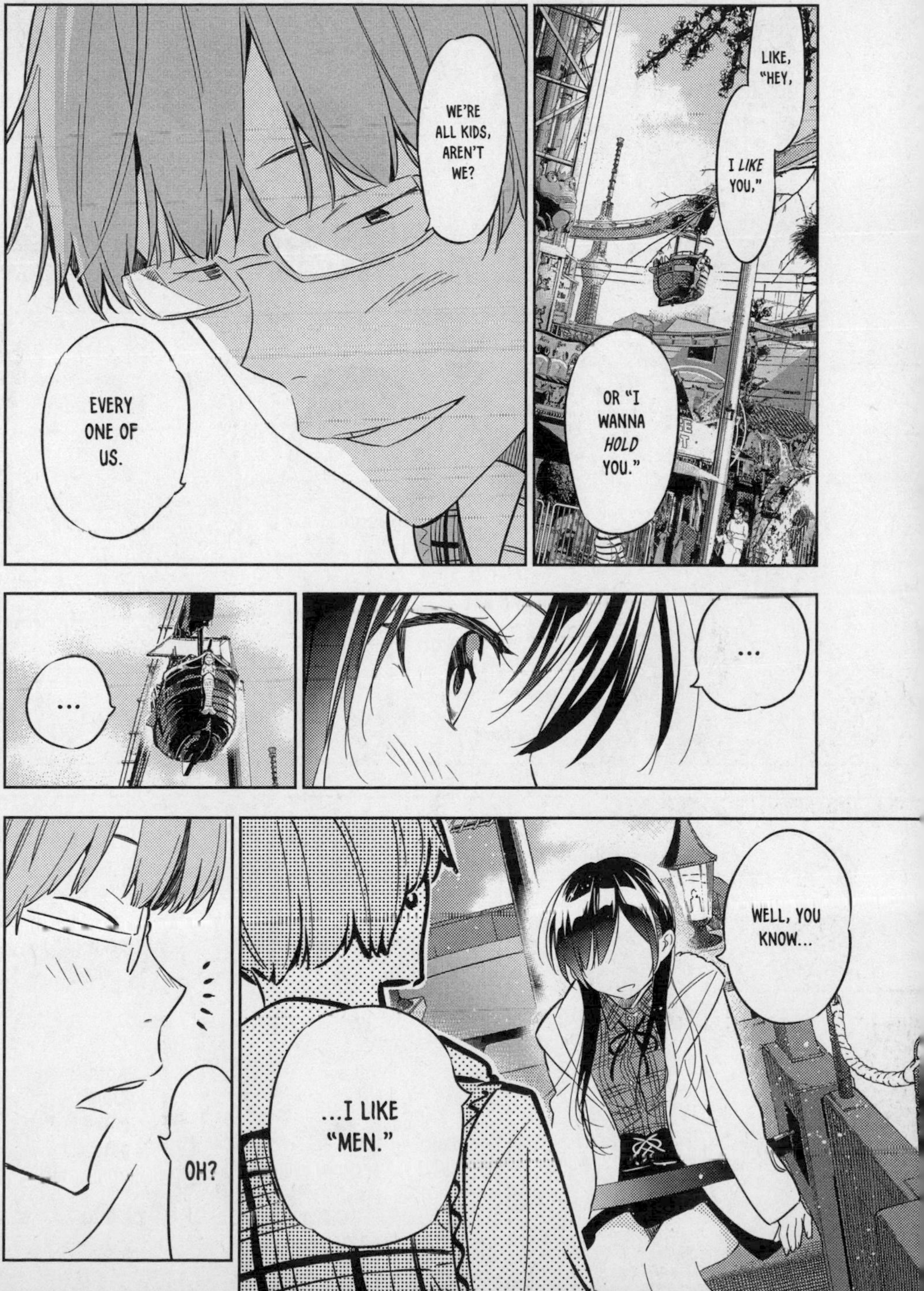
LIKE, "HEY,
I *LIKE* YOU,"
OR "I WANNA *HOLD* YOU."
WE'RE ALL KIDS, AREN'T WE?
EVERY ONE OF US.
...
...
WELL, YOU KNOW...
...I LIKE "MEN."
OH?

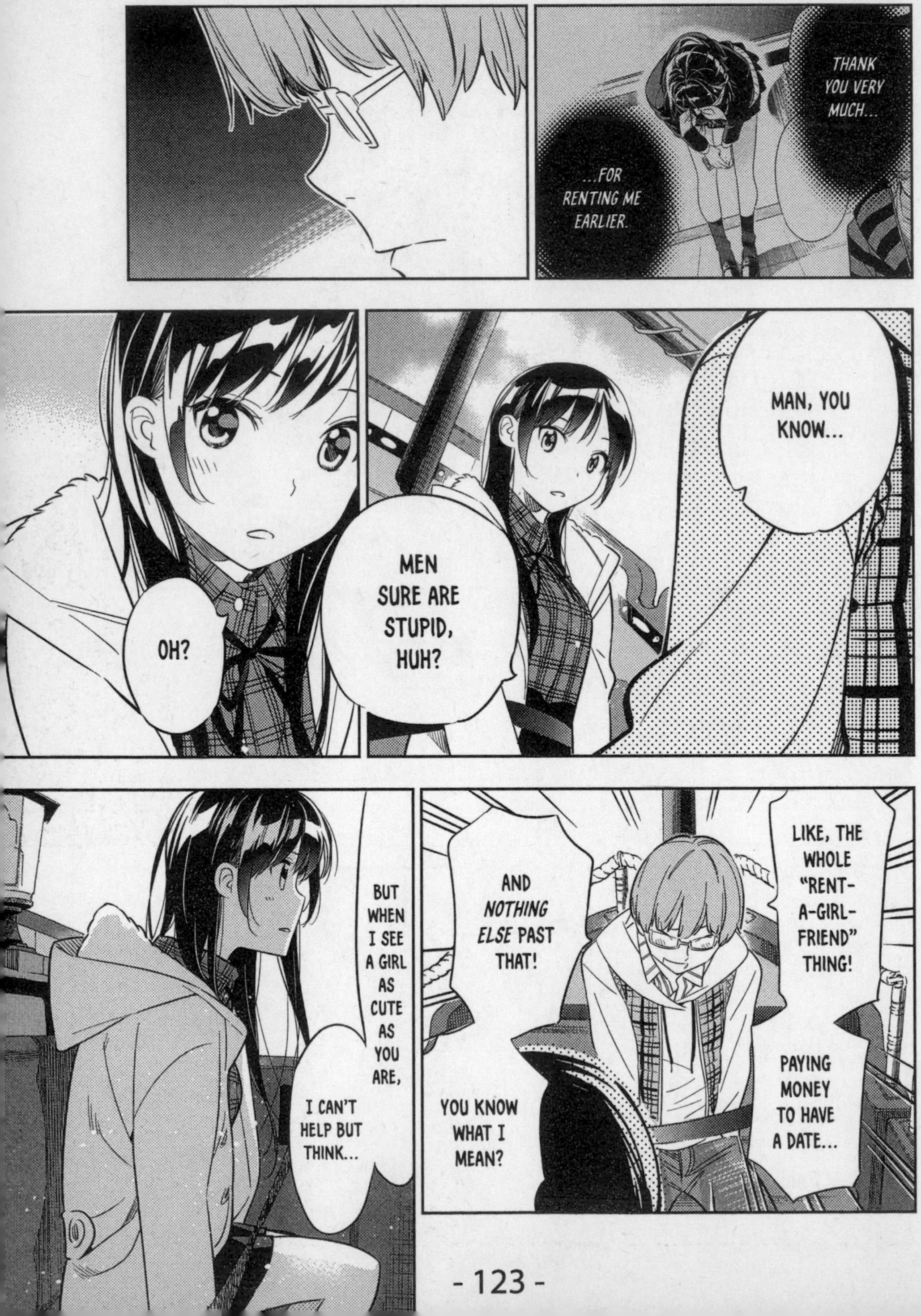
THANK YOU VERY MUCH...
...FOR RENTING ME EARLIER.
MAN, YOU KNOW...
MEN SURE ARE STUPID, HUH?
OH?
LIKE, THE WHOLE "RENT-A-GIRL-FRIEND" THING!
PAYING MONEY TO HAVE A DATE...
AND *NOTHING ELSE* PAST THAT!
YOU KNOW WHAT I MEAN?
BUT WHEN I SEE A GIRL AS CUTE AS YOU ARE,
I CAN'T HELP BUT THINK...

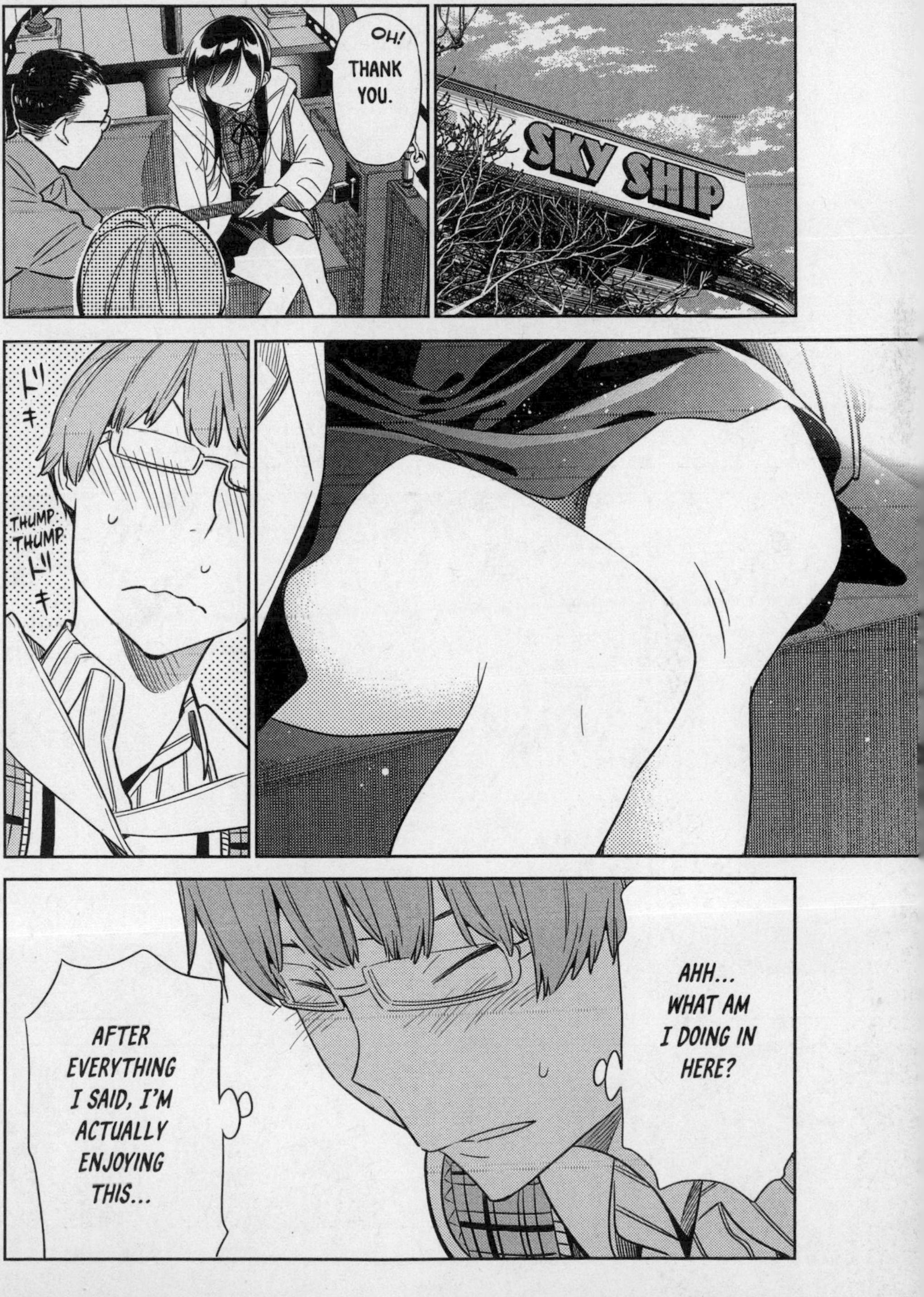
SKY SHIP
OH! THANK YOU.
ドキ
THUMP THUMP
ドキ
AHH... WHAT AM I DOING IN HERE?
AFTER EVERYTHING I SAID, I'M ACTUALLY ENJOYING THIS...

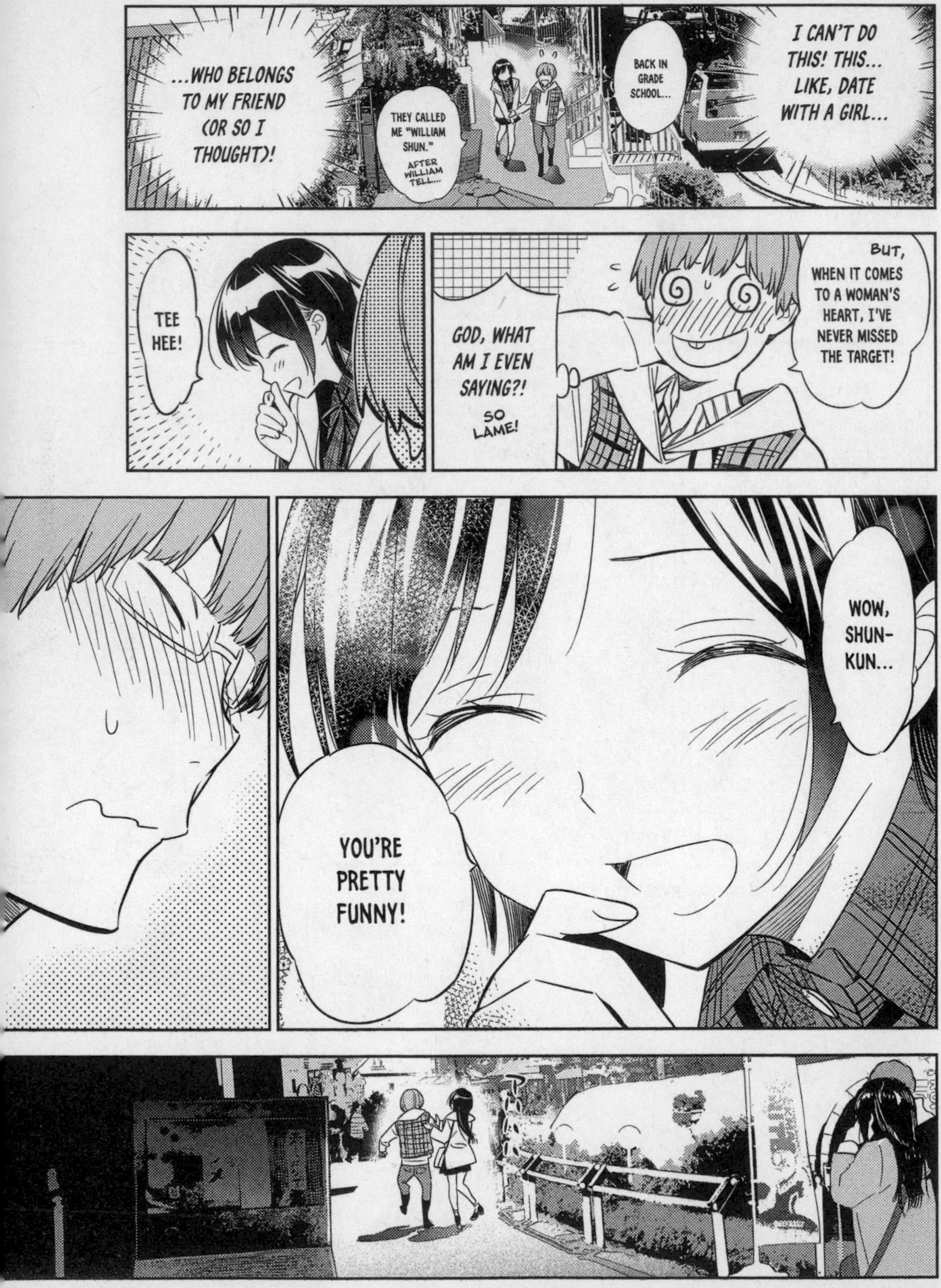
I CAN'T DO THIS! THIS... LIKE, DATE WITH A GIRL...
BACK IN GRADE SCHOOL...
THEY CALLED ME "WILLIAM SHUN."
AFTER WILLIAM TELL...
...WHO BELONGS TO MY FRIEND (OR SO I THOUGHT)!
BUT, WHEN IT COMES TO A WOMAN'S HEART, I'VE NEVER MISSED THE TARGET!
GOD, WHAT AM I EVEN SAYING?!
SO LAME!
TEE HEE!
WOW, SHUN-KUN...
YOU'RE PRETTY FUNNY!

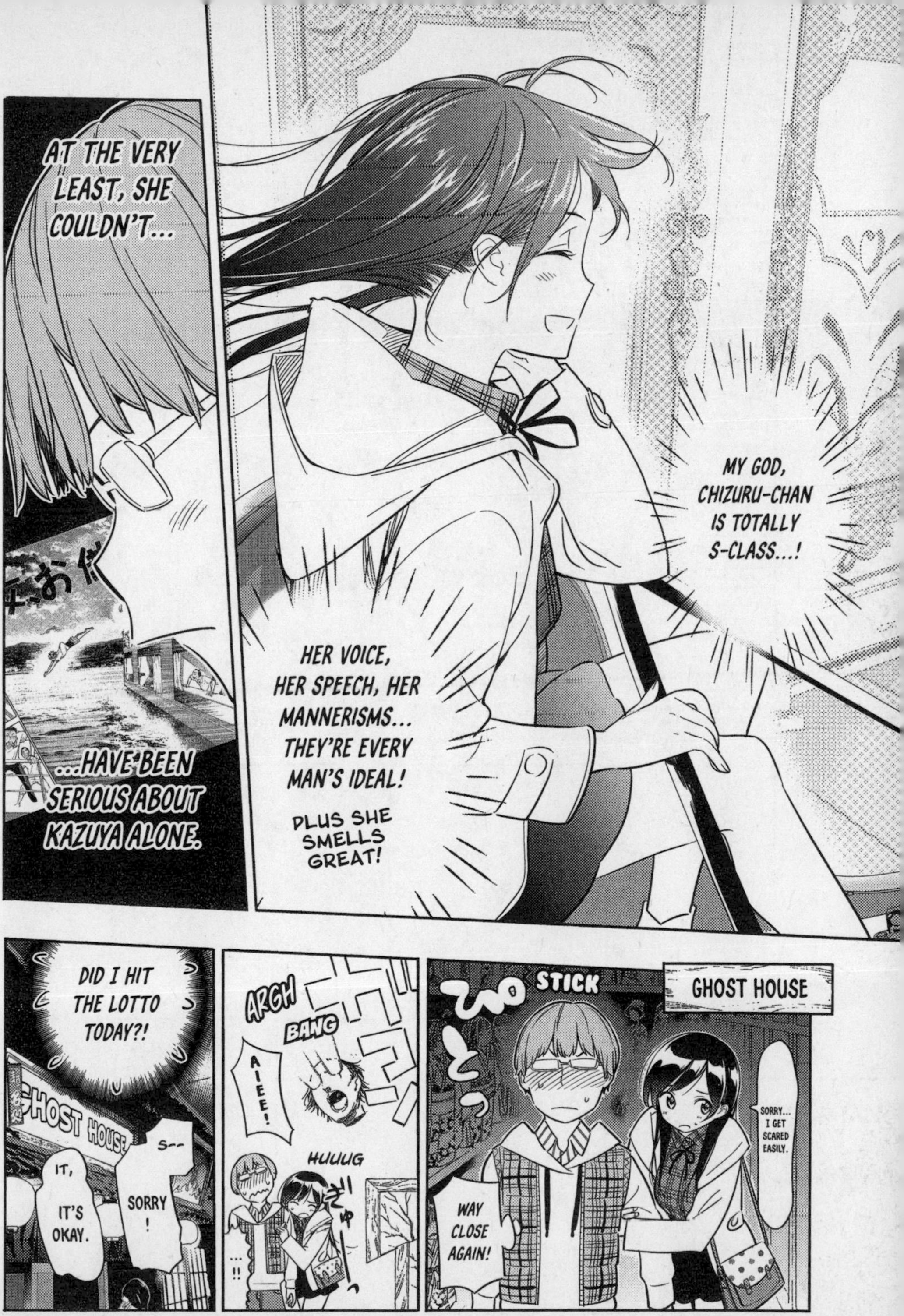
MY GOD, CHIZURU-CHAN IS TOTALLY S-CLASS...!
HER VOICE, HER SPEECH, HER MANNERISMS... THEY'RE EVERY MAN'S IDEAL!
PLUS SHE SMELLS GREAT!
AT THE VERY LEAST, SHE COULDN'T...
...HAVE BEEN SERIOUS ABOUT KAZUYA ALONE.
GHOST HOUSE
STICK
SORRY... I GET SCARED EASILY.
WAY CLOSE AGAIN!
ARGH
BANG
AIEEE!
HUUUG
...!!
DID I HIT THE LOTTO TODAY?!
GHOST HOUSE
S-- SORRY!
IT, IT'S OKAY.

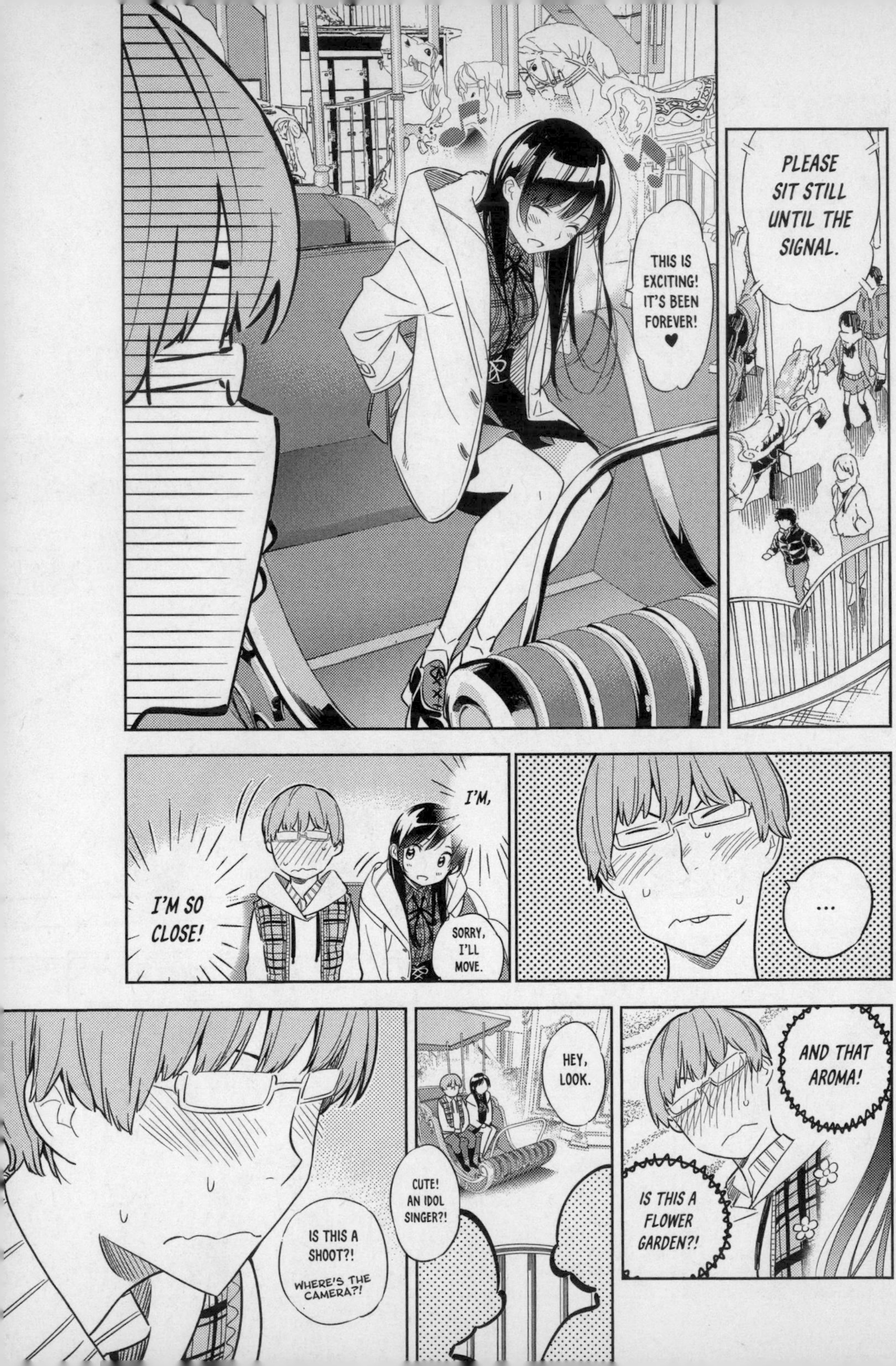
PLEASE SIT STILL UNTIL THE SIGNAL.
THIS IS EXCITING! IT'S BEEN FOREVER! ♥
...
I'M,
I'M SO CLOSE!
SORRY, I'LL MOVE.
AND THAT AROMA!
IS THIS A FLOWER GARDEN?!
HEY, LOOK.
CUTE! AN IDOL SINGER?!
IS THIS A SHOOT?!
WHERE'S THE CAMERA?!

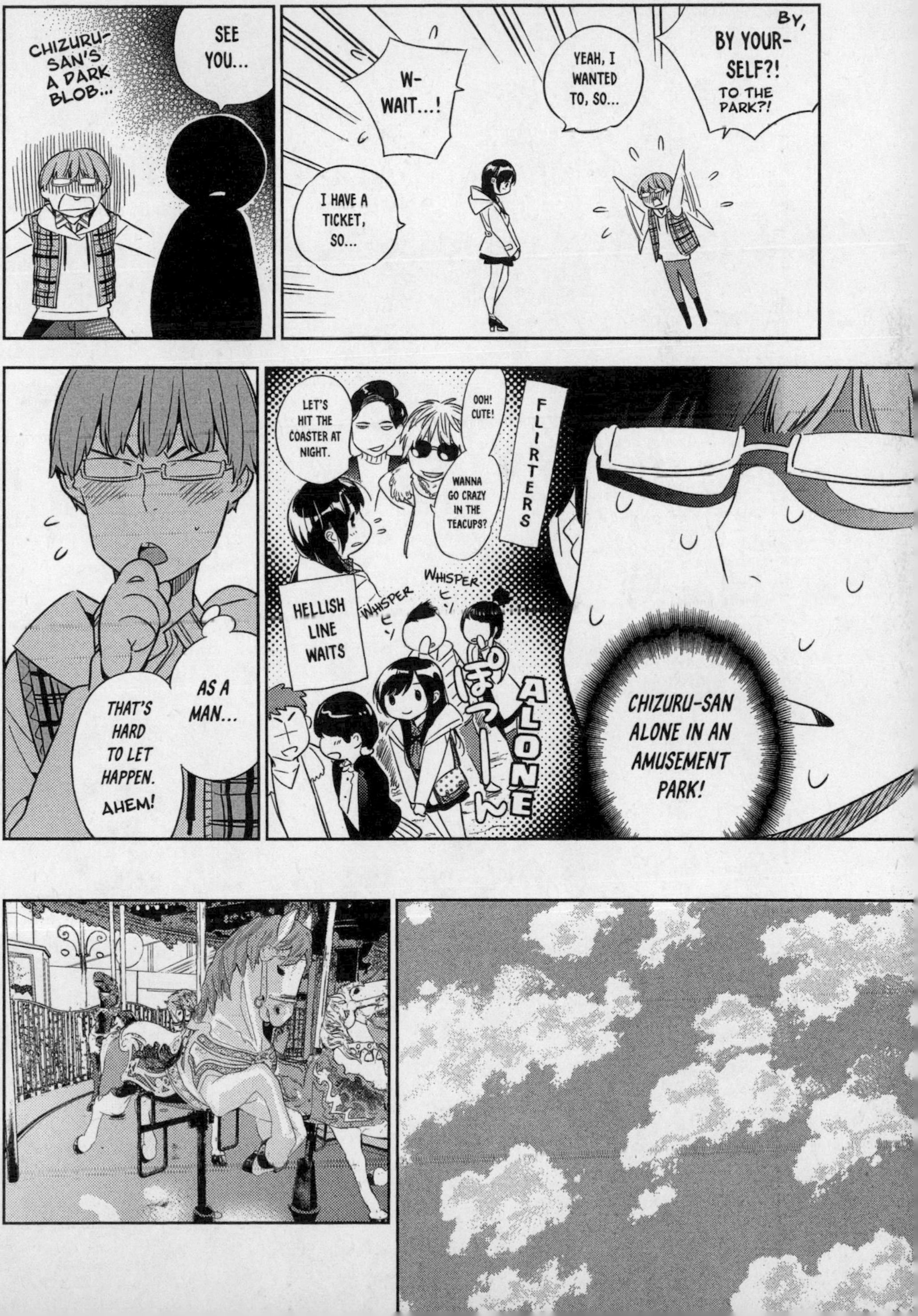
BY, BY YOUR-SELF?! TO THE PARK?!
YEAH, I WANTED TO, SO...
W-WAIT...!
I HAVE A TICKET, SO...
SEE YOU...
CHIZURU-SAN'S A DARK BLOB...
CHIZURU-SAN ALONE IN AN AMUSEMENT PARK!
FLIRTERS
OOH! CUTE!
LET'S HIT THE COASTER AT NIGHT.
WANNA GO CRAZY IN THE TEACUPS?
WHISPER
WHISPER
HELLISH LINE WAITS
ALONE
ぽつーん
AS A MAN...
THAT'S HARD TO LET HAPPEN.
AHEM!

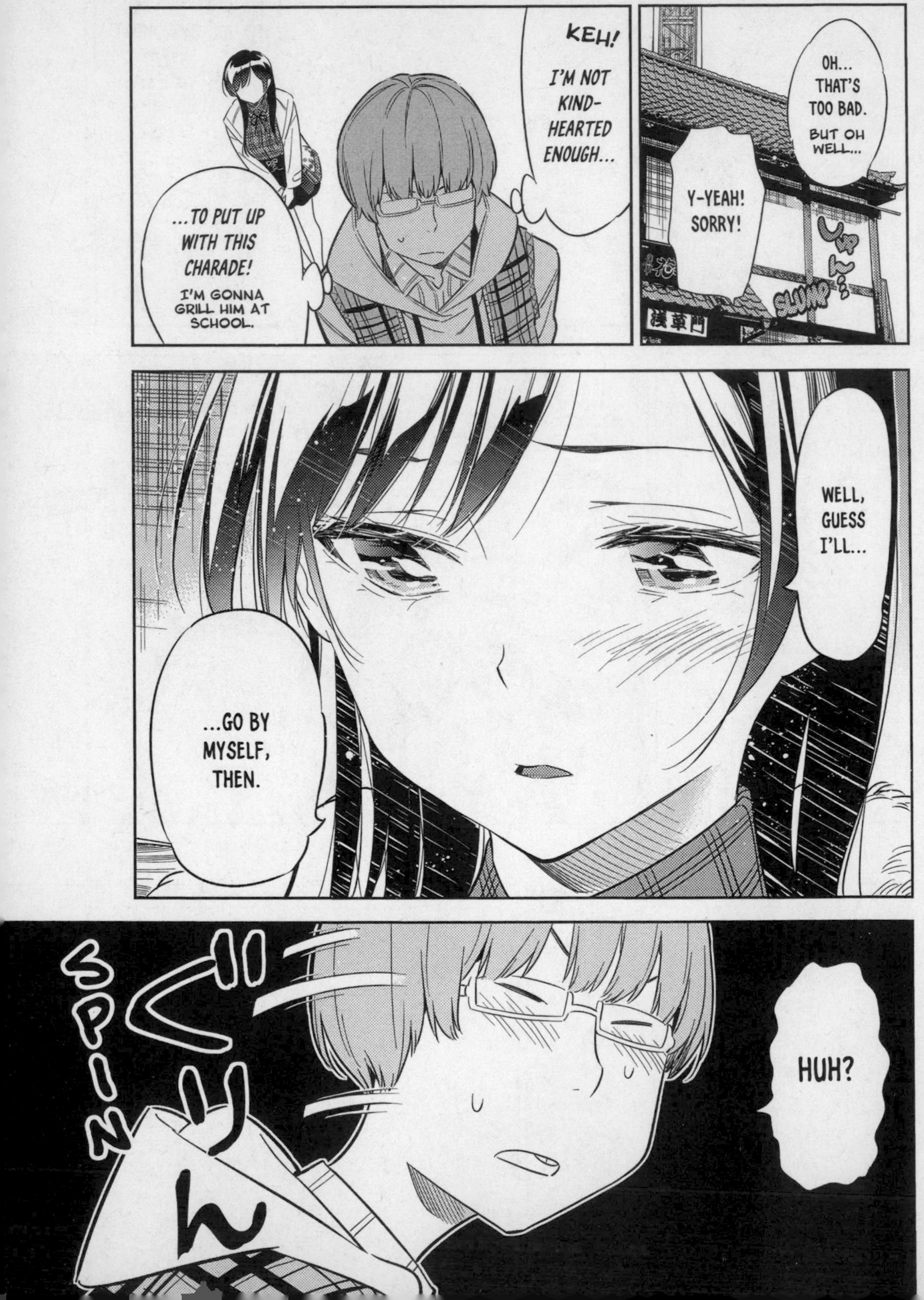
OH... THAT'S TOO BAD.
BUT OH WELL...
Y-YEAH! SORRY!
SLUMP
KEH!
I'M NOT KIND-HEARTED ENOUGH...
...TO PUT UP WITH THIS CHARADE!
I'M GONNA GRILL HIM AT SCHOOL.
WELL, GUESS I'LL...
...GO BY MYSELF, THEN.
HUH?
SPIN

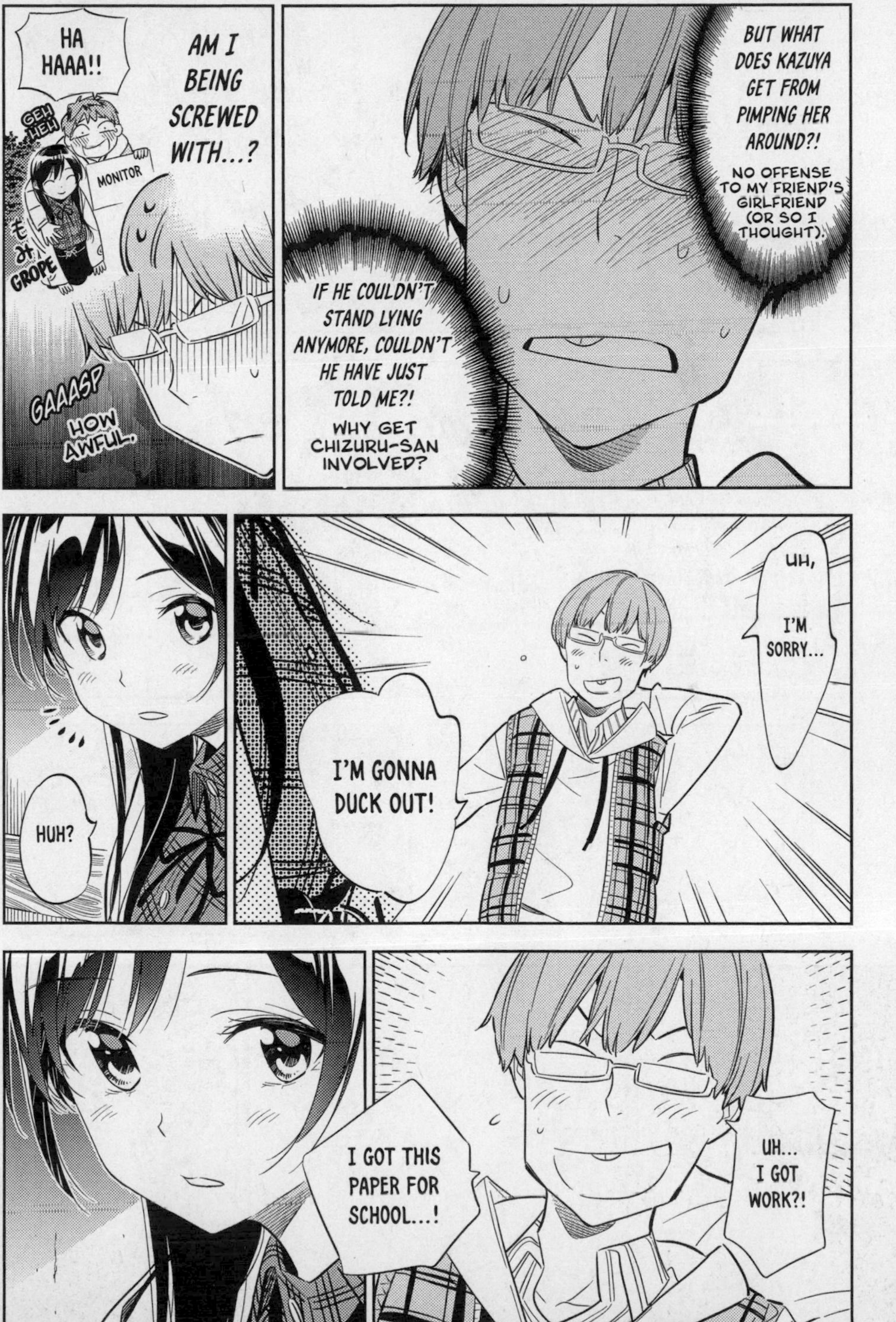
BUT WHAT DOES KAZUYA GET FROM PIMPING HER AROUND?!
NO OFFENSE TO MY FRIEND'S GIRLFRIEND (OR SO I THOUGHT).
IF HE COULDN'T STAND LYING ANYMORE, COULDN'T HE HAVE JUST TOLD ME?!
WHY GET CHIZURU-SAN INVOLVED?
AM I BEING SCREWED WITH...?
HA HAAA!!
GEH HEH
MONITOR
もみ
GROPE
GAAASP
HOW AWFUL.
UH,
I'M SORRY...
I'M GONNA DUCK OUT!
HUH?
UH... I GOT WORK?!
I GOT THIS PAPER FOR SCHOOL...!

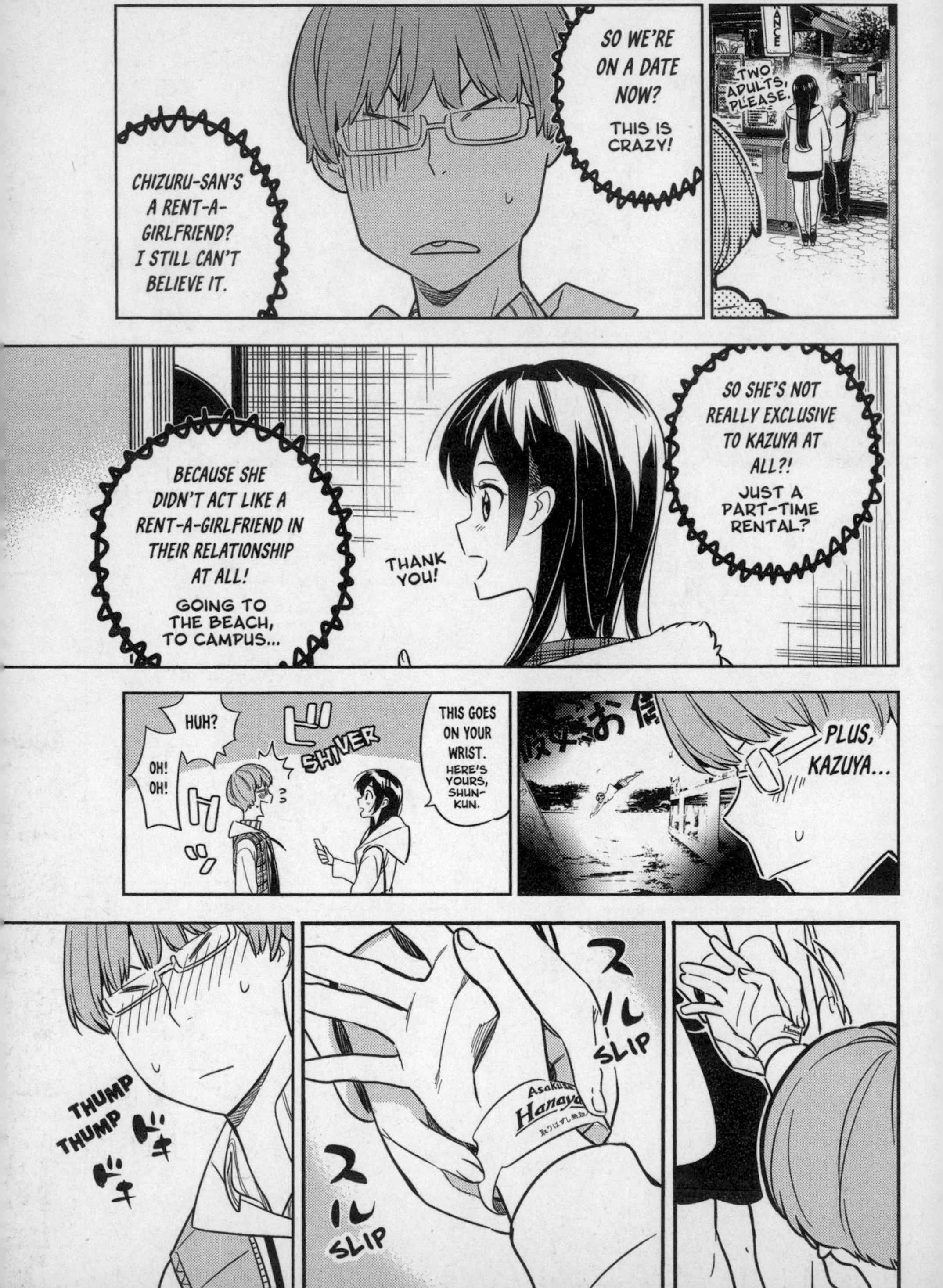
TWO ADULTS, PLEASE.
SO WE'RE ON A DATE NOW?
THIS IS CRAZY!
CHIZURU-SAN'S A RENT-A-GIRLFRIEND? I STILL CAN'T BELIEVE IT.
SO SHE'S NOT REALLY EXCLUSIVE TO KAZUYA AT ALL?!
JUST A PART-TIME RENTAL?
THANK YOU!
BECAUSE SHE DIDN'T ACT LIKE A RENT-A-GIRLFRIEND IN THEIR RELATIONSHIP AT ALL!
GOING TO THE BEACH, TO CAMPUS...
PLUS, KAZUYA...
THIS GOES ON YOUR WRIST.
HERE'S YOURS, SHUN-KUN.
ビ SHIVER
HUH?
OH! OH!
スル SLIP
スル SLIP
THUMP THUMP
ドキ ドキ

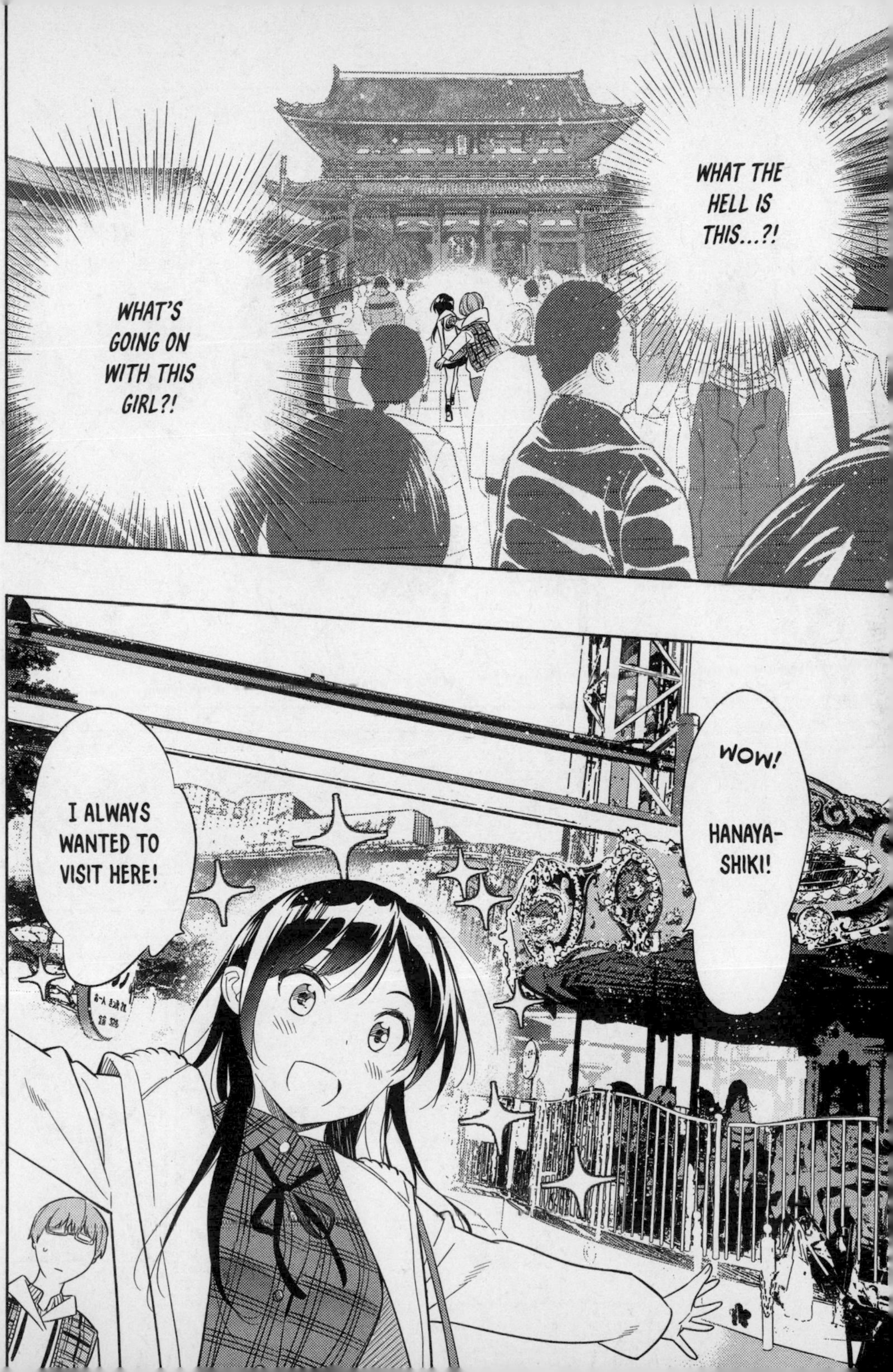
WHAT THE HELL IS THIS...?!
WHAT'S GOING ON WITH THIS GIRL?!
WOW! HANAYA-SHIKI!
I ALWAYS WANTED TO VISIT HERE!

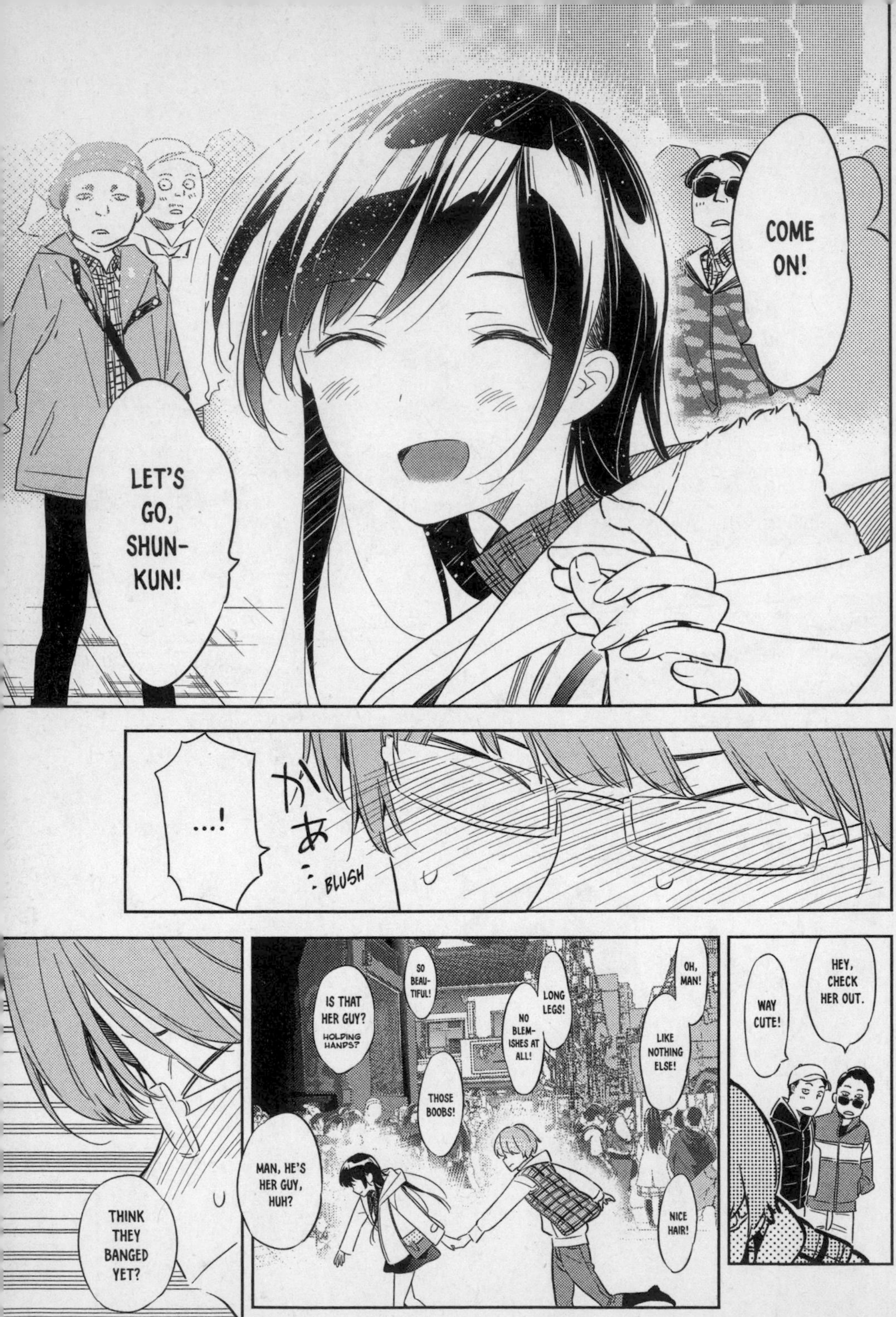
COME ON!
LET'S GO, SHUN-KUN!
...!
がぁ BLUSH
HEY, CHECK HER OUT.
WAY CUTE!
OH, MAN!
LIKE NOTHING ELSE!
LONG LEGS!
NO BLEMISHES AT ALL!
SO BEAUTIFUL!
IS THAT HER GUY? HOLDING HANDS?
THOSE BOOBS!
NICE HAIR!
MAN, HE'S HER GUY, HUH?
THINK THEY BANGED YET?

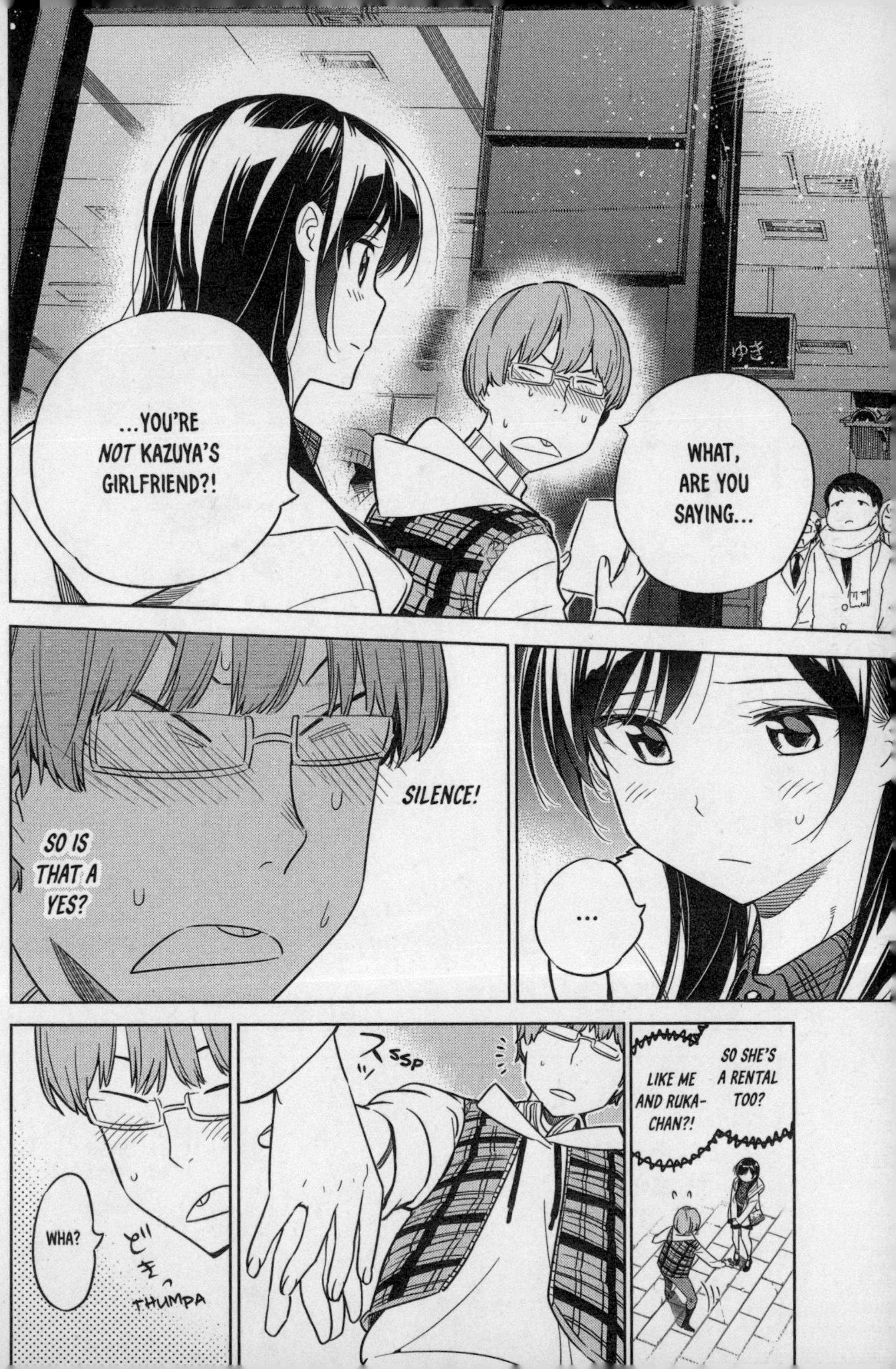
WHAT, ARE YOU SAYING...
ゆき
...YOU'RE *NOT* KAZUYA'S GIRLFRIEND?!
...
SILENCE!
SO IS THAT A YES?
SO SHE'S A RENTAL TOO?
LIKE ME AND RUKA-CHAN?!
スッ SSP
WHA?
どきっ THUMPA

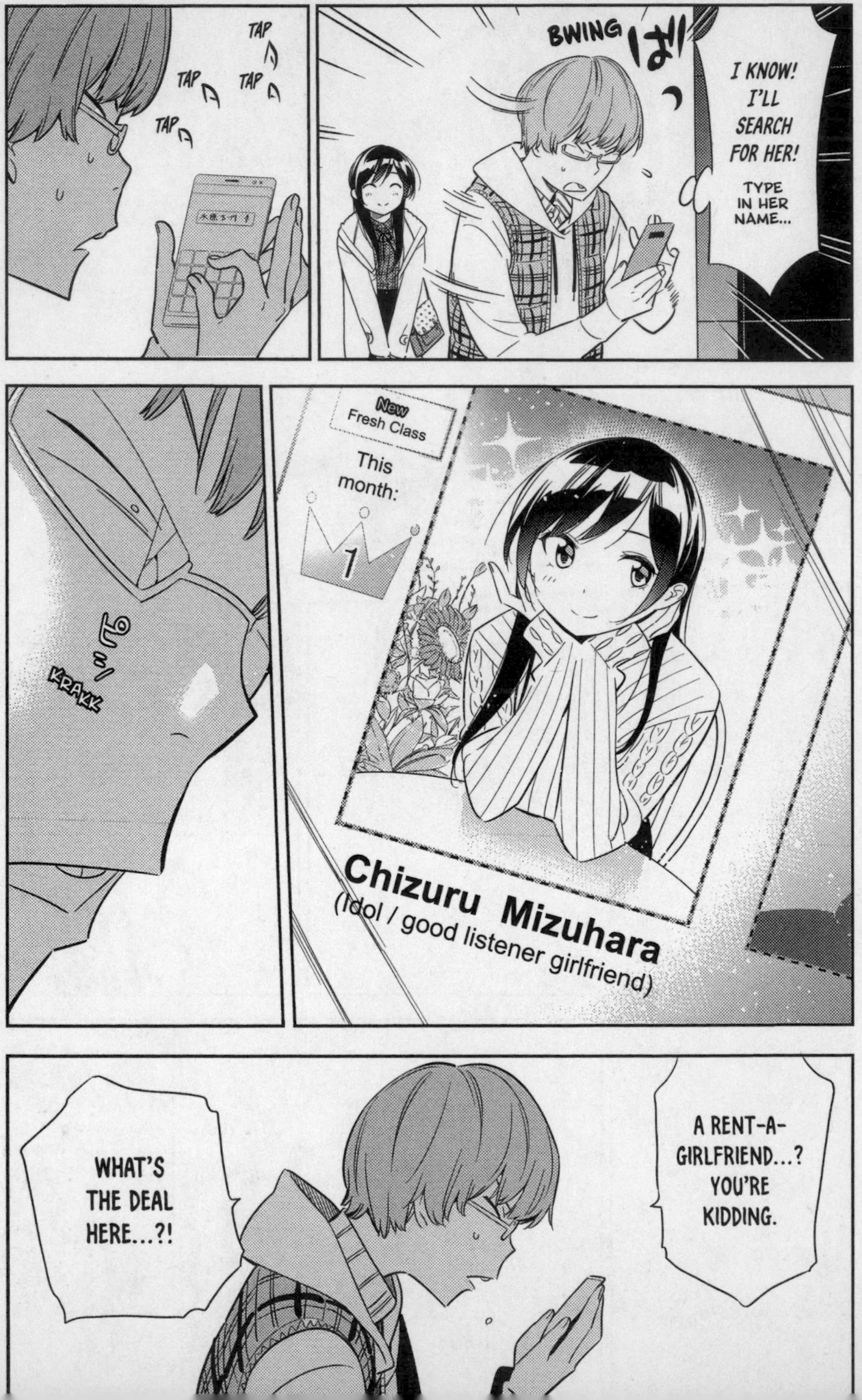

BWING
I KNOW! I'LL SEARCH FOR HER!
TYPE IN HER NAME...
TAP
TAP
TAP
TAP
New
Fresh Class
This month:
1
Chizuru Mizuhara
(Idol / good listener girlfriend)
KRAKK
A RENT-A-GIRLFRIEND...? YOU'RE KIDDING.
WHAT'S THE DEAL HERE...?!

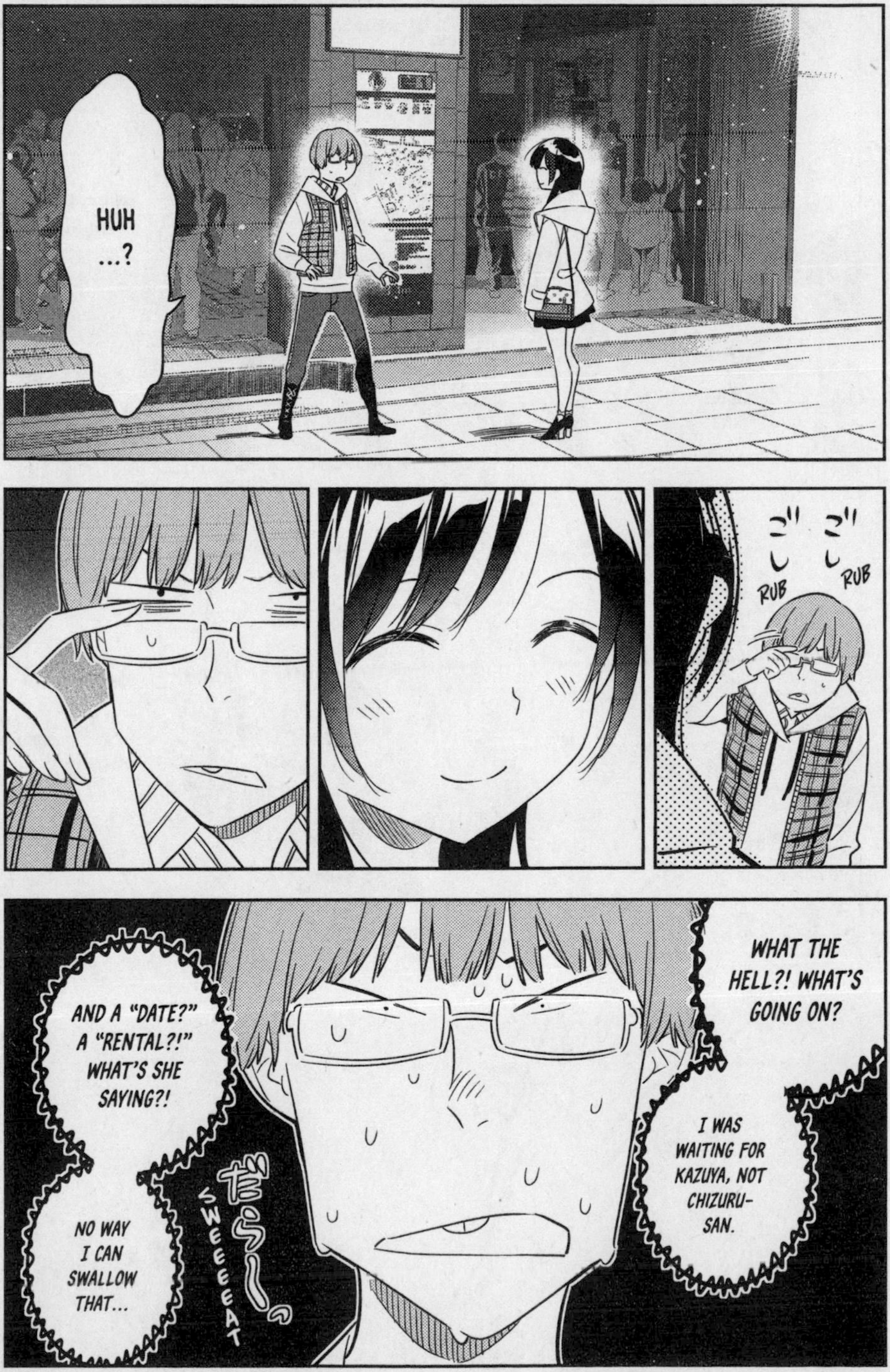
HUH ...?
ごし ごし
RUB RUB
WHAT THE HELL?! WHAT'S GOING ON?
I WAS WAITING FOR KAZUYA, NOT CHIZURU-SAN.
AND A "DATE?" A "RENTAL?!" WHAT'S SHE SAYING?!
SWEEEAT
NO WAY I CAN SWALLOW THAT...

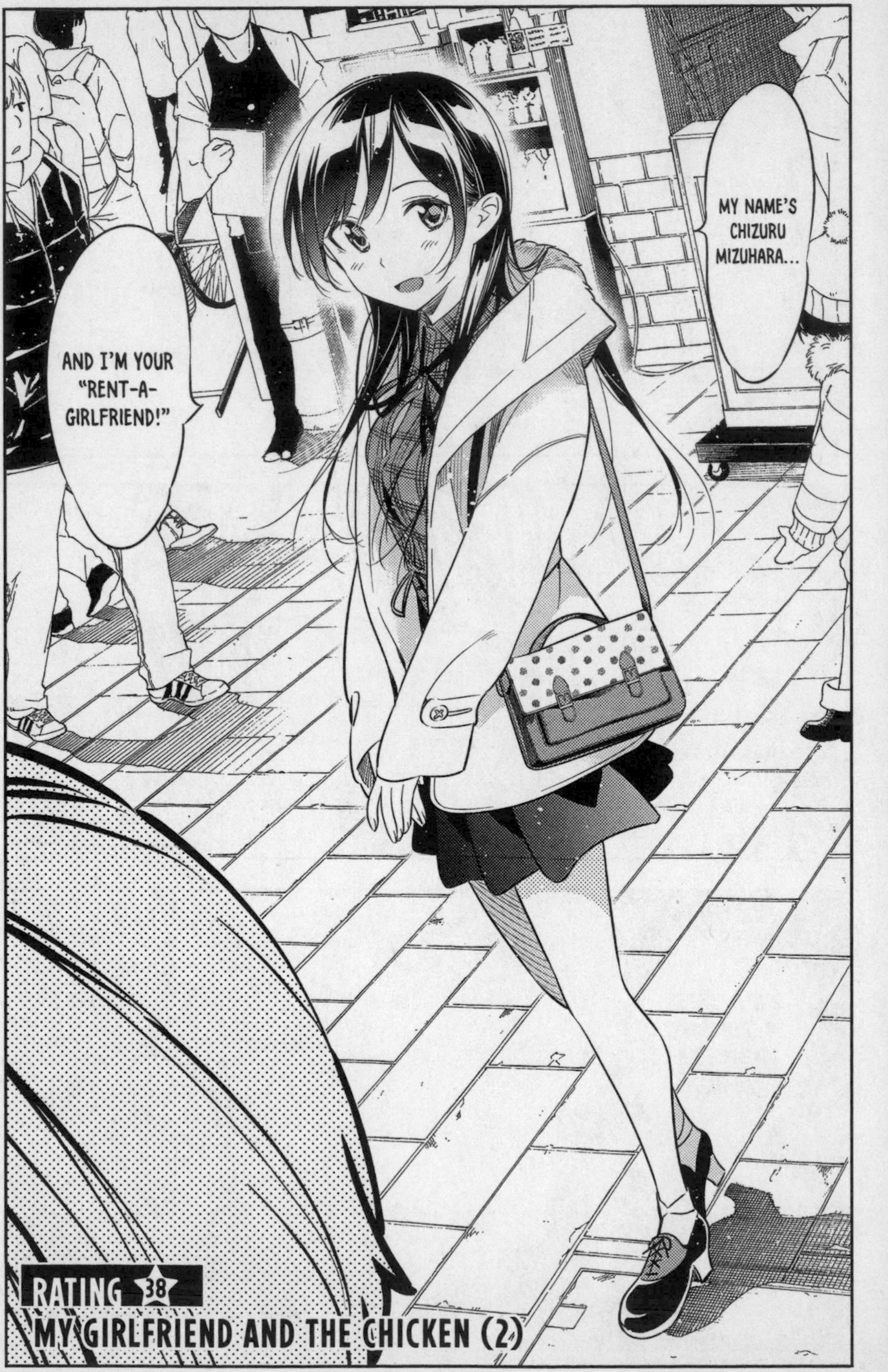
MY NAME'S CHIZURU MIZUHARA...
AND I'M YOUR "RENT-A-GIRLFRIEND!"
RATING 38
MY GIRLFRIEND AND THE CHICKEN (2)

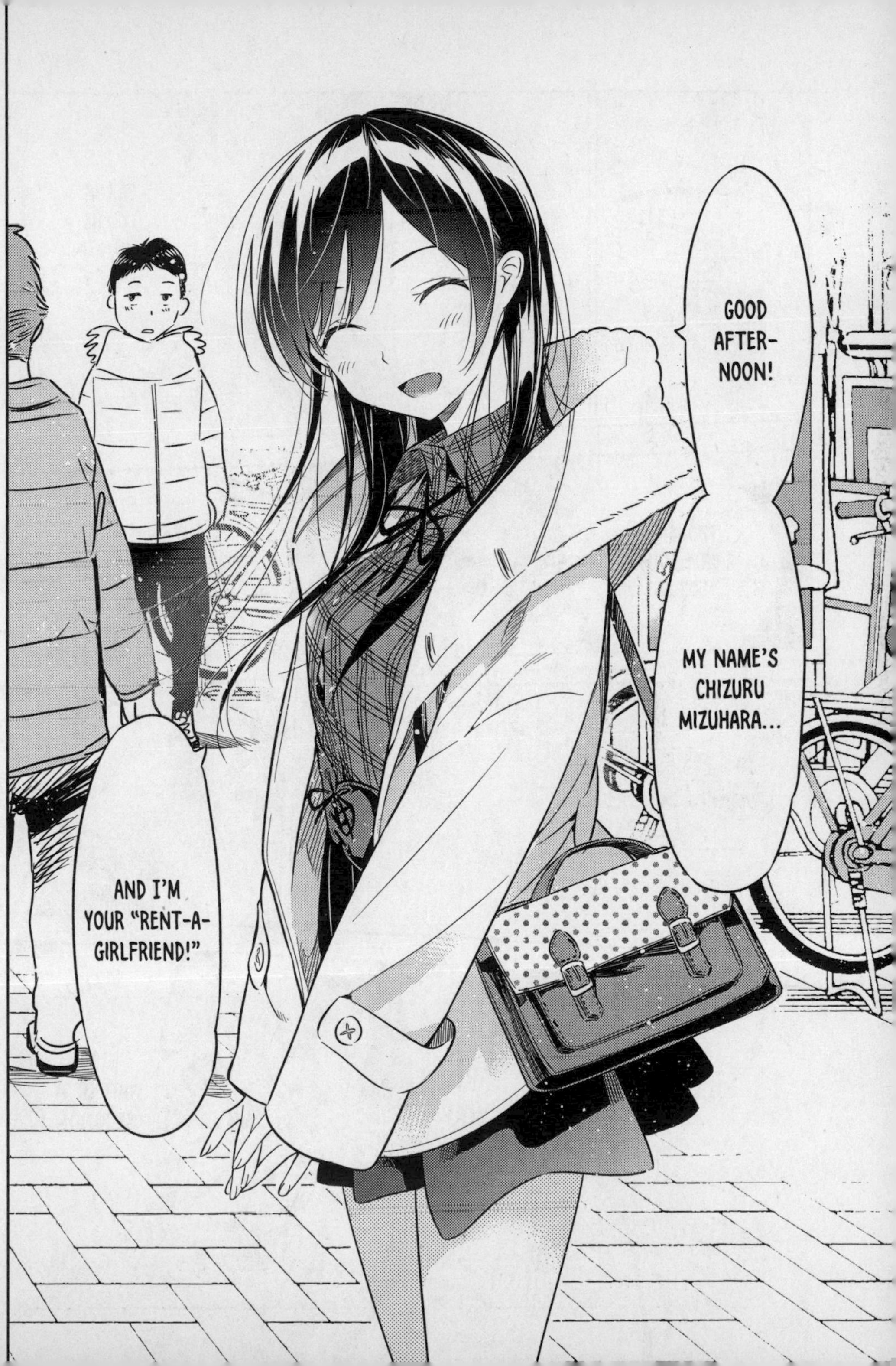
GOOD AFTER-NOON!
MY NAME'S CHIZURU MIZUHARA...
AND I'M YOUR "RENT-A-GIRLFRIEND!"

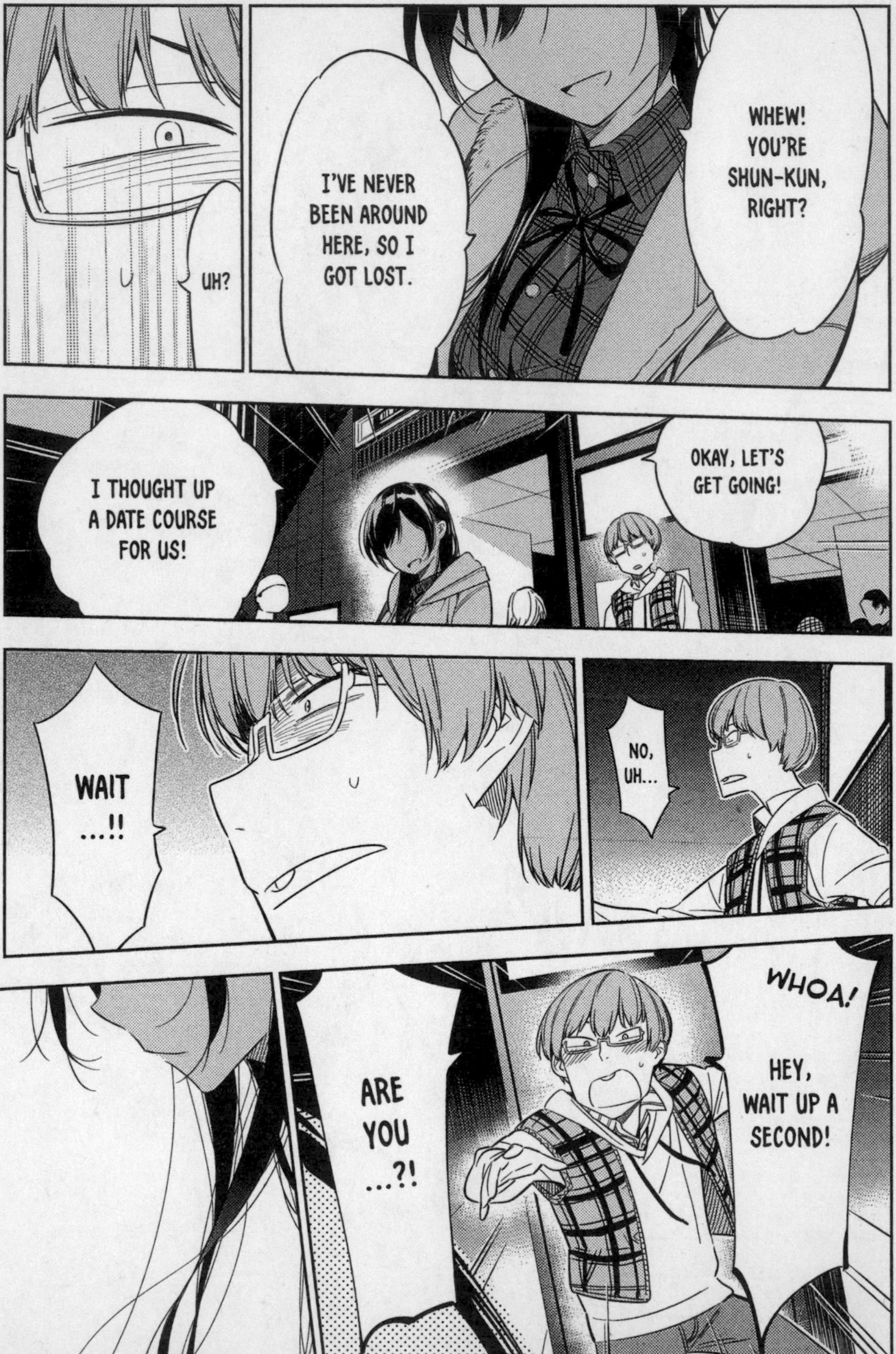
WHEW! YOU'RE SHUN-KUN, RIGHT?
I'VE NEVER BEEN AROUND HERE, SO I GOT LOST.
UH?
OKAY, LET'S GET GOING!
I THOUGHT UP A DATE COURSE FOR US!
NO, UH...
WAIT ...!!
WHOA!
HEY, WAIT UP A SECOND!
ARE YOU ...?!

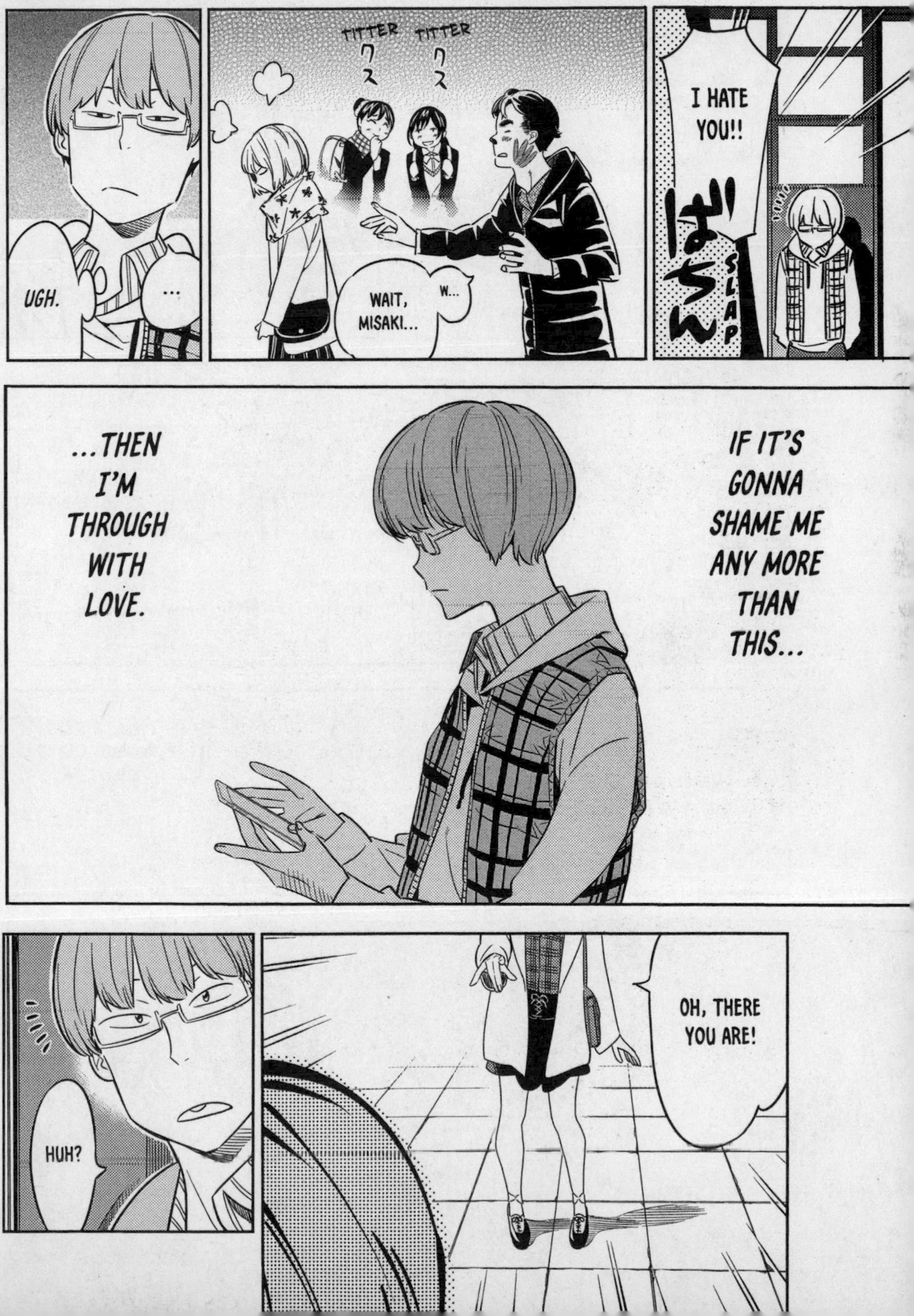
I HATE YOU!!
ぱちん
SLAP
TITTER
クス
TITTER
クス
W...
WAIT, MISAKI...
...
UGH.
IF IT'S GONNA SHAME ME ANY MORE THAN THIS...
...THEN I'M THROUGH WITH LOVE.
OH, THERE YOU ARE!
HUH?

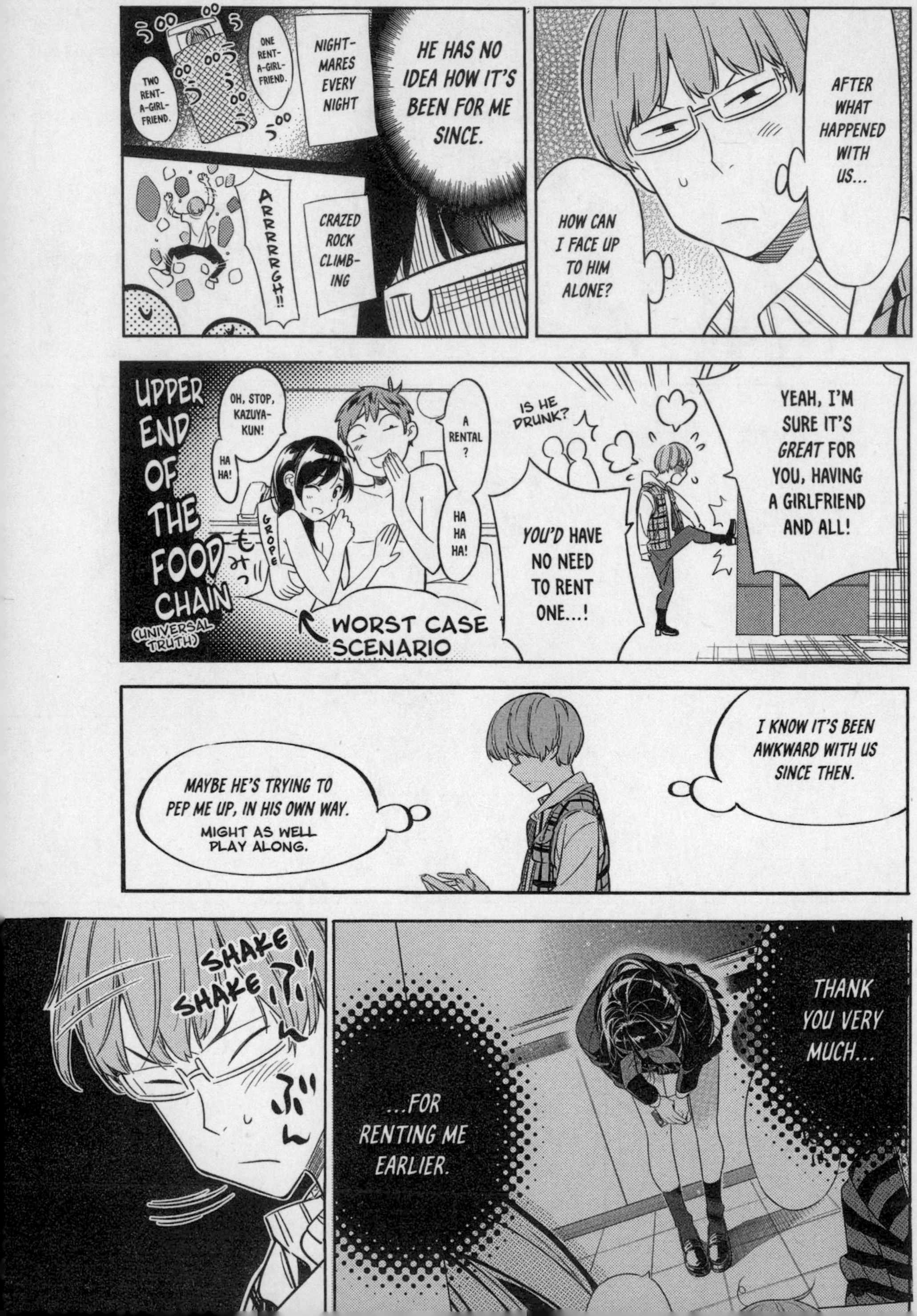
AFTER WHAT HAPPENED WITH US...
HOW CAN I FACE UP TO HIM ALONE?
HE HAS NO IDEA HOW IT'S BEEN FOR ME SINCE.
NIGHTMARES EVERY NIGHT
ONE RENT-A-GIRLFRIEND.
TWO RENT-A-GIRLFRIEND.
CRAZED ROCK CLIMBING
ARRRRRGH!!
YEAH, I'M SURE IT'S GREAT FOR YOU, HAVING A GIRLFRIEND AND ALL!
YOU'D HAVE NO NEED TO RENT ONE...!
IS HE DRUNK?
A RENTAL?
HA HA HA!
OH, STOP, KAZUYA-KUN!
HA HA!
GROPE
UPPER END OF THE FOOD CHAIN
(UNIVERSAL TRUTH)
WORST CASE SCENARIO
I KNOW IT'S BEEN AWKWARD WITH US SINCE THEN.
MAYBE HE'S TRYING TO PEP ME UP, IN HIS OWN WAY.
MIGHT AS WELL PLAY ALONG.
THANK YOU VERY MUCH...
...FOR RENTING ME EARLIER.
SHAKE SHAKE

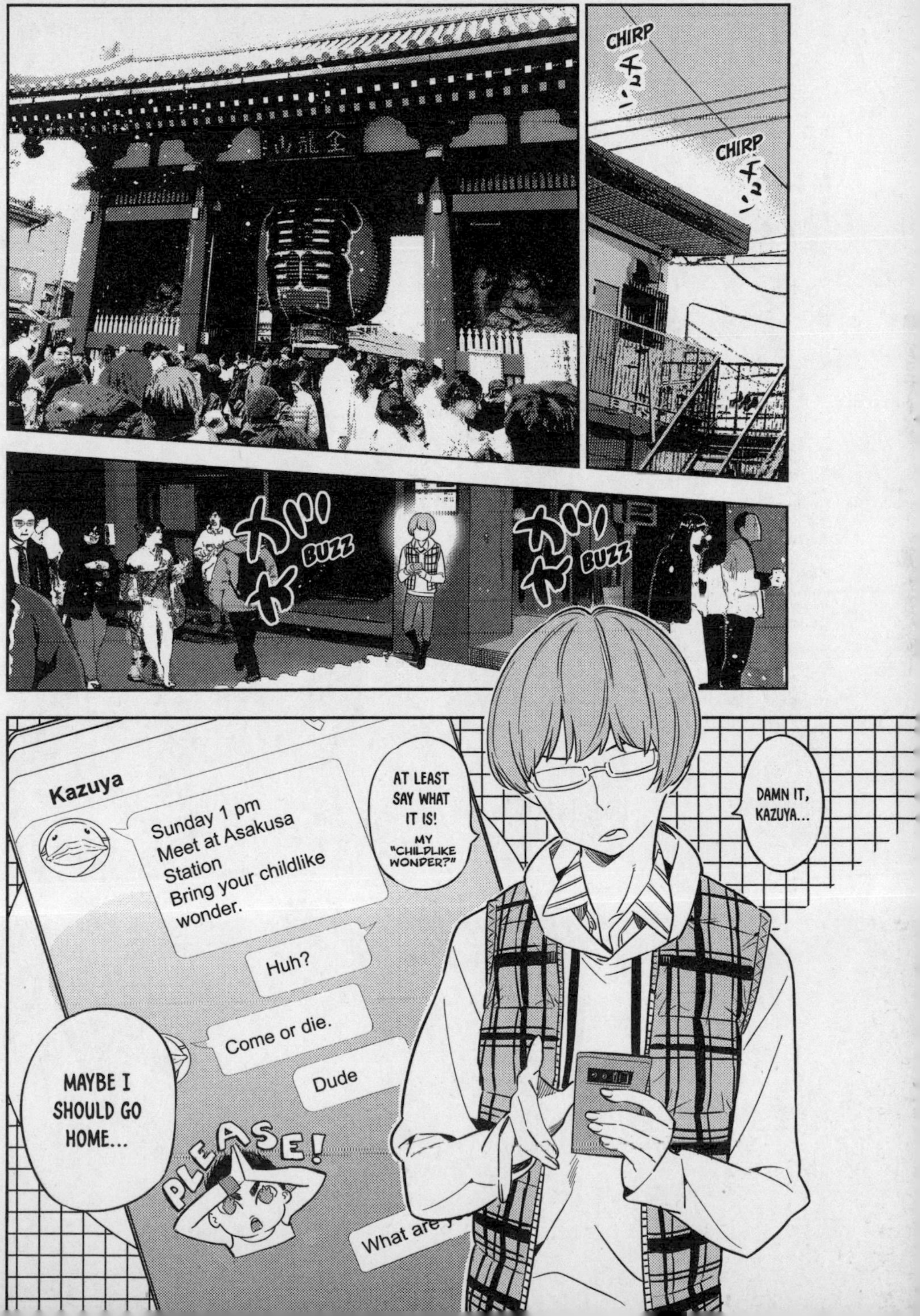
CHIRP
チュン
CHIRP
チュン
BUZZ
BUZZ
DAMN IT, KAZUYA...
AT LEAST SAY WHAT IT IS!
MY "CHILDLIKE WONDER?"
Kazuya
Sunday 1 pm Meet at Asakusa Station Bring your childlike wonder.
Huh?
Come or die.
Dude
What are
MAYBE I SHOULD GO HOME...
PLEASE!

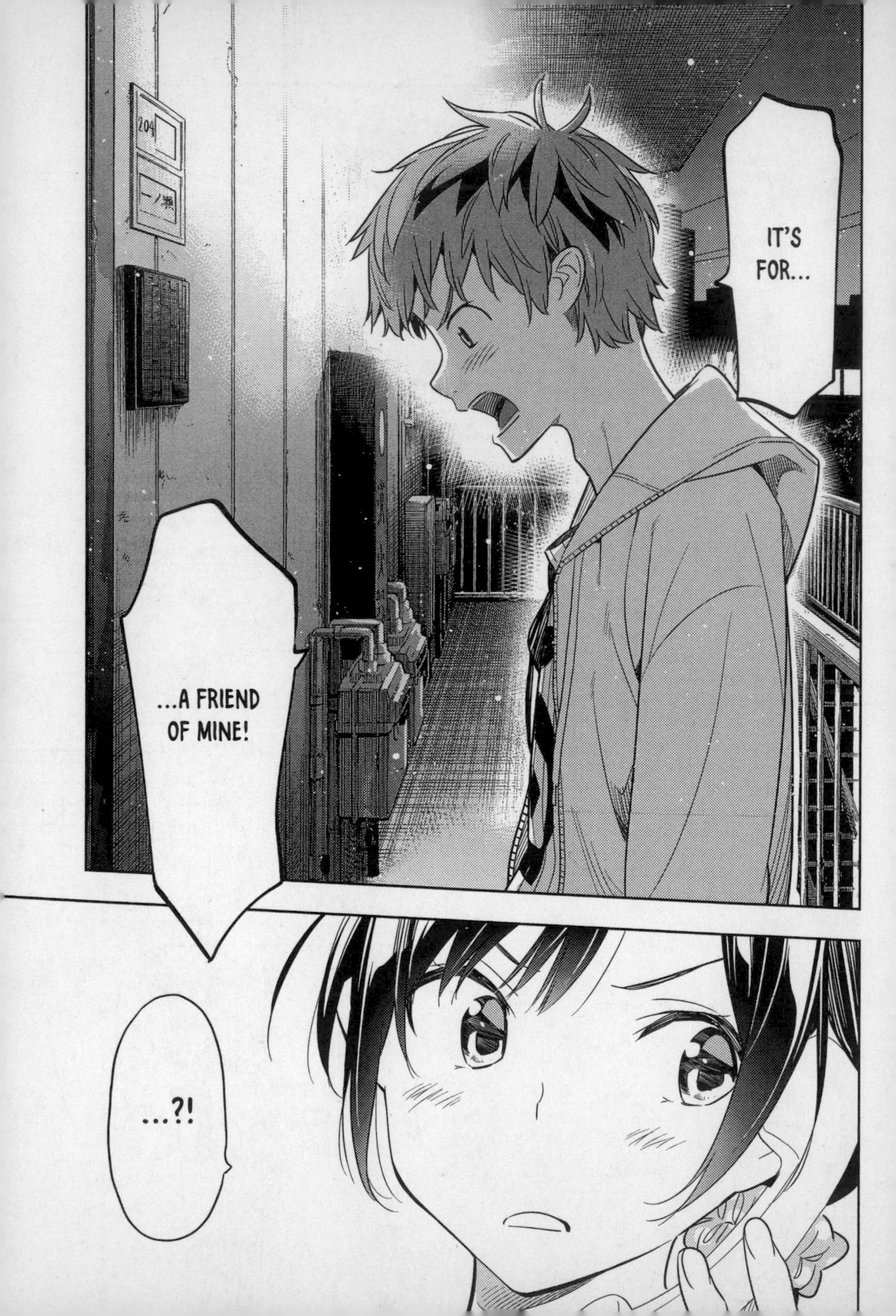
204
一ノ瀬
IT'S FOR...
...A FRIEND OF MINE!
...?!

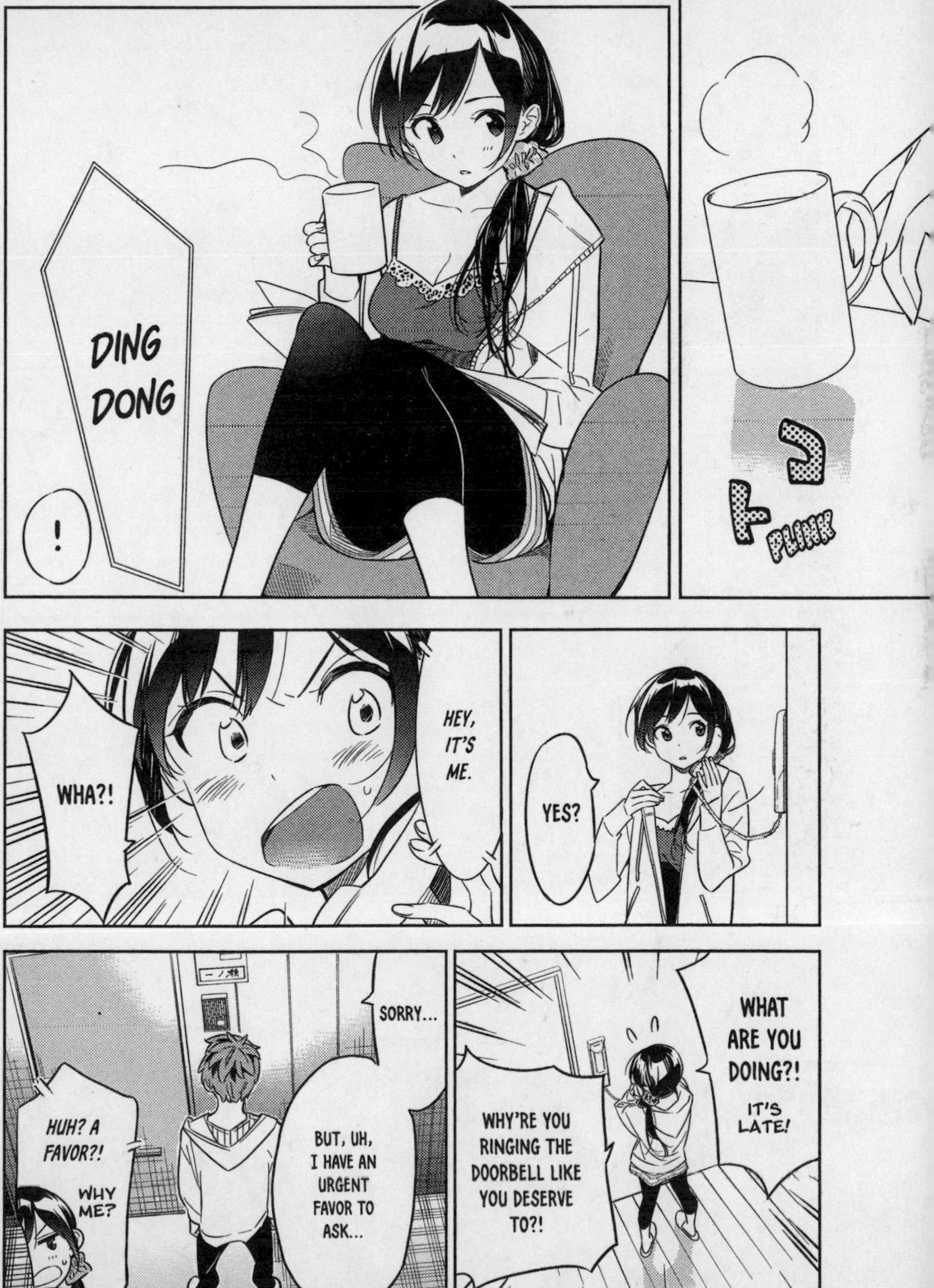
コト
PLINK
DING DONG
!
YES?
HEY, IT'S ME.
WHA?!
WHAT ARE YOU DOING?!
IT'S LATE!
WHY'RE YOU RINGING THE DOORBELL LIKE YOU DESERVE TO?!
一ノ瀬
SORRY...
BUT, UH, I HAVE AN URGENT FAVOR TO ASK...
HUH? A FAVOR?!
WHY ME?

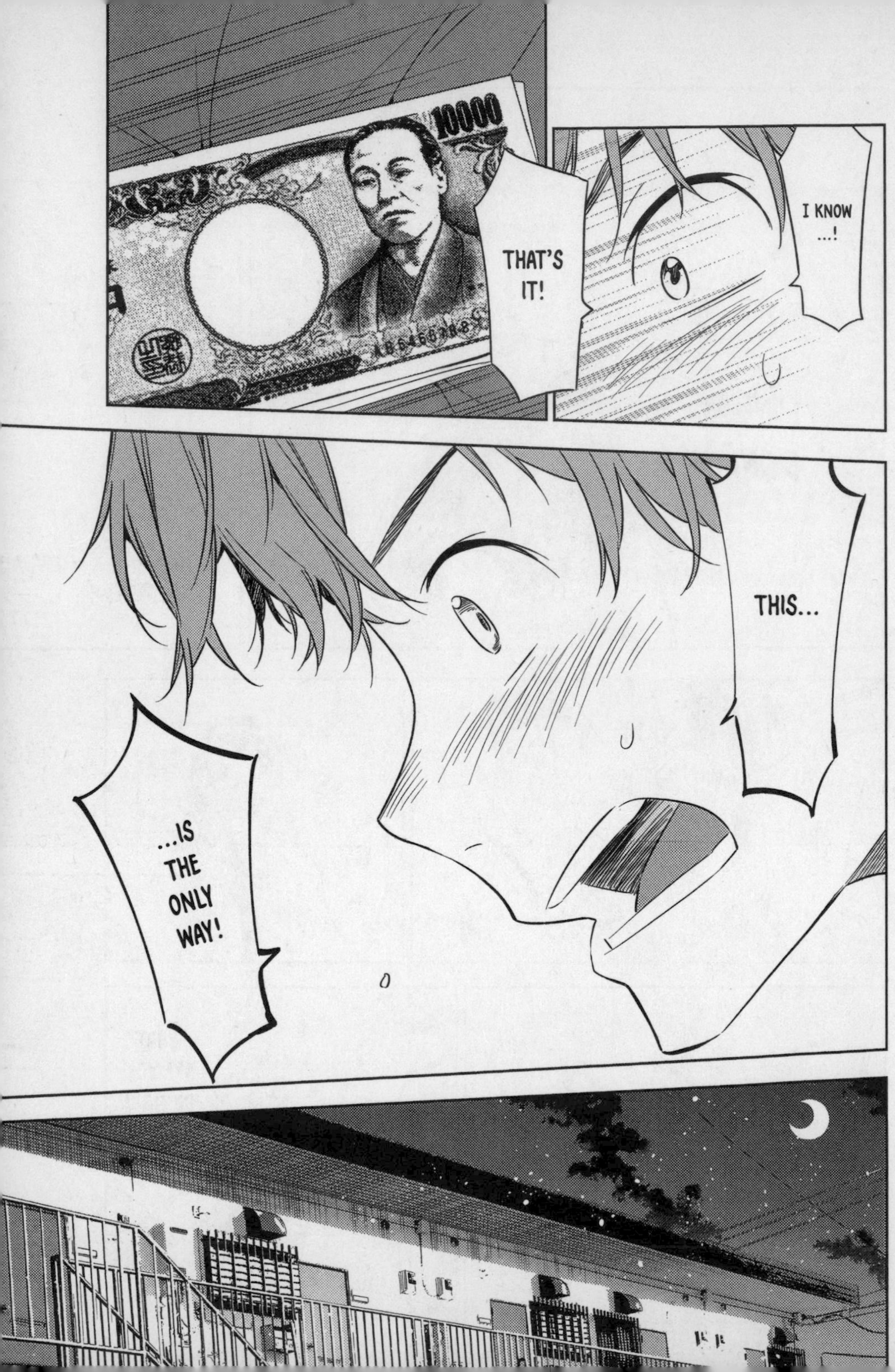
I KNOW ...!
THAT'S IT!
10000
THIS...
...IS THE ONLY WAY!

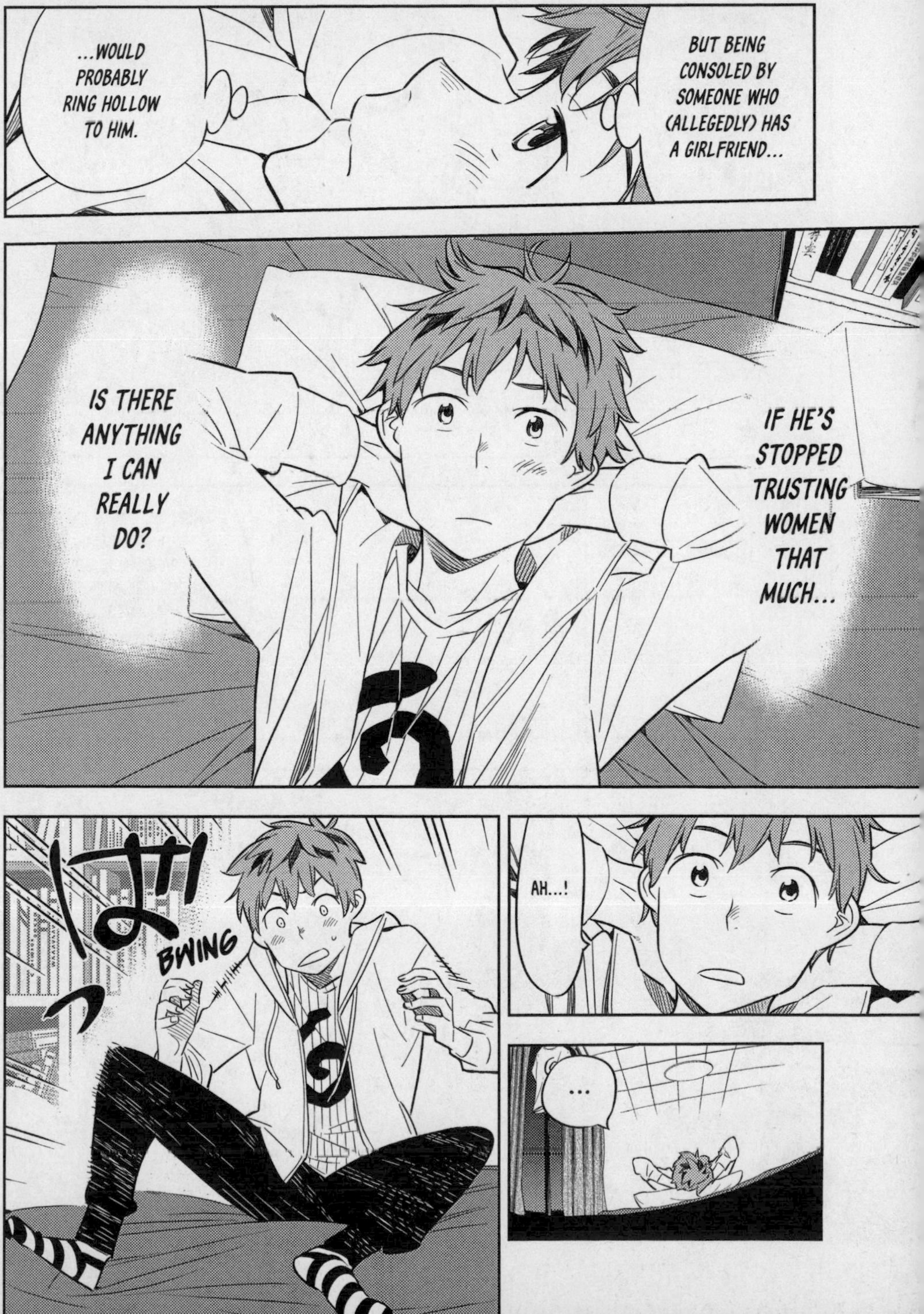
BUT BEING CONSOLED BY SOMEONE WHO (ALLEGEDLY) HAS A GIRLFRIEND...
...WOULD PROBABLY RING HOLLOW TO HIM.
IF HE'S STOPPED TRUSTING WOMEN THAT MUCH...
IS THERE ANYTHING I CAN REALLY DO?
AH...!
...
BWING

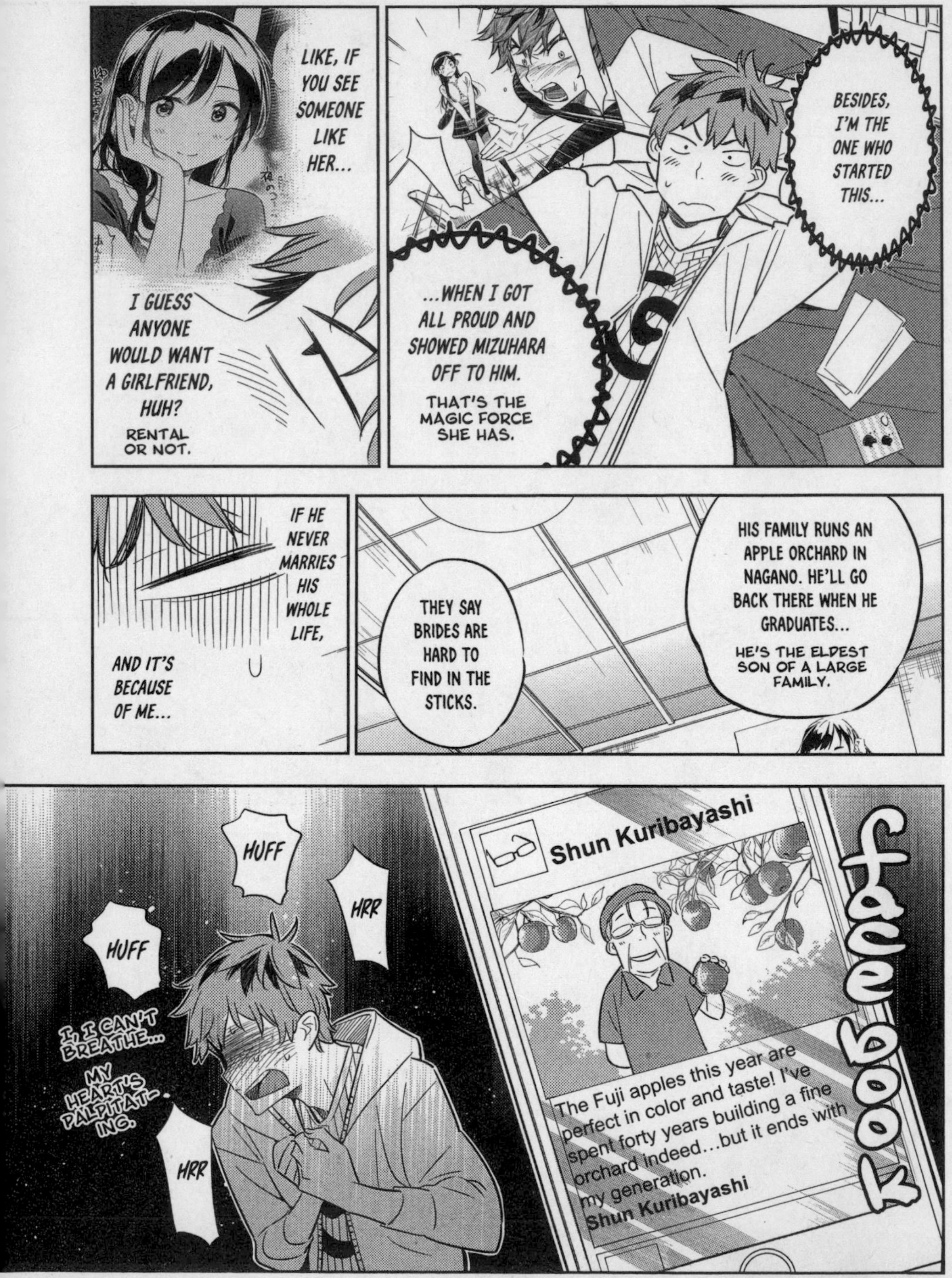
BESIDES, I'M THE ONE WHO STARTED THIS...
...WHEN I GOT ALL PROUD AND SHOWED MIZUHARA OFF TO HIM.
THAT'S THE MAGIC FORCE SHE HAS.
LIKE, IF YOU SEE SOMEONE LIKE HER...
I GUESS ANYONE WOULD WANT A GIRLFRIEND, HUH?
RENTAL OR NOT.
HIS FAMILY RUNS AN APPLE ORCHARD IN NAGANO. HE'LL GO BACK THERE WHEN HE GRADUATES...
HE'S THE ELDEST SON OF A LARGE FAMILY.
THEY SAY BRIDES ARE HARD TO FIND IN THE STICKS.
IF HE NEVER MARRIES HIS WHOLE LIFE,
AND IT'S BECAUSE OF ME...
facebook
Shun Kuribayashi
The Fuji apples this year are perfect in color and taste! I've spent forty years building a fine orchard indeed...but it ends with my generation.
Shun Kuribayashi
HRR
HUFF
HUFF
I, I CAN'T BREATHE...
MY HEART'S PALPITATING.
HRR

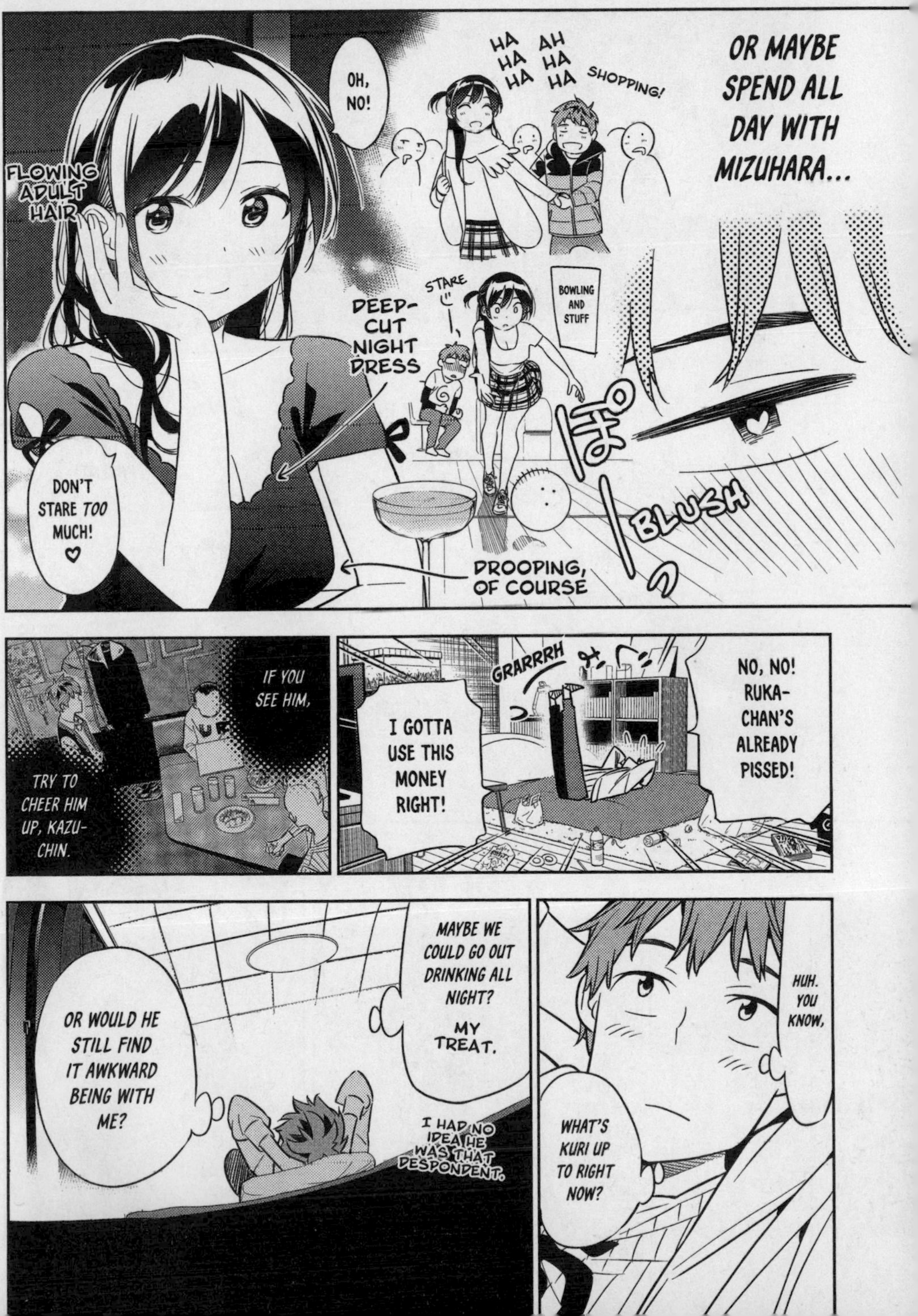
OR MAYBE SPEND ALL DAY WITH MIZUHARA...
SHOPPING!
AH HA HA
HA HA HA
OH, NO!
FLOWING ADULT HAIR
BOWLING AND STUFF
STARE
DEEP-CUT NIGHT DRESS
BLUSH
DON'T STARE *TOO* MUCH! ♡
DROOPING, OF COURSE
NO, NO! RUKA-CHAN'S ALREADY PISSED!
GRARRRH
I GOTTA USE THIS MONEY RIGHT!
IF YOU SEE HIM,
TRY TO CHEER HIM UP, KAZU-CHIN.
HUH. YOU KNOW,
WHAT'S KURI UP TO RIGHT NOW?
MAYBE WE COULD GO OUT DRINKING ALL NIGHT?
MY TREAT.
OR WOULD HE STILL FIND IT AWKWARD BEING WITH ME?
I HAD NO IDEA HE WAS THAT DESPONDENT.

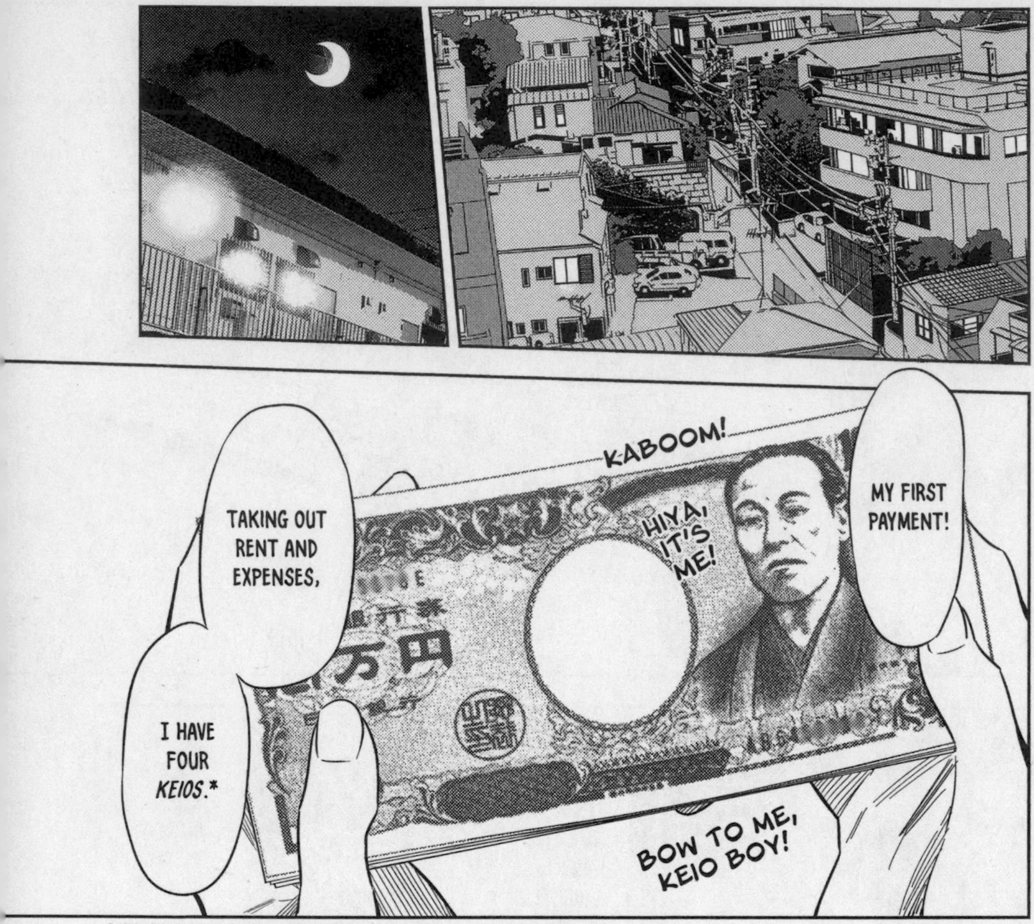
MY FIRST PAYMENT!
KABOOM!
HIYA, IT'S ME!
TAKING OUT RENT AND EXPENSES,
I HAVE FOUR *KEIOS*.*
BOW TO ME, KEIO BOY!

* YUKICHI FUKUZAWA, FOUNDER OF KEIO UNIVERSITY, IS ON THE 10,000 YEN BILL.

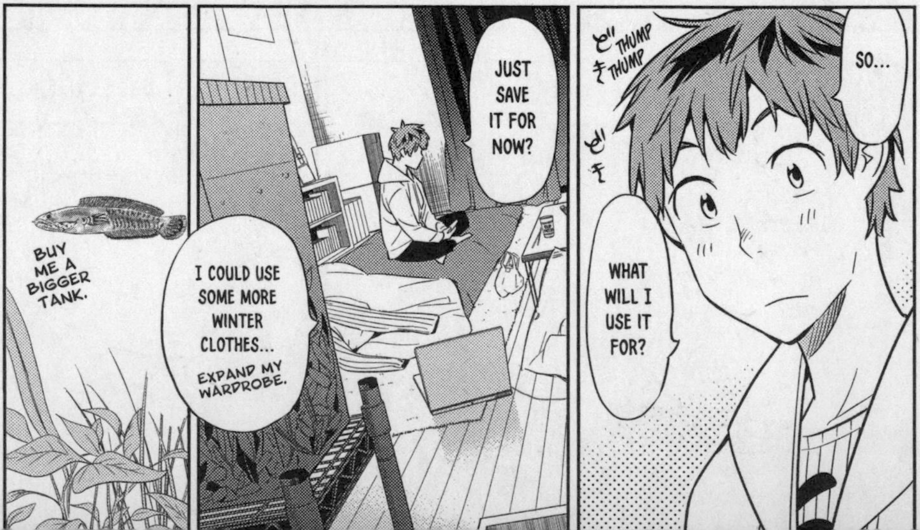
SO...
どき THUMP THUMP
どき
WHAT WILL I USE IT FOR?
JUST SAVE IT FOR NOW?
I COULD USE SOME MORE WINTER CLOTHES...
EXPAND MY WARDROBE.
BUY ME A BIGGER TANK.

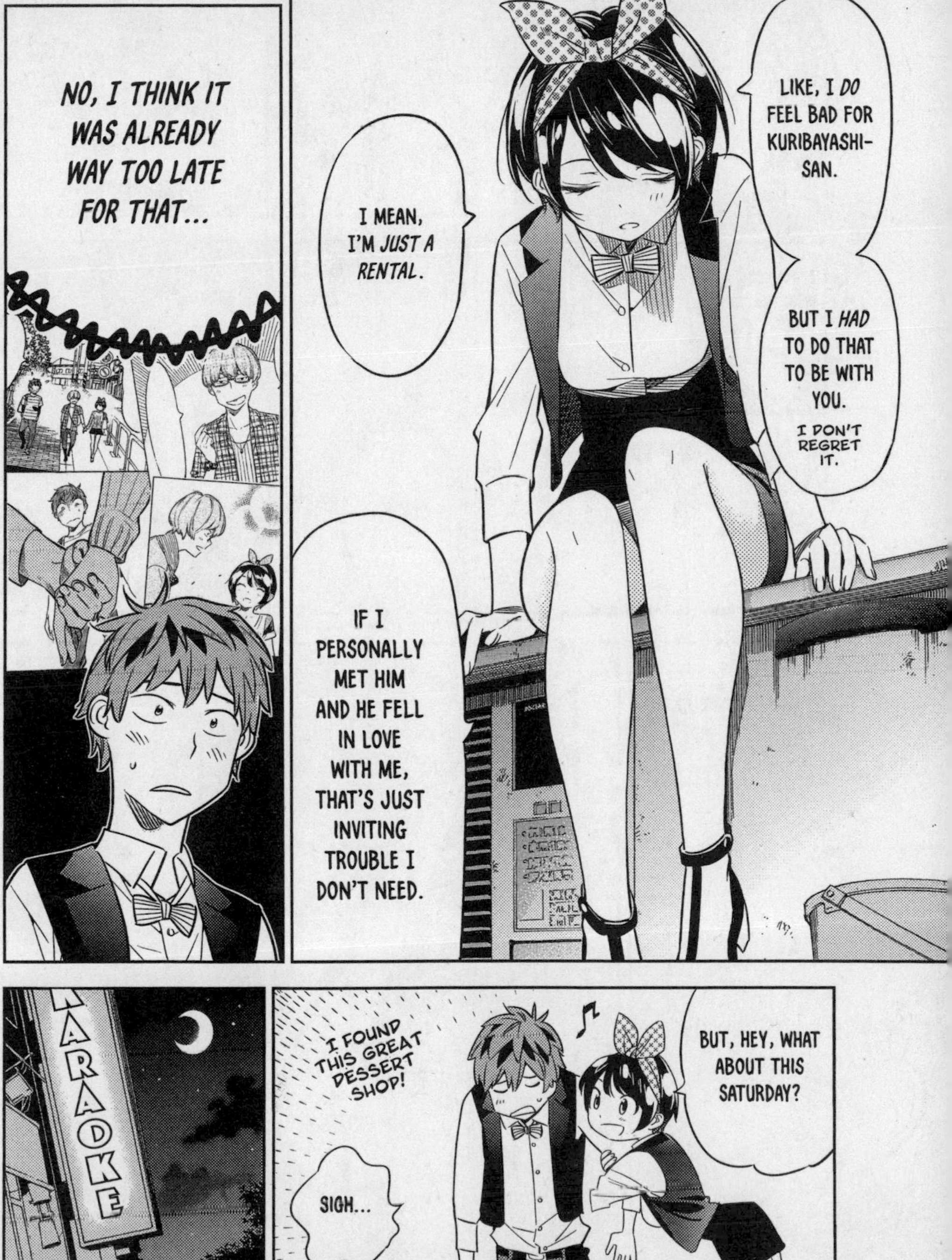
LIKE, I DO FEEL BAD FOR KURIBAYASHI-SAN.
BUT I HAD TO DO THAT TO BE WITH YOU.
I DON'T REGRET IT.
I MEAN, I'M JUST A RENTAL.
IF I PERSONALLY MET HIM AND HE FELL IN LOVE WITH ME, THAT'S JUST INVITING TROUBLE I DON'T NEED.
NO, I THINK IT WAS ALREADY WAY TOO LATE FOR THAT...
BUT, HEY, WHAT ABOUT THIS SATURDAY?
I FOUND THIS GREAT DESSERT SHOP!
SIGH...
KARAOKE

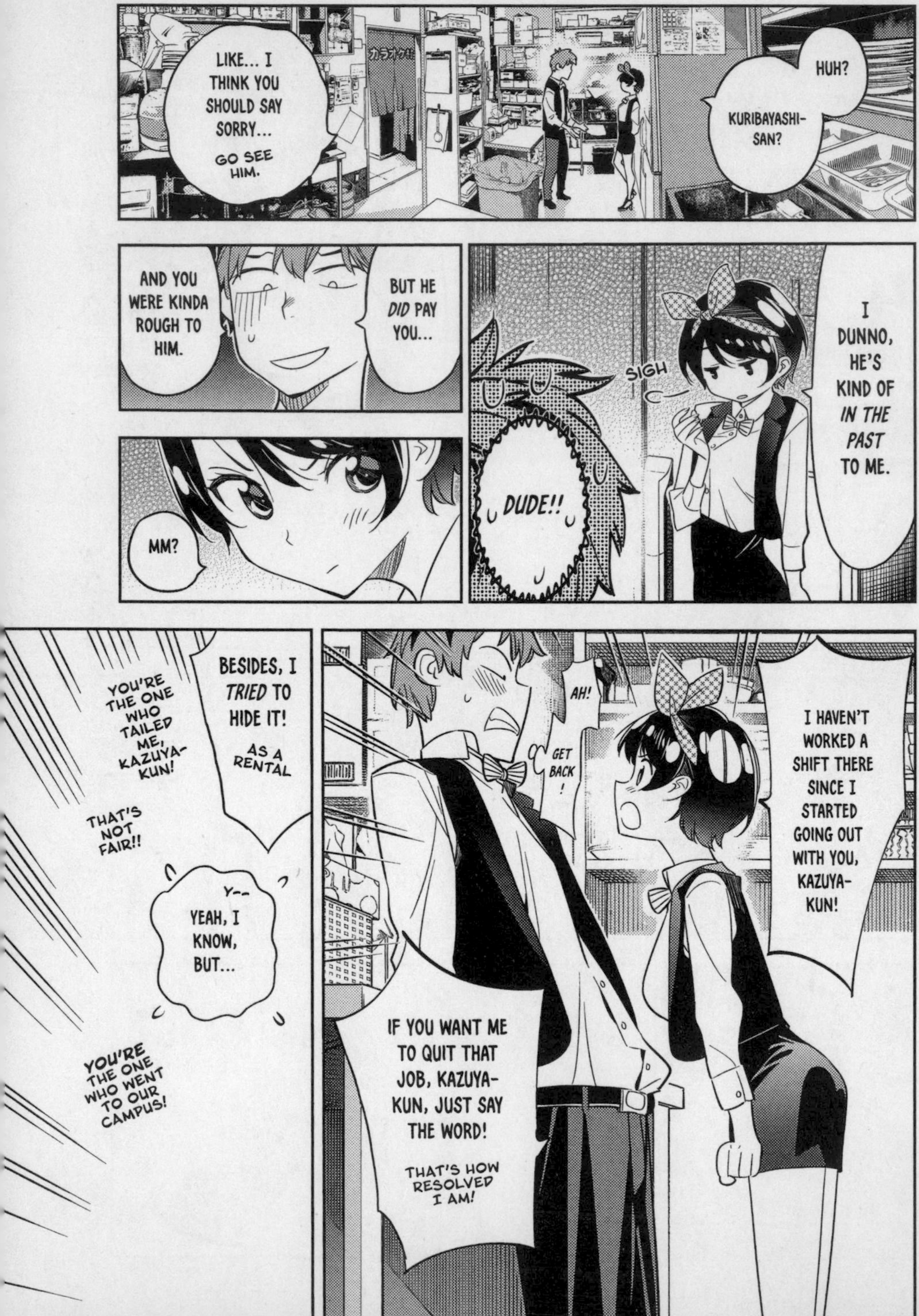
HUH?
KURIBAYASHI-SAN?
LIKE... I THINK YOU SHOULD SAY SORRY...
GO SEE HIM.
I DUNNO, HE'S KIND OF IN THE PAST TO ME.
SIGH
DUDE!!
BUT HE DID PAY YOU...
AND YOU WERE KINDA ROUGH TO HIM.
MM?
I HAVEN'T WORKED A SHIFT THERE SINCE I STARTED GOING OUT WITH YOU, KAZUYA-KUN!
AH!
GET BACK!
IF YOU WANT ME TO QUIT THAT JOB, KAZUYA-KUN, JUST SAY THE WORD!
THAT'S HOW RESOLVED I AM!
BESIDES, I TRIED TO HIDE IT!
AS A RENTAL
YOU'RE THE ONE WHO TAILED ME, KAZUYA-KUN!
THAT'S NOT FAIR!!
Y-- YEAH, I KNOW, BUT...
YOU'RE THE ONE WHO WENT TO OUR CAMPUS!

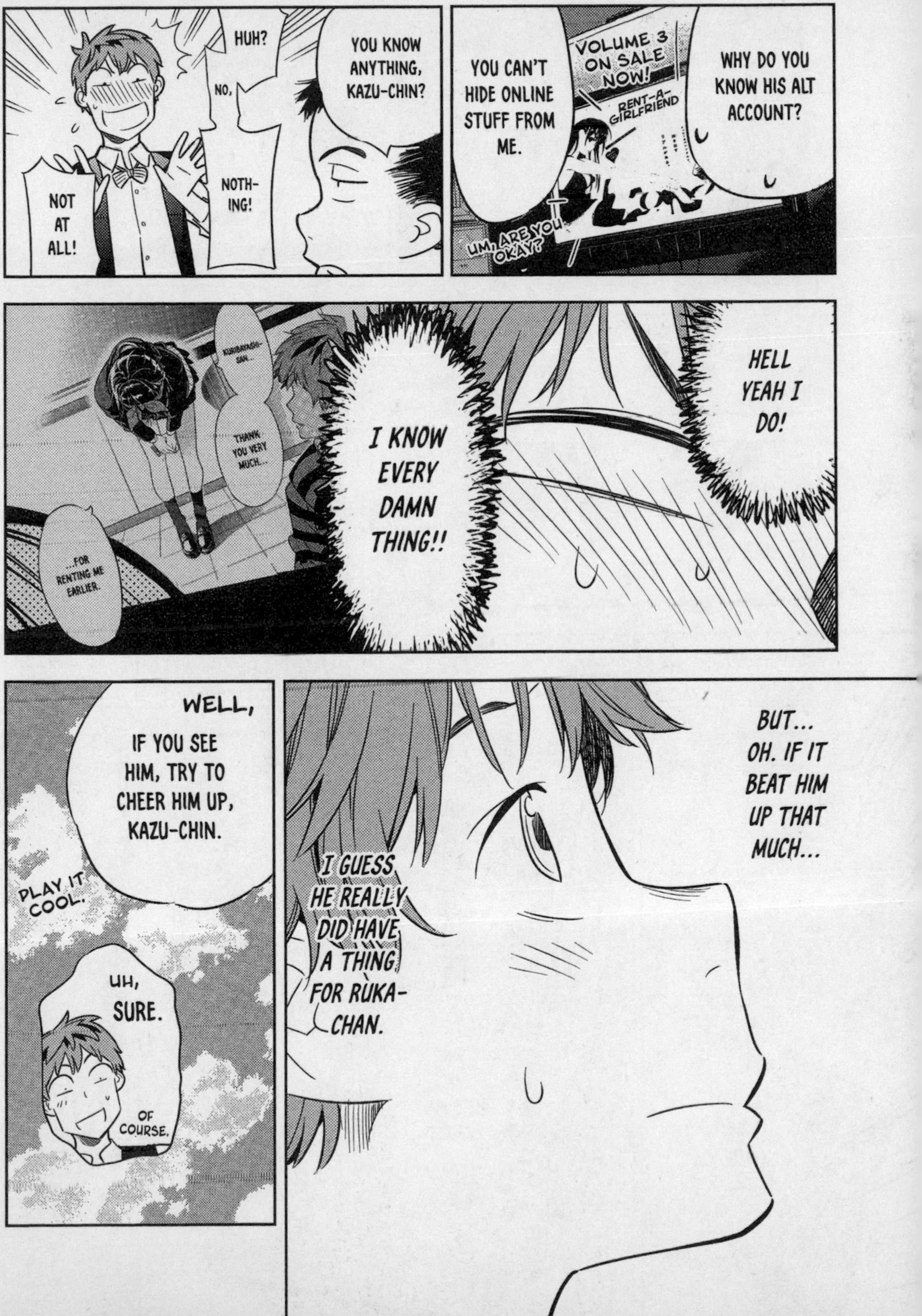
WHY DO YOU KNOW HIS ALT ACCOUNT?
VOLUME 3 ON SALE NOW!
RENT-A-GIRLFRIEND
YOU CAN'T HIDE ONLINE STUFF FROM ME.
UM, ARE YOU OKAY?
YOU KNOW ANYTHING, KAZU-CHIN?
HUH?
NO,
NOTH-ING!
NOT AT ALL!
HELL YEAH I DO!
I KNOW EVERY DAMN THING!!
KURIBAYASHI-SAN.
THANK YOU VERY MUCH...
...FOR RENTING ME EARLIER.
BUT... OH. IF IT BEAT HIM UP THAT MUCH...
I GUESS HE REALLY DID HAVE A THING FOR RUKA-CHAN.
WELL,
IF YOU SEE HIM, TRY TO CHEER HIM UP, KAZU-CHIN.
PLAY IT COOL.
UH, SURE.
OF COURSE.

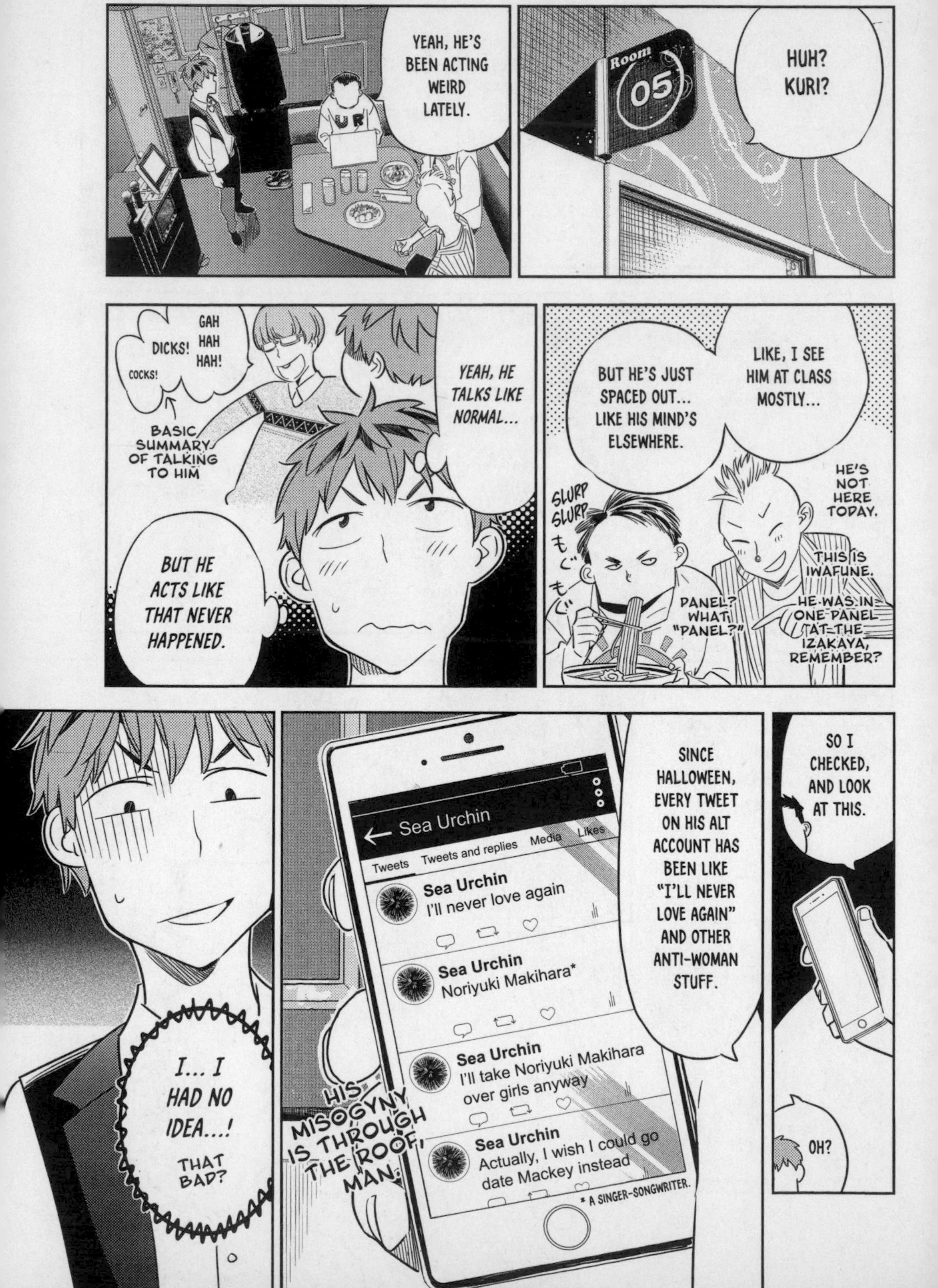

Room 05
HUH? KURI?
YEAH, HE'S BEEN ACTING WEIRD LATELY.
LIKE, I SEE HIM AT CLASS MOSTLY...
BUT HE'S JUST SPACED OUT... LIKE HIS MIND'S ELSEWHERE.
HE'S NOT HERE TODAY.
THIS IS IWAFUNE.
HE WAS IN ONE PANEL AT THE IZAKAYA, REMEMBER?
PANEL? WHAT "PANEL?"
SLURP SLURP
もぐもぐ
YEAH, HE TALKS LIKE NORMAL...
GAH HAH HAH!
DICKS!
COCKS!
BASIC SUMMARY OF TALKING TO HIM
BUT HE ACTS LIKE THAT NEVER HAPPENED.
SO I CHECKED, AND LOOK AT THIS.
OH?
SINCE HALLOWEEN, EVERY TWEET ON HIS ALT ACCOUNT HAS BEEN LIKE "I'LL NEVER LOVE AGAIN" AND OTHER ANTI-WOMAN STUFF.
Sea Urchin
Tweets Tweets and replies Media Likes
Sea Urchin
I'll never love again
Sea Urchin
Noriyuki Makihara*
Sea Urchin
I'll take Noriyuki Makihara over girls anyway
Sea Urchin
Actually, I wish I could go date Mackey instead
* A SINGER-SONGWRITER.
HIS MISOGYNY IS THROUGH THE ROOF, MAN.
I... I HAD NO IDEA...!
THAT BAD?

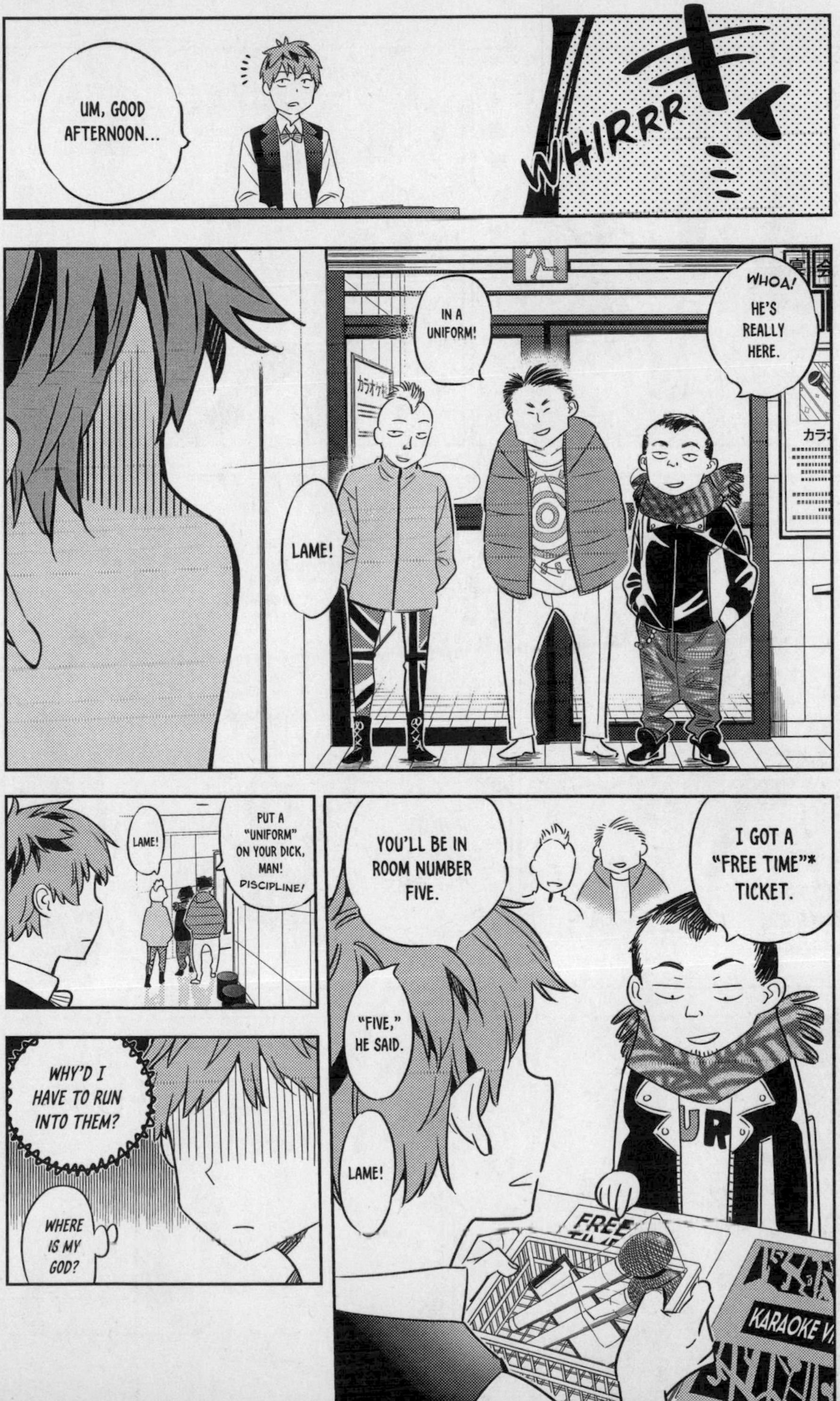
WHIRRR
UM, GOOD AFTERNOON...
WHOA! HE'S REALLY HERE.
IN A UNIFORM!
LAME!
I GOT A "FREE TIME"* TICKET.
YOU'LL BE IN ROOM NUMBER FIVE.
"FIVE," HE SAID.
LAME!
FREE
KARAOKE V
PUT A "UNIFORM" ON YOUR DICK, MAN! DISCIPLINE!
LAME!
WHY'D I HAVE TO RUN INTO THEM?
WHERE IS MY GOD?

* A TICKET THAT LETS YOU USE A ROOM AS LONG AS YOU WANT, AS LONG AS ALL ROOMS AREN'T FULL.

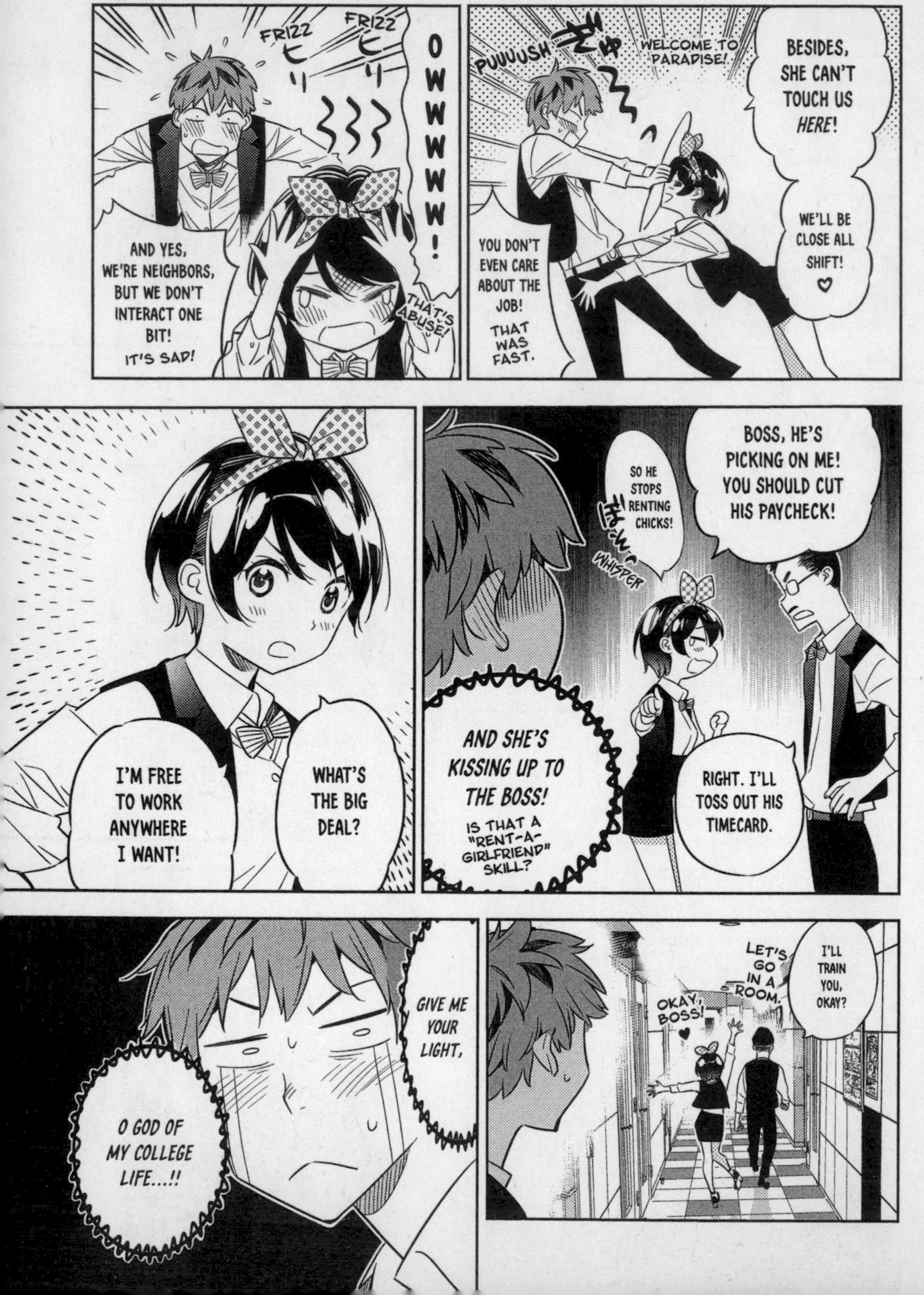
PUUUUSH
WELCOME TO PARADISE!
BESIDES, SHE CAN'T TOUCH US *HERE*!
WE'LL BE CLOSE ALL SHIFT! ♥
YOU DON'T EVEN CARE ABOUT THE JOB!
THAT WAS FAST.
FRIZZ
FRIZZ
OWWWWWW!
THAT'S ABUSE!
AND YES, WE'RE NEIGHBORS, BUT WE DON'T INTERACT ONE BIT!
IT'S SAD!
BOSS, HE'S PICKING ON ME! YOU SHOULD CUT HIS PAYCHECK!
SO HE STOPS RENTING CHICKS!
WHISPER
RIGHT. I'LL TOSS OUT HIS TIMECARD.
AND SHE'S KISSING UP TO THE BOSS!
IS THAT A "RENT-A-GIRLFRIEND" SKILL?
WHAT'S THE BIG DEAL?
I'M FREE TO WORK ANYWHERE I WANT!
I'LL TRAIN YOU, OKAY?
LET'S GO IN A ROOM.
OKAY, BOSS! ♥
GIVE ME YOUR LIGHT,
O GOD OF MY COLLEGE LIFE...!!

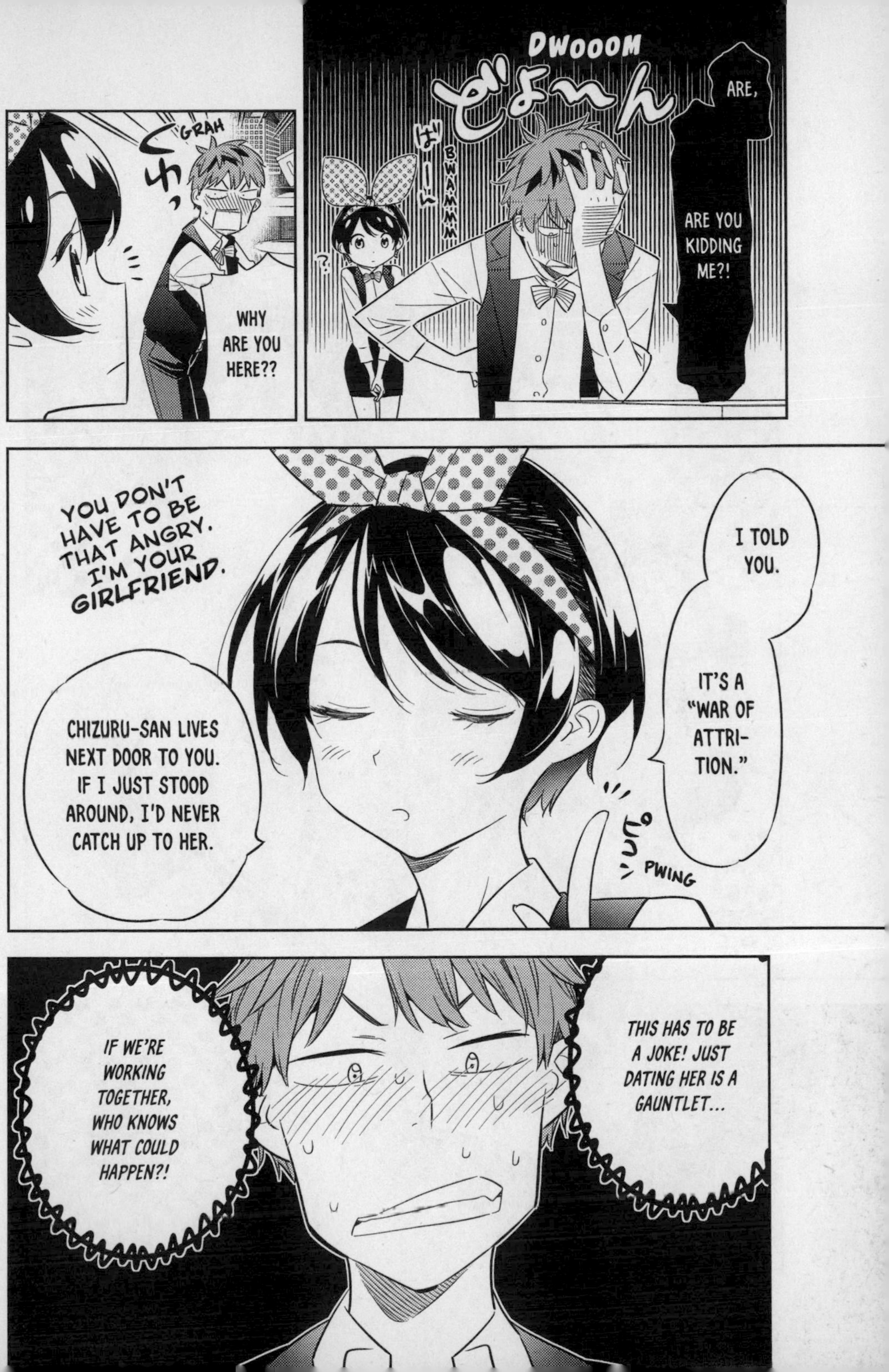
DWOOOM
BWAMMM
ARE,
ARE YOU KIDDING ME?!
GRAH
WHY ARE YOU HERE??
I TOLD YOU.
IT'S A "WAR OF ATTRITION."
PWING
CHIZURU-SAN LIVES NEXT DOOR TO YOU. IF I JUST STOOD AROUND, I'D NEVER CATCH UP TO HER.
YOU DON'T HAVE TO BE THAT ANGRY. I'M YOUR GIRLFRIEND.
THIS HAS TO BE A JOKE! JUST DATING HER IS A GAUNTLET...
IF WE'RE WORKING TOGETHER, WHO KNOWS WHAT COULD HAPPEN?!

RATING 37

MY GIRLFRIEND AND THE CHICKEN (1)

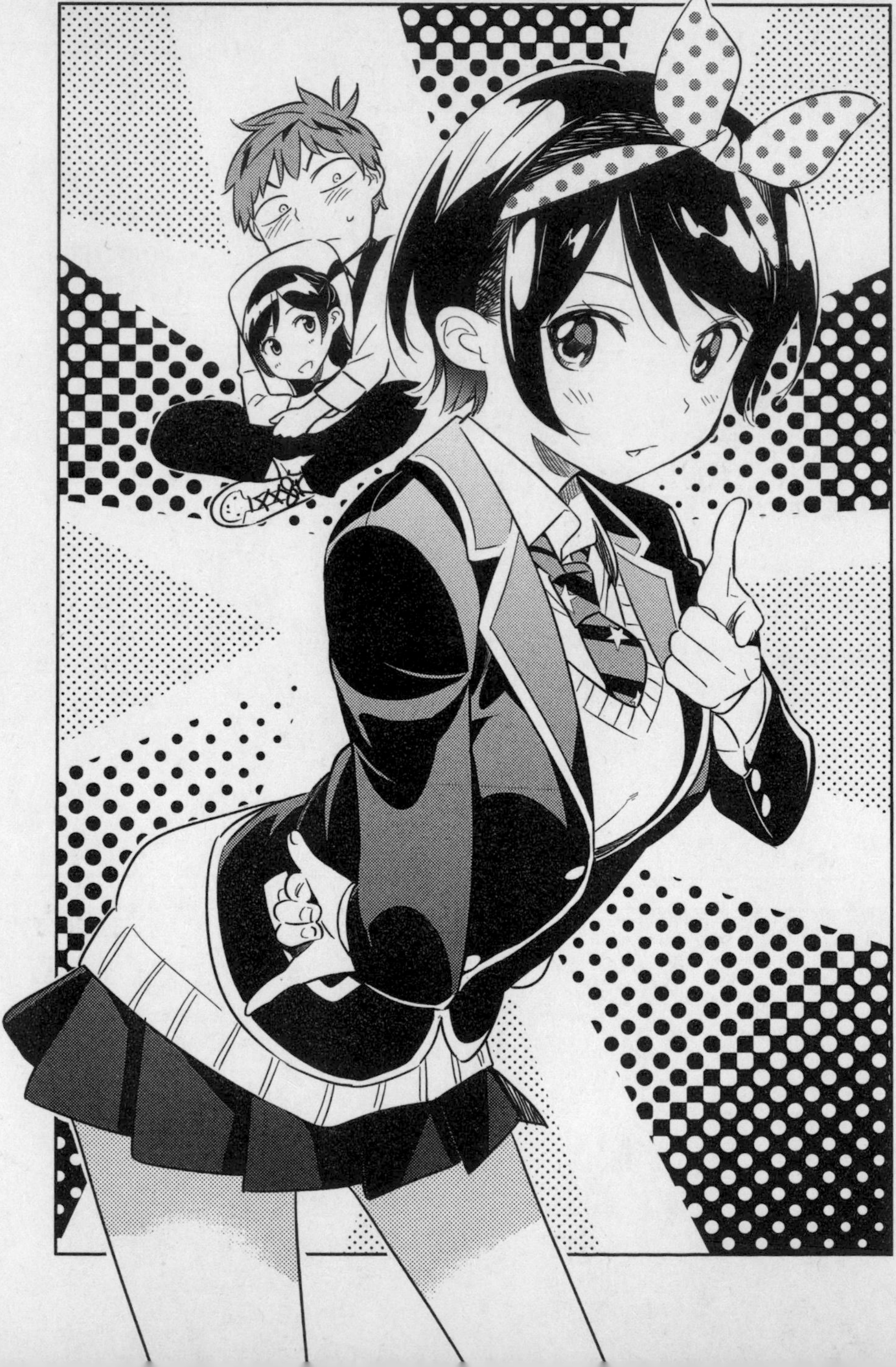

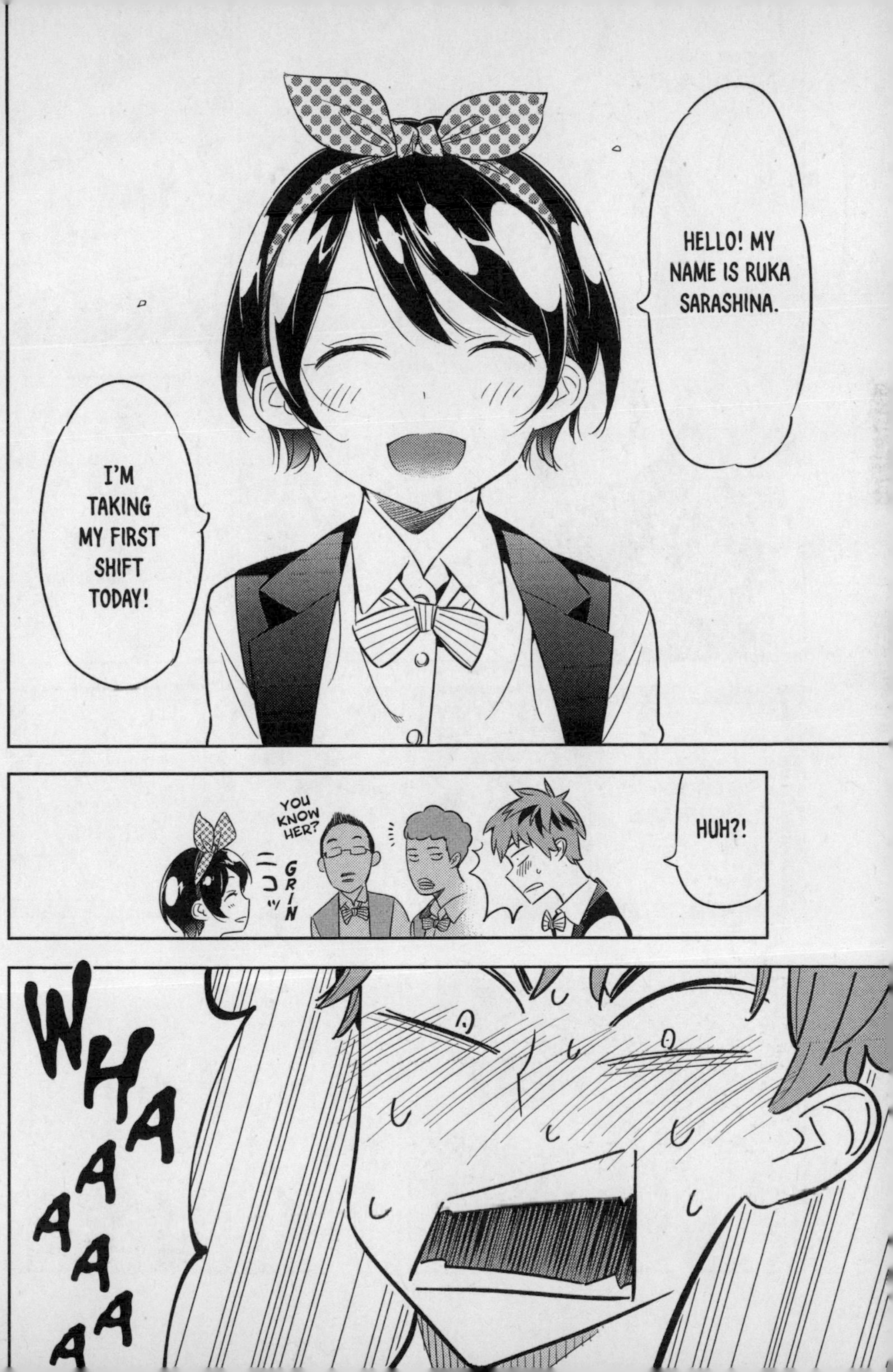
HELLO! MY NAME IS RUKA SARASHINA.
I'M TAKING MY FIRST SHIFT TODAY!
HUH?!
YOU KNOW HER?
ニコッ
GRIN
WHAAAAAA

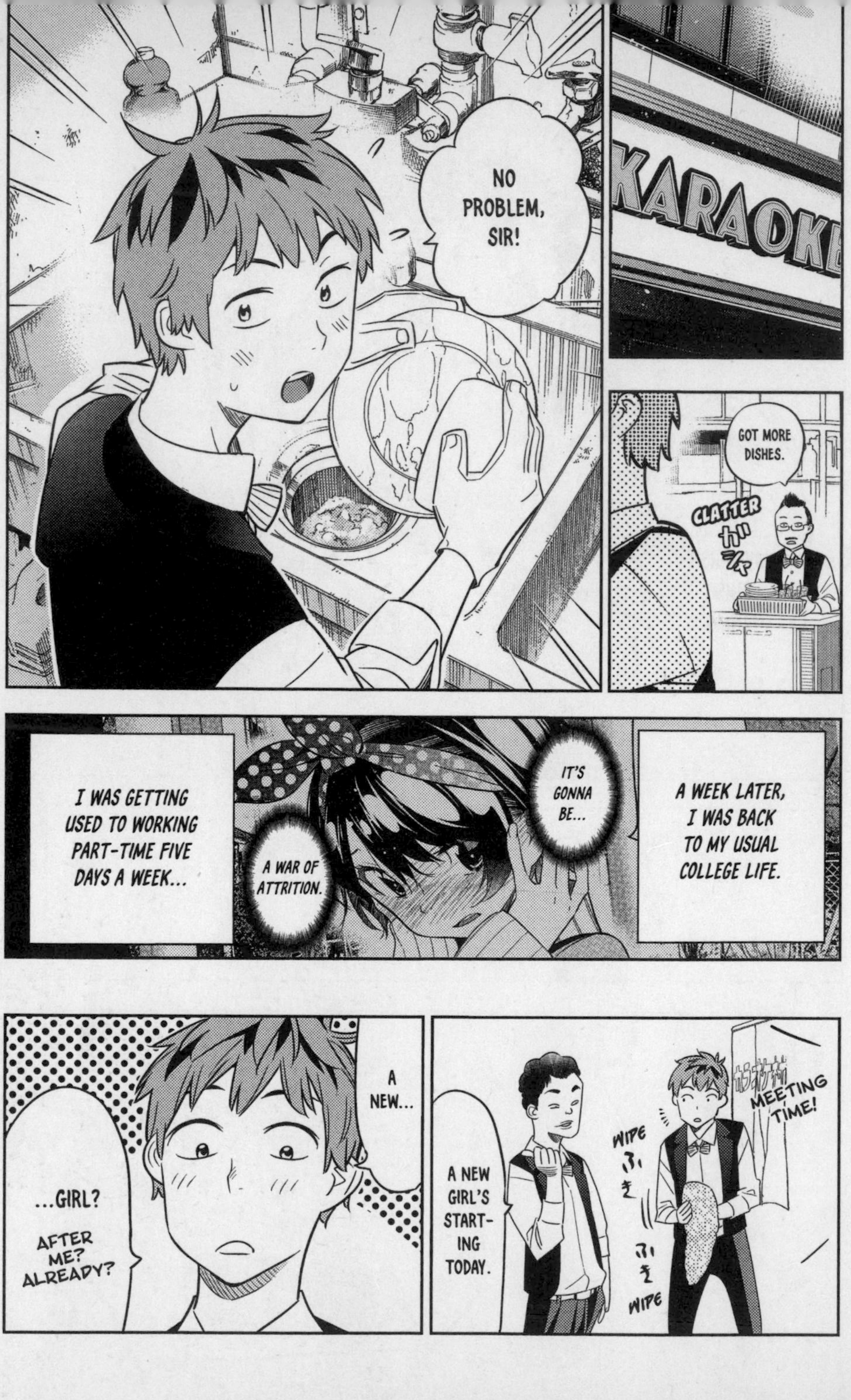
KARAOKE
GOT MORE DISHES.
CLATTER
ガシャ
NO PROBLEM, SIR!
A WEEK LATER, I WAS BACK TO MY USUAL COLLEGE LIFE.
IT'S GONNA BE...
A WAR OF ATTRITION.
I WAS GETTING USED TO WORKING PART-TIME FIVE DAYS A WEEK...
MEETING TIME!
A NEW GIRL'S START-ING TODAY.
WIPE
ふき
ふき
WIPE
A NEW...
...GIRL?
AFTER ME? ALREADY?

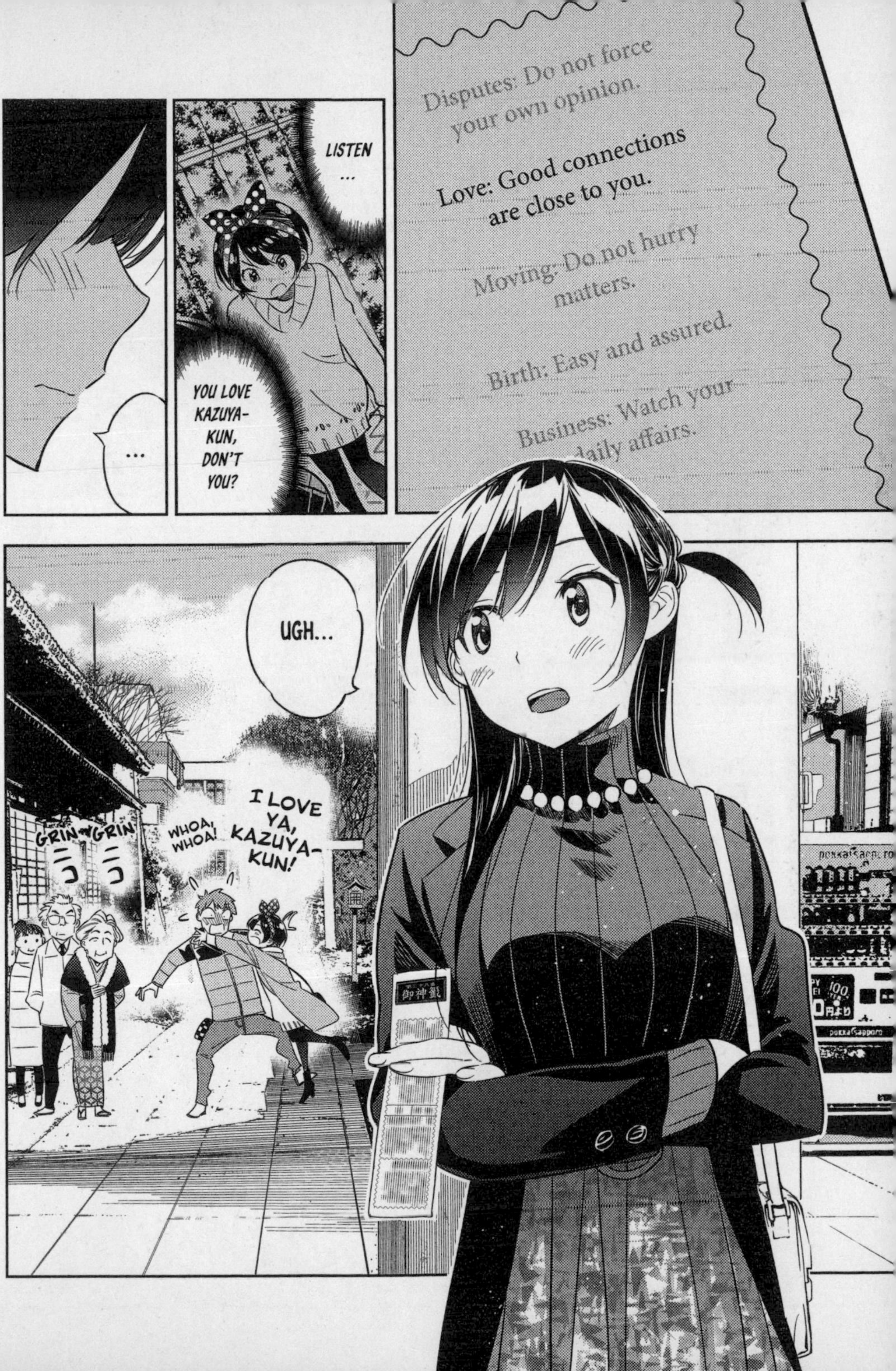

Disputes: Do not force your own opinion.
Love: Good connections are close to you.
Moving: Do not hurry matters.
Birth: Easy and assured.
Business: Watch your daily affairs.
LISTEN ...
YOU LOVE KAZUYA-KUN, DON'T YOU?
...
UGH...
I LOVE YA, KAZUYA-KUN!
WHOA, WHOA!
GRIN GRIN
ニコ ニコ

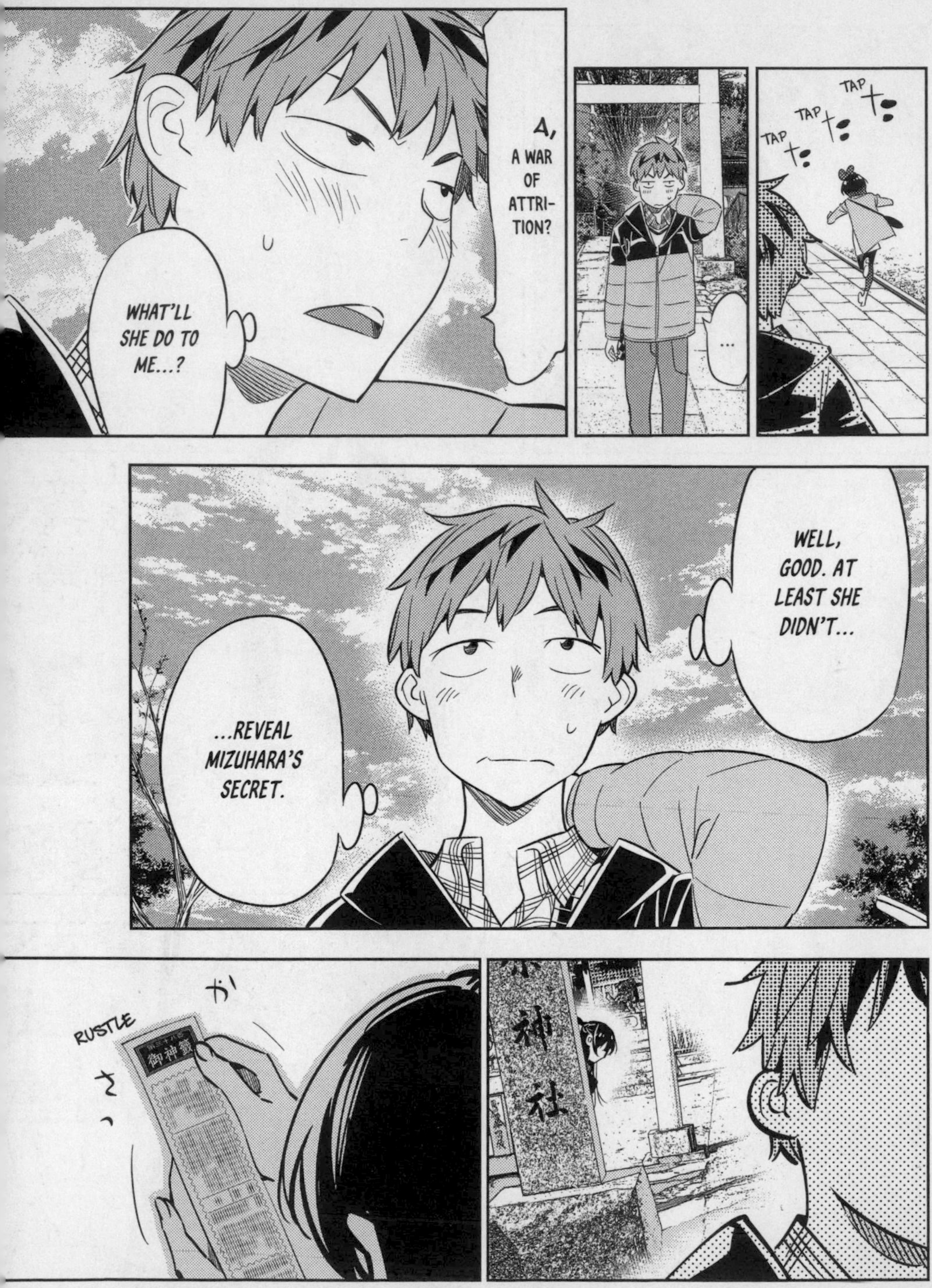
TAP
TAP
TAP
...
A, A WAR OF ATTRITION?
WHAT'LL SHE DO TO ME...?
WELL, GOOD. AT LEAST SHE DIDN'T...
...REVEAL MIZUHARA'S SECRET.
神社
RUSTLE

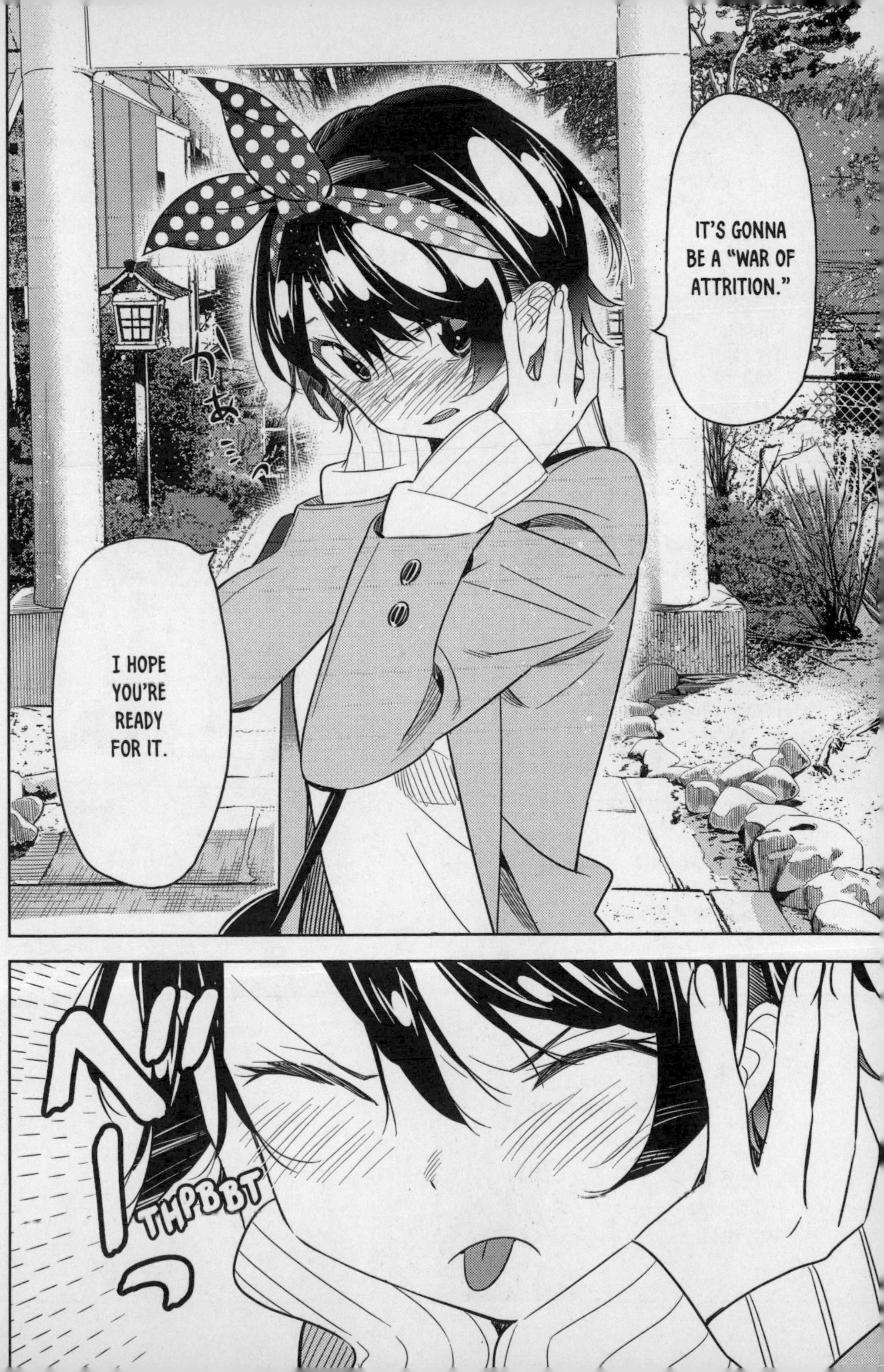
IT'S GONNA BE A "WAR OF ATTRITION."
I HOPE YOU'RE READY FOR IT.
THPBBT

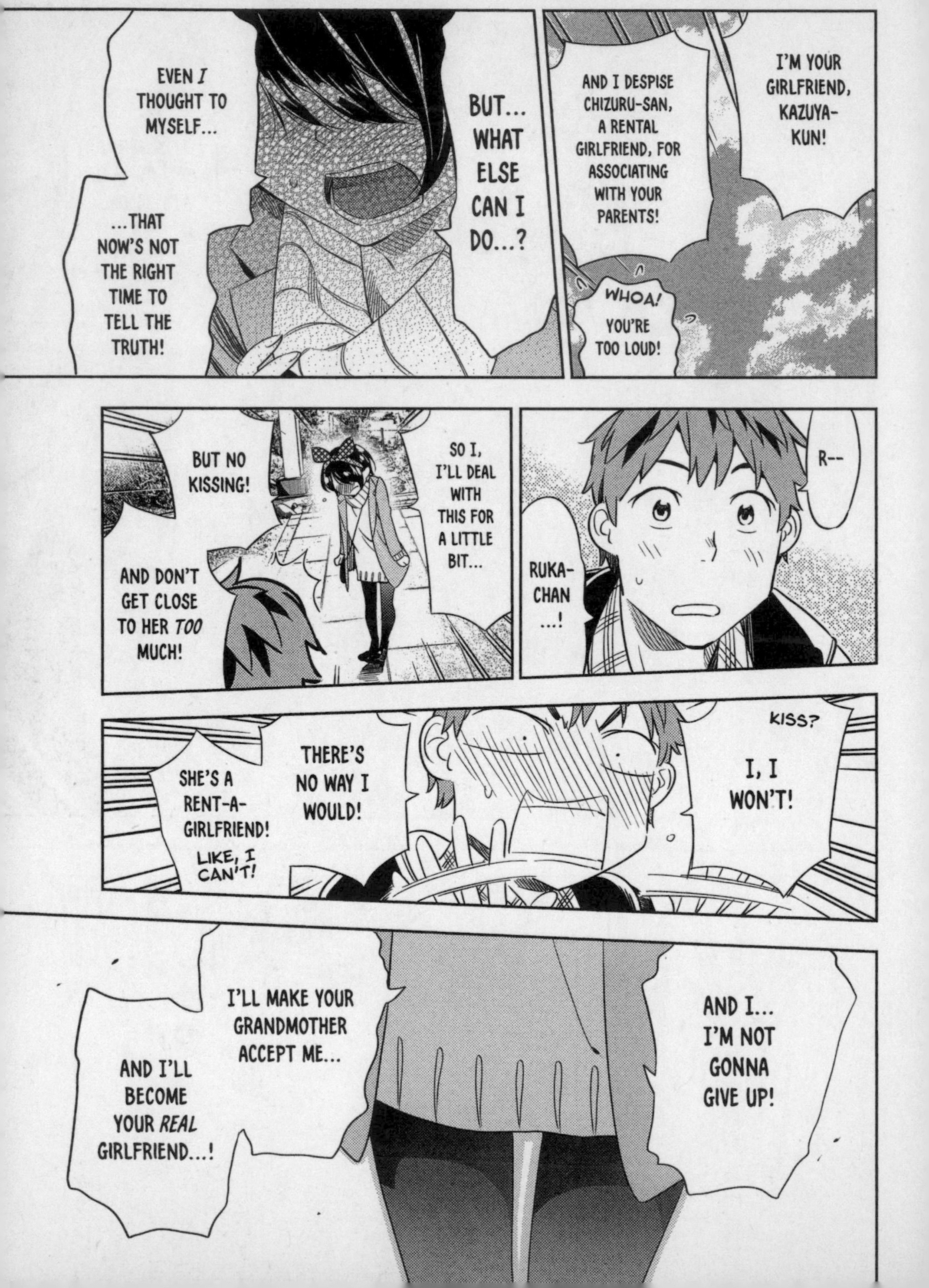
I'M YOUR GIRLFRIEND, KAZUYA-KUN!
AND I DESPISE CHIZURU-SAN, A RENTAL GIRLFRIEND, FOR ASSOCIATING WITH YOUR PARENTS!
WHOA! YOU'RE TOO LOUD!
BUT... WHAT ELSE CAN I DO...?
EVEN *I* THOUGHT TO MYSELF...
...THAT NOW'S NOT THE RIGHT TIME TO TELL THE TRUTH!
R--
RUKA-CHAN...!
SO I, I'LL DEAL WITH THIS FOR A LITTLE BIT...
BUT NO KISSING!
AND DON'T GET CLOSE TO HER *TOO* MUCH!
KISS?
I, I WON'T!
THERE'S NO WAY I WOULD!
SHE'S A RENT-A-GIRLFRIEND!
LIKE, I CAN'T!
AND I... I'M NOT GONNA GIVE UP!
I'LL MAKE YOUR GRANDMOTHER ACCEPT ME...
AND I'LL BECOME YOUR *REAL* GIRLFRIEND...!

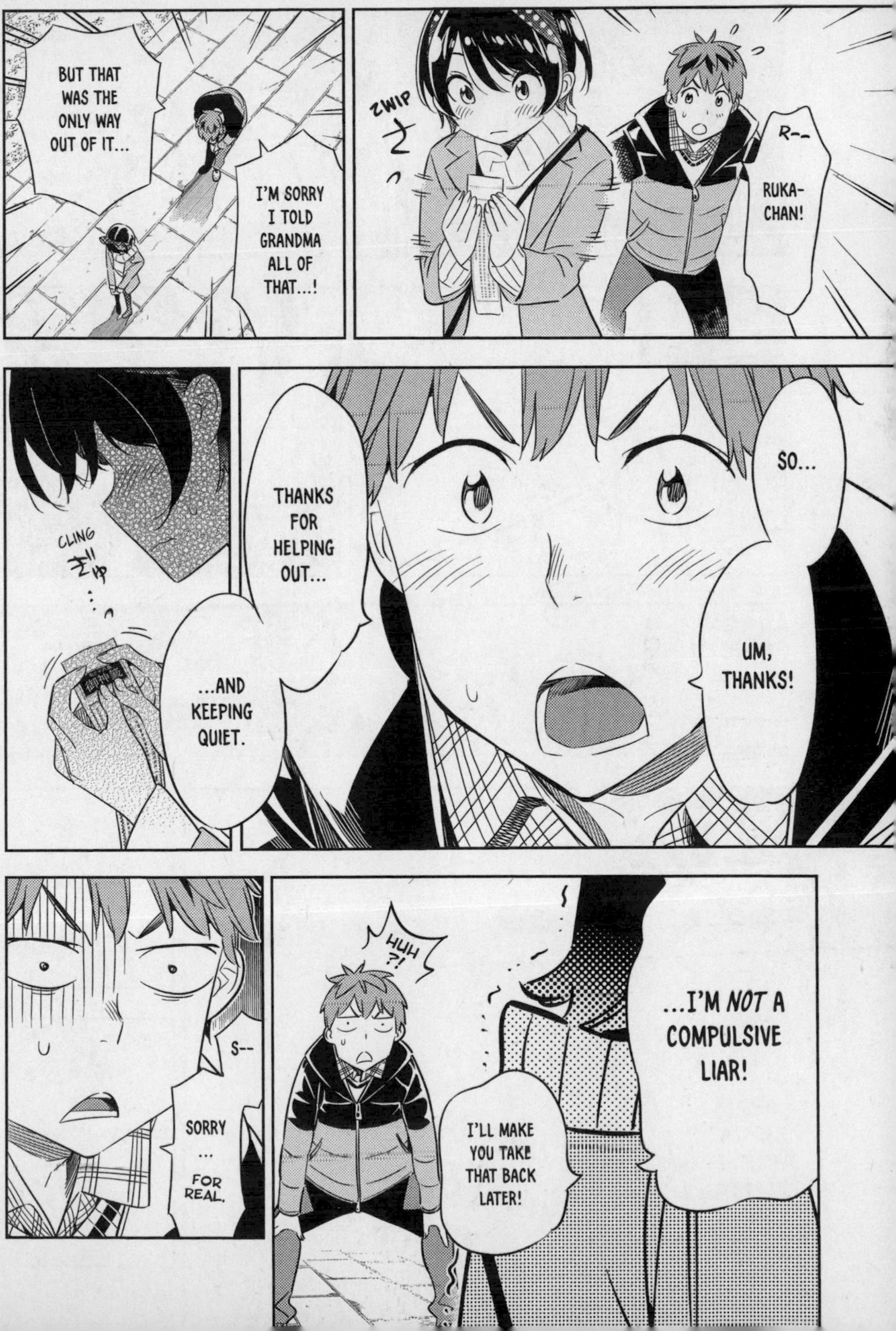
R--
RUKA-CHAN!
ZWIP
I'M SORRY I TOLD GRANDMA ALL OF THAT...!
BUT THAT WAS THE ONLY WAY OUT OF IT...
SO...
UM, THANKS!
THANKS FOR HELPING OUT...
...AND KEEPING QUIET.
CLING
...I'M *NOT* A COMPULSIVE LIAR!
I'LL MAKE YOU TAKE THAT BACK LATER!
HUH ?!
S--
SORRY ... FOR REAL.

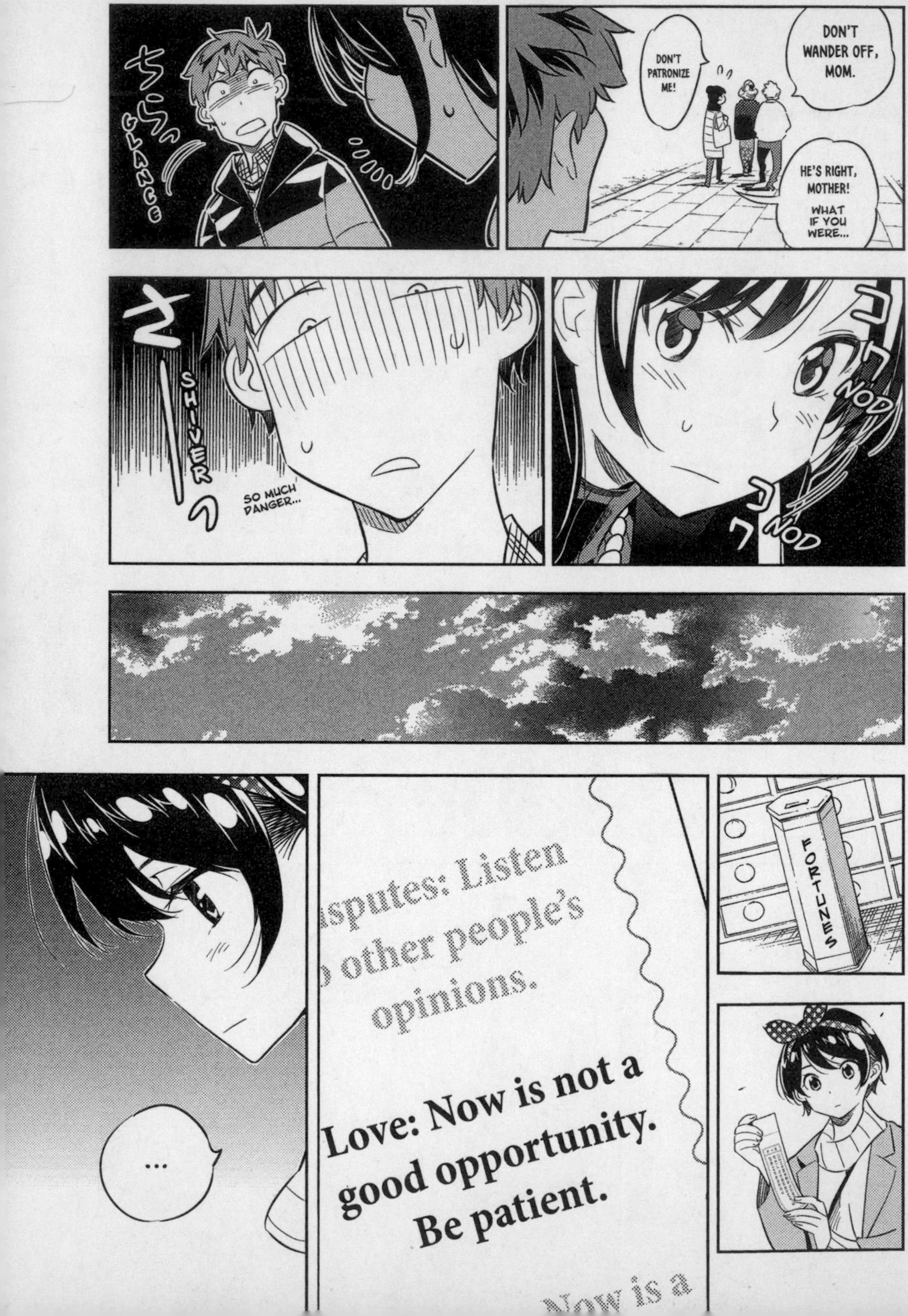
DON'T WANDER OFF, MOM.
DON'T PATRONIZE ME!
HE'S RIGHT, MOTHER!
WHAT IF YOU WERE...
ちらっ
GLANCE
コク
NOD
コク
NOD
さー
SHIVER
SO MUCH DANGER...
FORTUNES
isputes: Listen
o other people's
opinions.
Love: Now is not a
good opportunity.
Be patient.
Now is a
...

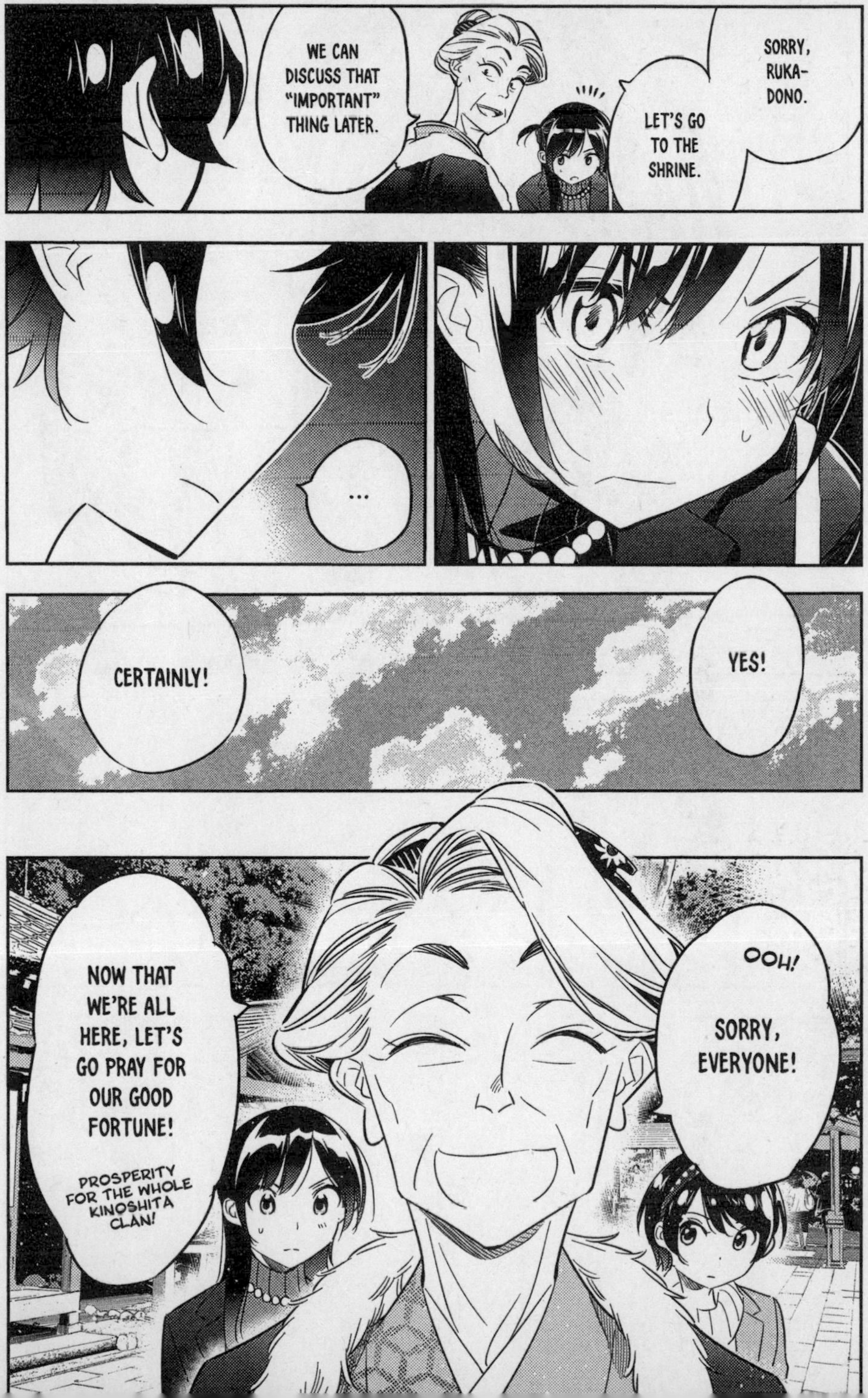
SORRY, RUKA-DONO.
LET'S GO TO THE SHRINE.
WE CAN DISCUSS THAT "IMPORTANT" THING LATER.
...
YES!
CERTAINLY!
OOH!
SORRY, EVERYONE!
NOW THAT WE'RE ALL HERE, LET'S GO PRAY FOR OUR GOOD FORTUNE!
PROSPERITY FOR THE WHOLE KINOSHITA CLAN!

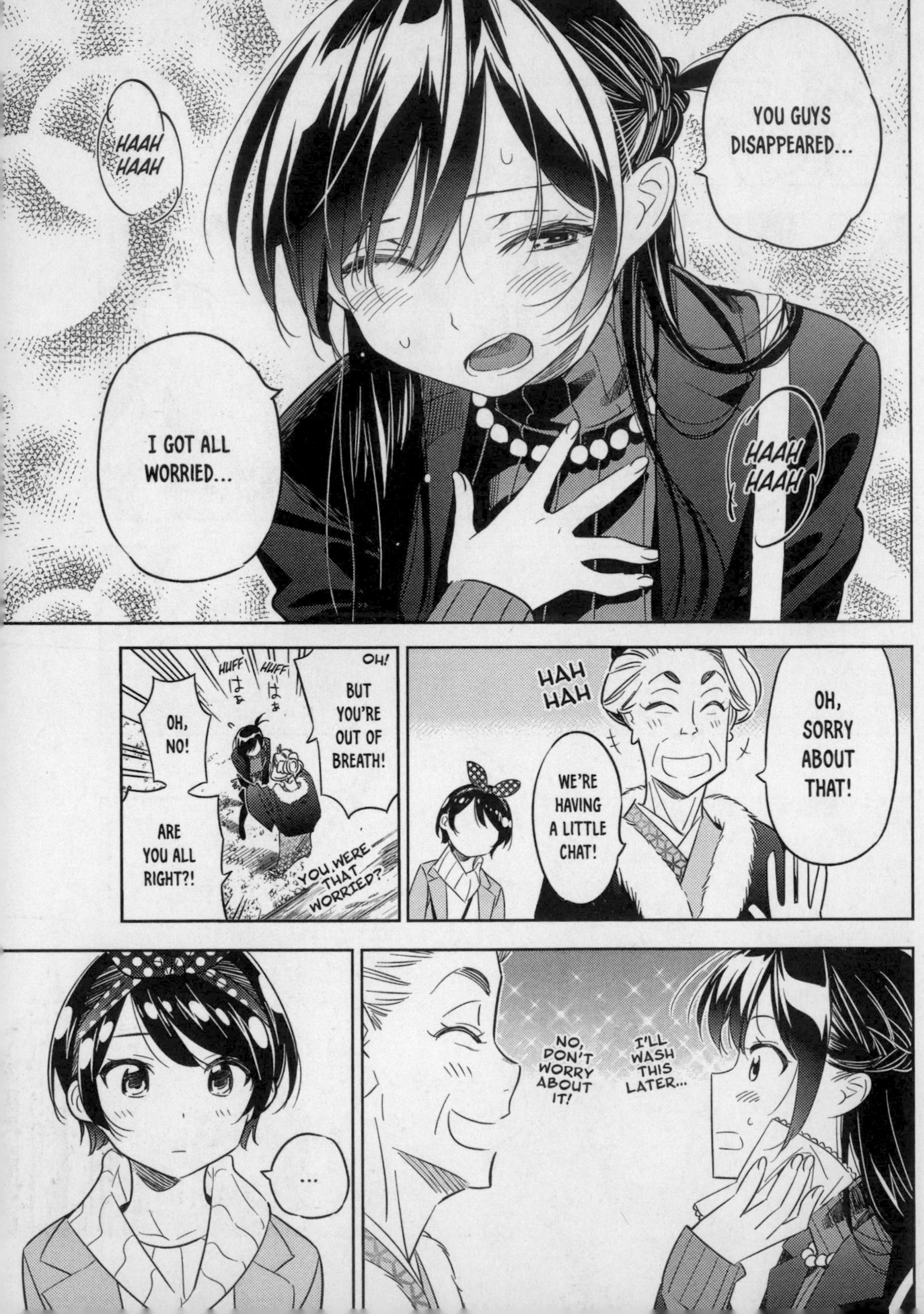
YOU GUYS DISAPPEARED...
HAAH HAAH
HAAH HAAH
I GOT ALL WORRIED...
OH, SORRY ABOUT THAT!
HAH HAH
WE'RE HAVING A LITTLE CHAT!
OH! BUT YOU'RE OUT OF BREATH!
HUFF はぁ
HUFF はぁ
OH, NO!
ARE YOU ALL RIGHT?!
YOU WERE THAT WORRIED?
I'LL WASH THIS LATER...
NO, DON'T WORRY ABOUT IT!
...

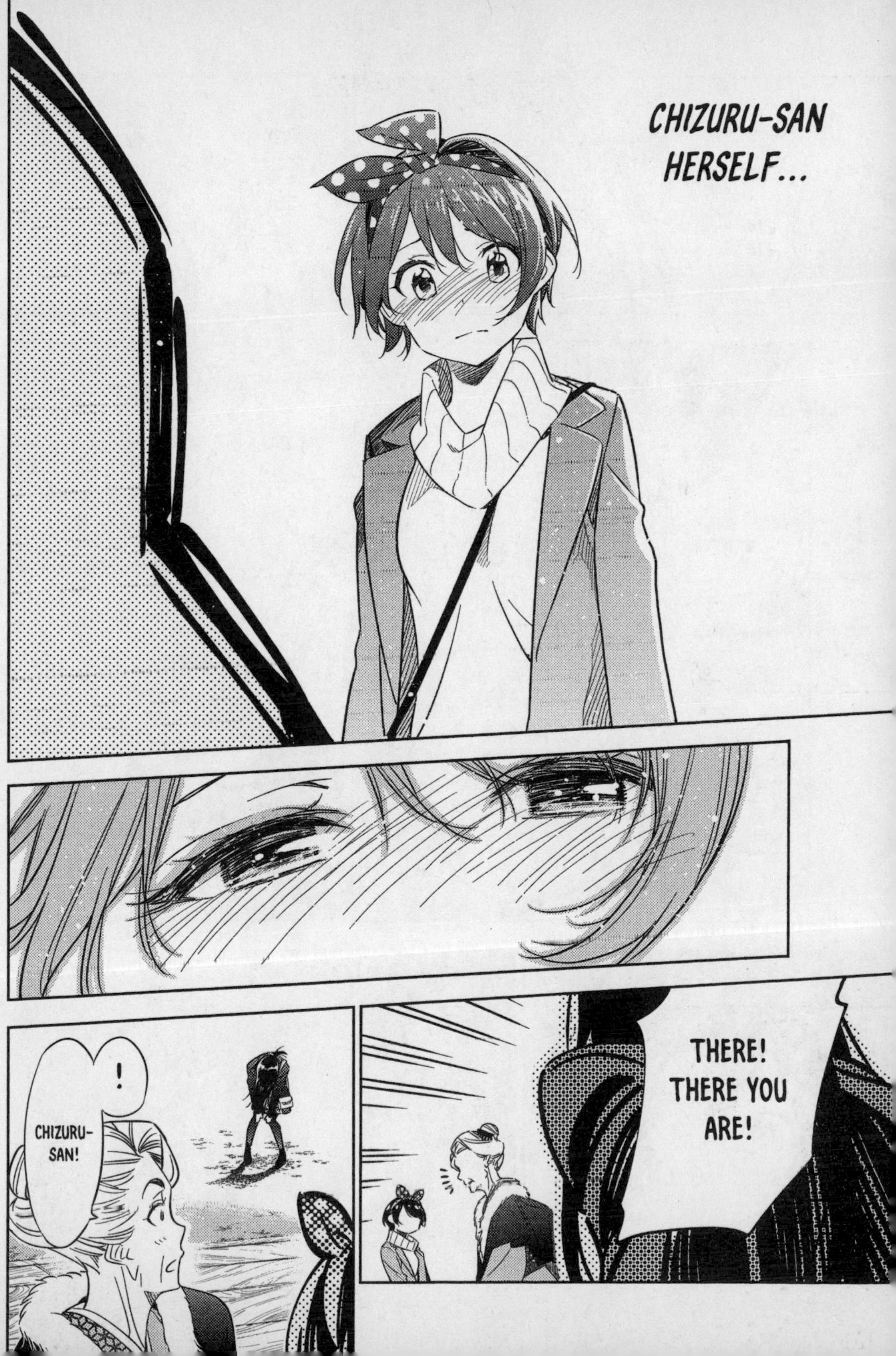
CHIZURU-SAN HERSELF...
THERE! THERE YOU ARE!
!
CHIZURU-SAN!

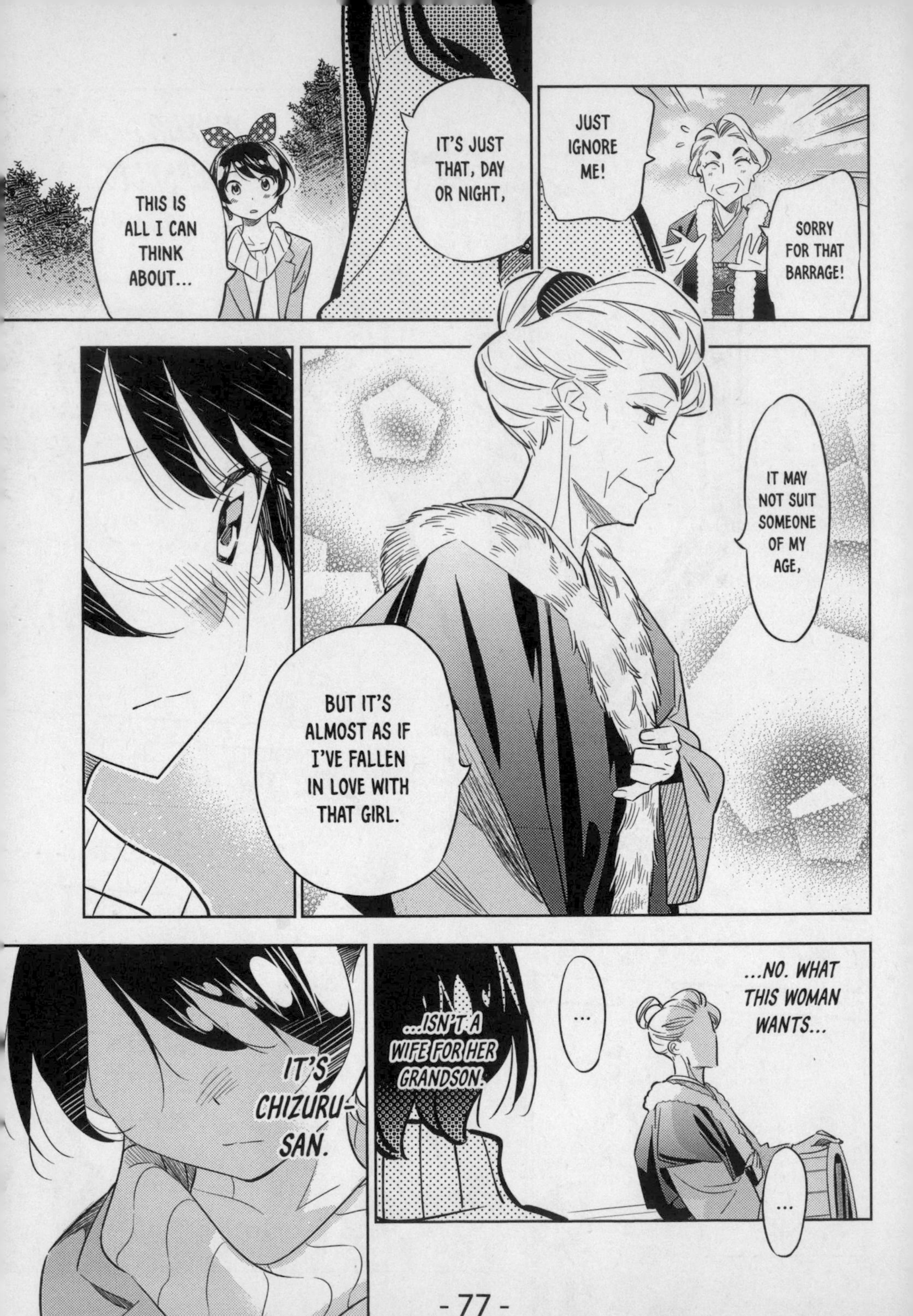
SORRY FOR THAT BARRAGE!
JUST IGNORE ME!
IT'S JUST THAT, DAY OR NIGHT,
THIS IS ALL I CAN THINK ABOUT...
IT MAY NOT SUIT SOMEONE OF MY AGE,
BUT IT'S ALMOST AS IF I'VE FALLEN IN LOVE WITH THAT GIRL.
...NO. WHAT THIS WOMAN WANTS...
...
...
...ISN'T A WIFE FOR HER GRANDSON.
IT'S CHIZURU-SAN.

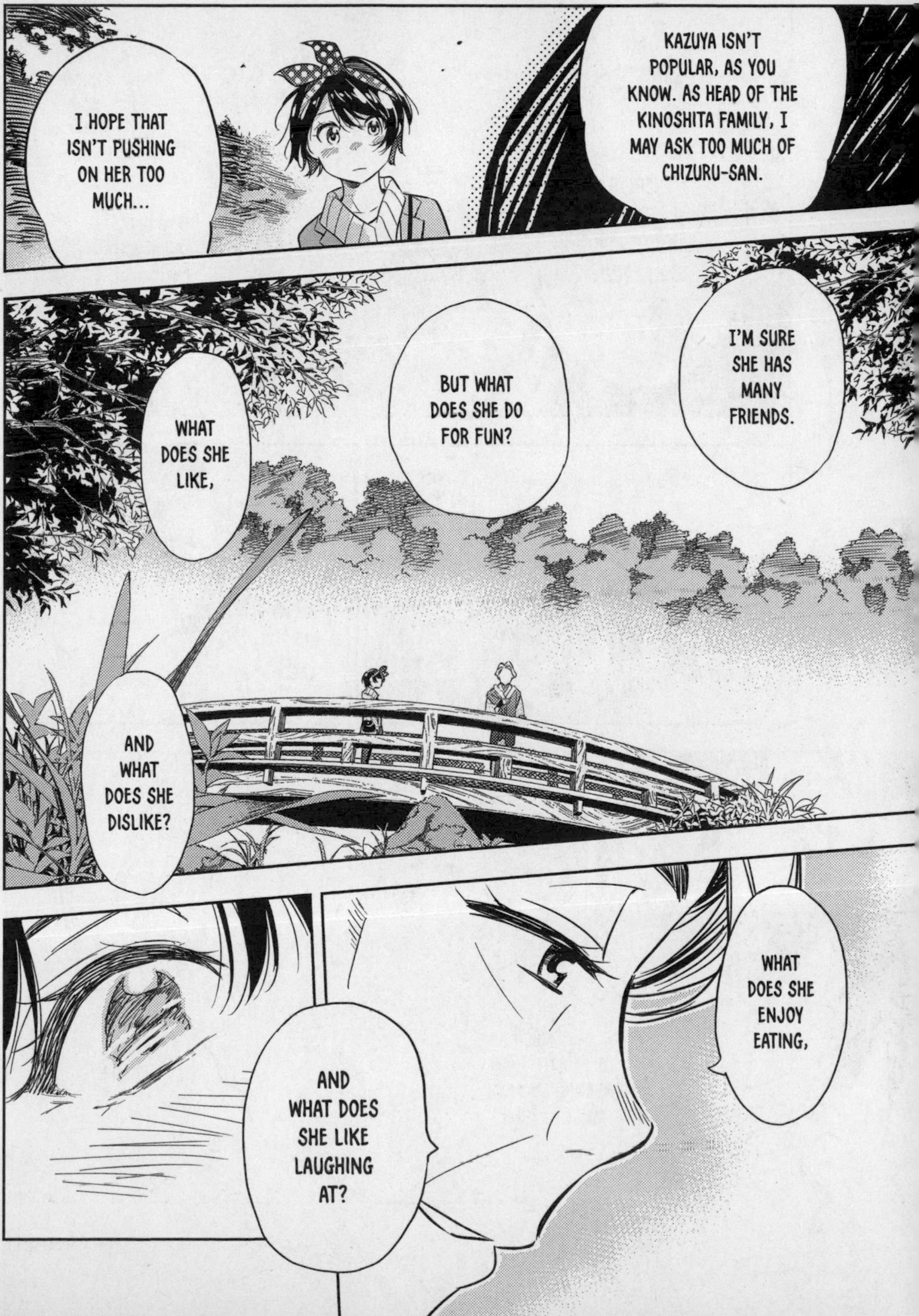
KAZUYA ISN'T POPULAR, AS YOU KNOW. AS HEAD OF THE KINOSHITA FAMILY, I MAY ASK TOO MUCH OF CHIZURU-SAN.
I HOPE THAT ISN'T PUSHING ON HER TOO MUCH...
I'M SURE SHE HAS MANY FRIENDS.
BUT WHAT DOES SHE DO FOR FUN?
WHAT DOES SHE LIKE,
AND WHAT DOES SHE DISLIKE?
WHAT DOES SHE ENJOY EATING,
AND WHAT DOES SHE LIKE LAUGHING AT?

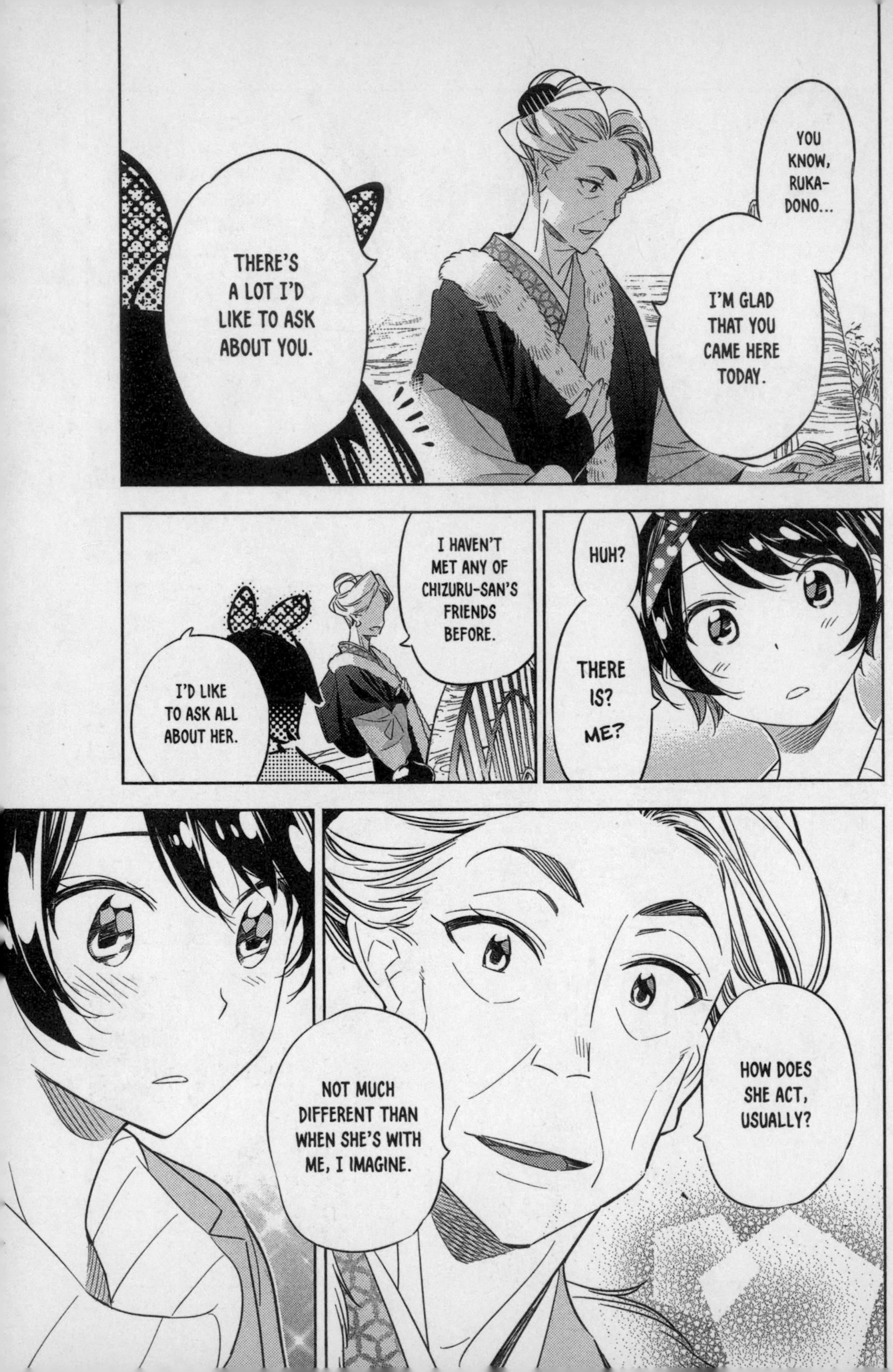
YOU KNOW, RUKA-DONO...
I'M GLAD THAT YOU CAME HERE TODAY.
THERE'S A LOT I'D LIKE TO ASK ABOUT YOU.
HUH?
THERE IS? ME?
I HAVEN'T MET ANY OF CHIZURU-SAN'S FRIENDS BEFORE.
I'D LIKE TO ASK ALL ABOUT HER.
HOW DOES SHE ACT, USUALLY?
NOT MUCH DIFFERENT THAN WHEN SHE'S WITH ME, I IMAGINE.

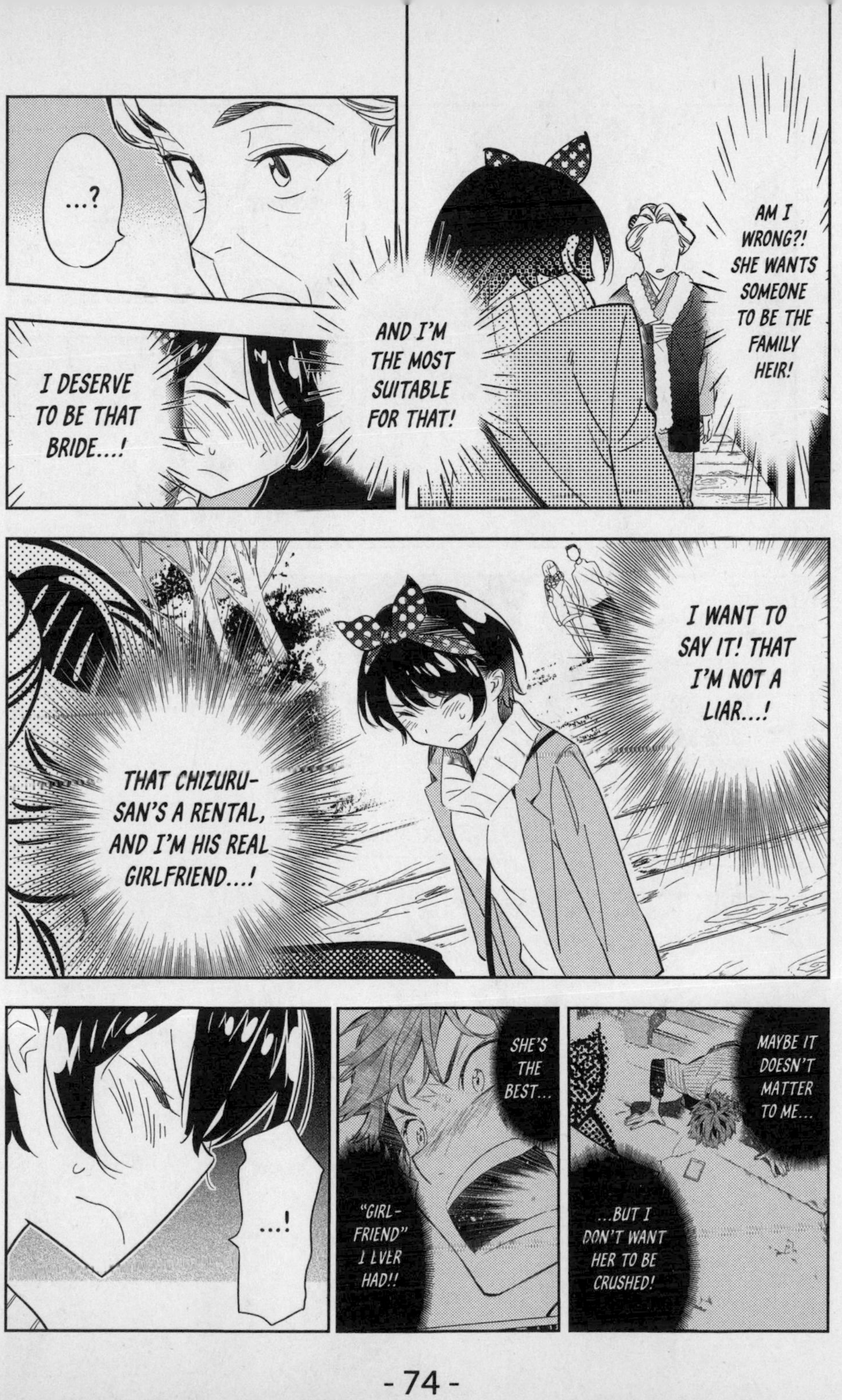
AM I WRONG?! SHE WANTS SOMEONE TO BE THE FAMILY HEIR!
AND I'M THE MOST SUITABLE FOR THAT!
...?
I DESERVE TO BE THAT BRIDE...!
I WANT TO SAY IT! THAT I'M NOT A LIAR...!
THAT CHIZURU-SAN'S A RENTAL, AND I'M HIS REAL GIRLFRIEND...!
MAYBE IT DOESN'T MATTER TO ME...
...BUT I DON'T WANT HER TO BE CRUSHED!
SHE'S THE BEST...
"GIRL-FRIEND" I EVER HAD!!
...!

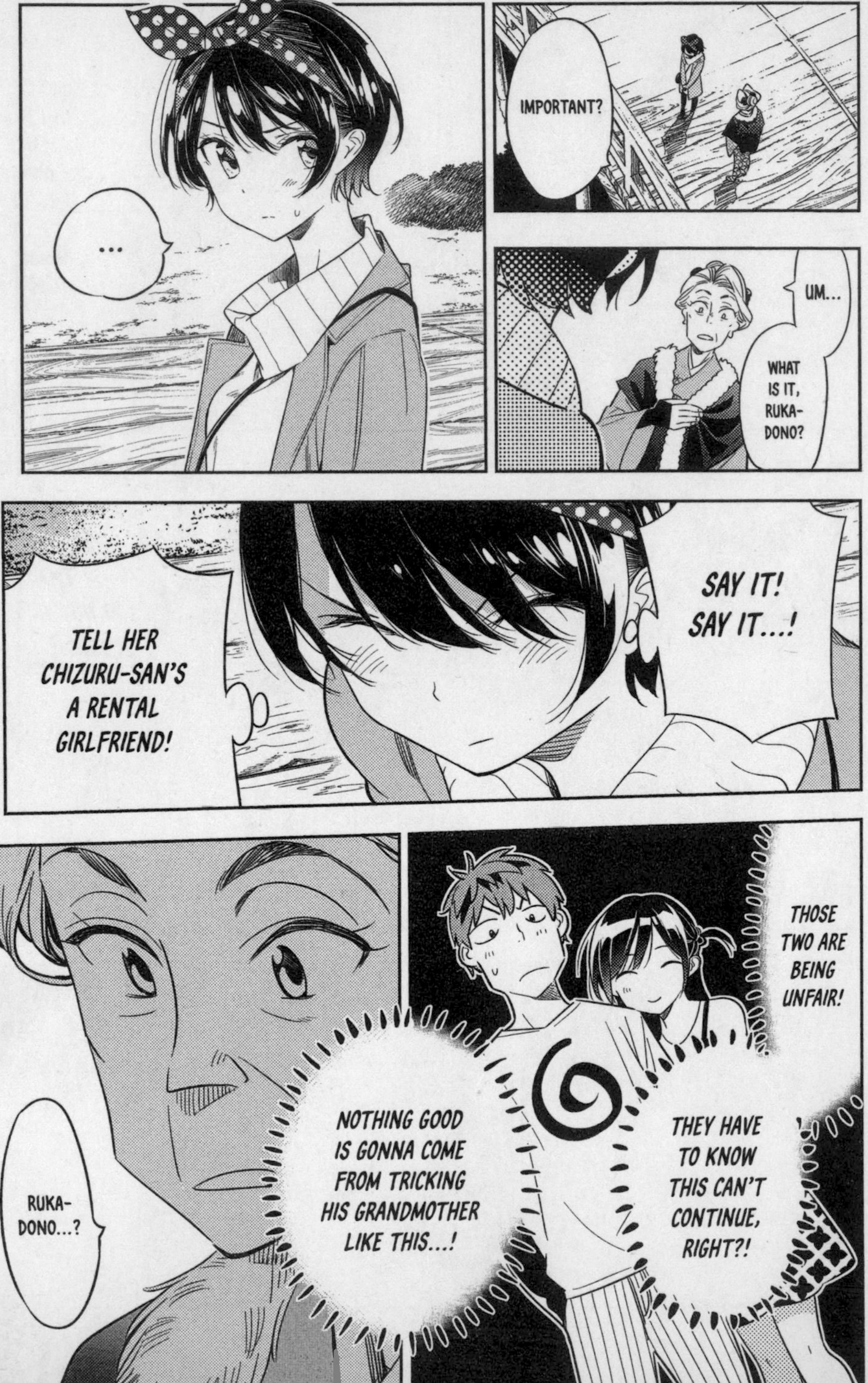
IMPORTANT?
UM...
WHAT IS IT, RUKA-DONO?
...
SAY IT! SAY IT...!
TELL HER CHIZURU-SAN'S A RENTAL GIRLFRIEND!
THOSE TWO ARE BEING UNFAIR!
THEY HAVE TO KNOW THIS CAN'T CONTINUE, RIGHT?!
NOTHING GOOD IS GONNA COME FROM TRICKING HIS GRANDMOTHER LIKE THIS...!
RUKA-DONO...?

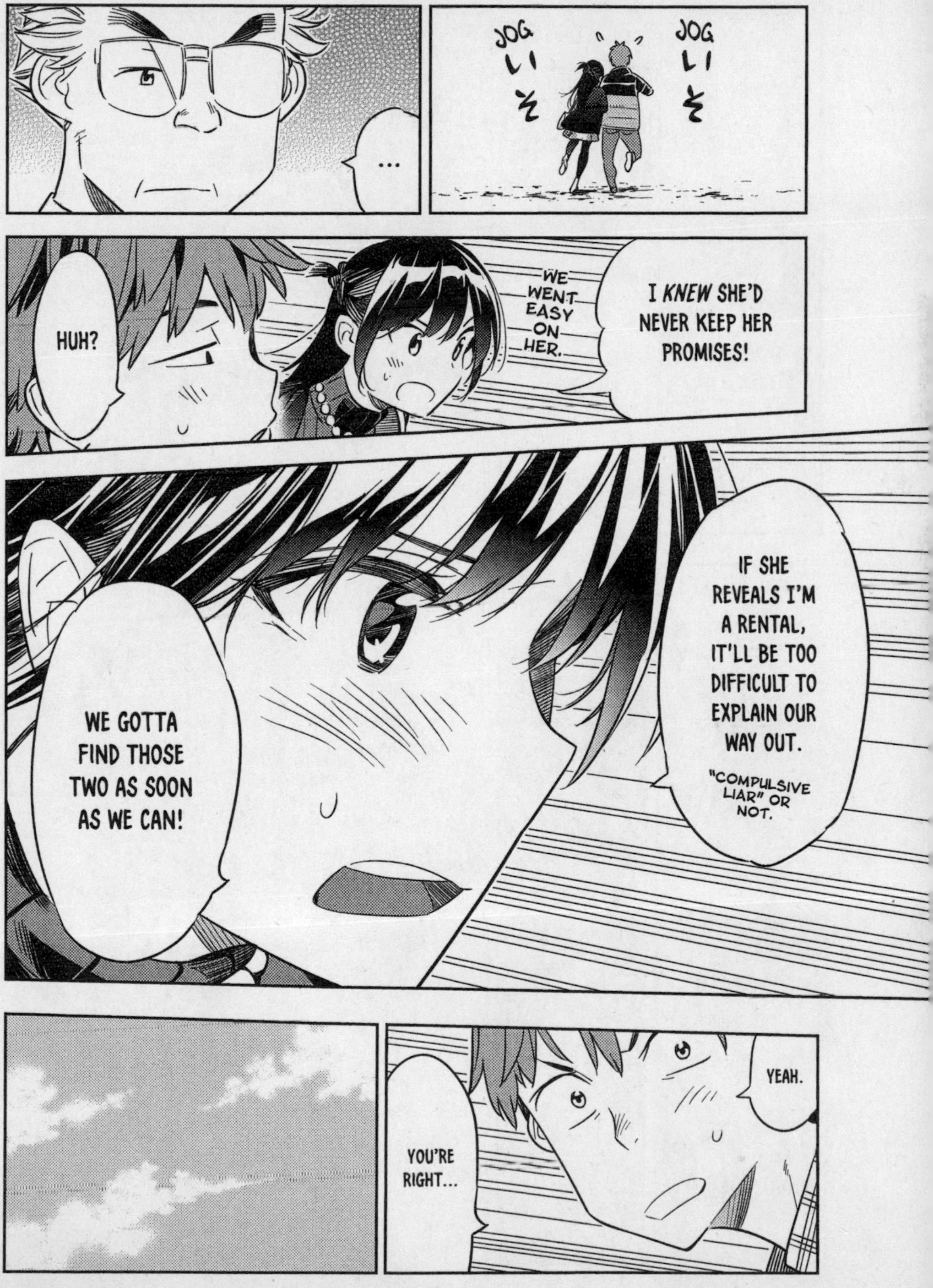
JOG
JOG
...
I *KNEW* SHE'D NEVER KEEP HER PROMISES!
WE WENT EASY ON HER.
HUH?
IF SHE REVEALS I'M A RENTAL, IT'LL BE TOO DIFFICULT TO EXPLAIN OUR WAY OUT.
"COMPULSIVE LIAR" OR NOT.
WE GOTTA FIND THOSE TWO AS SOON AS WE CAN!
YEAH.
YOU'RE RIGHT...

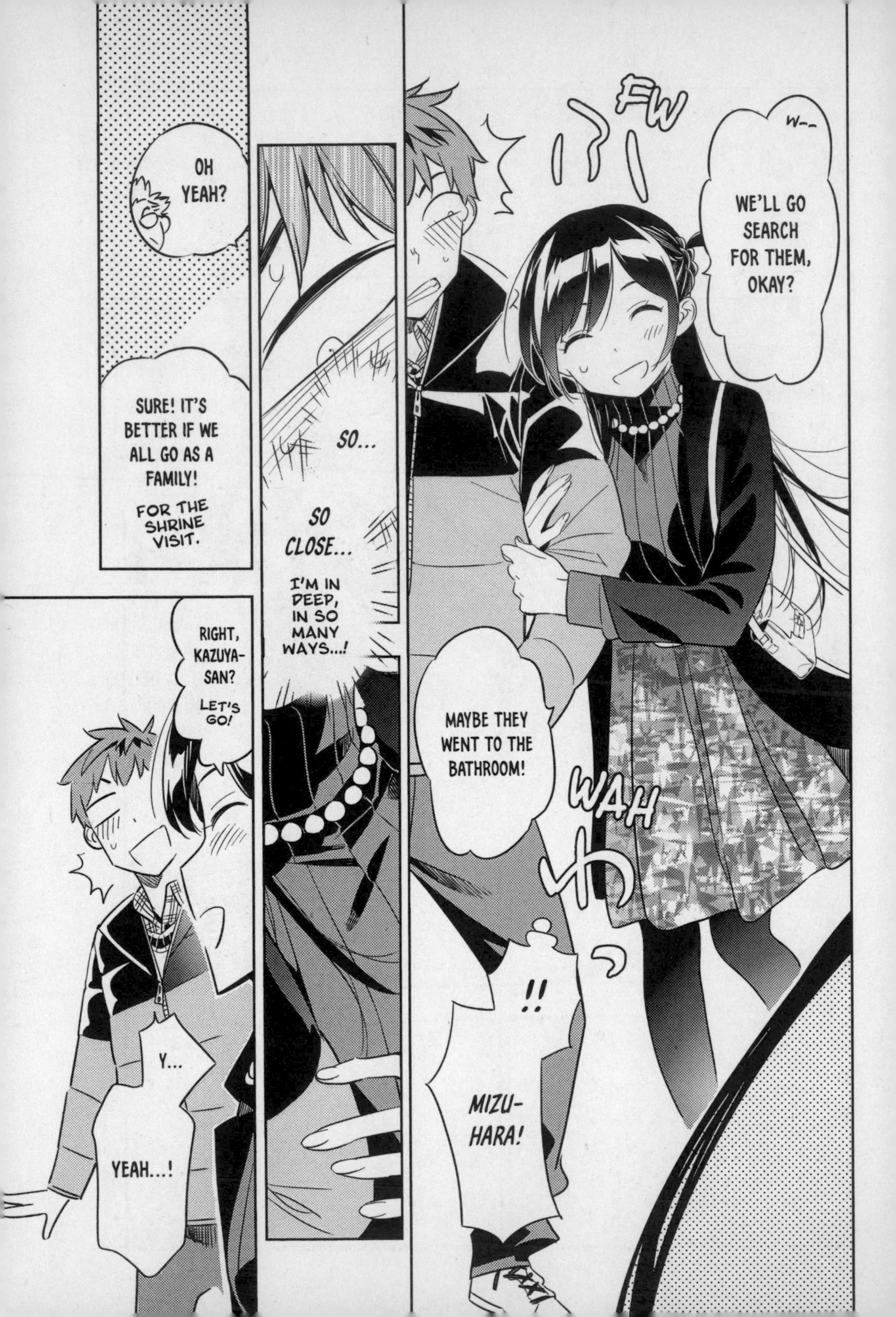
W--
FW
WE'LL GO SEARCH FOR THEM, OKAY?
MAYBE THEY WENT TO THE BATHROOM!
WAH
!!
MIZU-HARA!
SO...
SO CLOSE...
I'M IN DEEP, IN SO MANY WAYS...!
OH YEAH?
SURE! IT'S BETTER IF WE ALL GO AS A FAMILY!
FOR THE SHRINE VISIT.
RIGHT, KAZUYA-SAN?
LET'S GO!
Y...
YEAH...!

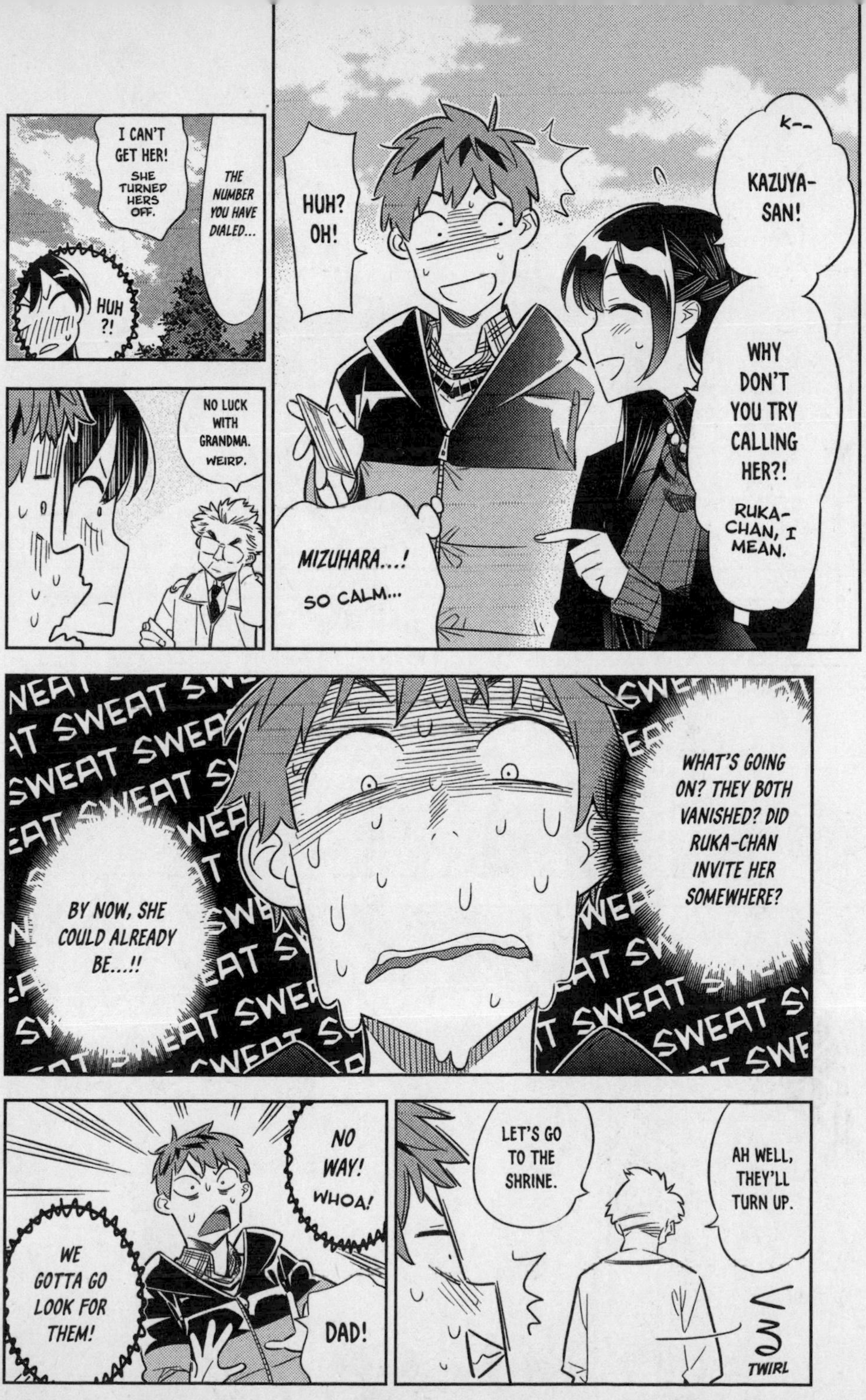
K-- KAZUYA-SAN!
WHY DON'T YOU TRY CALLING HER?! RUKA-CHAN, I MEAN.
HUH? OH!
MIZUHARA...!
SO CALM...
THE NUMBER YOU HAVE DIALED...
I CAN'T GET HER! SHE TURNED HERS OFF.
HUH ?!
NO LUCK WITH GRANDMA. WEIRD.
WHAT'S GOING ON? THEY BOTH VANISHED? DID RUKA-CHAN INVITE HER SOMEWHERE?
BY NOW, SHE COULD ALREADY BE...!!
SWEAT SWEAT SWEAT
AH WELL, THEY'LL TURN UP.
LET'S GO TO THE SHRINE.
TWIRL
NO WAY! WHOA!
DAD!
WE GOTTA GO LOOK FOR THEM!

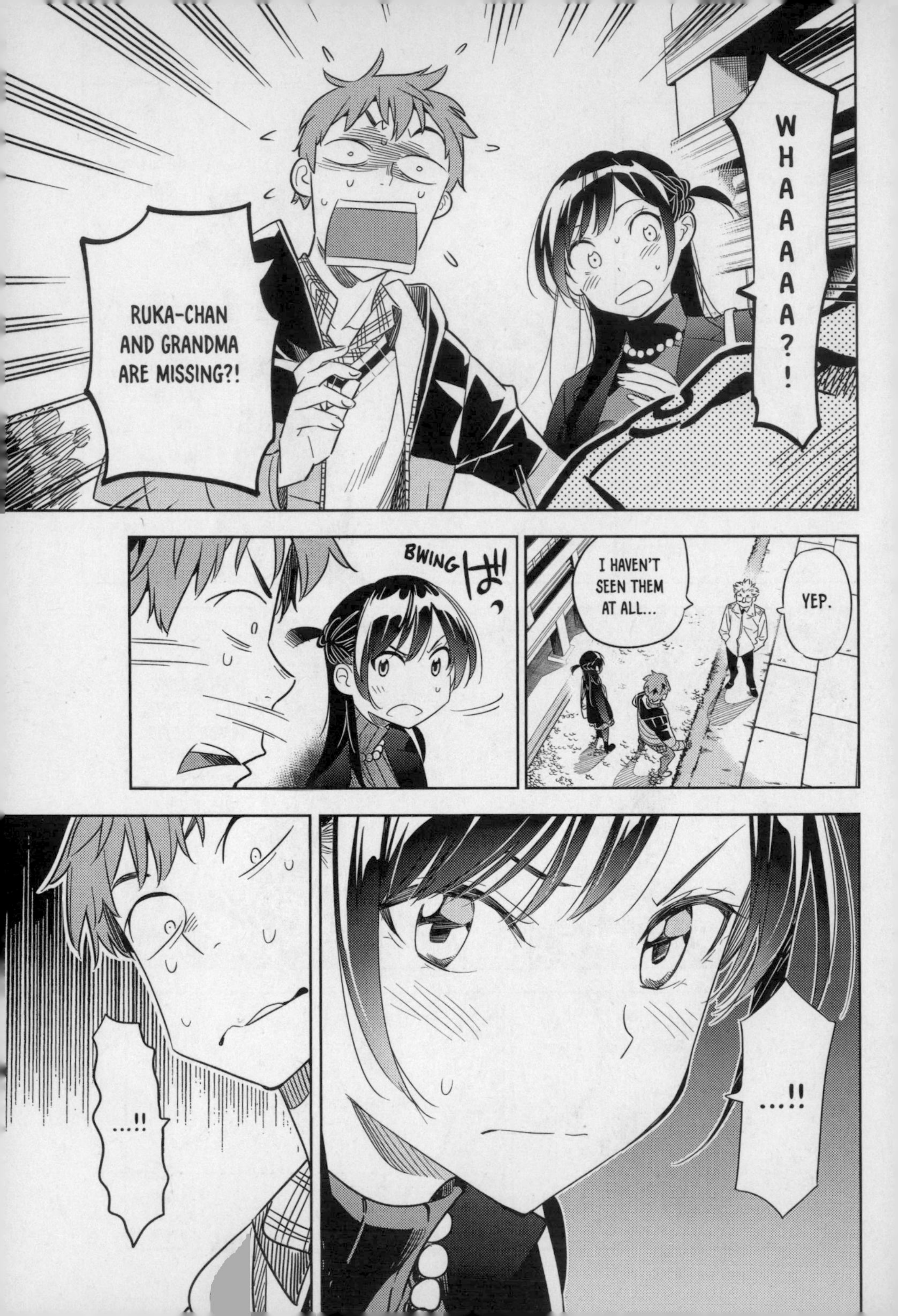
WHAAAAAA?!
RUKA-CHAN AND GRANDMA ARE MISSING?!
YEP.
I HAVEN'T SEEN THEM AT ALL...
BWING ば
...!!
...!!

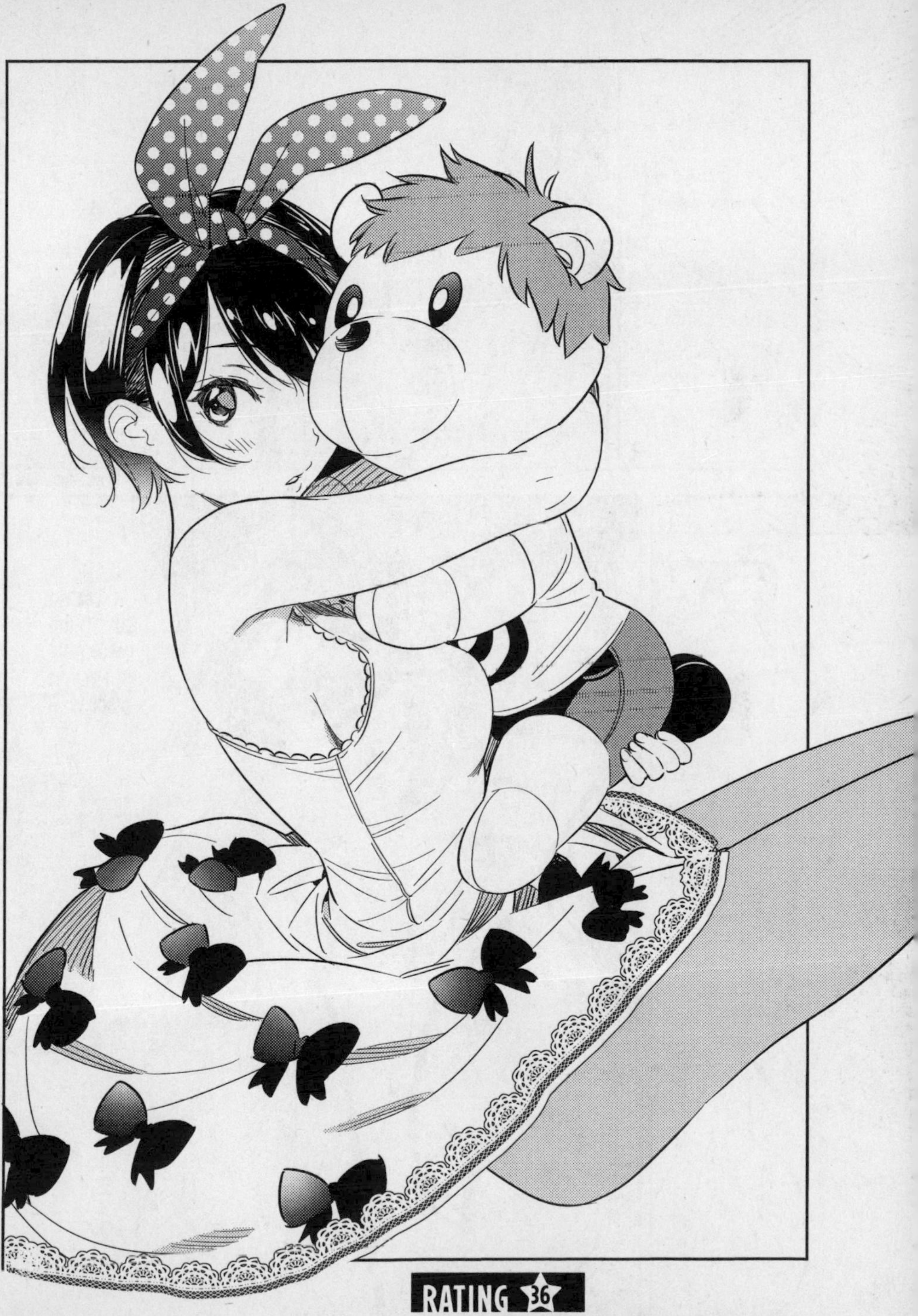

RATING 36

MY TWO GIRLFRIENDS (5)

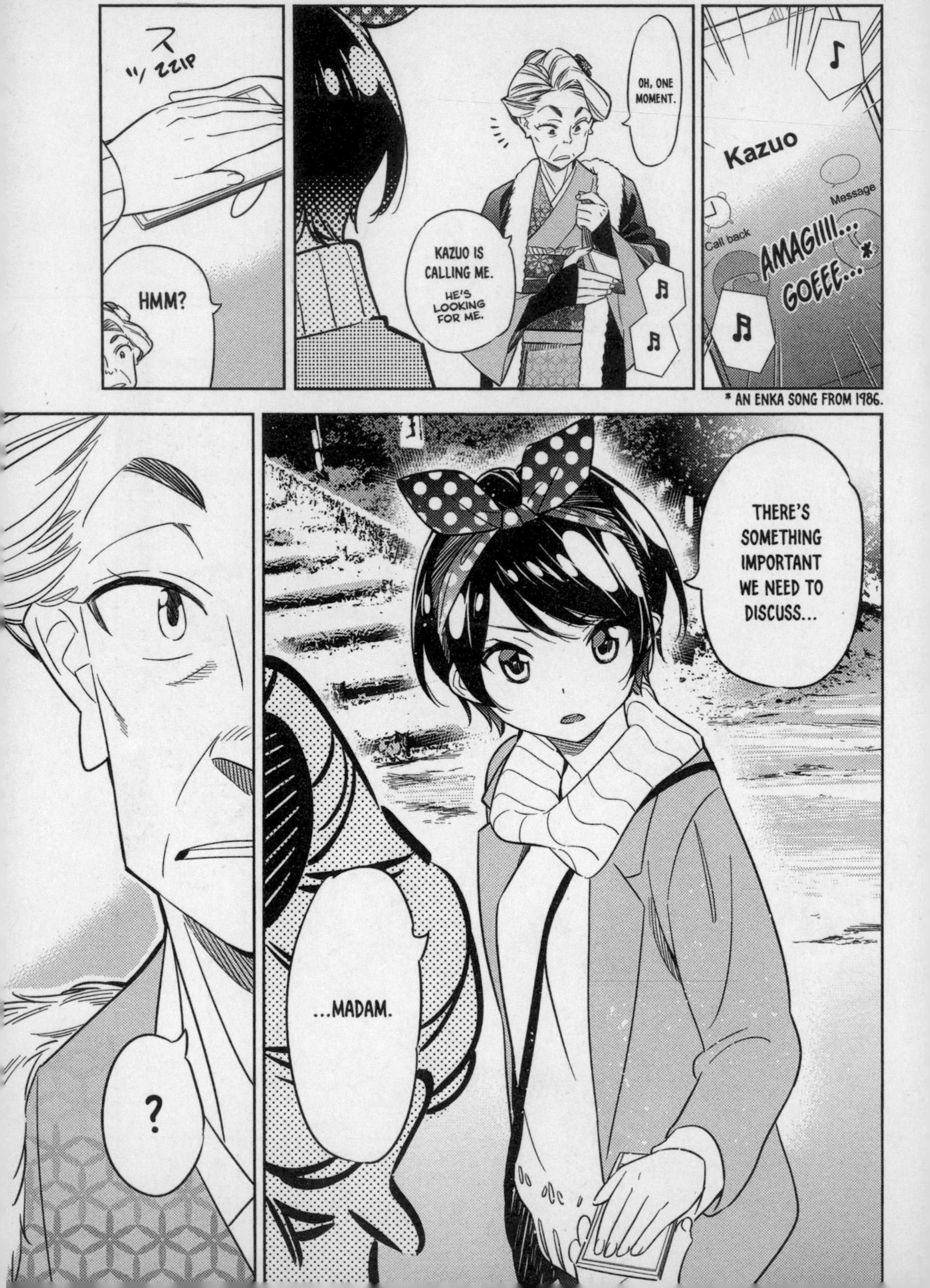
♪
Kazuo
Message
Call back
AMAGIIII... GOEEE...*
♫
OH, ONE MOMENT.
KAZUO IS CALLING ME. HE'S LOOKING FOR ME.
♬
♬
ZZIP
HMM?
THERE'S SOMETHING IMPORTANT WE NEED TO DISCUSS...
...MADAM.
?

* AN ENKA SONG FROM 1986.

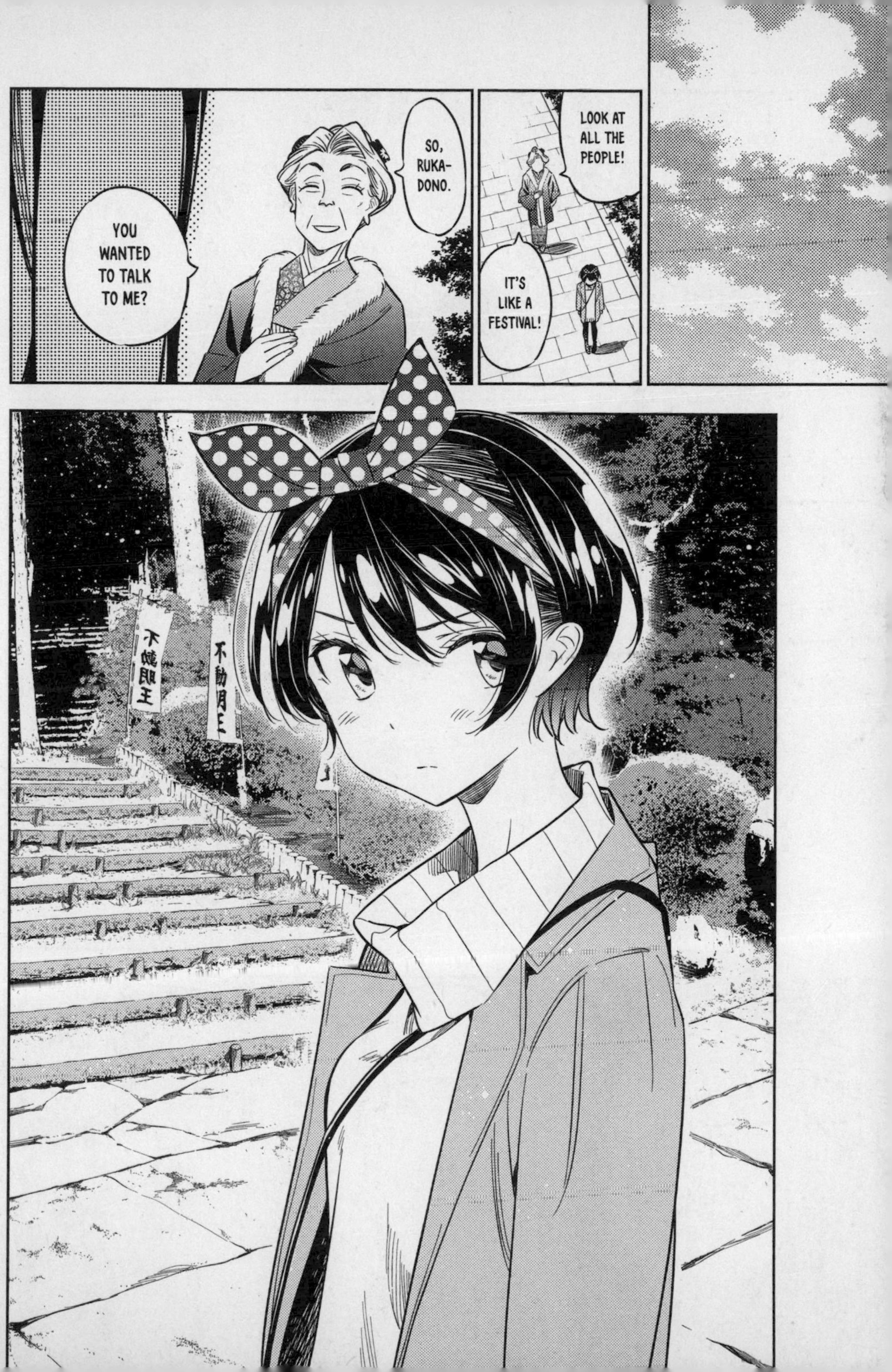
LOOK AT ALL THE PEOPLE!
IT'S LIKE A FESTIVAL!
SO, RUKA-DONO.
YOU WANTED TO TALK TO ME?

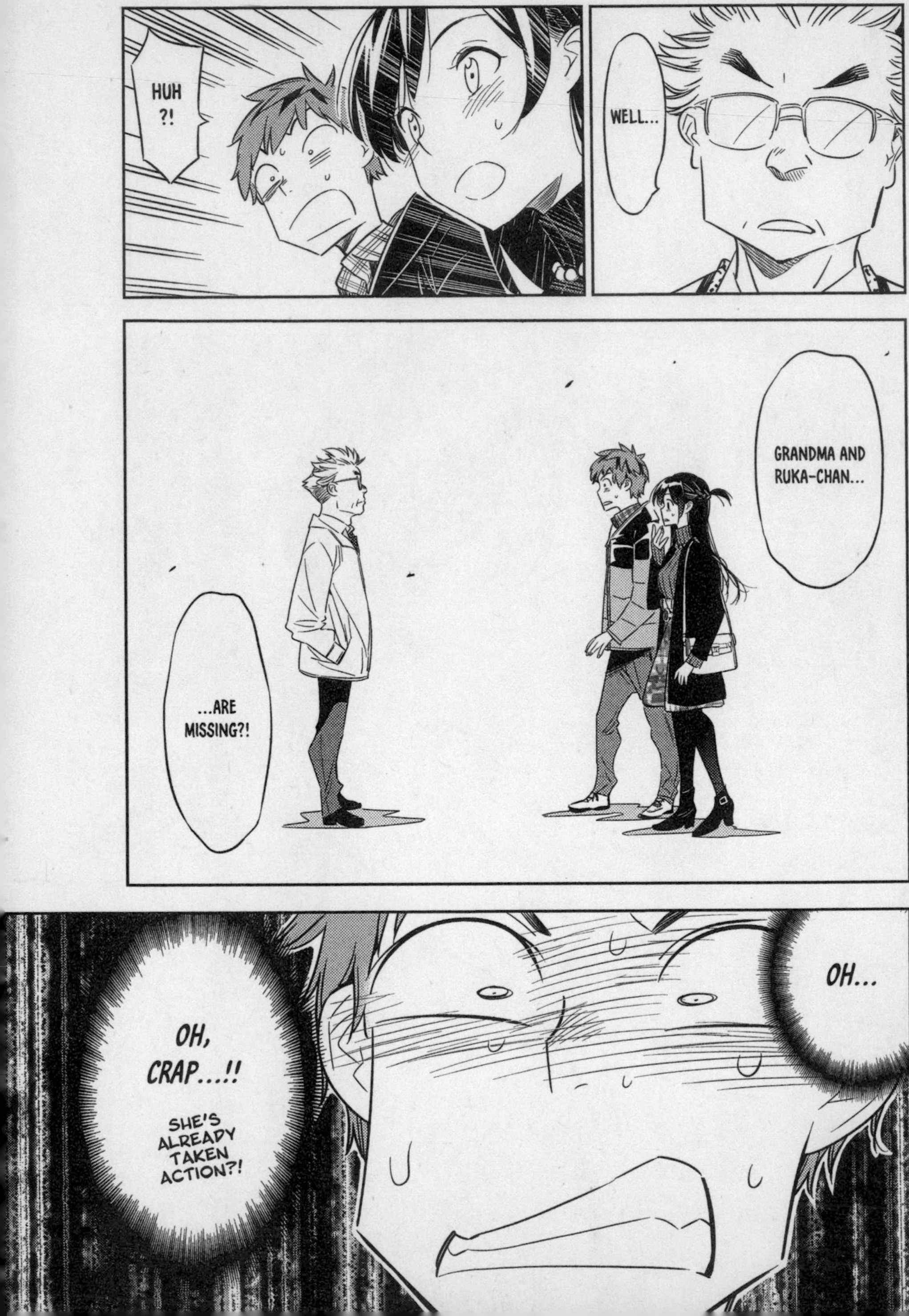
WELL...
HUH ?!
GRANDMA AND RUKA-CHAN...
...ARE MISSING?!
OH...
OH, CRAP...!!
SHE'S ALREADY TAKEN ACTION?!

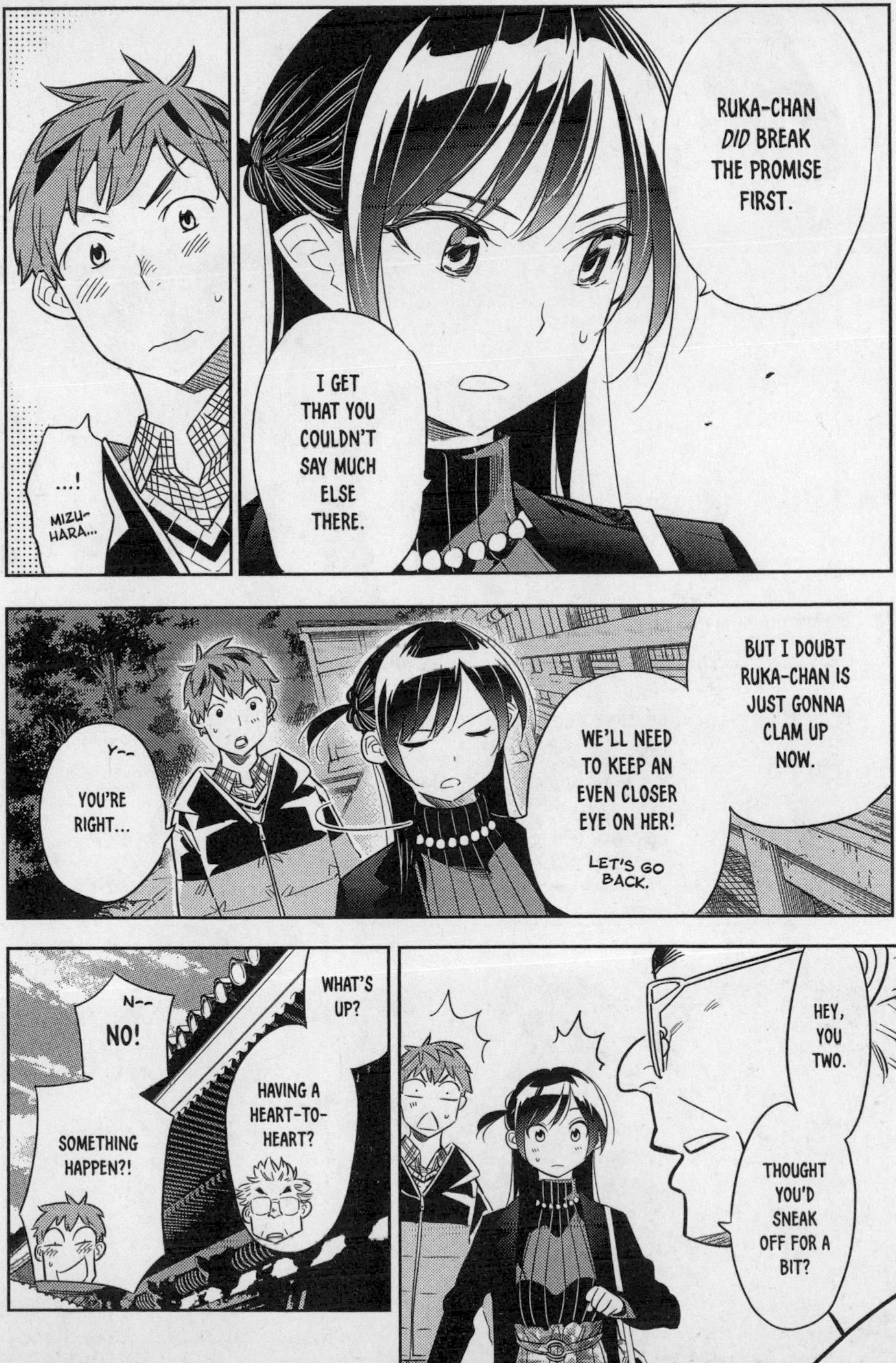
RUKA-CHAN DID BREAK THE PROMISE FIRST.
I GET THAT YOU COULDN'T SAY MUCH ELSE THERE.
...!
MIZU-HARA...
BUT I DOUBT RUKA-CHAN IS JUST GONNA CLAM UP NOW.
WE'LL NEED TO KEEP AN EVEN CLOSER EYE ON HER!
LET'S GO BACK.
Y--
YOU'RE RIGHT...
HEY, YOU TWO.
THOUGHT YOU'D SNEAK OFF FOR A BIT?
WHAT'S UP?
HAVING A HEART-TO-HEART?
N--
NO!
SOMETHING HAPPEN?!

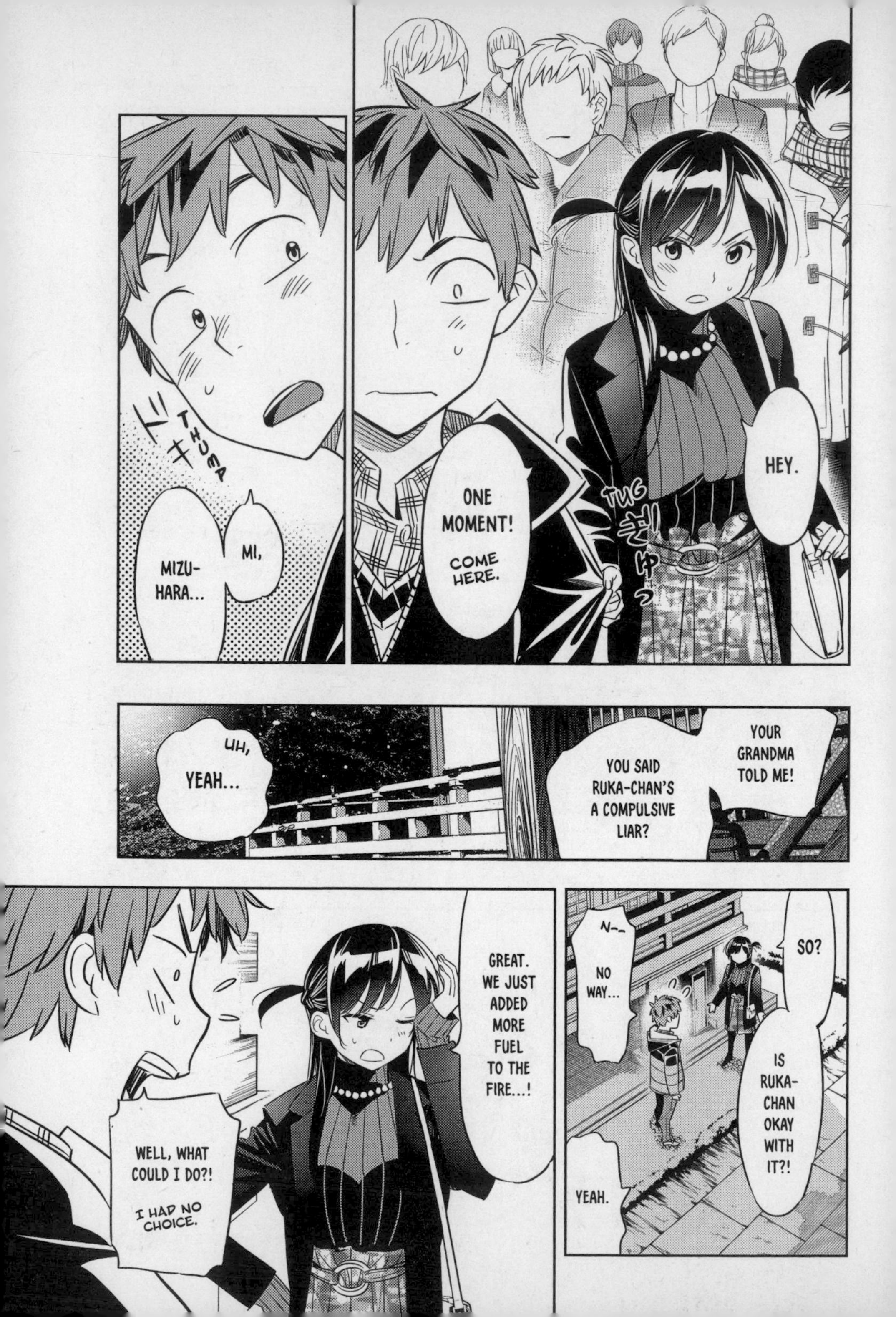
HEY.
TUG ぎゅっ
ONE MOMENT!
COME HERE.
THUMP ドキ
MI,
MIZU-HARA...
YOUR GRANDMA TOLD ME!
YOU SAID RUKA-CHAN'S A COMPULSIVE LIAR?
UH, YEAH...
SO?
IS RUKA-CHAN OKAY WITH IT?!
N--
NO WAY...
YEAH.
GREAT. WE JUST ADDED MORE FUEL TO THE FIRE...!
WELL, WHAT COULD I DO?!
I HAD NO CHOICE.

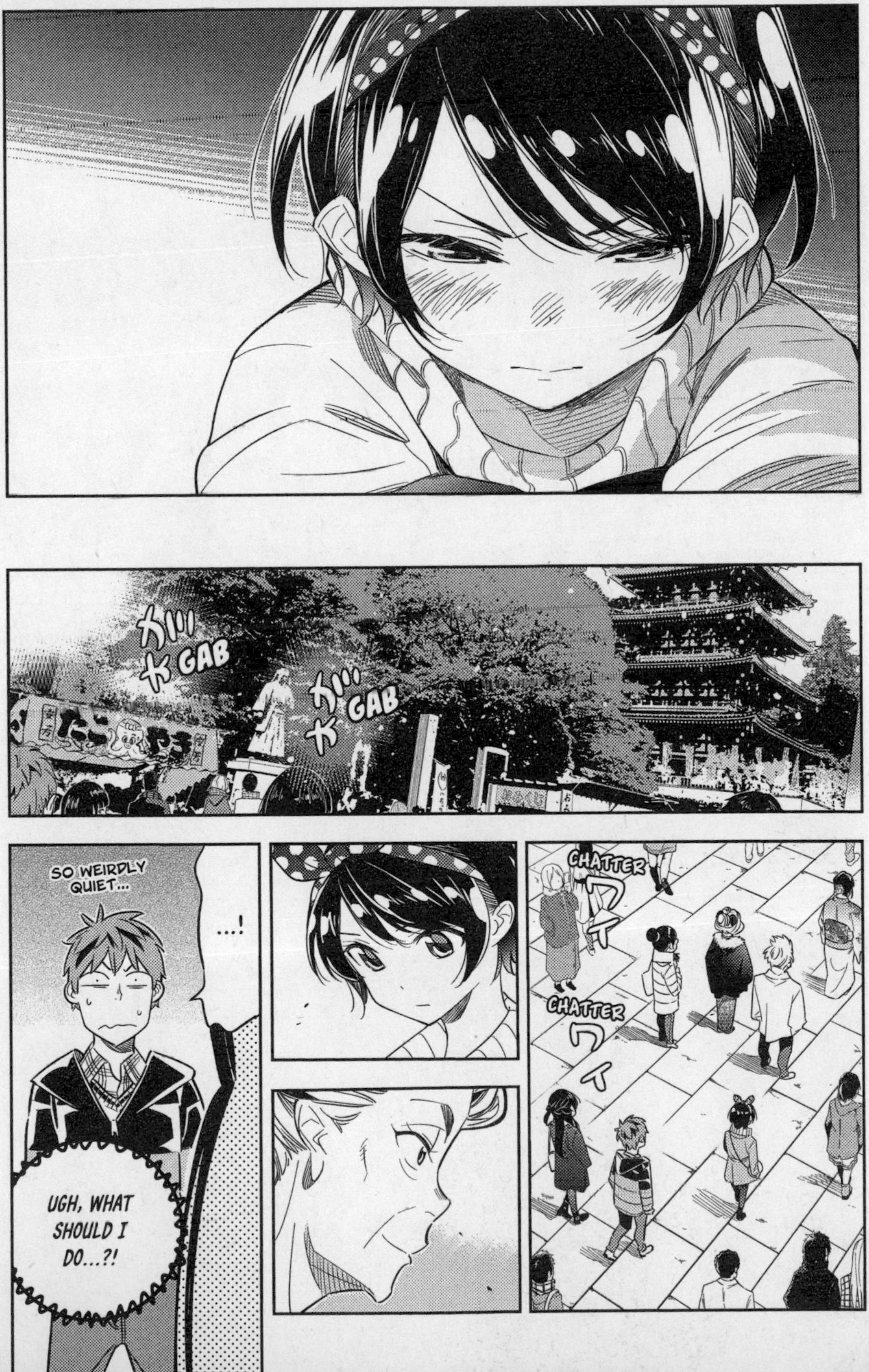
がや GAB
がや GAB
CHATTER ワイ
CHATTER ワイ
...!
SO WEIRDLY QUIET...
UGH, WHAT SHOULD I DO...?!

I'M SORRY.

YOU GO ON AHEAD.

?!

UM, OKAY...

I'M FINE!

I'M FINE, SO...!

ARE, ARE YOU OKAY? IF NOT...

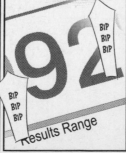

92
BIP BIP BIP
BIP BIP BIP
Results Range

ZZIP
ス

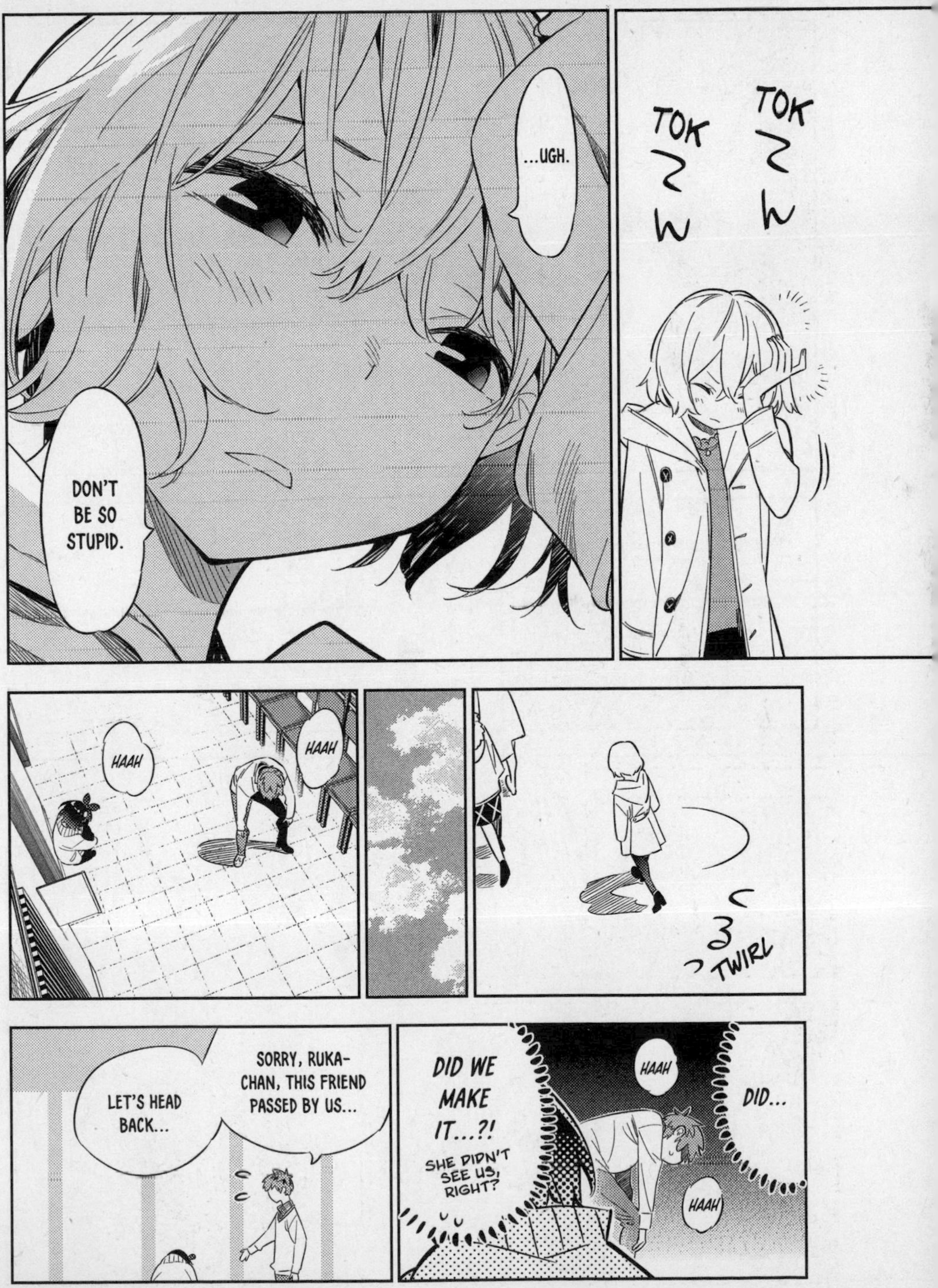
TOK TOK
TOK TOK
...UGH.
DON'T BE SO STUPID.
TWIRL
HAAH
HAAH
DID...
HAAH
DID WE MAKE IT...?!
SHE DIDN'T SEE US, RIGHT?
HAAH
SORRY, RUKA-CHAN, THIS FRIEND PASSED BY US...
LET'S HEAD BACK...

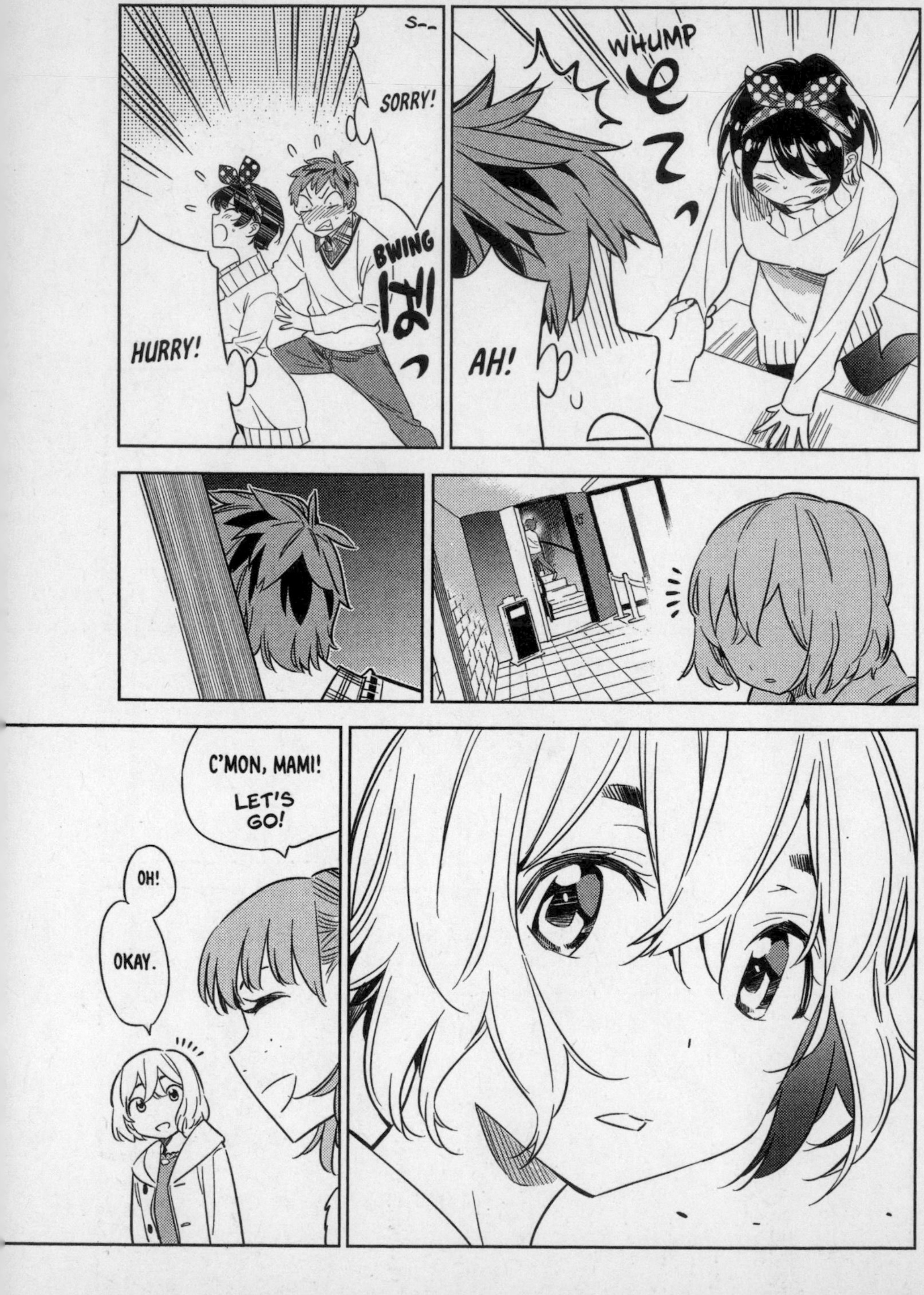
WHUMP
AH!
S--
SORRY!
BWING
ばっ
HURRY!
C'MON, MAMI!
LET'S GO!
OH!
OKAY.

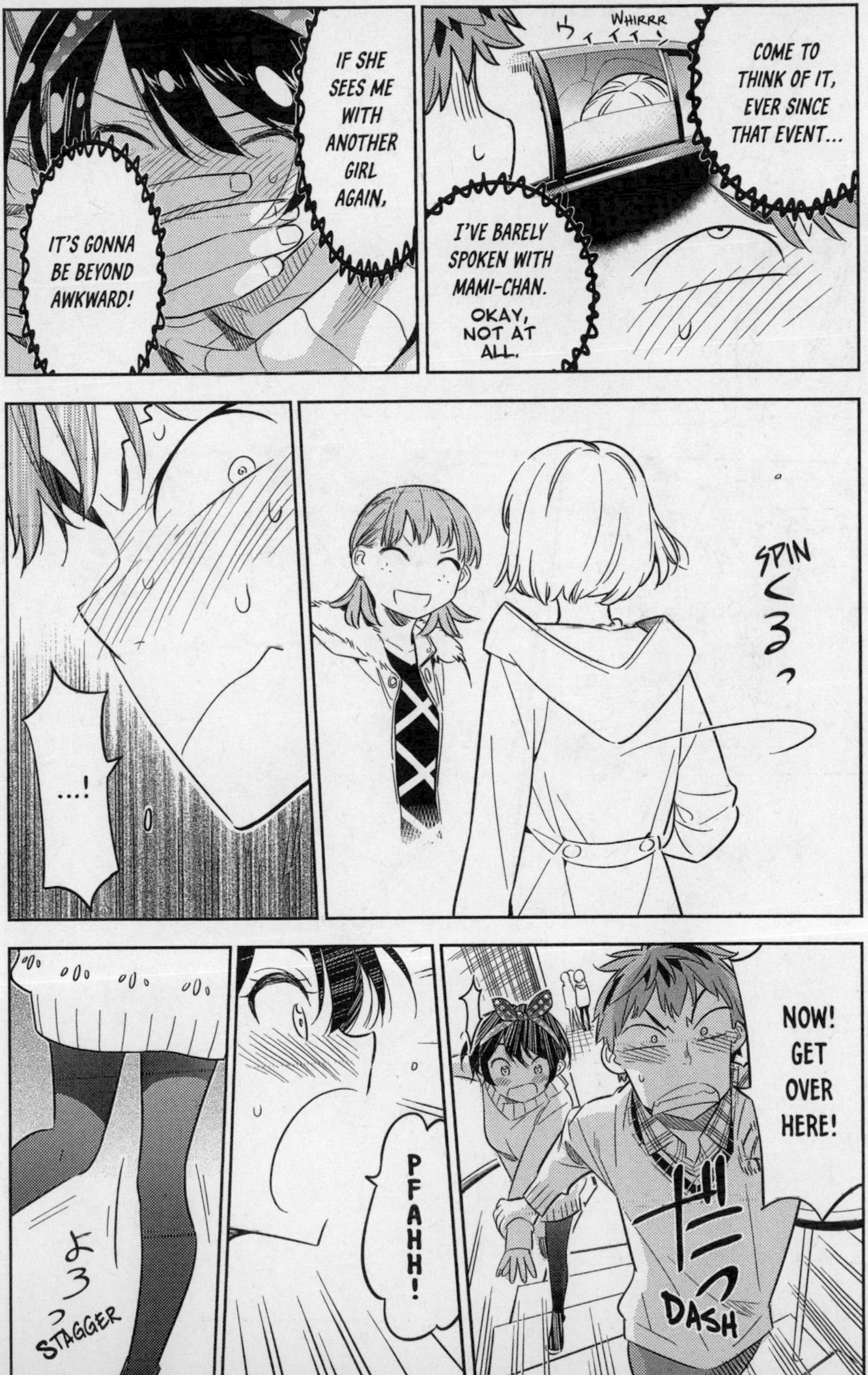
WHIRRR
COME TO THINK OF IT, EVER SINCE THAT EVENT...
I'VE BARELY SPOKEN WITH MAMI-CHAN.
OKAY, NOT AT ALL.
IF SHE SEES ME WITH ANOTHER GIRL AGAIN,
IT'S GONNA BE BEYOND AWKWARD!
くるっ
SPIN
...!
NOW! GET OVER HERE!
DASH
PFAHH!
よろっ
STAGGER

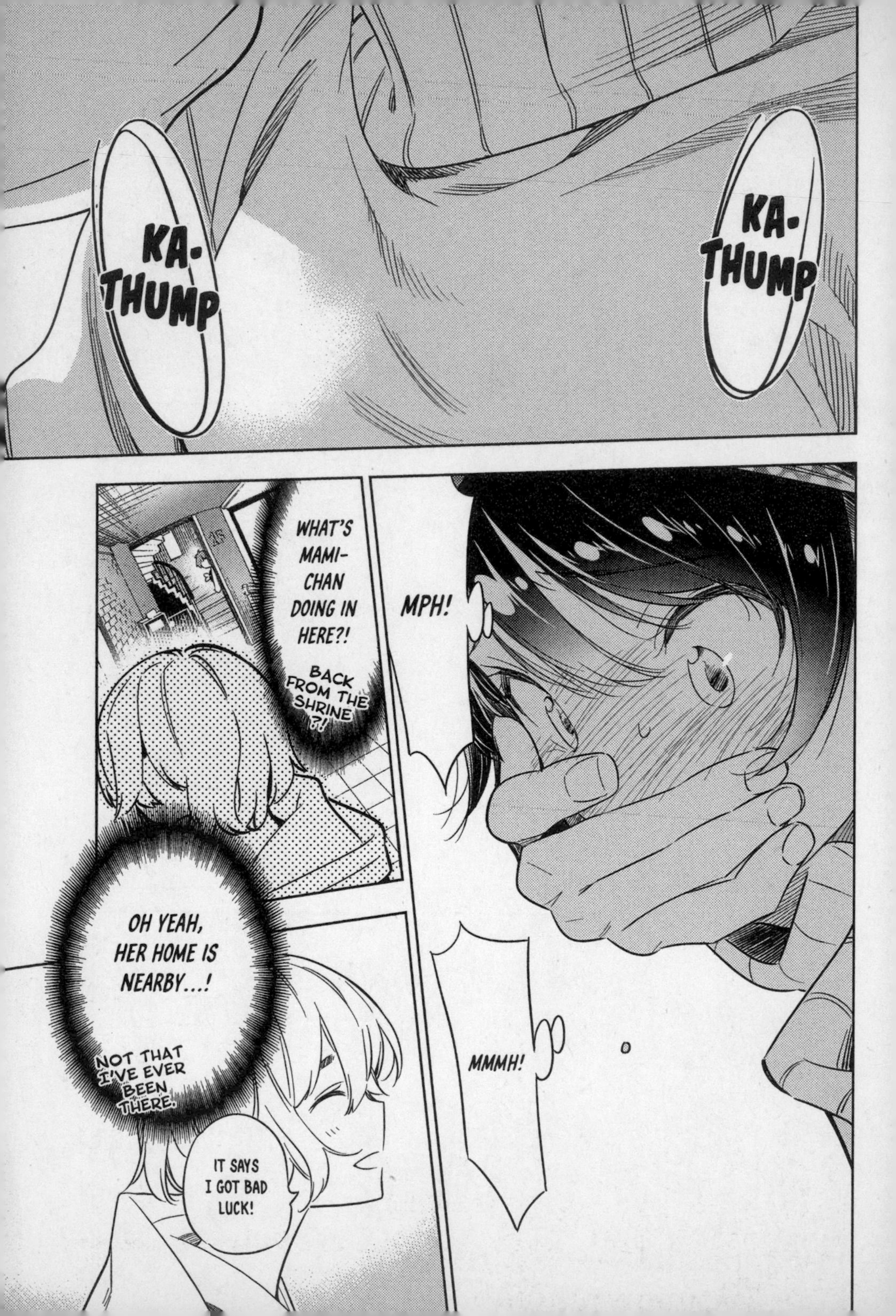
KA-THUMP
KA-THUMP
MPH!
MMMH!
WHAT'S MAMI-CHAN DOING IN HERE?!
BACK FROM THE SHRINE?!
OH YEAH, HER HOME IS NEARBY...!
NOT THAT I'VE EVER BEEN THERE.
IT SAYS I GOT BAD LUCK!

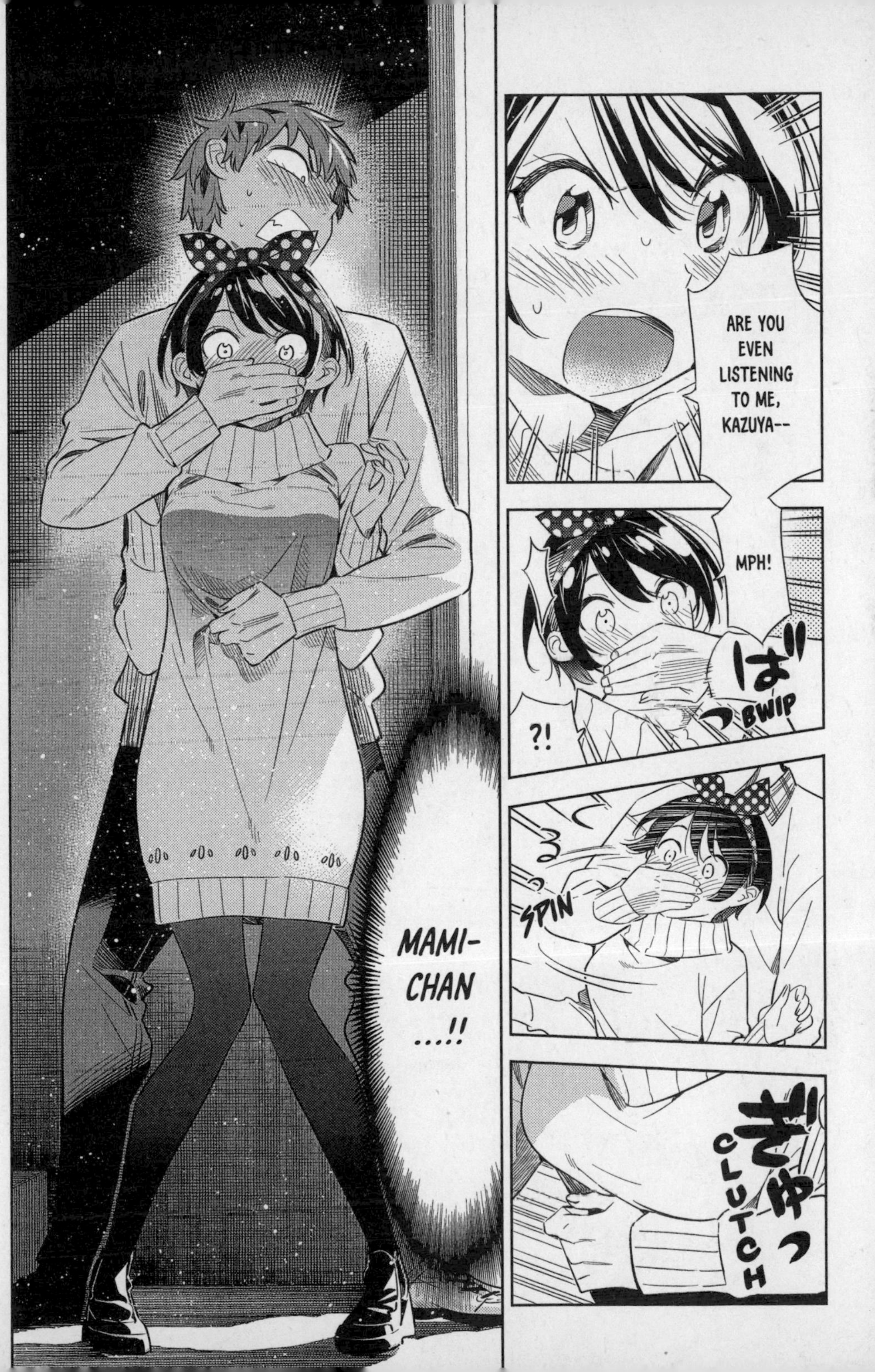
ARE YOU EVEN LISTENING TO ME, KAZUYA--
MPH!
ばっ
BWIP
?!
くるっ
SPIN
ぎゅっ
CLUTCH
MAMI-CHAN ...!!

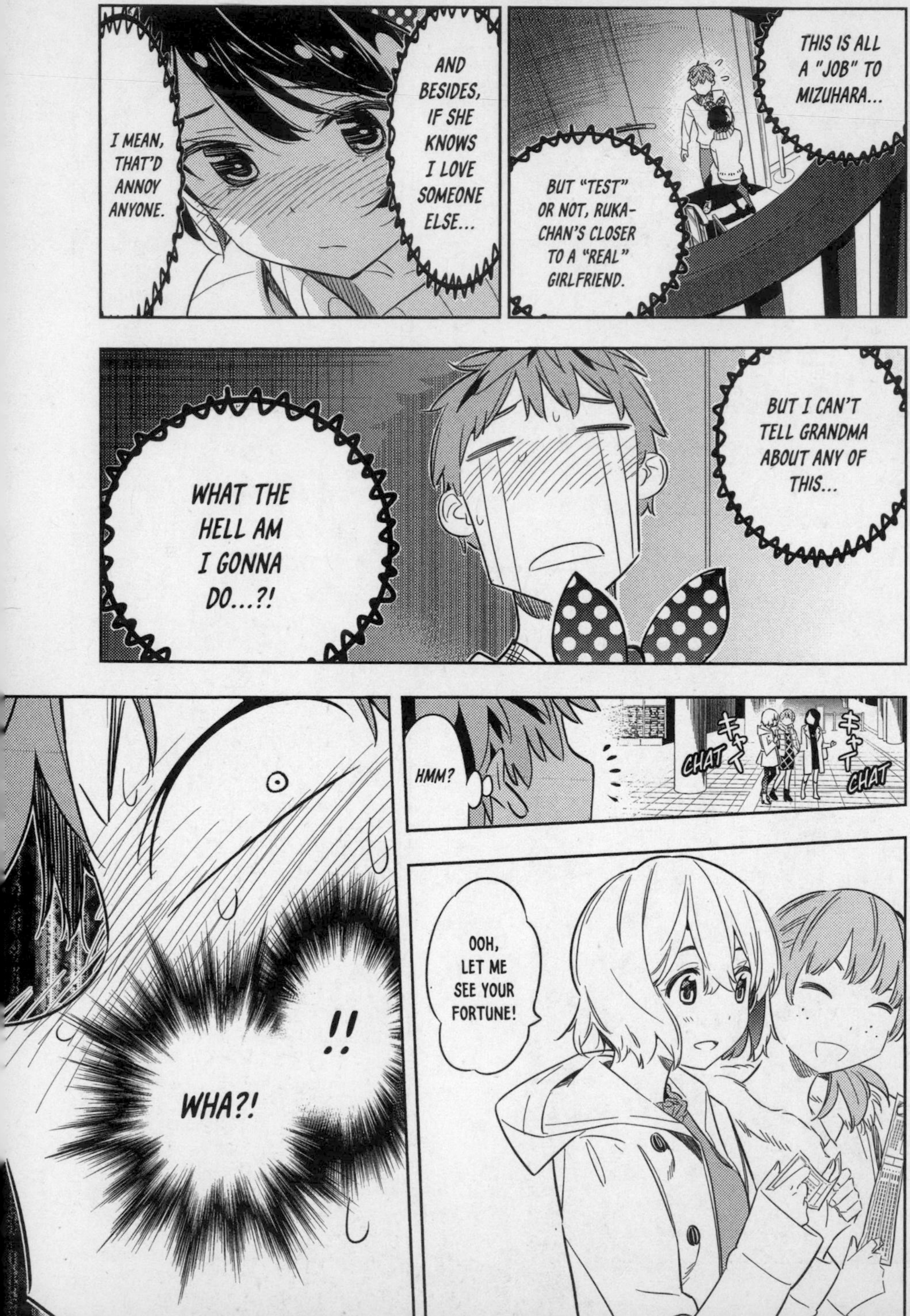
THIS IS ALL A "JOB" TO MIZUHARA...
BUT "TEST" OR NOT, RUKA-CHAN'S CLOSER TO A "REAL" GIRLFRIEND.
AND BESIDES, IF SHE KNOWS I LOVE SOMEONE ELSE...
I MEAN, THAT'D ANNOY ANYONE.
BUT I CAN'T TELL GRANDMA ABOUT ANY OF THIS...
WHAT THE HELL AM I GONNA DO...?!
キャイ
CHAT
キャイ
CHAT
HMM?
OOH, LET ME SEE YOUR FORTUNE!
!!
WHA?!

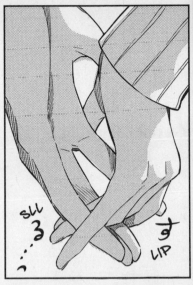

SLL
...2

すLIP

...!

THE ONLY
"GIRL-
FRIEND"
...

THE ONLY
"GIRL-
FRIEND"
YOU
NEED
IS
ME...!

MAN...

I'M
SUNK...!

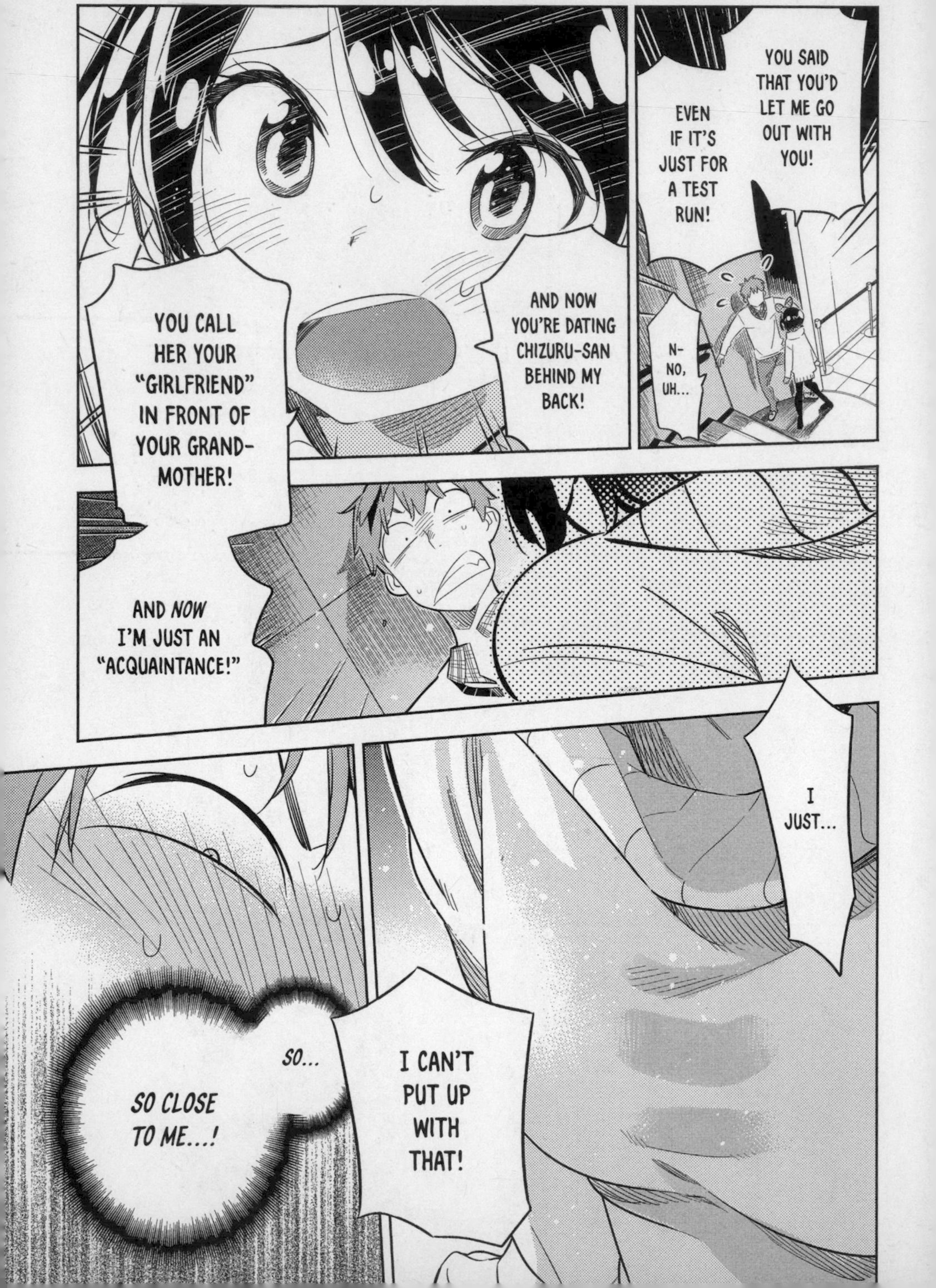
YOU SAID THAT YOU'D LET ME GO OUT WITH YOU!
EVEN IF IT'S JUST FOR A TEST RUN!
N-NO, UH...
AND NOW YOU'RE DATING CHIZURU-SAN BEHIND MY BACK!
YOU CALL HER YOUR "GIRLFRIEND" IN FRONT OF YOUR GRAND-MOTHER!
AND *NOW* I'M JUST AN "ACQUAINTANCE!"
I JUST...
I CAN'T PUT UP WITH THAT!
SO...
SO CLOSE TO ME...!

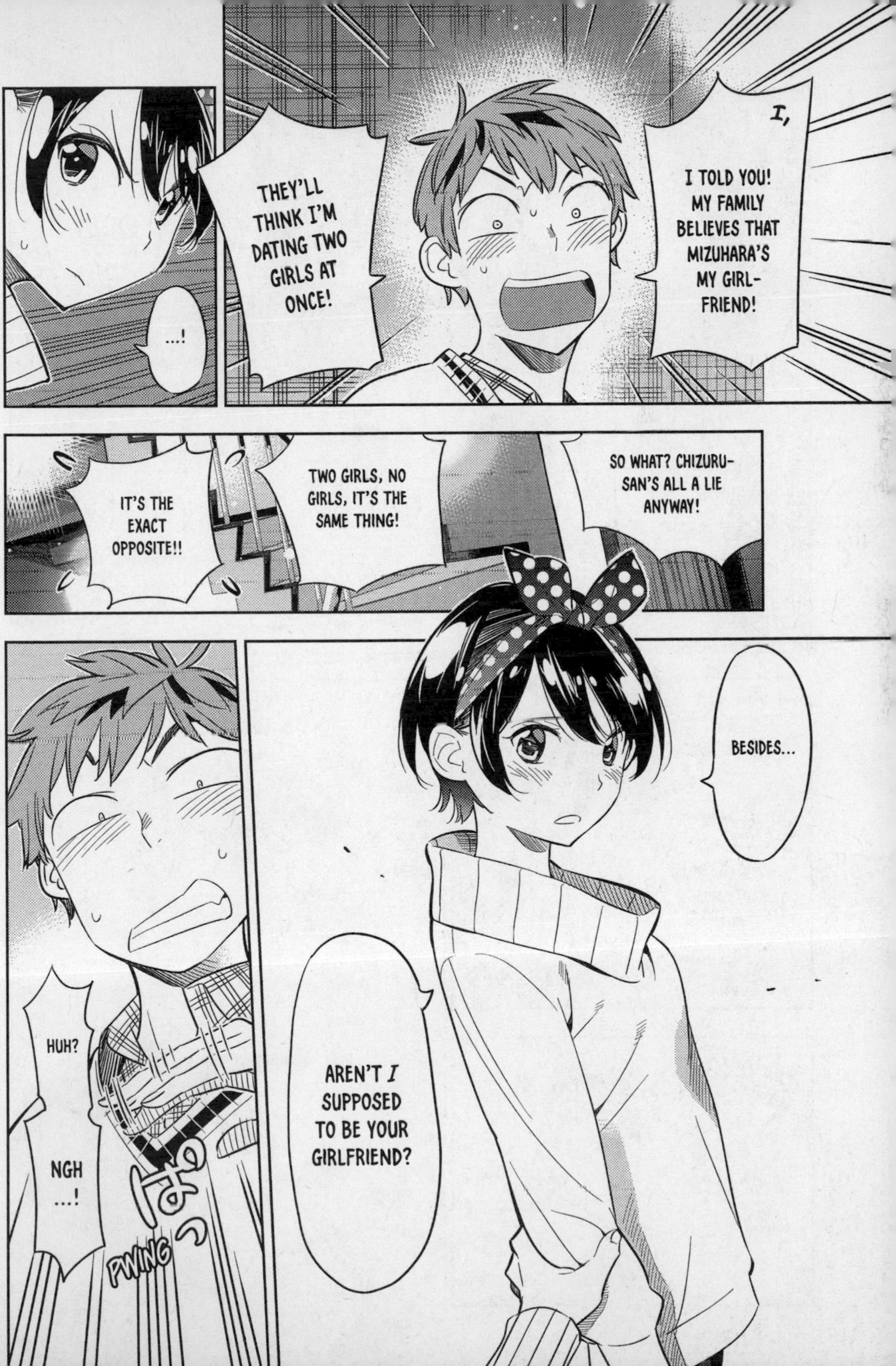
I,
I TOLD YOU! MY FAMILY BELIEVES THAT MIZUHARA'S MY GIRL-FRIEND!
THEY'LL THINK I'M DATING TWO GIRLS AT ONCE!
...!
SO WHAT? CHIZURU-SAN'S ALL A LIE ANYWAY!
TWO GIRLS, NO GIRLS, IT'S THE SAME THING!
IT'S THE EXACT OPPOSITE!!
BESIDES...
AREN'T *I* SUPPOSED TO BE YOUR GIRLFRIEND?
HUH?
はっ
PWING
NGH ...!

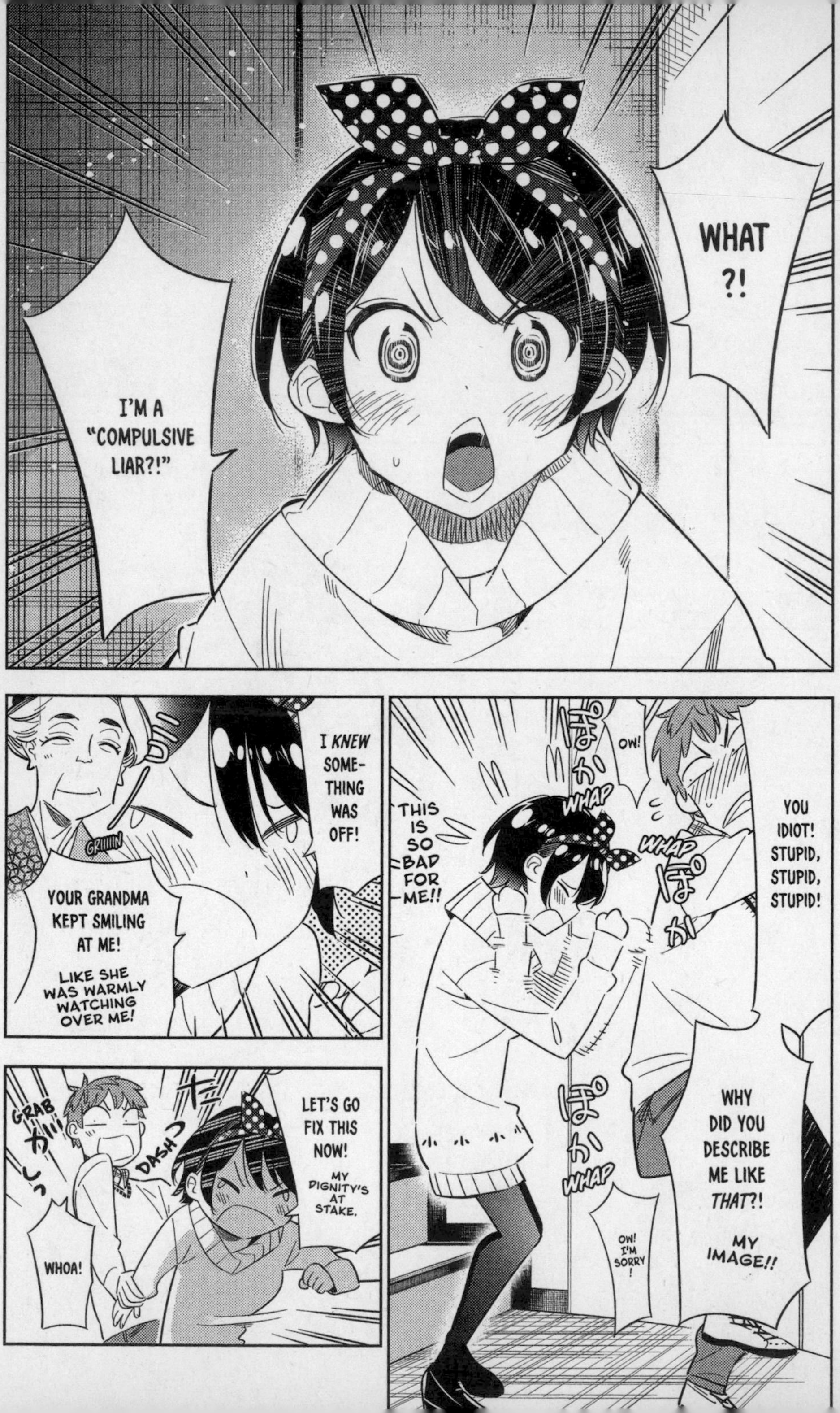
WHAT ?!
I'M A "COMPULSIVE LIAR?!"
YOU IDIOT! STUPID, STUPID, STUPID!
OW!
ぽか
WHAP
ぽか
WHAP
THIS IS SO BAD FOR ME!!
WHY DID YOU DESCRIBE ME LIKE *THAT*?!
MY IMAGE!!
OW! I'M SORRY!
ぽか
WHAP
I *KNEW* SOMETHING WAS OFF!
GRIIIIN
YOUR GRANDMA KEPT SMILING AT ME!
LIKE SHE WAS WARMLY WATCHING OVER ME!
LET'S GO FIX THIS NOW!
MY DIGNITY'S AT STAKE.
DASH
GRAB
WHOA!

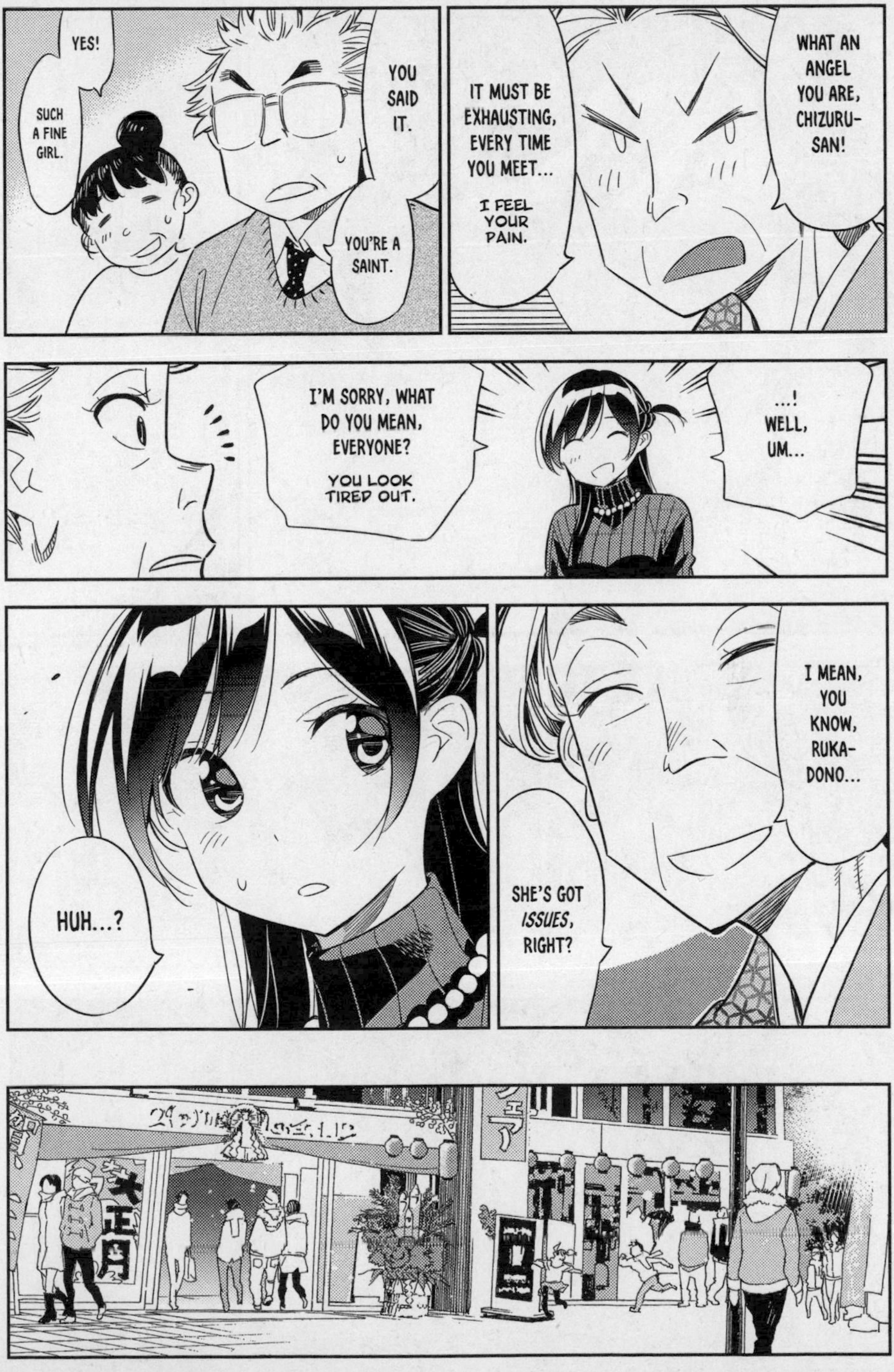
WHAT AN ANGEL YOU ARE, CHIZURU-SAN!
IT MUST BE EXHAUSTING, EVERY TIME YOU MEET...
I FEEL YOUR PAIN.
YOU SAID IT.
YOU'RE A SAINT.
YES!
SUCH A FINE GIRL.
...! WELL, UM...
I'M SORRY, WHAT DO YOU MEAN, EVERYONE?
YOU LOOK TIRED OUT.
I MEAN, YOU KNOW, RUKA-DONO...
SHE'S GOT *ISSUES*, RIGHT?
HUH...?

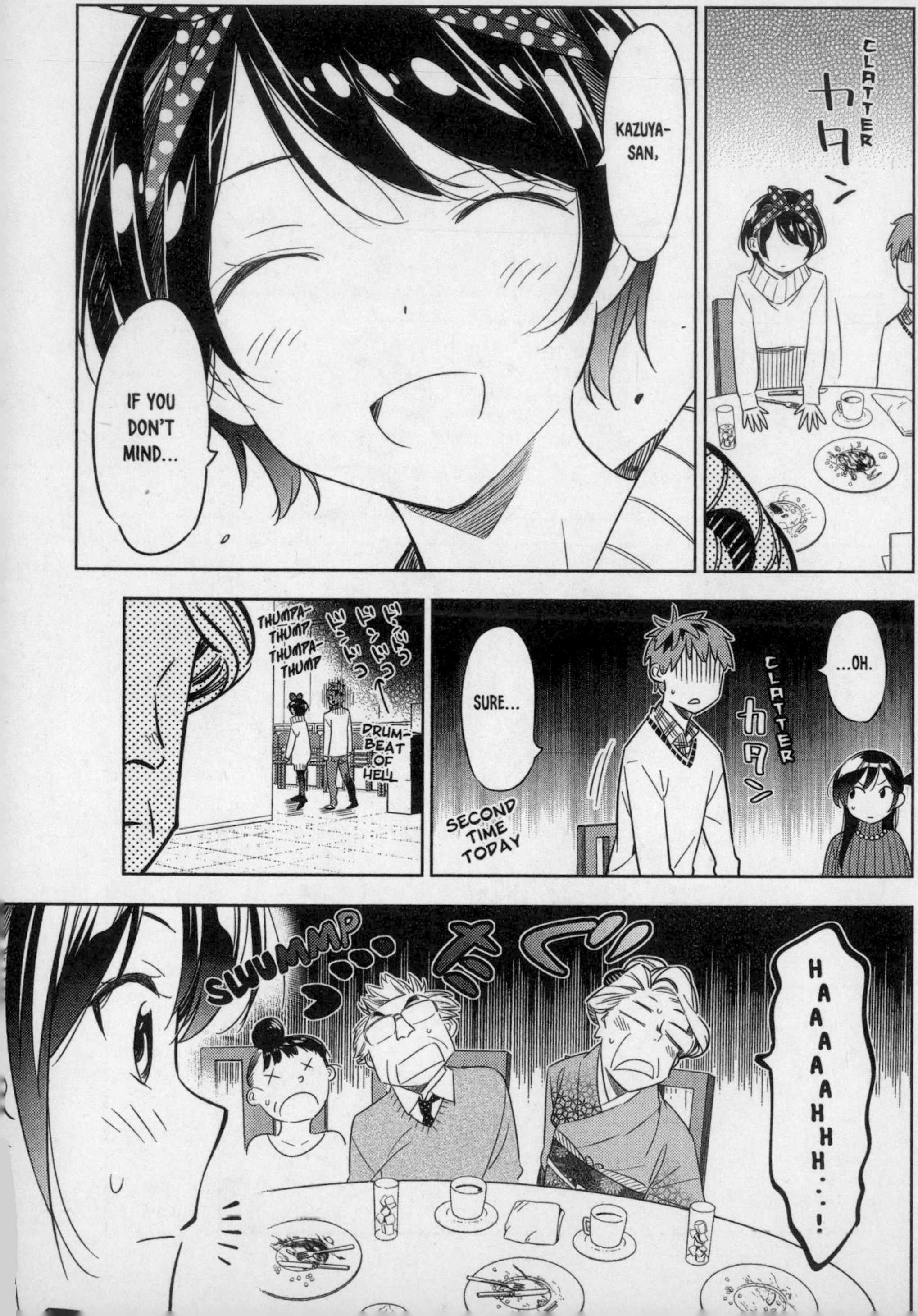
CLATTER
カタン
KAZUYA-SAN,
IF YOU DON'T MIND...
...OH.
CLATTER
カタン
SURE...
SECOND TIME TODAY
THUMPA-THUMP THUMPA-THUMP
DRUMBEAT OF HELL
HAAAAAHHH...!
SLUUMMP

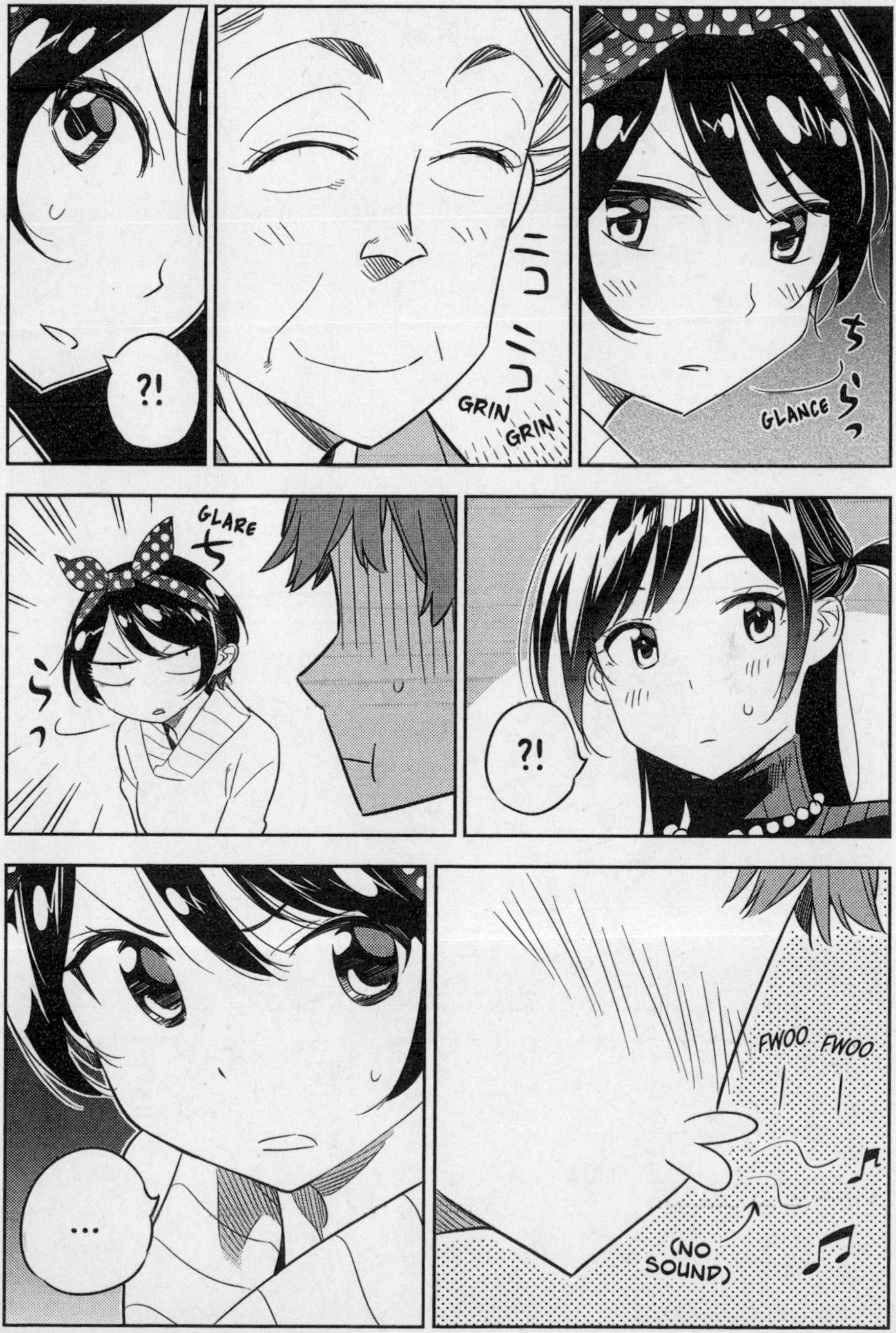
ちらっ
GLANCE
ニコニコ
GRIN GRIN
?!
?!
GLARE
ち
らっ
FWOO FWOO
(NO SOUND)
...

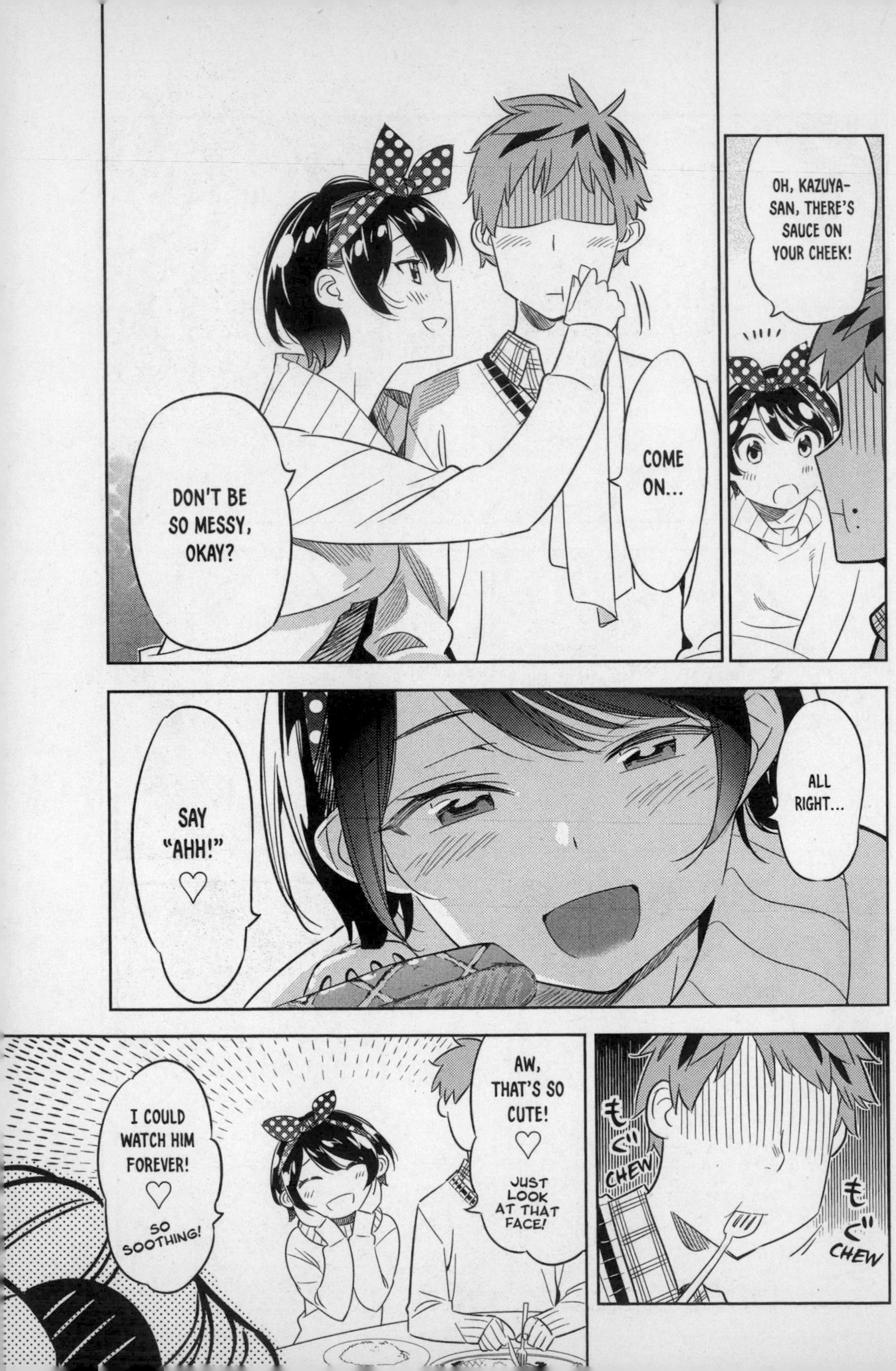
OH, KAZUYA-SAN, THERE'S SAUCE ON YOUR CHEEK!
COME ON...
DON'T BE SO MESSY, OKAY?
ALL RIGHT...
SAY "AHH!" ♡
もぐ CHEW
もぐ CHEW
AW, THAT'S SO CUTE! ♡
JUST LOOK AT THAT FACE!
I COULD WATCH HIM FOREVER! ♡
SO SOOTHING!

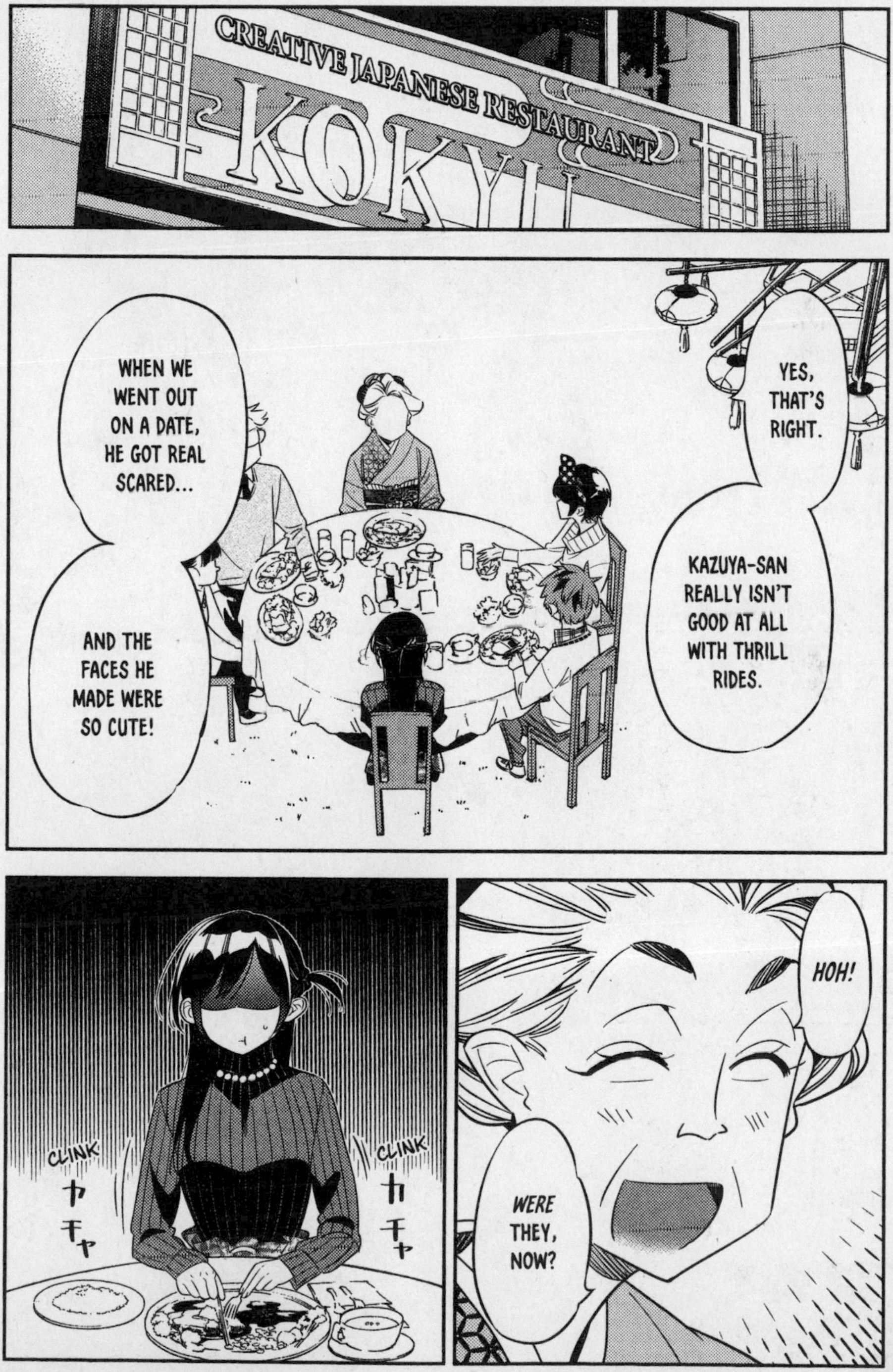
CREATIVE JAPANESE RESTAURANT
KOKYU
YES, THAT'S RIGHT.
KAZUYA-SAN REALLY ISN'T GOOD AT ALL WITH THRILL RIDES.
WHEN WE WENT OUT ON A DATE, HE GOT REAL SCARED...
AND THE FACES HE MADE WERE SO CUTE!
HOH!
WERE THEY, NOW?
CLINK
カチャ
CLINK
カチャ

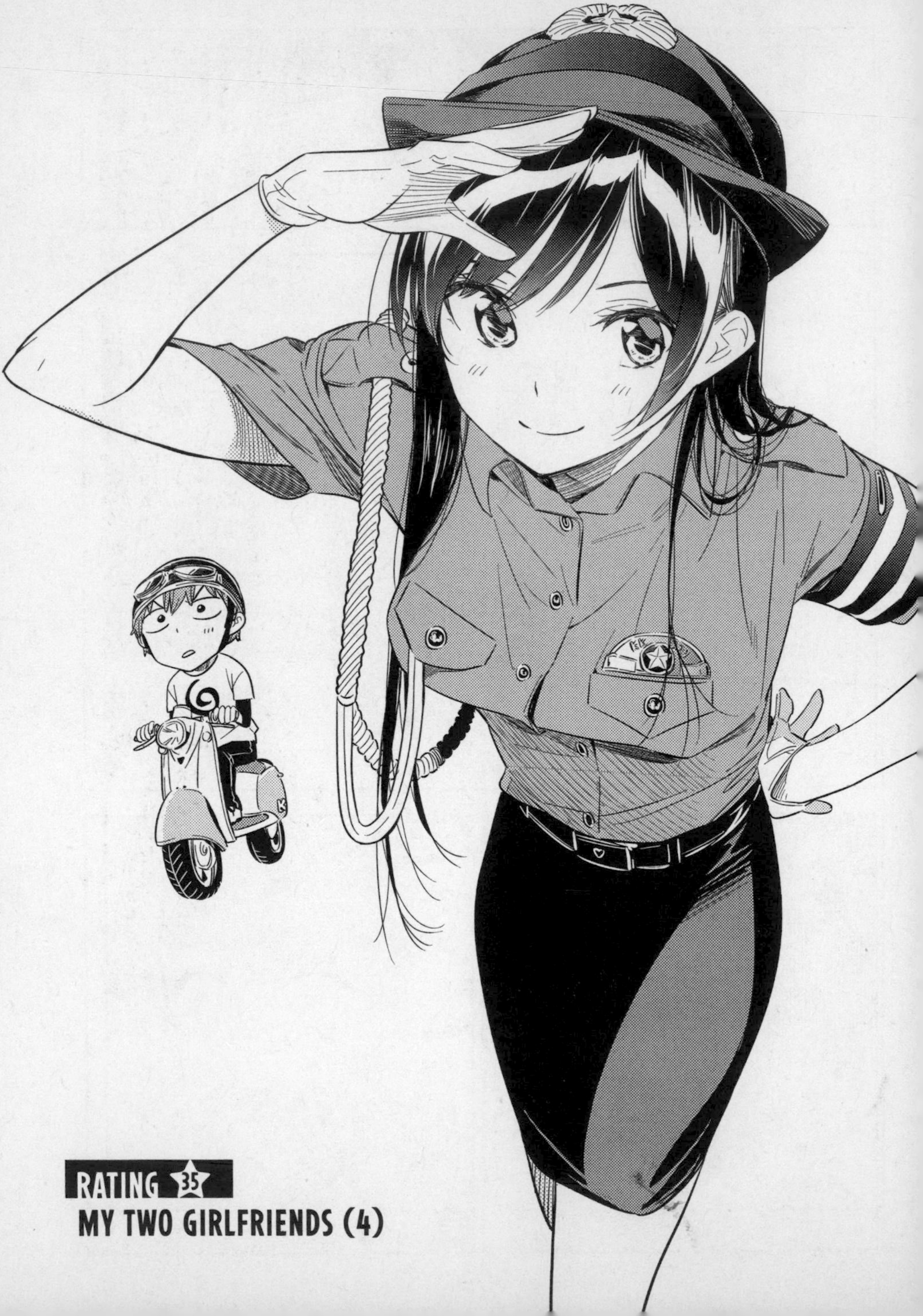

RATING 35
MY TWO GIRLFRIENDS (4)

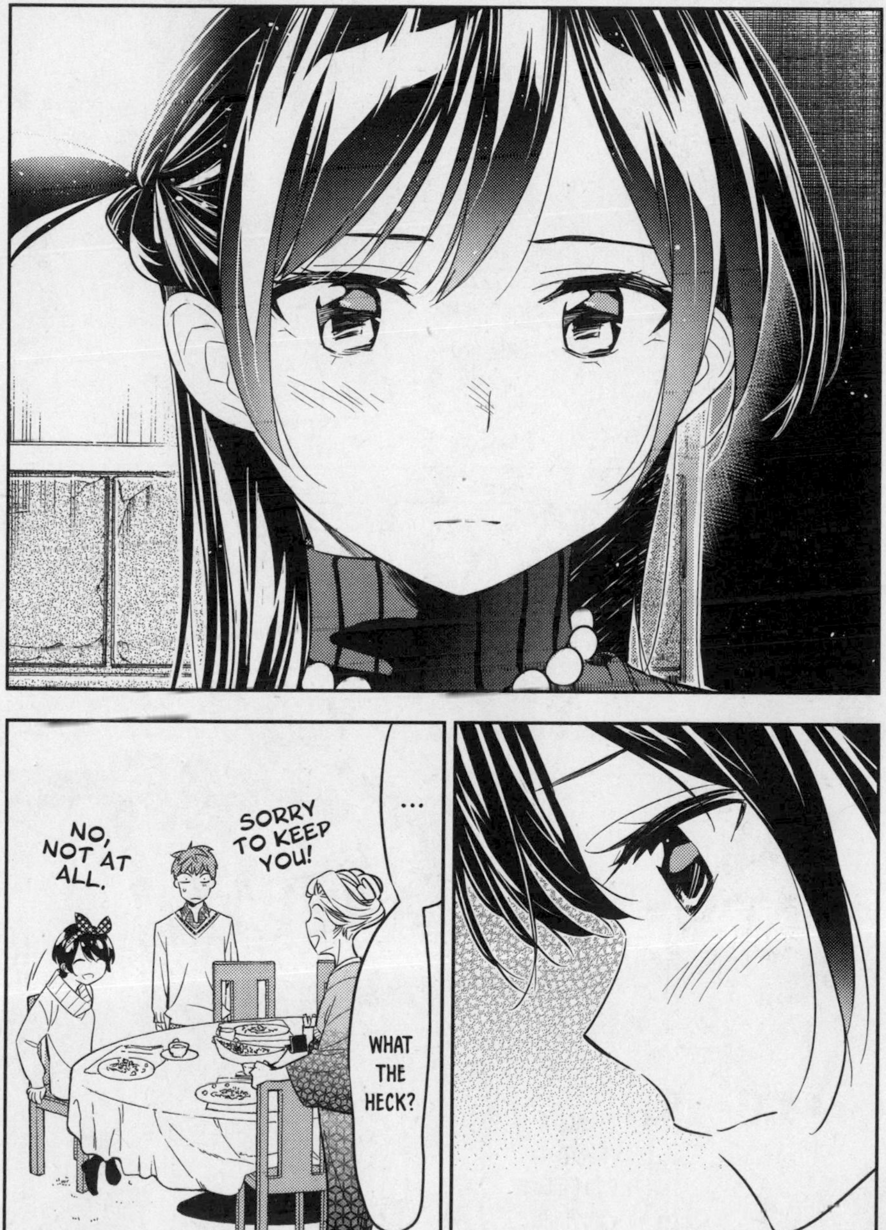
...
WHAT THE HECK?
SORRY TO KEEP YOU!
NO, NOT AT ALL.

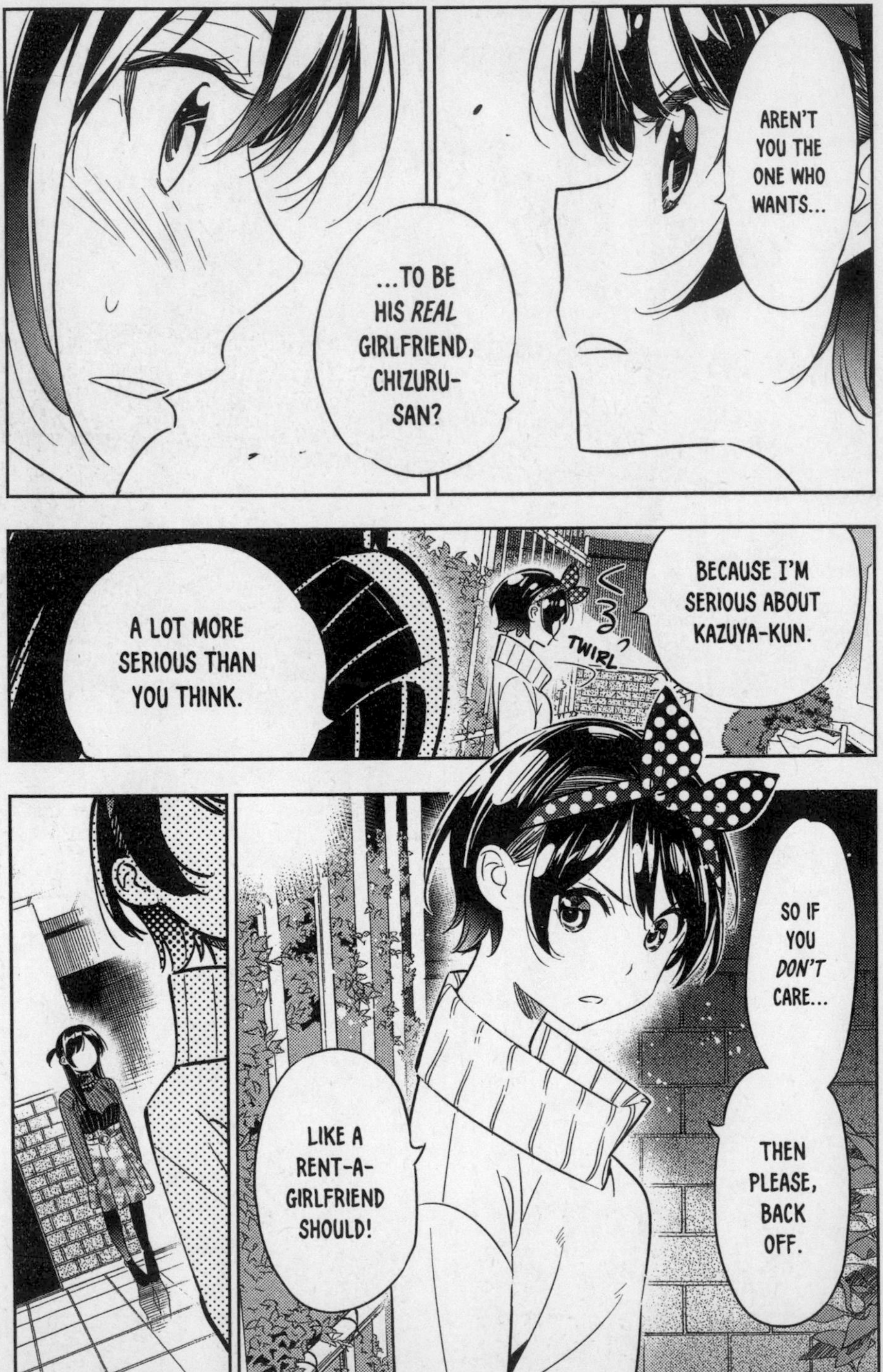
AREN'T YOU THE ONE WHO WANTS...
...TO BE HIS *REAL* GIRLFRIEND, CHIZURU-SAN?
BECAUSE I'M SERIOUS ABOUT KAZUYA-KUN.
TWIRL
A LOT MORE SERIOUS THAN YOU THINK.
SO IF YOU *DON'T* CARE...
THEN PLEASE, BACK OFF.
LIKE A RENT-A-GIRLFRIEND SHOULD!

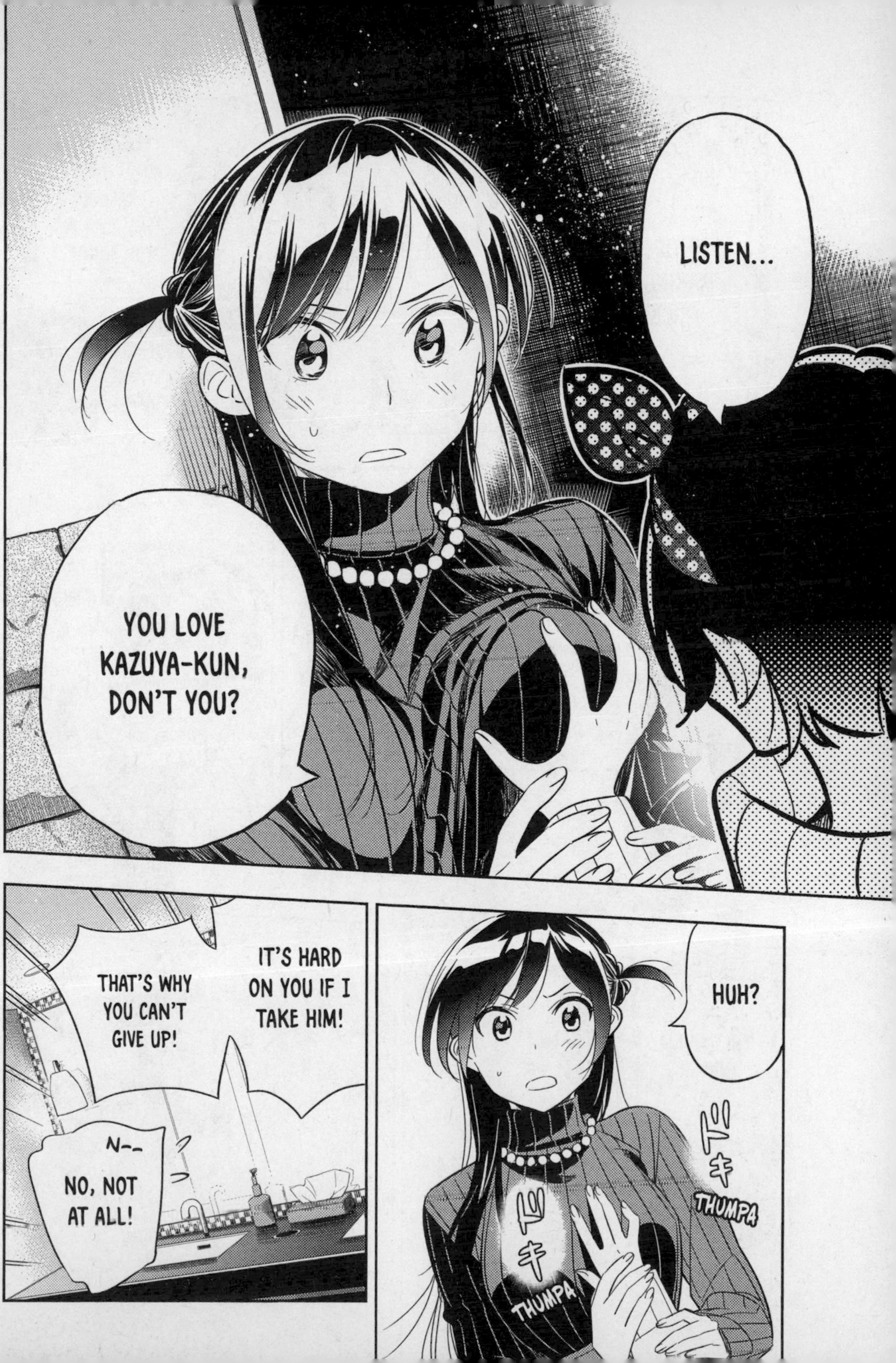
LISTEN...
YOU LOVE KAZUYA-KUN, DON'T YOU?
HUH?
ドキ
THUMPA
ドキ
THUMPA
IT'S HARD ON YOU IF I TAKE HIM!
THAT'S WHY YOU CAN'T GIVE UP!
N--
NO, NOT AT ALL!

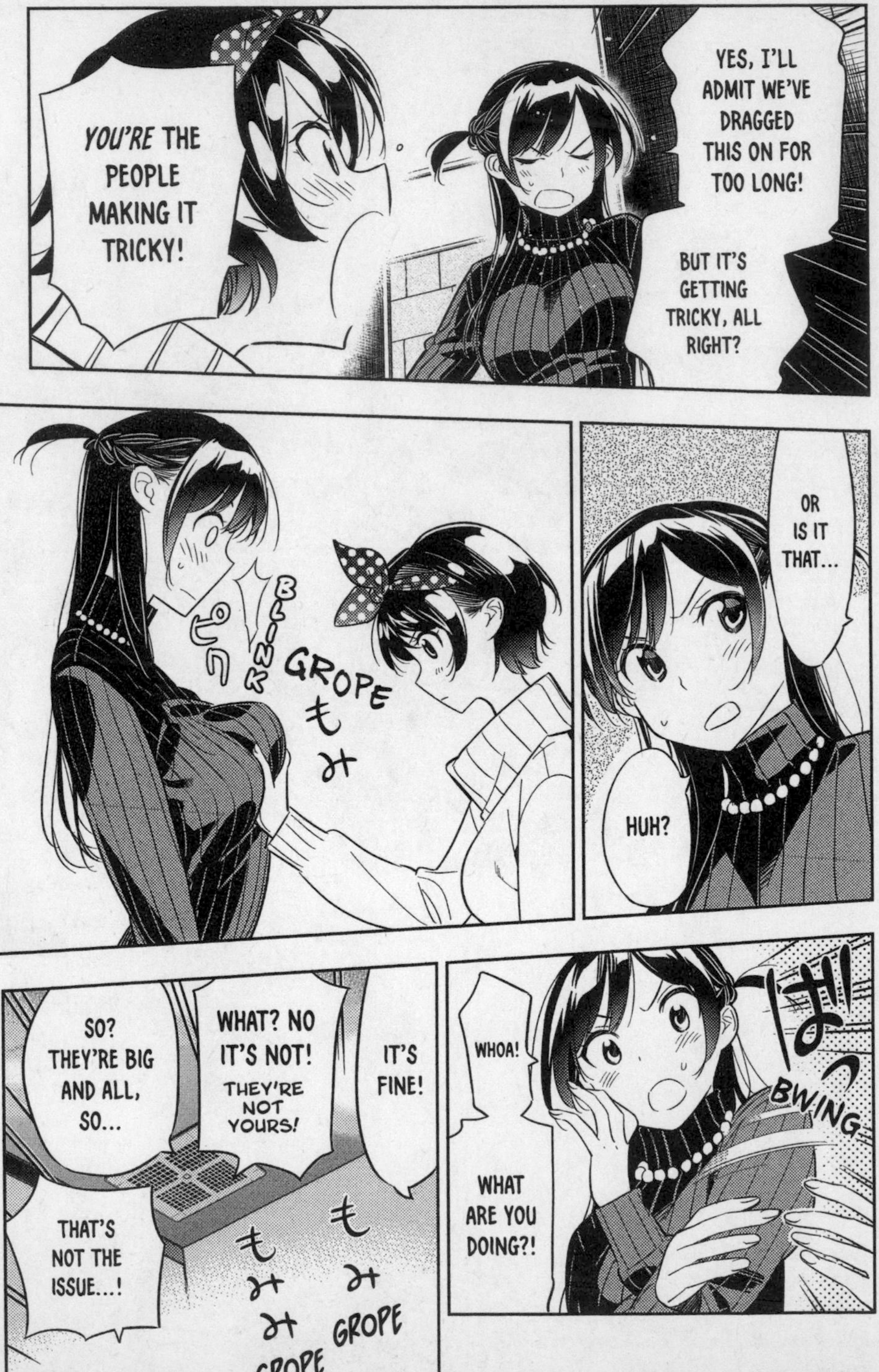
YES, I'LL ADMIT WE'VE DRAGGED THIS ON FOR TOO LONG!
BUT IT'S GETTING TRICKY, ALL RIGHT?
YOU'RE THE PEOPLE MAKING IT TRICKY!
OR IS IT THAT...
HUH?
ピク
BLINK
もみ
GROPE
ぱっ
BWING
WHOA!
WHAT ARE YOU DOING?!
IT'S FINE!
WHAT? NO IT'S NOT!
THEY'RE NOT YOURS!
SO? THEY'RE BIG AND ALL, SO...
THAT'S NOT THE ISSUE...!
もみ
GROPE
もみ
GROPE

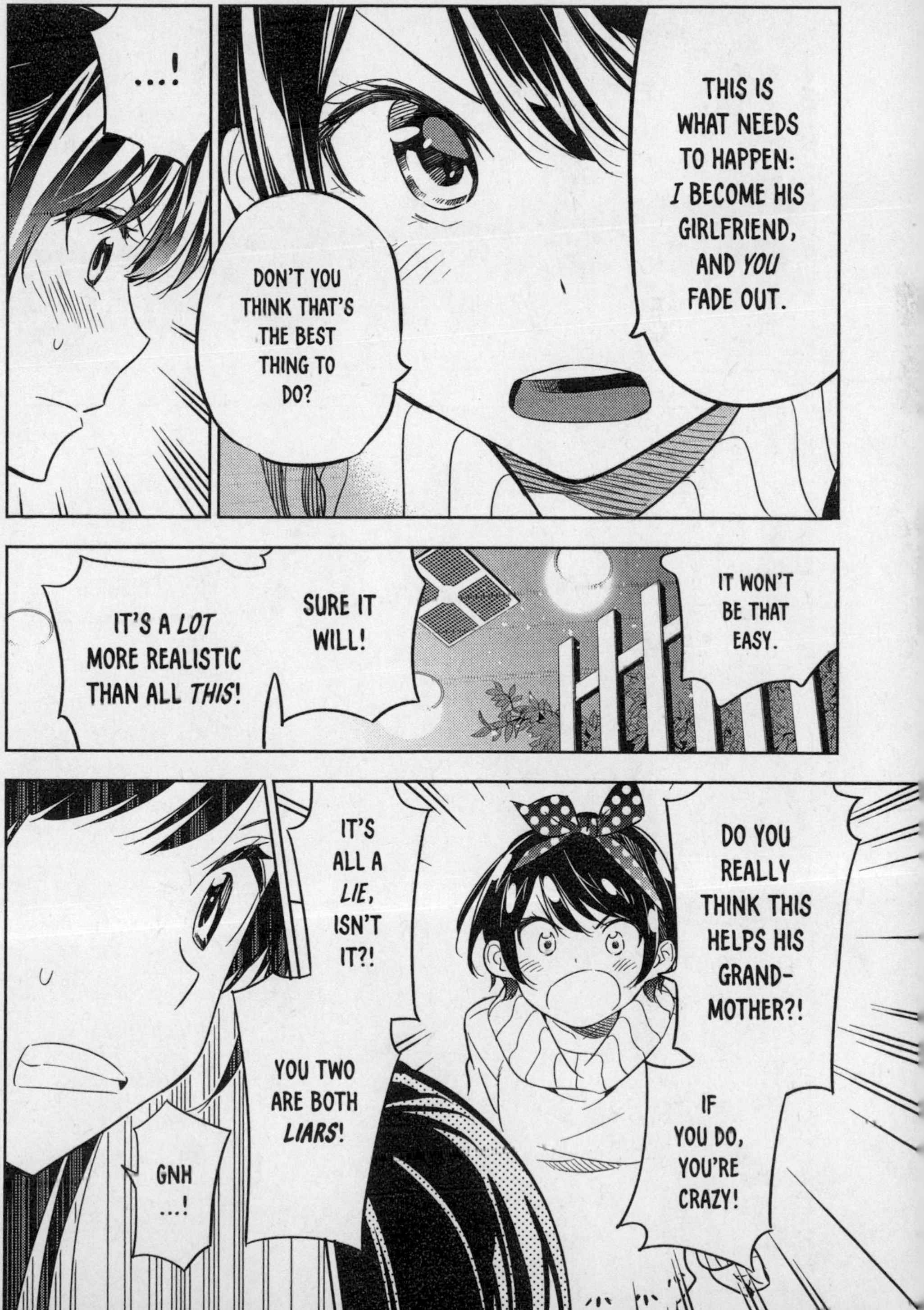
THIS IS WHAT NEEDS TO HAPPEN: *I* BECOME HIS GIRLFRIEND, AND *YOU* FADE OUT.
DON'T YOU THINK THAT'S THE BEST THING TO DO?
...!
IT WON'T BE THAT EASY.
SURE IT WILL!
IT'S A *LOT* MORE REALISTIC THAN ALL *THIS*!
DO YOU REALLY THINK THIS HELPS HIS GRAND-MOTHER?!
IT'S ALL A *LIE*, ISN'T IT?!
IF YOU DO, YOU'RE CRAZY!
YOU TWO ARE BOTH *LIARS*!
GNH ...!

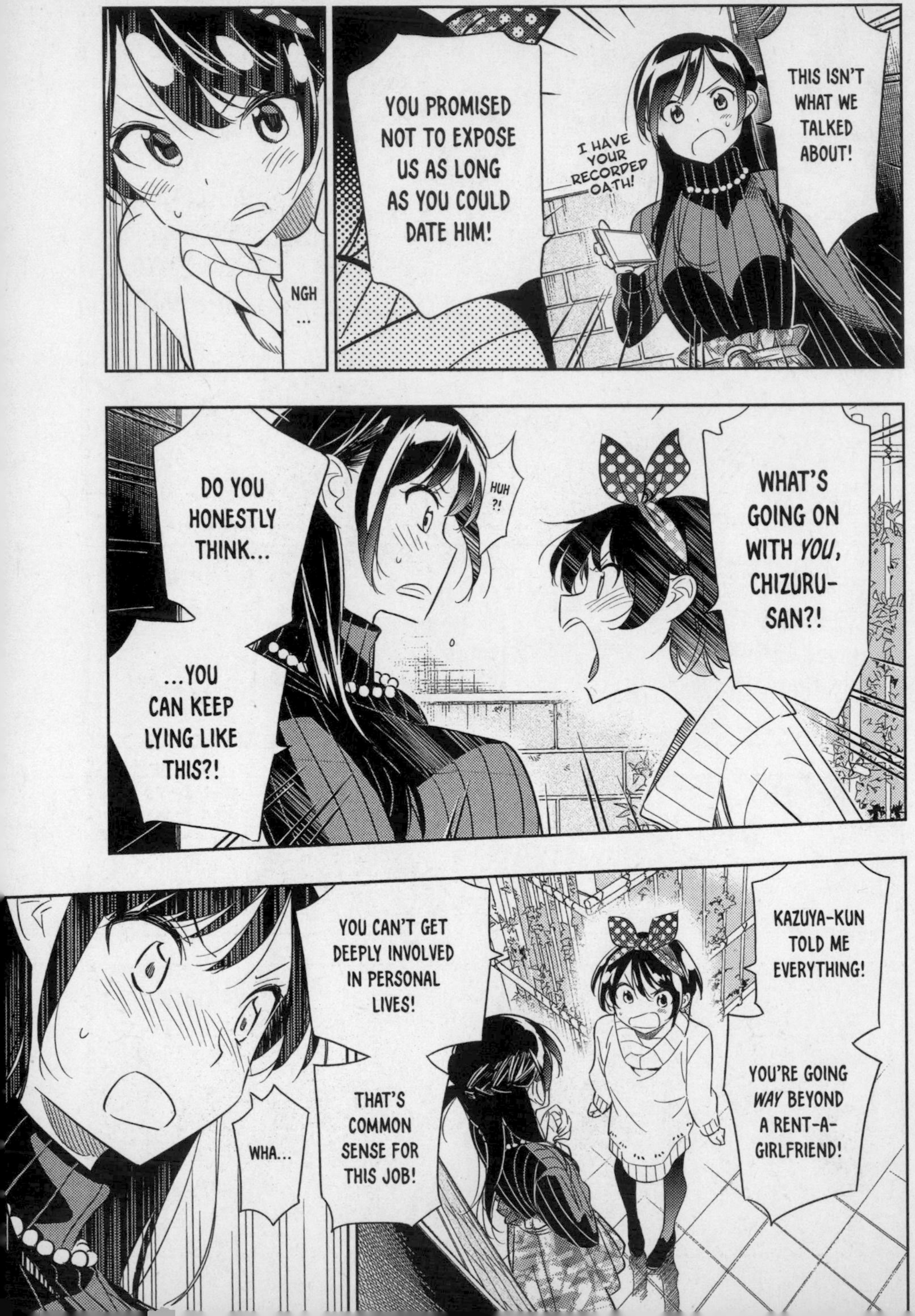
THIS ISN'T WHAT WE TALKED ABOUT!
I HAVE YOUR RECORDED OATH!
YOU PROMISED NOT TO EXPOSE US AS LONG AS YOU COULD DATE HIM!
NGH ...
WHAT'S GOING ON WITH *YOU*, CHIZURU-SAN?!
HUH ?!
DO YOU HONESTLY THINK...
...YOU CAN KEEP LYING LIKE THIS?!
KAZUYA-KUN TOLD ME EVERYTHING!
YOU'RE GOING *WAY* BEYOND A RENT-A-GIRLFRIEND!
YOU CAN'T GET DEEPLY INVOLVED IN PERSONAL LIVES!
THAT'S COMMON SENSE FOR THIS JOB!
WHA...

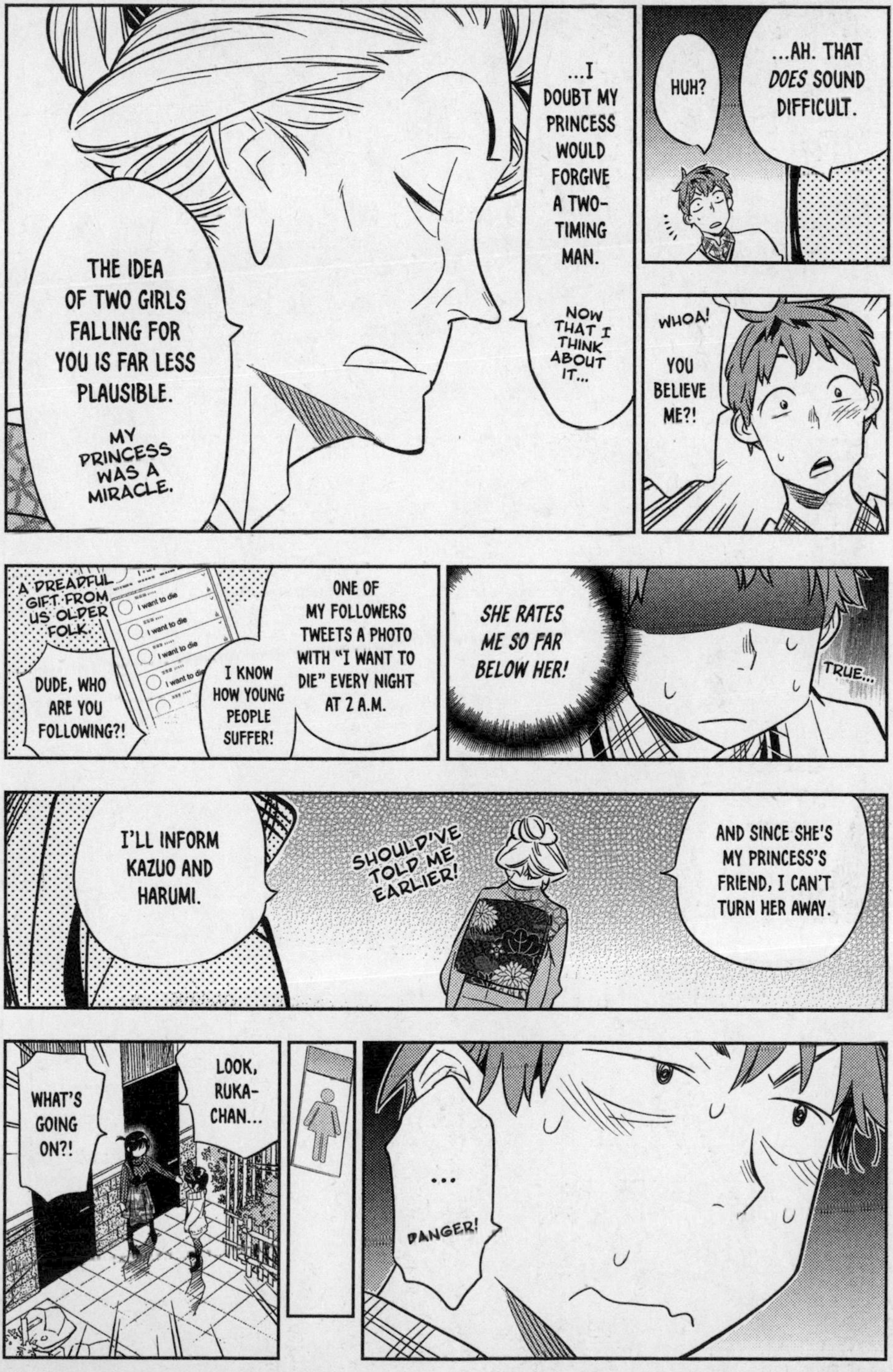

...AH. THAT *DOES* SOUND DIFFICULT.
HUH?
WHOA!
YOU BELIEVE ME?!
...I DOUBT MY PRINCESS WOULD FORGIVE A TWO-TIMING MAN.
NOW THAT I THINK ABOUT IT...
THE IDEA OF TWO GIRLS FALLING FOR YOU IS FAR LESS PLAUSIBLE.
MY PRINCESS WAS A MIRACLE.
SHE RATES ME SO FAR BELOW HER!
TRUE...
ONE OF MY FOLLOWERS TWEETS A PHOTO WITH "I WANT TO DIE" EVERY NIGHT AT 2 A.M.
I KNOW HOW YOUNG PEOPLE SUFFER!
A DREADFUL GIFT FROM US OLDER FOLK.
I want to die
I want to die
I want to die
I want to die
DUDE, WHO ARE YOU FOLLOWING?!
AND SINCE SHE'S MY PRINCESS'S FRIEND, I CAN'T TURN HER AWAY.
SHOULD'VE TOLD ME EARLIER!
I'LL INFORM KAZUO AND HARUMI.
...
DANGER!
LOOK, RUKA-CHAN...
WHAT'S GOING ON?!

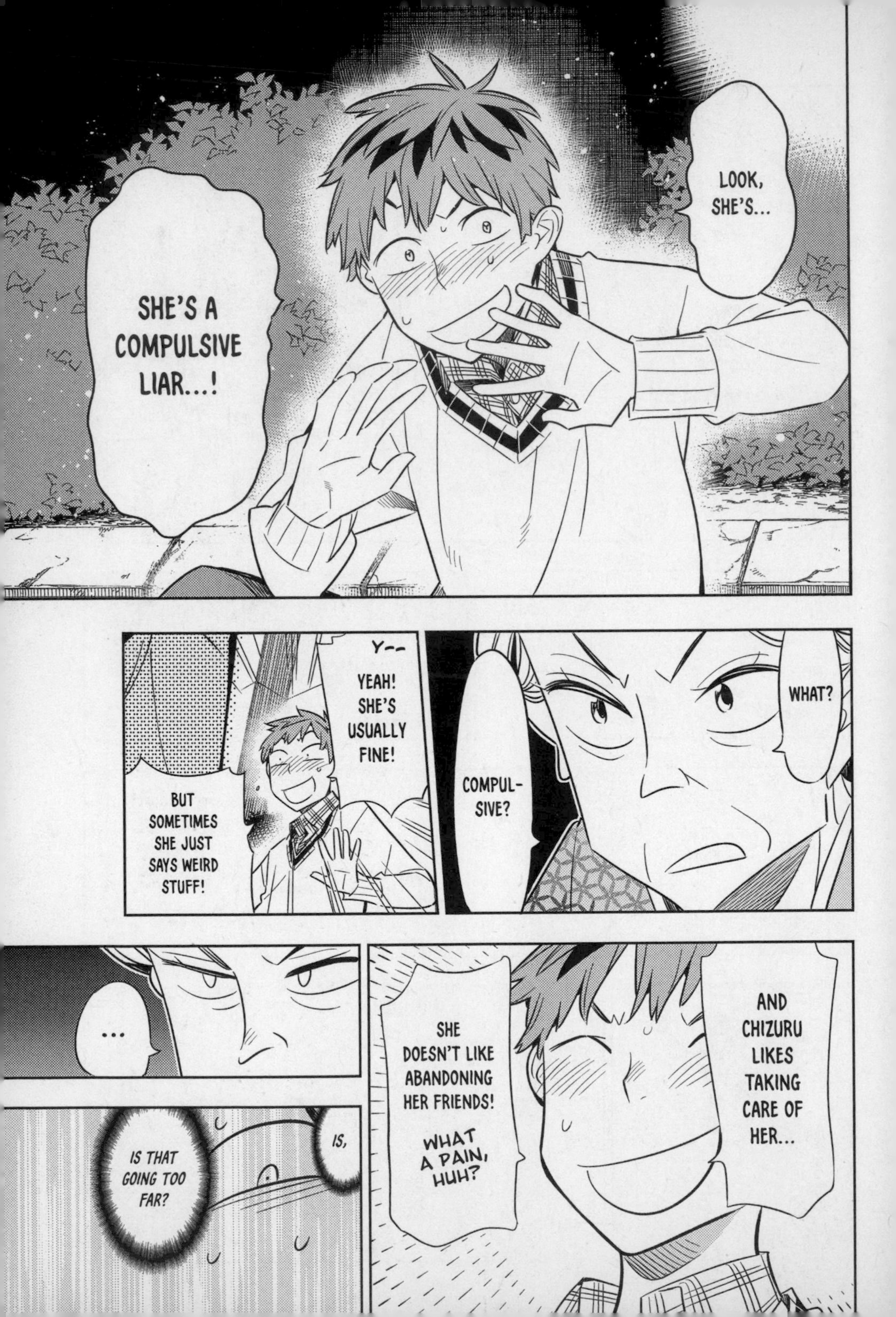
LOOK, SHE'S...
SHE'S A COMPULSIVE LIAR...!
WHAT?
COMPUL-SIVE?
Y--
YEAH! SHE'S USUALLY FINE!
BUT SOMETIMES SHE JUST SAYS WEIRD STUFF!
AND CHIZURU LIKES TAKING CARE OF HER...
SHE DOESN'T LIKE ABANDONING HER FRIENDS!
WHAT A PAIN, HUH?
...
IS,
IS THAT GOING TOO FAR?

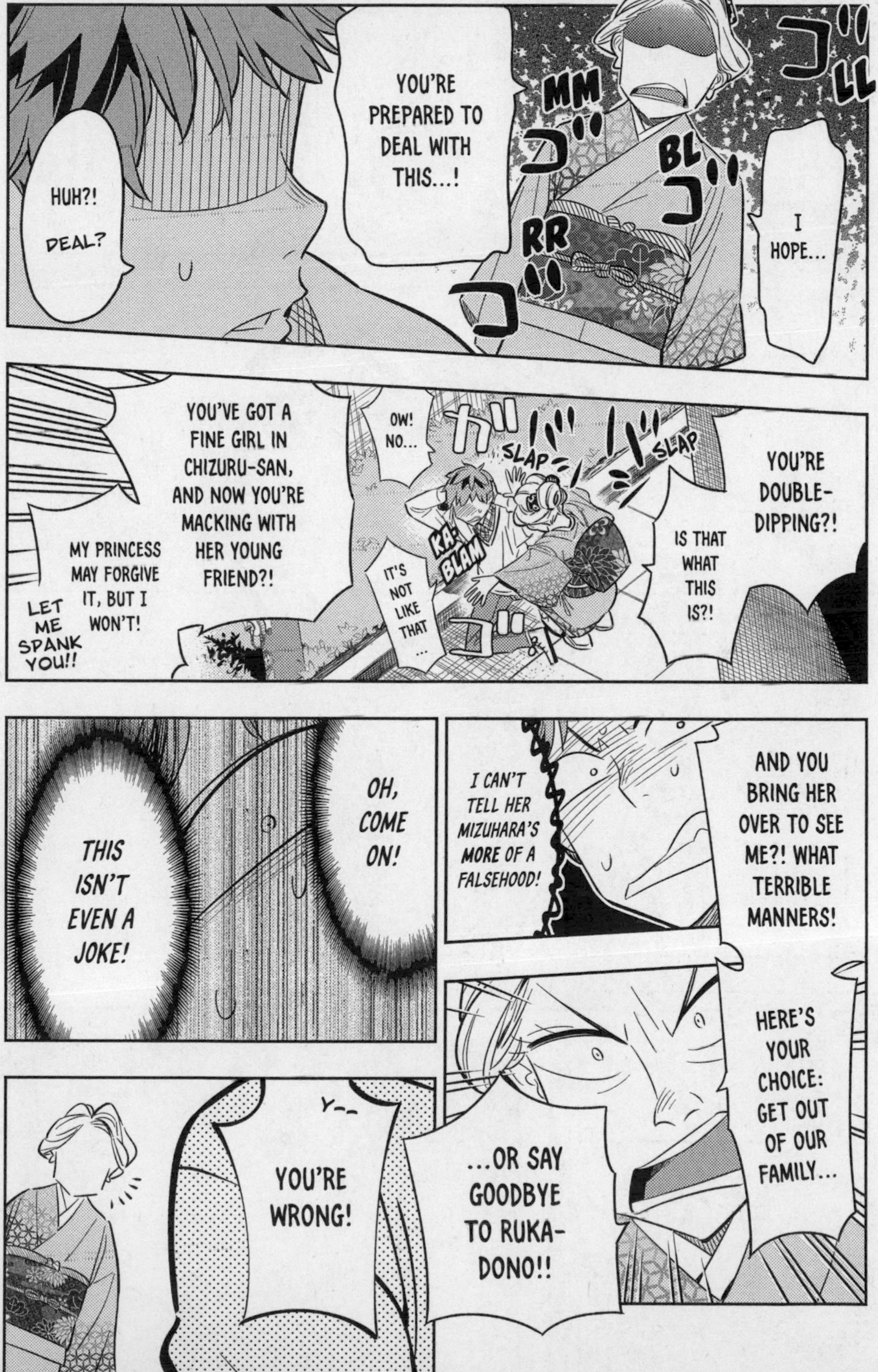
ゴLL
I HOPE...
YOU'RE PREPARED TO DEAL WITH THIS...!
MM ゴ
BL ゴ
RR ゴ
HUH?! DEAL?
YOU'RE DOUBLE-DIPPING?!
IS THAT WHAT THIS IS?!
SLAP
SLAP
OW! NO...
IT'S NOT LIKE THAT...
KA-BLAM
YOU'VE GOT A FINE GIRL IN CHIZURU-SAN, AND NOW YOU'RE MACKING WITH HER YOUNG FRIEND?!
MY PRINCESS MAY FORGIVE IT, BUT I WON'T!
LET ME SPANK YOU!!
AND YOU BRING HER OVER TO SEE ME?! WHAT TERRIBLE MANNERS!
I CAN'T TELL HER MIZUHARA'S MORE OF A FALSEHOOD!
OH, COME ON!
THIS ISN'T EVEN A JOKE!
HERE'S YOUR CHOICE: GET OUT OF OUR FAMILY...
...OR SAY GOODBYE TO RUKA-DONO!!
Y--
YOU'RE WRONG!

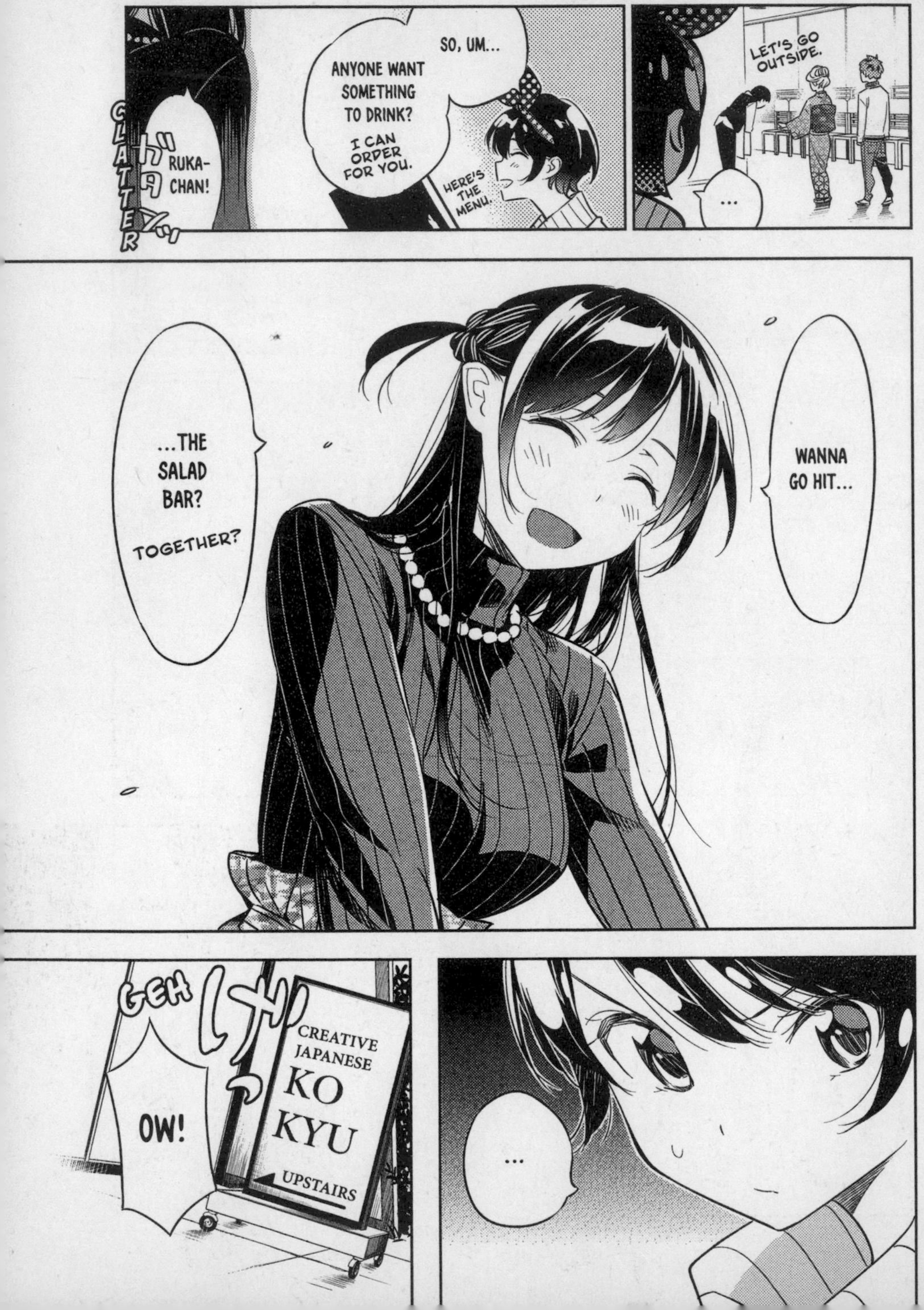
LET'S GO OUTSIDE.
...
SO, UM...
ANYONE WANT SOMETHING TO DRINK?
I CAN ORDER FOR YOU.
HERE'S THE MENU.
RUKA-CHAN!
CLATTER
WANNA GO HIT...
...THE SALAD BAR?
TOGETHER?
...
GEH
OW!
CREATIVE JAPANESE
KO KYU
UPSTAIRS

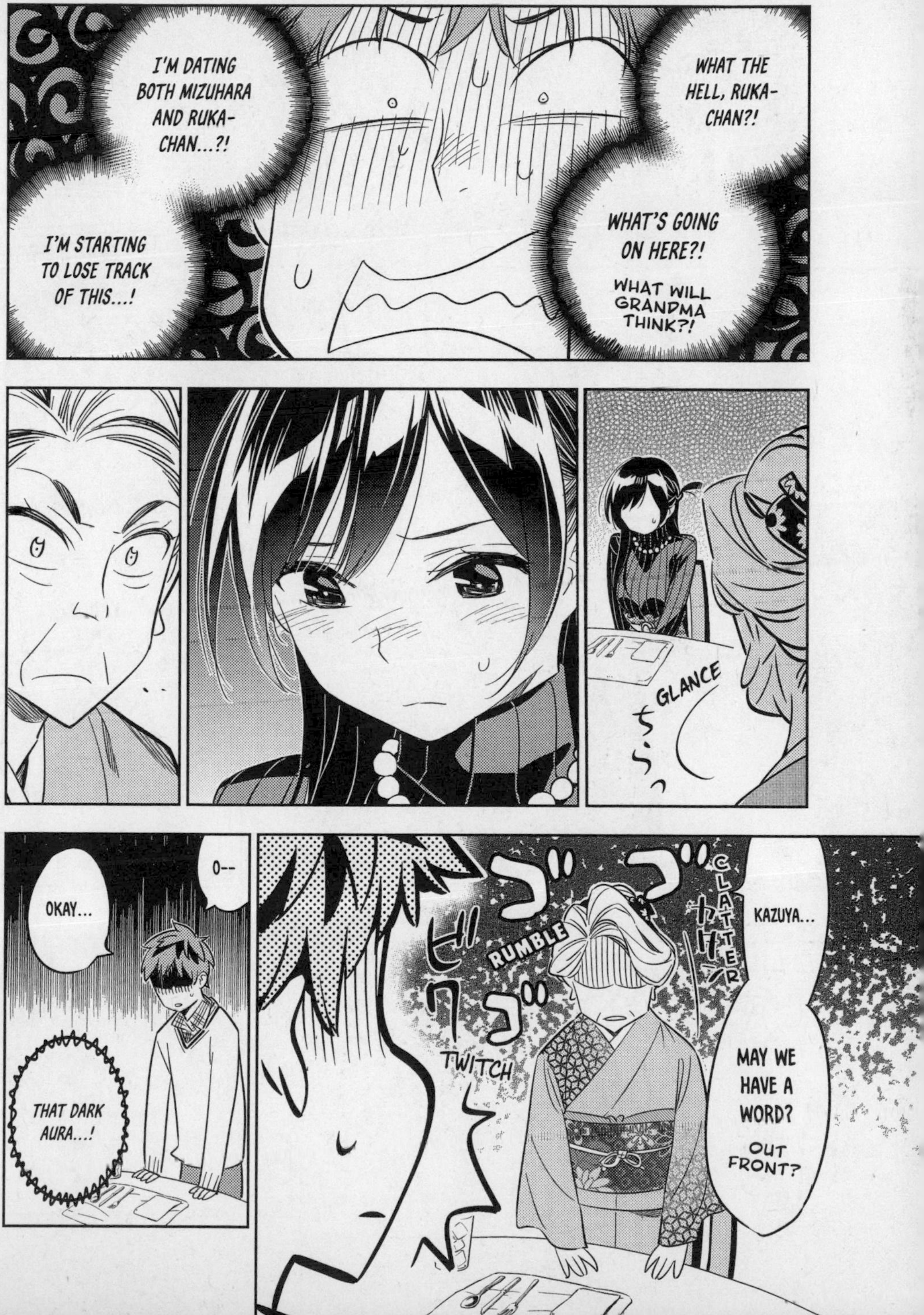
WHAT THE HELL, RUKA-CHAN?!
I'M DATING BOTH MIZUHARA AND RUKA-CHAN...?!
WHAT'S GOING ON HERE?!
WHAT WILL GRANDMA THINK?!
I'M STARTING TO LOSE TRACK OF THIS...!
GLANCE
KAZUYA...
MAY WE HAVE A WORD?
OUT FRONT?
CLATTER
RUMBLE
TWITCH
O--
OKAY...
THAT DARK AURA...!

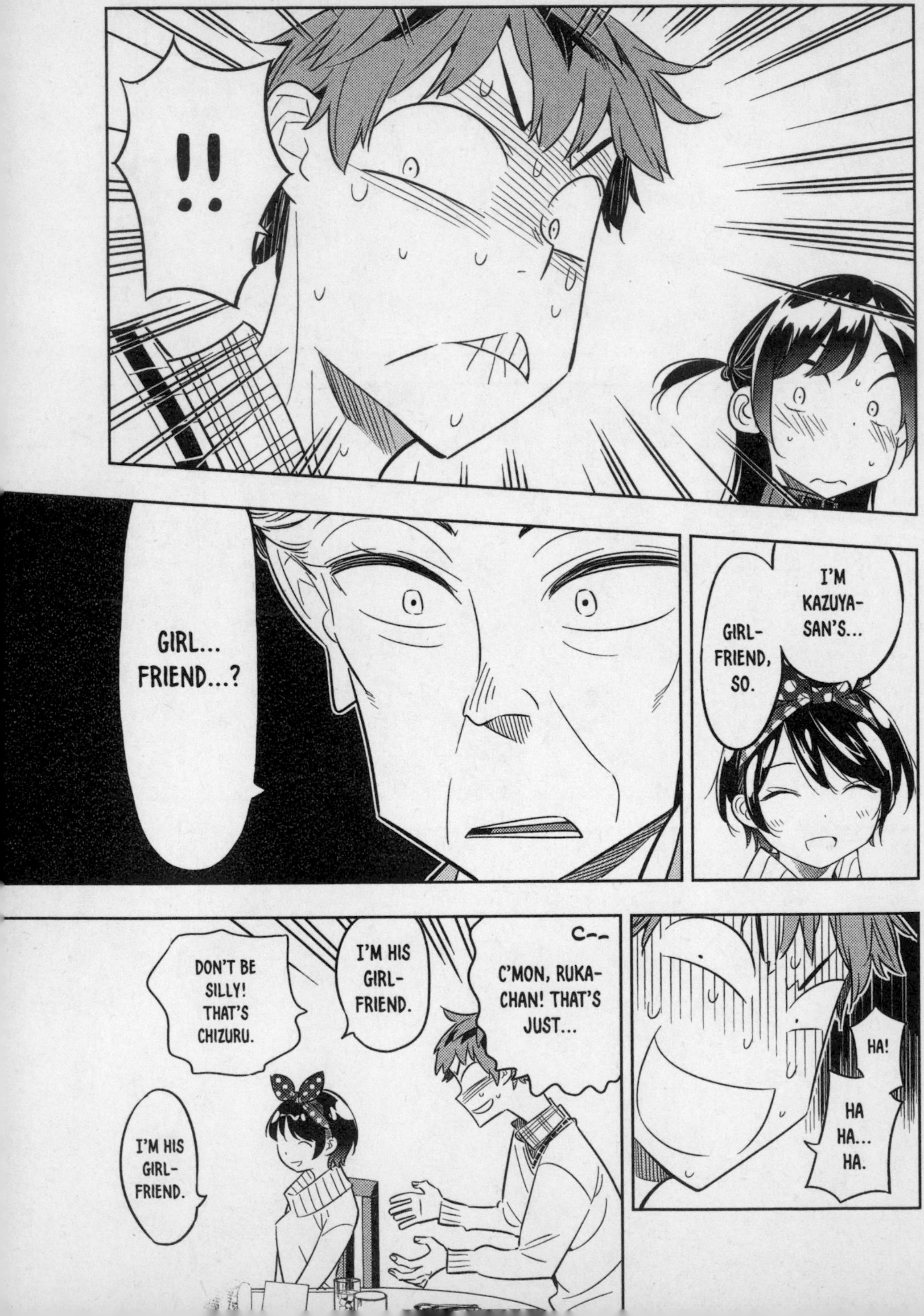
!!
I'M KAZUYA-SAN'S...
GIRL-FRIEND, SO.
GIRL... FRIEND...?
HA!
HA HA... HA.
C--
C'MON, RUKA-CHAN! THAT'S JUST...
I'M HIS GIRL-FRIEND.
DON'T BE SILLY! THAT'S CHIZURU.
I'M HIS GIRL-FRIEND.

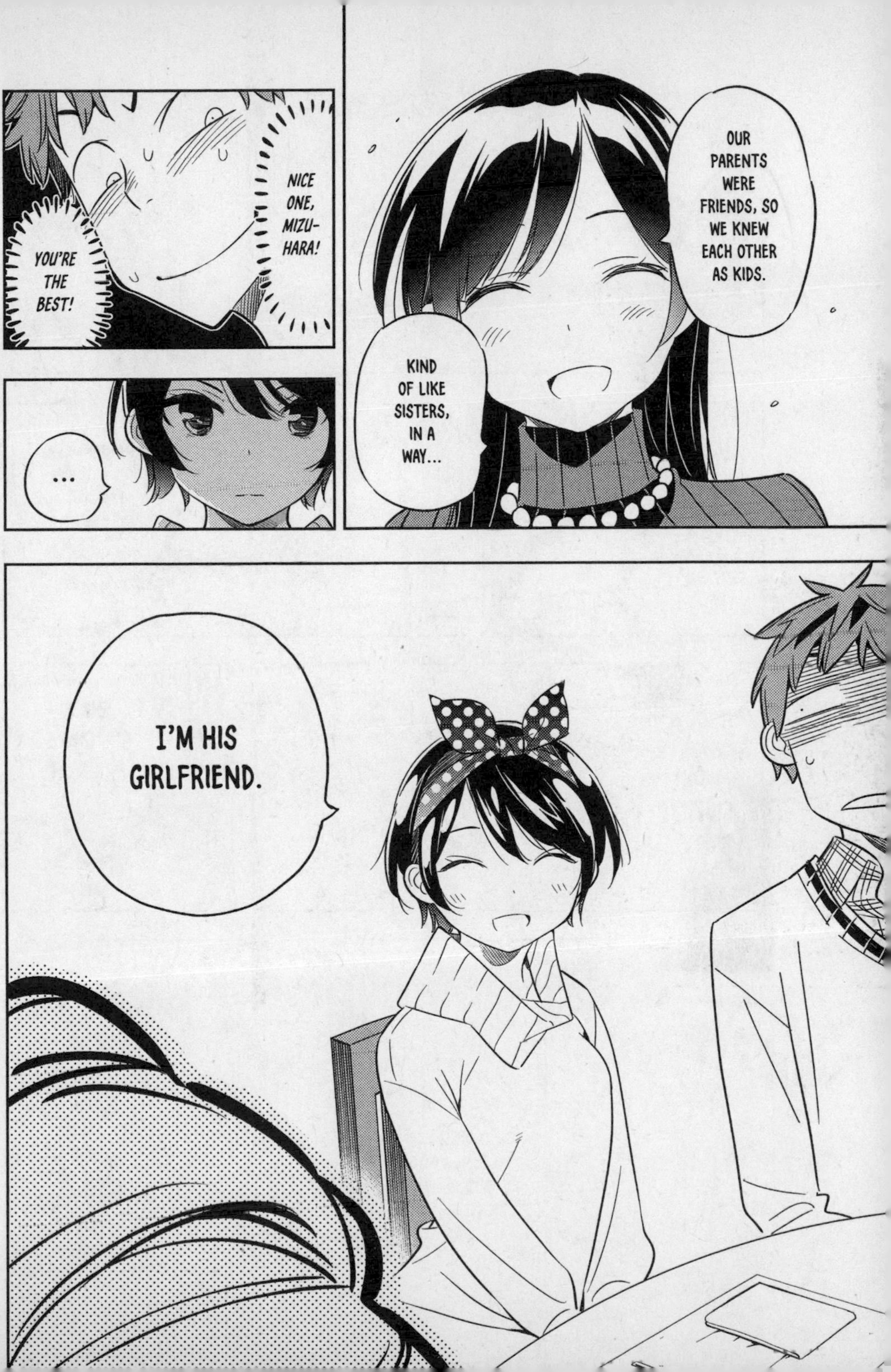
OUR PARENTS WERE FRIENDS, SO WE KNEW EACH OTHER AS KIDS.
KIND OF LIKE SISTERS, IN A WAY...
NICE ONE, MIZU-HARA!
YOU'RE THE BEST!
...
I'M HIS GIRLFRIEND.

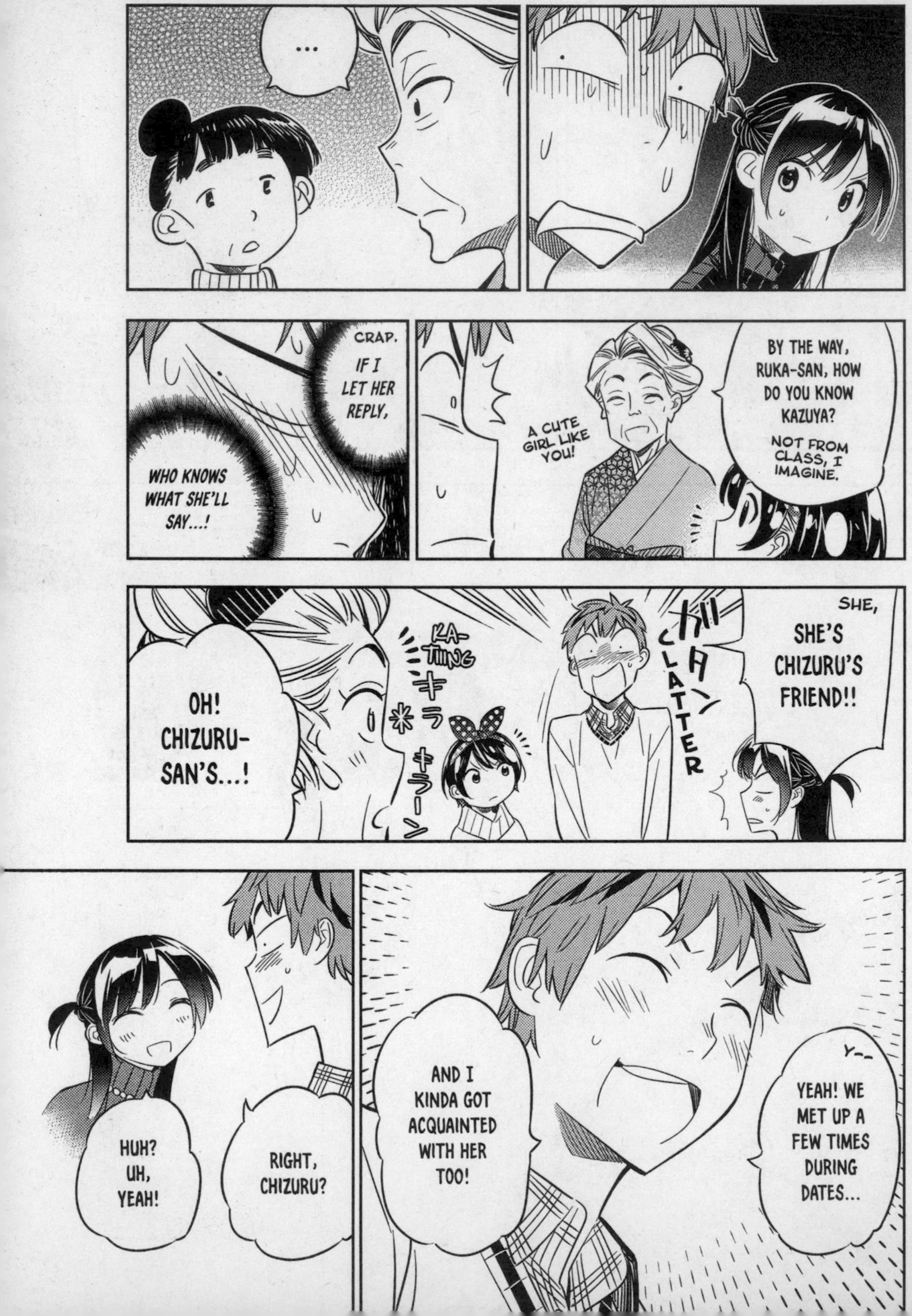
...
BY THE WAY, RUKA-SAN, HOW DO YOU KNOW KAZUYA?
NOT FROM CLASS, I IMAGINE.
A CUTE GIRL LIKE YOU!
CRAP.
IF I LET HER REPLY,
WHO KNOWS WHAT SHE'LL SAY...!
SHE,
SHE'S CHIZURU'S FRIEND!!
ガタン
CLATTER
KA-TIING
キラキラーン
OH! CHIZURU-SAN'S...!
Y--
YEAH! WE MET UP A FEW TIMES DURING DATES...
AND I KINDA GOT ACQUAINTED WITH HER TOO!
RIGHT, CHIZURU?
HUH? UH, YEAH!

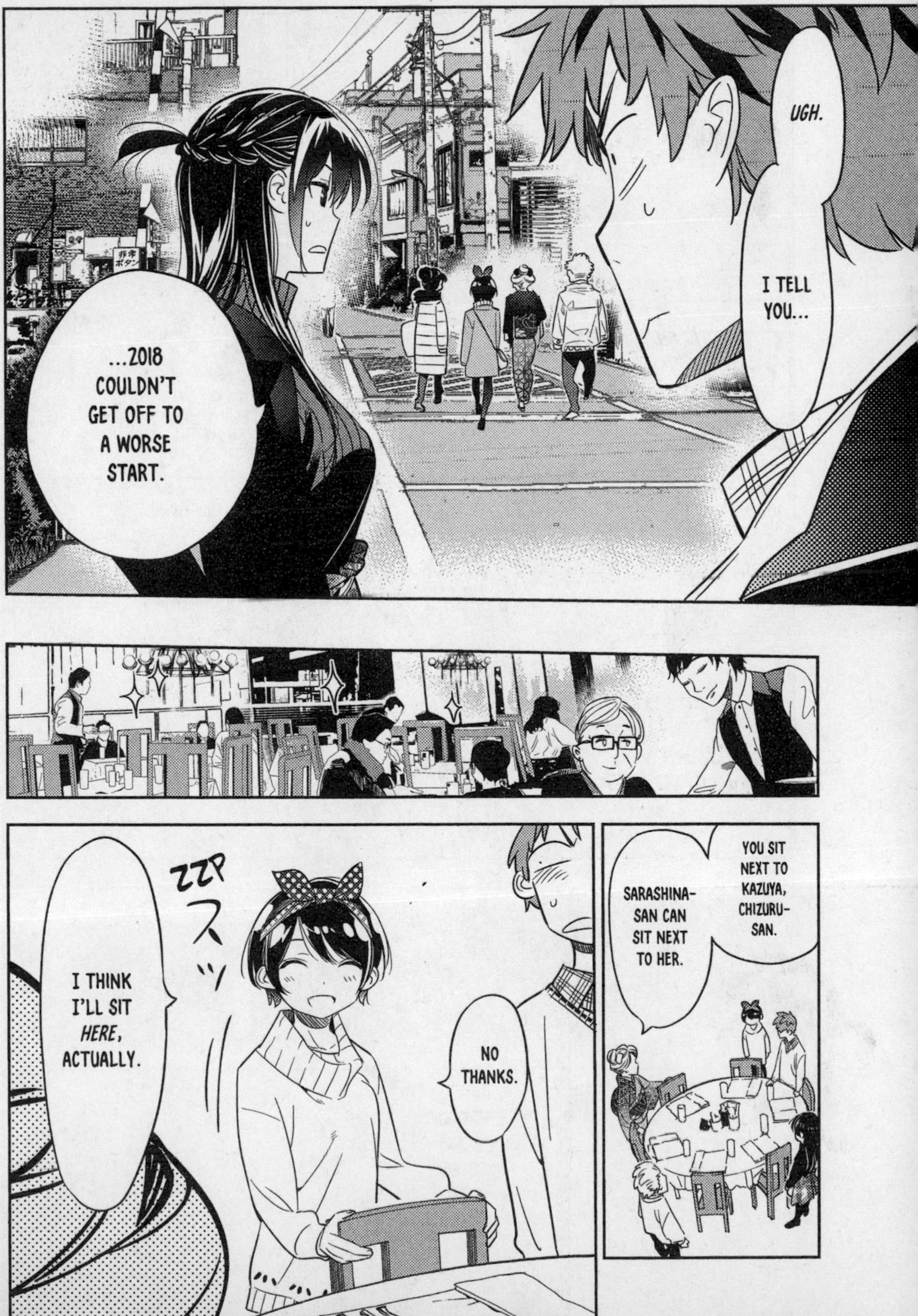
UGH.
I TELL YOU...
...2018 COULDN'T GET OFF TO A WORSE START.
YOU SIT NEXT TO KAZUYA, CHIZURU-SAN.
SARASHINA-SAN CAN SIT NEXT TO HER.
NO THANKS.
ZZP
スッ
I THINK I'LL SIT *HERE*, ACTUALLY.

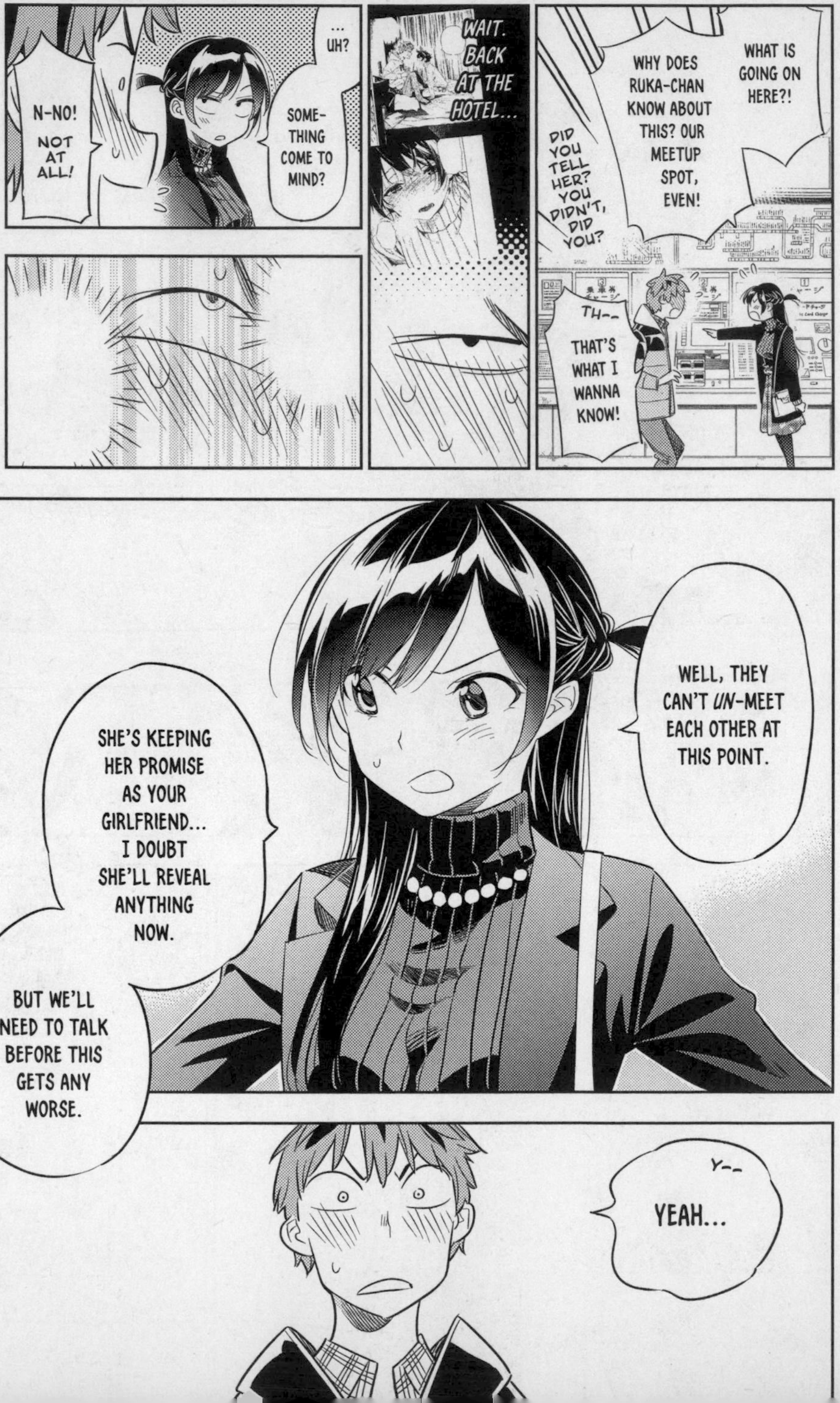
WHAT IS GOING ON HERE?!
WHY DOES RUKA-CHAN KNOW ABOUT THIS? OUR MEETUP SPOT, EVEN!
DID YOU TELL HER? YOU DIDN'T, DID YOU?
TH-- THAT'S WHAT I WANNA KNOW!
WAIT. BACK AT THE HOTEL...
... UH?
SOME-THING COME TO MIND?
N-NO! NOT AT ALL!
WELL, THEY CAN'T *UN*-MEET EACH OTHER AT THIS POINT.
SHE'S KEEPING HER PROMISE AS YOUR GIRLFRIEND... I DOUBT SHE'LL REVEAL ANYTHING NOW.
BUT WE'LL NEED TO TALK BEFORE THIS GETS ANY WORSE.
Y-- YEAH...

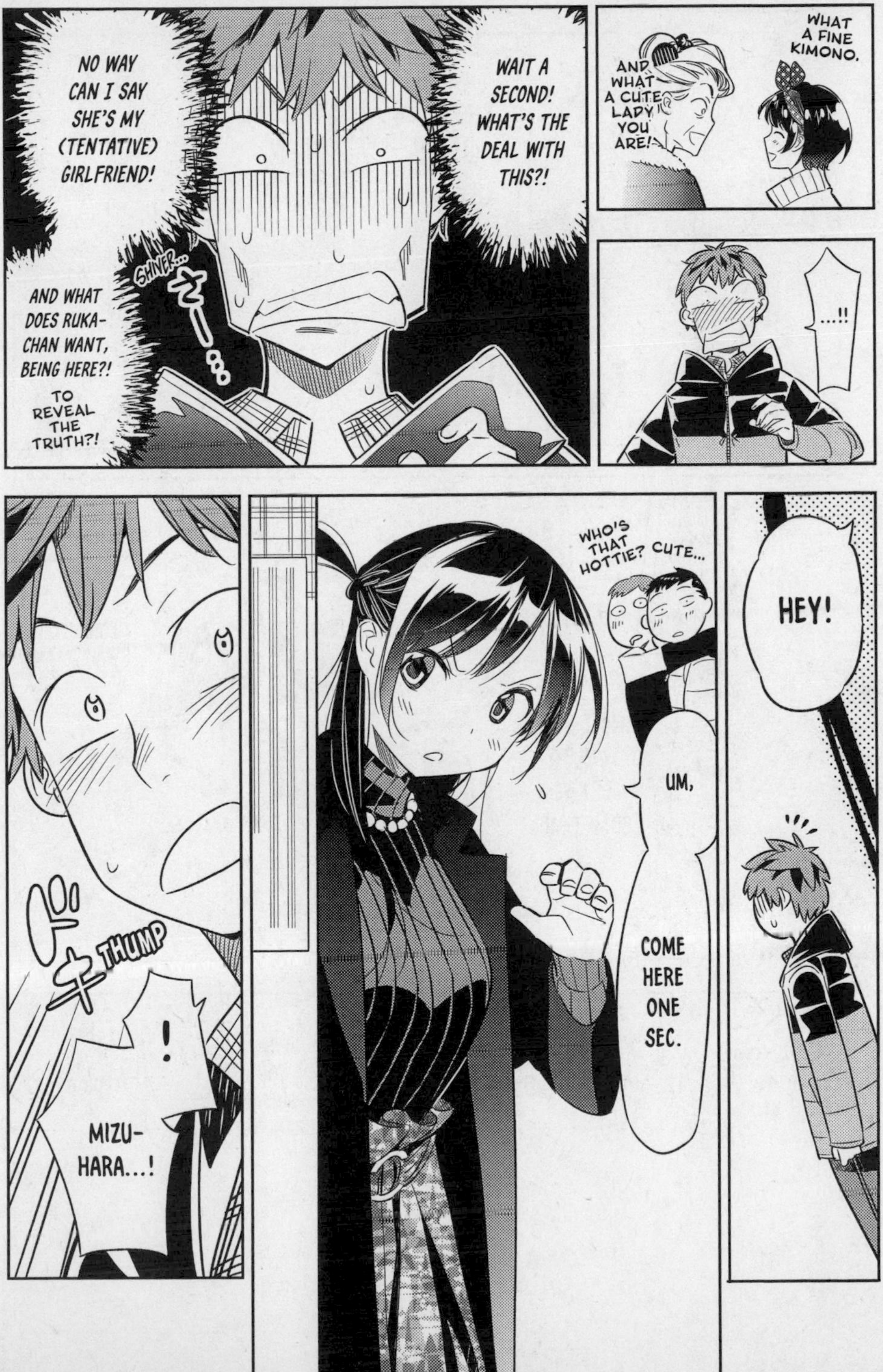
WHAT A FINE KIMONO.
AND WHAT A CUTE LADY YOU ARE!
...!!
WAIT A SECOND! WHAT'S THE DEAL WITH THIS?!
NO WAY CAN I SAY SHE'S MY (TENTATIVE) GIRLFRIEND!
SHIVER...
AND WHAT DOES RUKA-CHAN WANT, BEING HERE?!
TO REVEAL THE TRUTH?!
HEY!
WHO'S THAT HOTTIE? CUTE...
UM,
COME HERE ONE SEC.
THUMP
!
MIZU-HARA...!

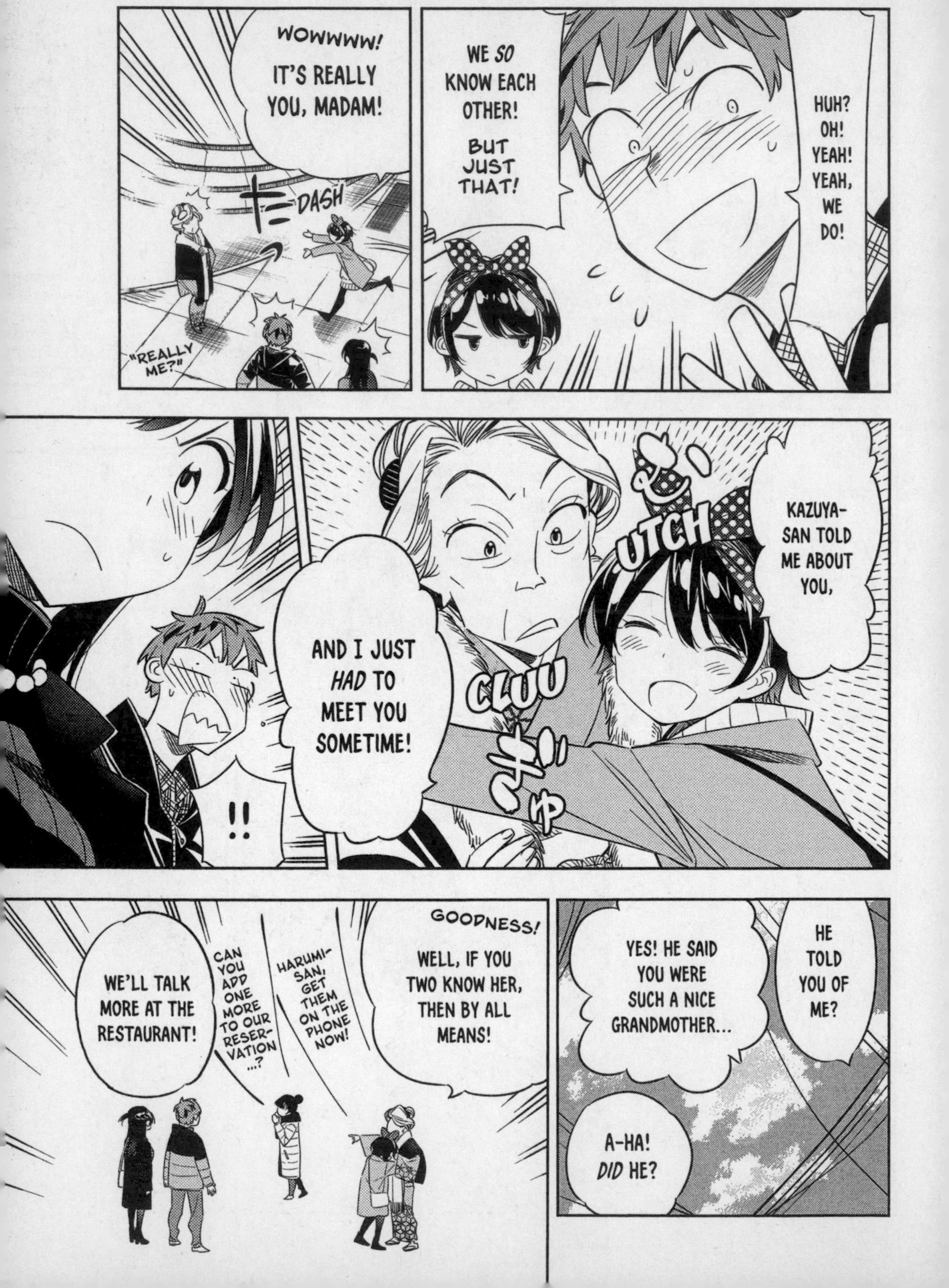
HUH? OH! YEAH! YEAH, WE DO!
WE *SO* KNOW EACH OTHER!
BUT JUST THAT!
WOWWWW!
IT'S REALLY YOU, MADAM!
DASH
"REALLY ME?"
KAZUYA-SAN TOLD ME ABOUT YOU,
UTCH
CLUU
ぎゅ
AND I JUST *HAD* TO MEET YOU SOMETIME!
!!
HE TOLD YOU OF ME?
YES! HE SAID YOU WERE SUCH A NICE GRANDMOTHER...
A-HA! *DID* HE?
GOODNESS!
WELL, IF YOU TWO KNOW HER, THEN BY ALL MEANS!
HARUMI-SAN, GET THEM ON THE PHONE NOW!
CAN YOU ADD ONE MORE TO OUR RESERVATION...?
WE'LL TALK MORE AT THE RESTAURANT!

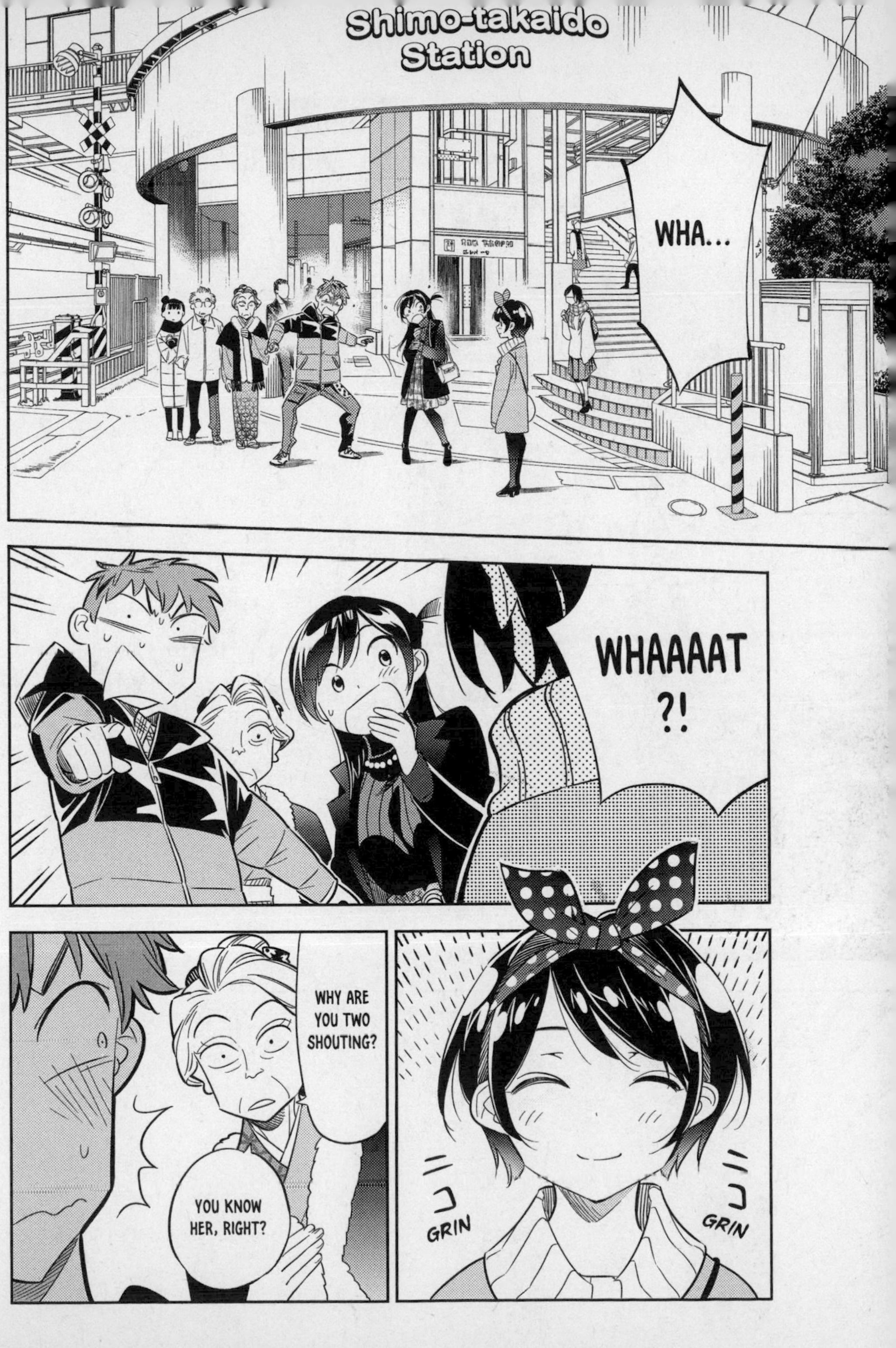
Shimo-takaido Station
WHA...
WHAAAAT ?!
GRIN GRIN
WHY ARE YOU TWO SHOUTING?
YOU KNOW HER, RIGHT?

RATING 34
MY TWO GIRLFRIENDS (3)

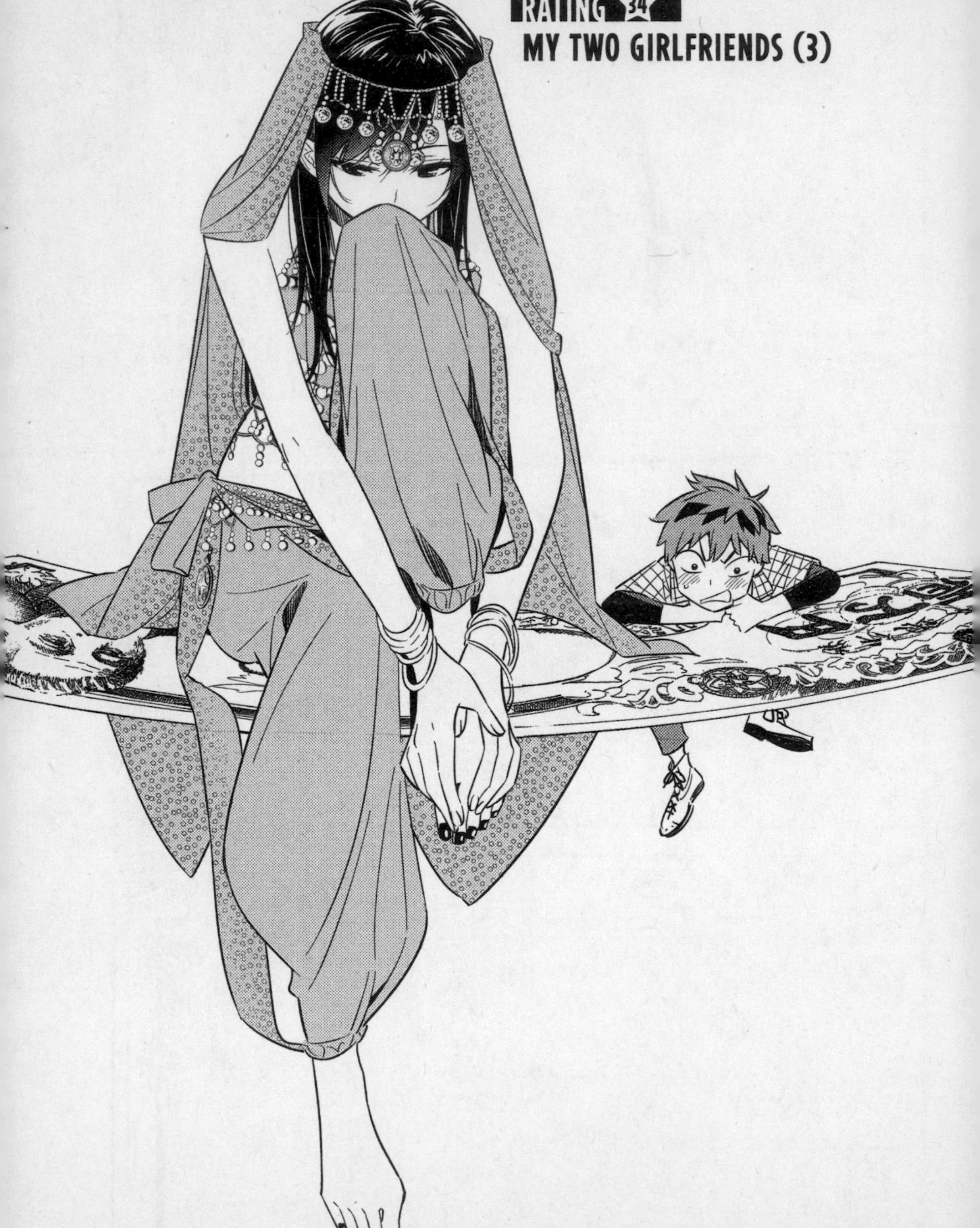

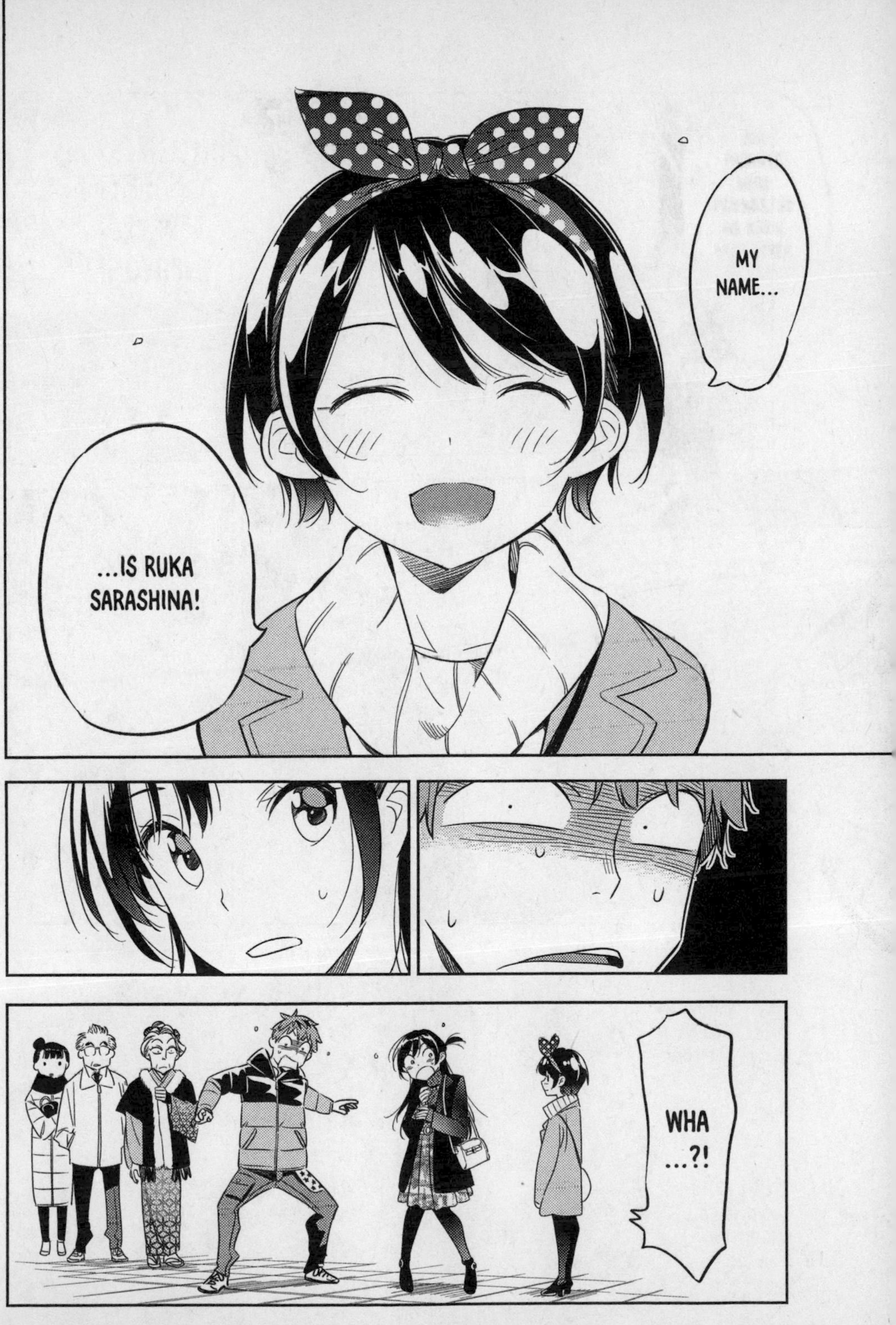
MY NAME...
...IS RUKA SARASHINA!
WHA ...?!

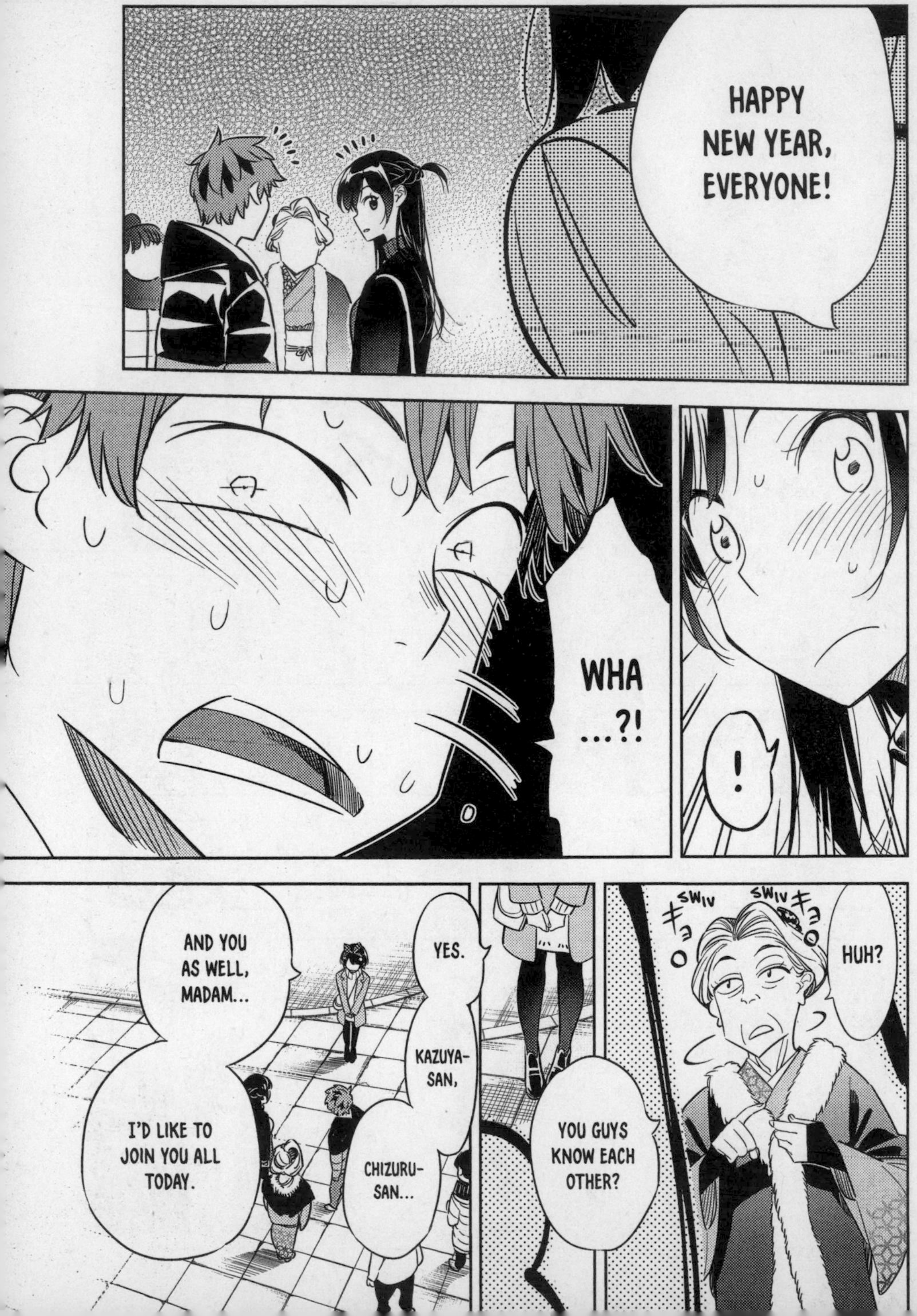
HAPPY NEW YEAR, EVERYONE!
!
WHA ...?!
SWIV
SWIV
HUH?
YOU GUYS KNOW EACH OTHER?
YES.
KAZUYA-SAN,
CHIZURU-SAN...
AND YOU AS WELL, MADAM...
I'D LIKE TO JOIN YOU ALL TODAY.

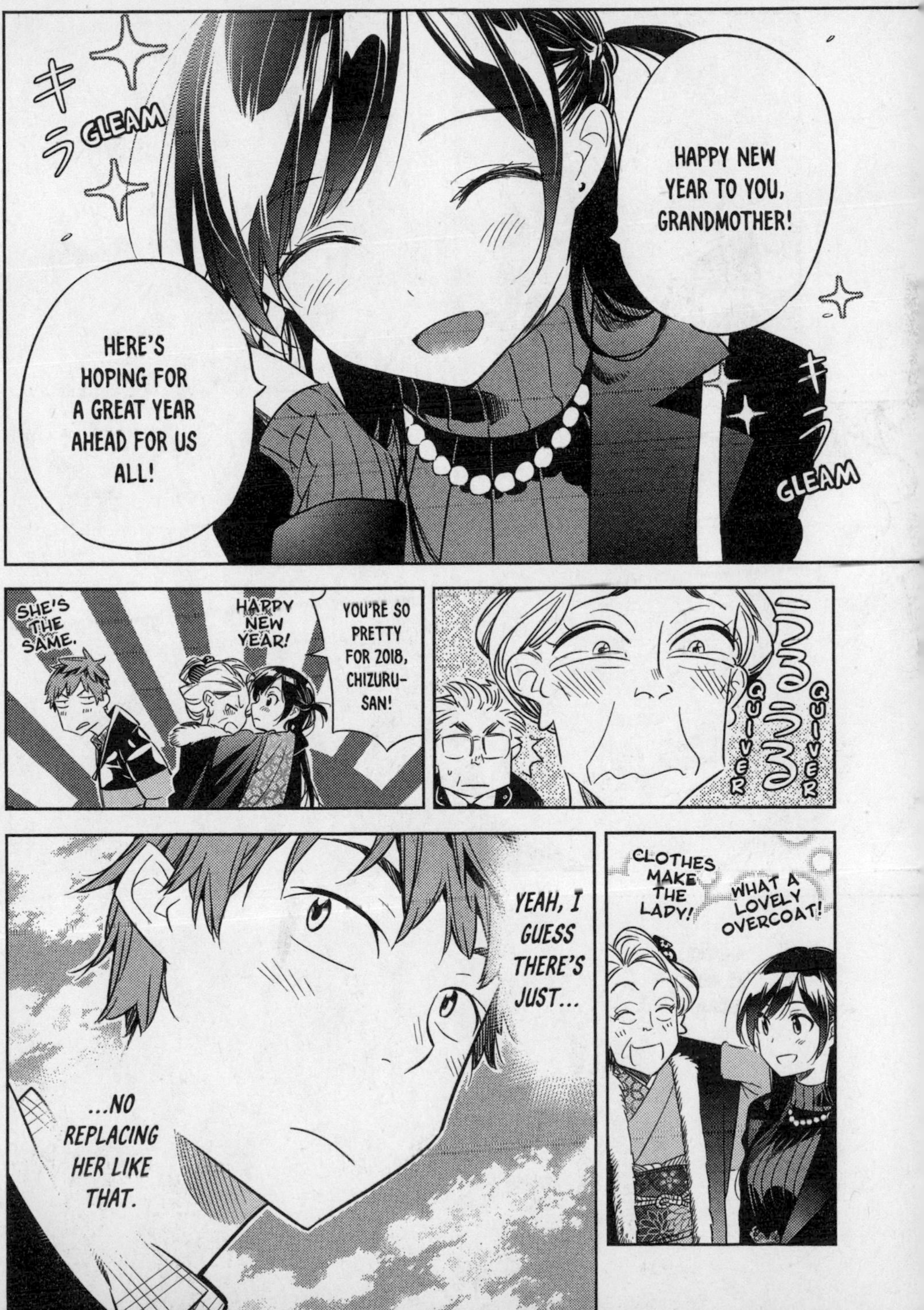
HAPPY NEW YEAR TO YOU, GRANDMOTHER!
キラ GLEAM
キラ GLEAM
HERE'S HOPING FOR A GREAT YEAR AHEAD FOR US ALL!
うるうる QUIVER QUIVER
YOU'RE SO PRETTY FOR 2018, CHIZURU-SAN!
HAPPY NEW YEAR!
SHE'S THE SAME.
WHAT A LOVELY OVERCOAT!
CLOTHES MAKE THE LADY!
YEAH, I GUESS THERE'S JUST...
...NO REPLACING HER LIKE THAT.

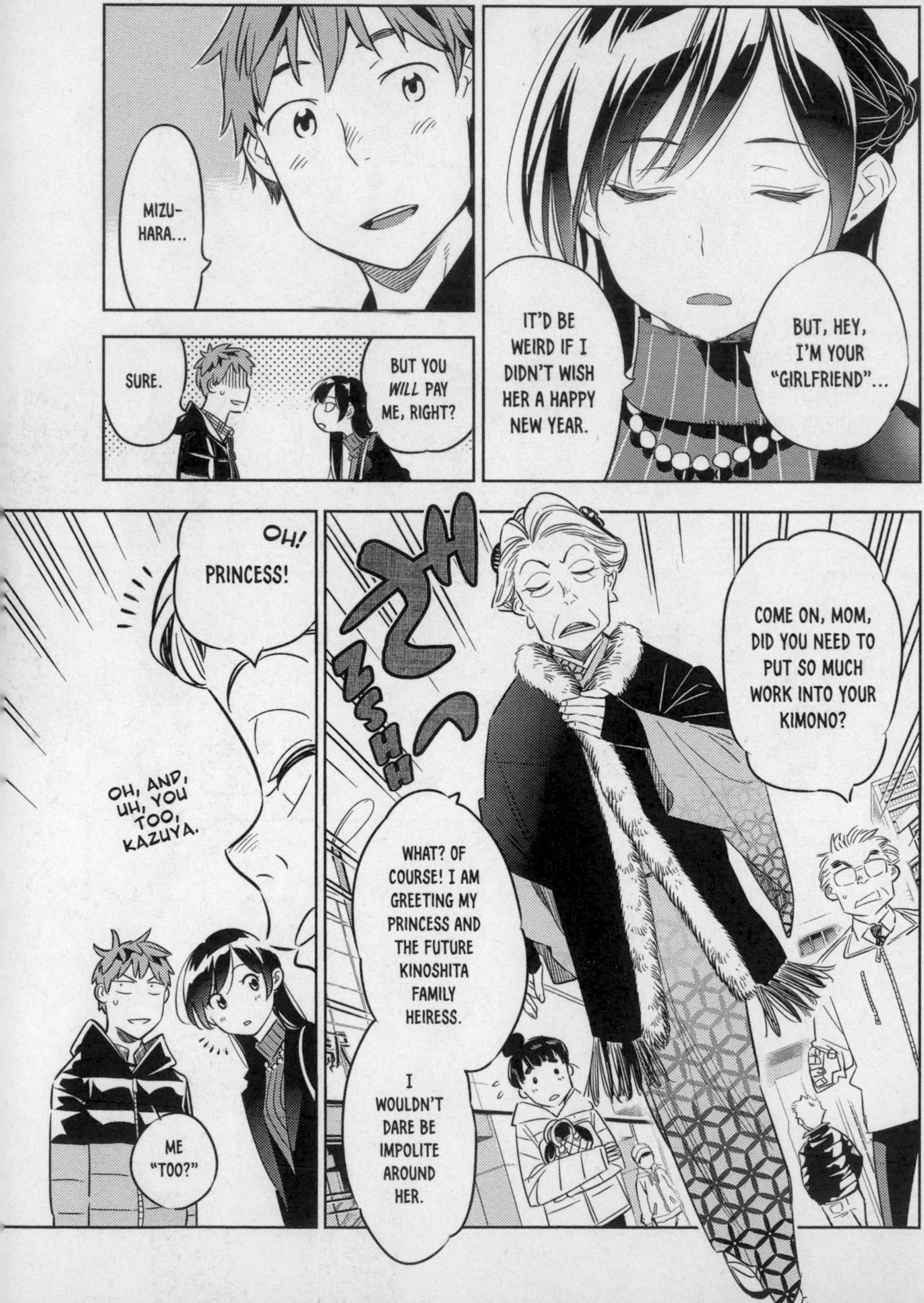
BUT, HEY, I'M YOUR "GIRLFRIEND"...
IT'D BE WEIRD IF I DIDN'T WISH HER A HAPPY NEW YEAR.
MIZU-HARA...
BUT YOU *WILL* PAY ME, RIGHT?
SURE.
ZSHH
COME ON, MOM, DID YOU NEED TO PUT SO MUCH WORK INTO YOUR KIMONO?
WHAT? OF COURSE! I AM GREETING MY PRINCESS AND THE FUTURE KINOSHITA FAMILY HEIRESS.
I WOULDN'T DARE BE IMPOLITE AROUND HER.
OH! PRINCESS!
OH, AND, UH, YOU TOO, KAZUYA.
ME "TOO?"

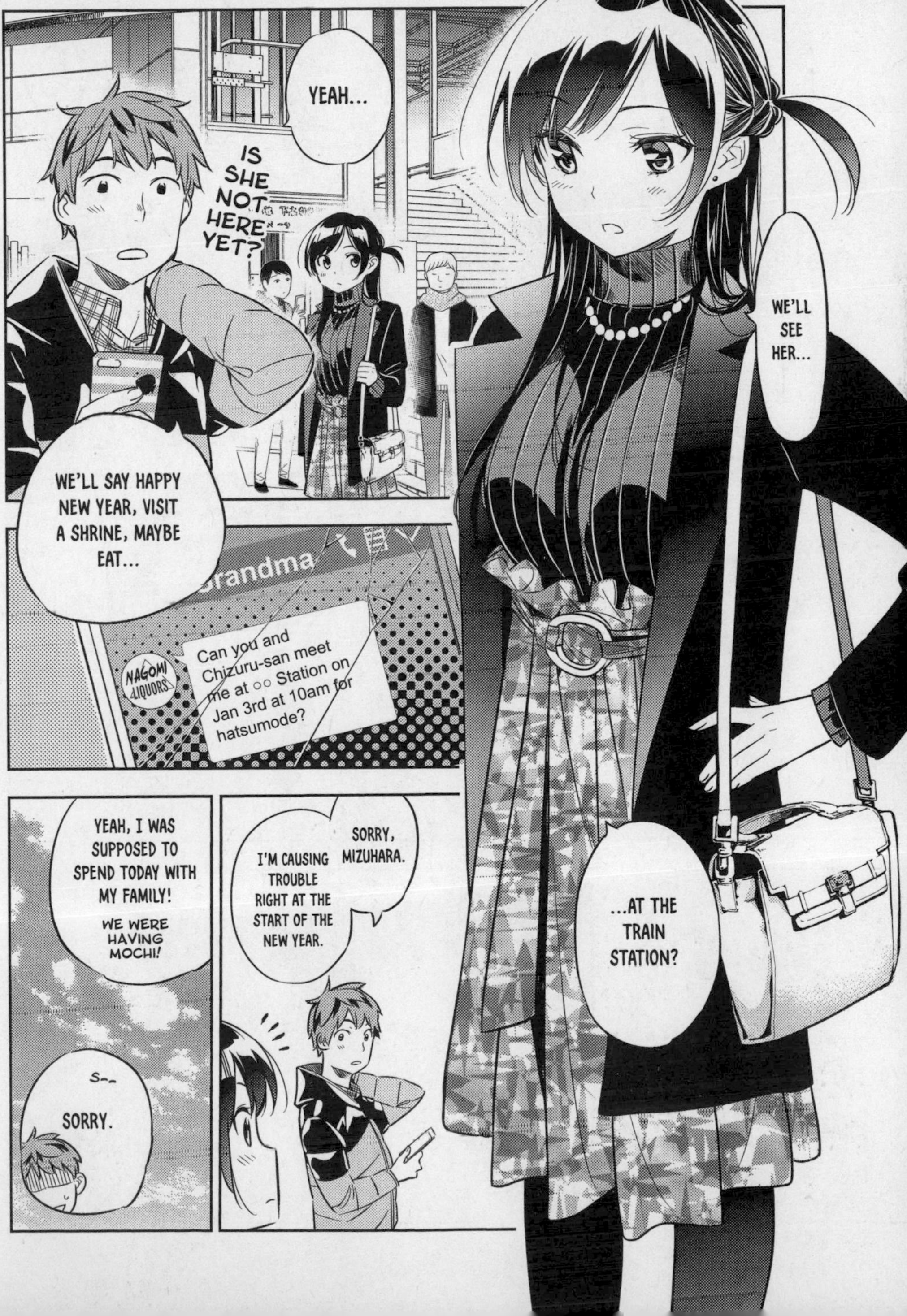
WE'LL SEE HER...
...AT THE TRAIN STATION?
YEAH...
IS SHE NOT HERE YET?
WE'LL SAY HAPPY NEW YEAR, VISIT A SHRINE, MAYBE EAT...
Grandma
NAGOMI LIQUORS
Can you and Chizuru-san meet me at ○○ Station on Jan 3rd at 10am for hatsumode?
SORRY, MIZUHARA.
I'M CAUSING TROUBLE RIGHT AT THE START OF THE NEW YEAR.
YEAH, I WAS SUPPOSED TO SPEND TODAY WITH MY FAMILY!
WE WERE HAVING MOCHI!
S--
SORRY.

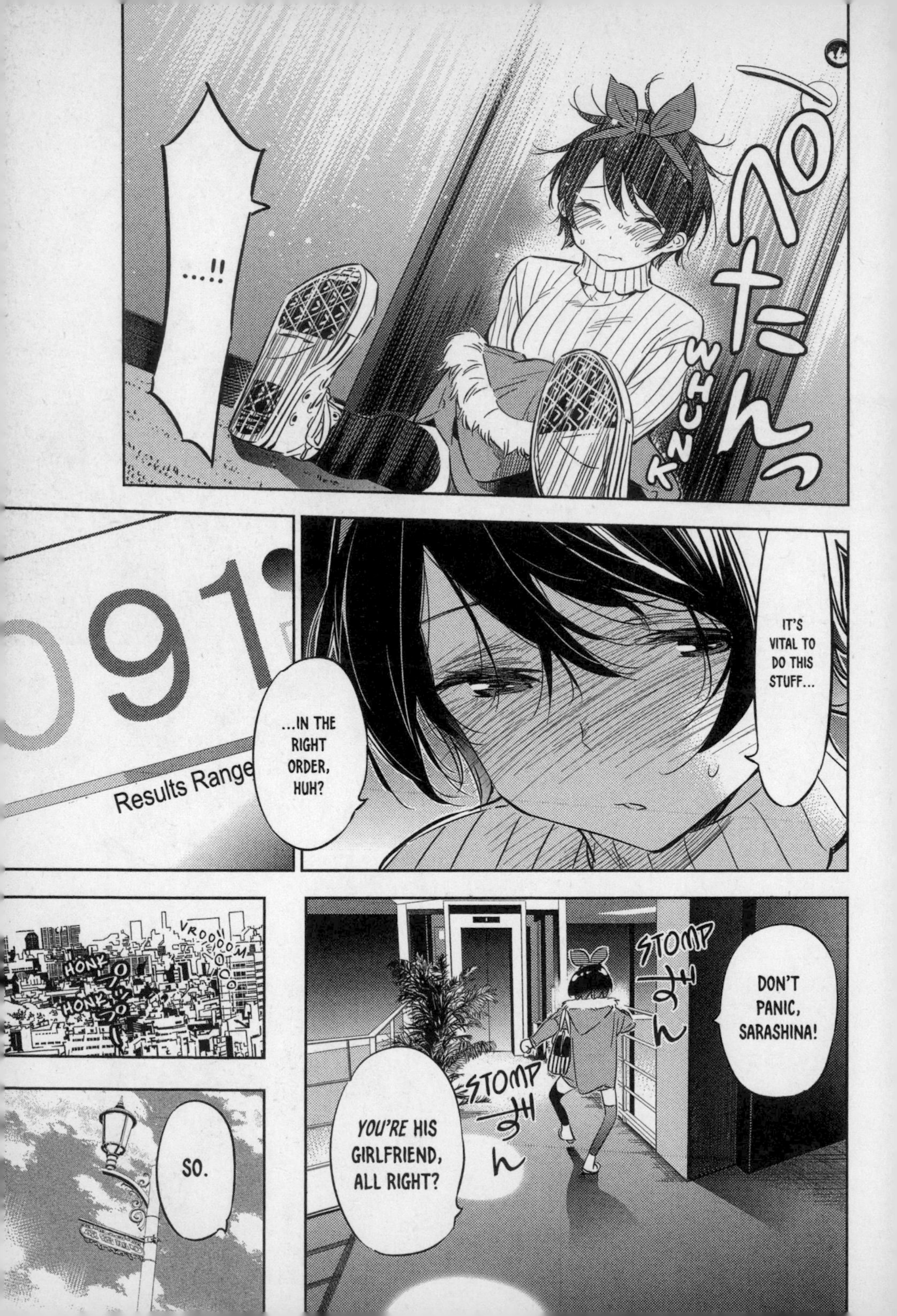

へたんっ
WHUNK
...!!
IT'S VITAL TO DO THIS STUFF...
...IN THE RIGHT ORDER, HUH?
091
Results Range
STOMP
ずん
DON'T PANIC, SARASHINA!
STOMP
ずん
YOU'RE HIS GIRLFRIEND, ALL RIGHT?
VROOOOM
HONK
HONK
SO.

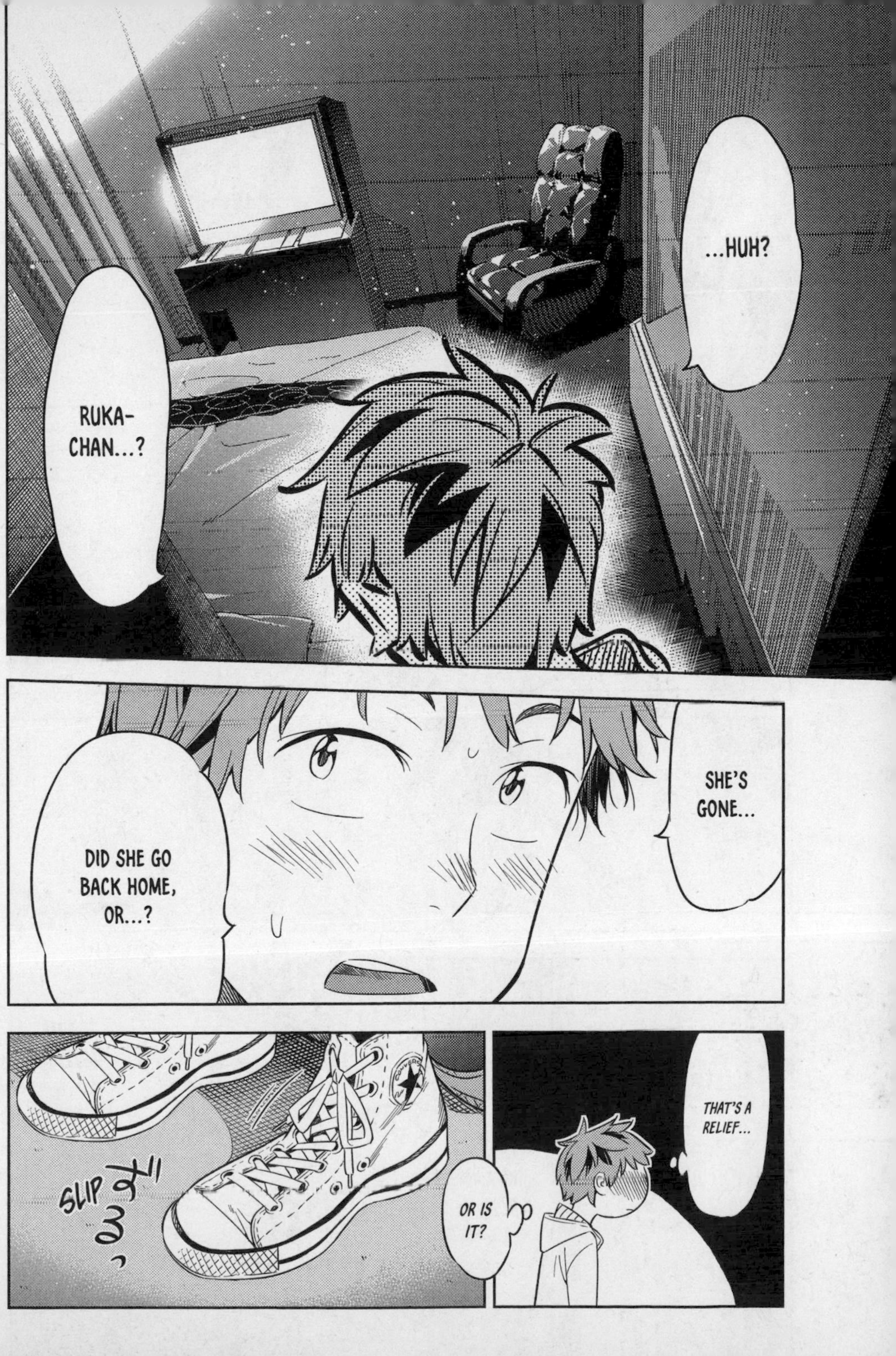
...HUH?
RUKA-CHAN...?
SHE'S GONE...
DID SHE GO BACK HOME, OR...?
THAT'S A RELIEF...
OR IS IT?
SLIP

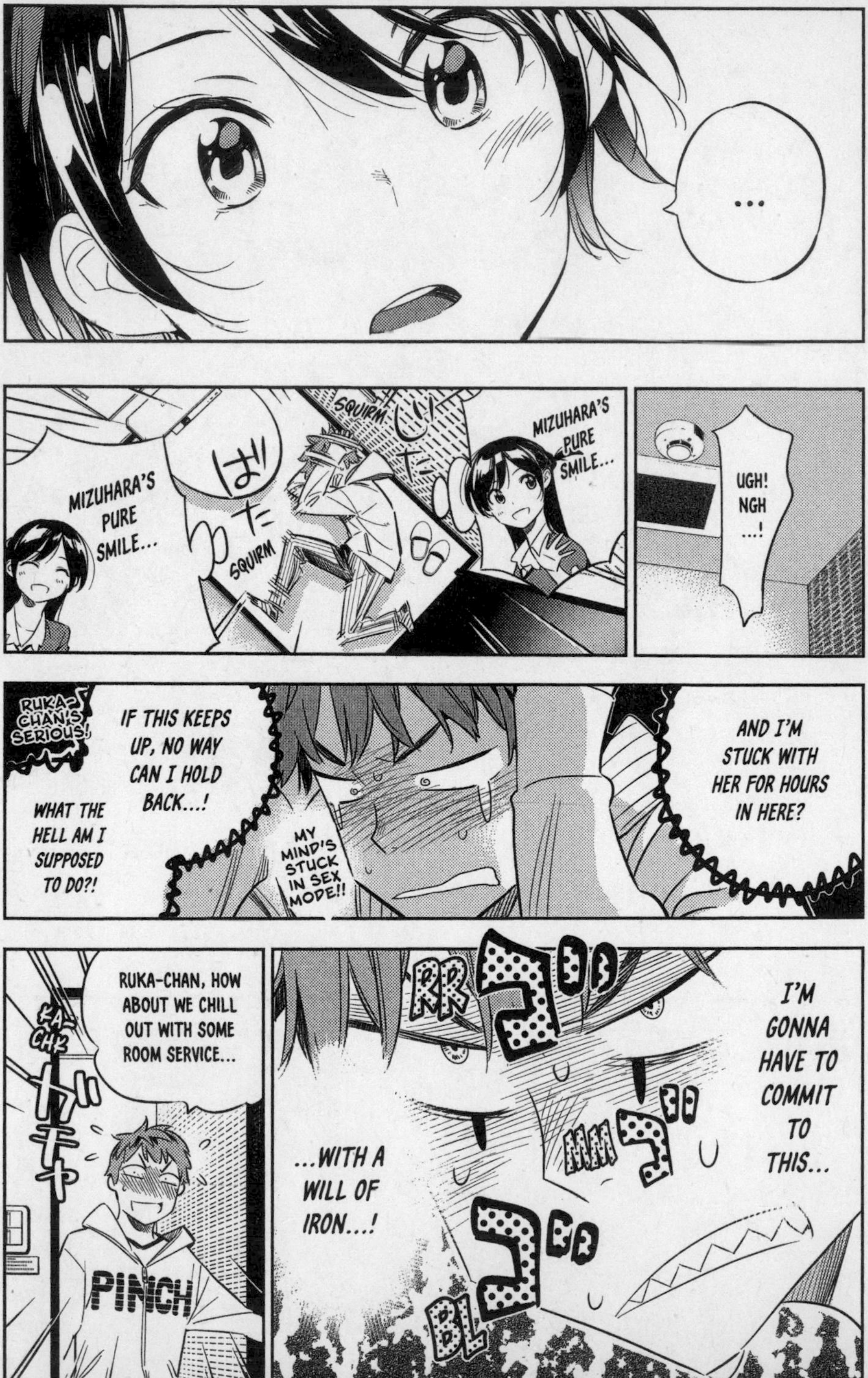
...
UGH! NGH ...!
MIZUHARA'S PURE SMILE...
SQUIRM
SQUIRM
MIZUHARA'S PURE SMILE...
AND I'M STUCK WITH HER FOR HOURS IN HERE?
MY MIND'S STUCK IN SEX MODE!!
IF THIS KEEPS UP, NO WAY CAN I HOLD BACK...!
RUKA-CHAN'S SERIOUS!
WHAT THE HELL AM I SUPPOSED TO DO?!
I'M GONNA HAVE TO COMMIT TO THIS...
RR
MM
...WITH A WILL OF IRON...!
DL
RUKA-CHAN, HOW ABOUT WE CHILL OUT WITH SOME ROOM SERVICE...
KA-CHK
PINCH

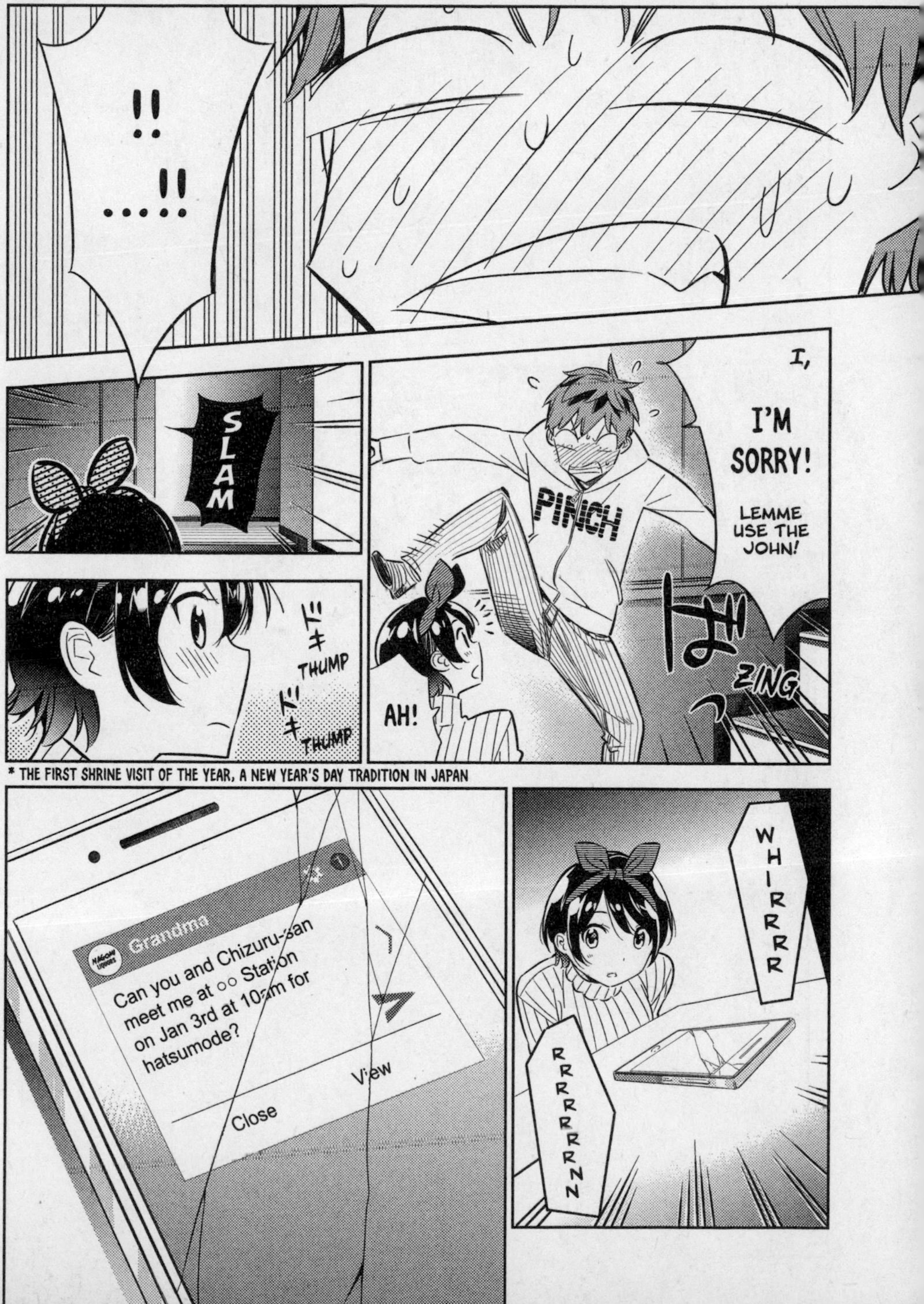
!!
...!!
I,
I'M SORRY!
LEMME USE THE JOHN!
ぱっ
ZING
AH!
SLAM
ドキ
THUMP
ドキ
THUMP
WHIRRR
RRRRRRN
Grandma
Can you and Chizuru-san meet me at ○○ Station on Jan 3rd at 10am for hatsumode?
View
Close

* THE FIRST SHRINE VISIT OF THE YEAR, A NEW YEAR'S DAY TRADITION IN JAPAN

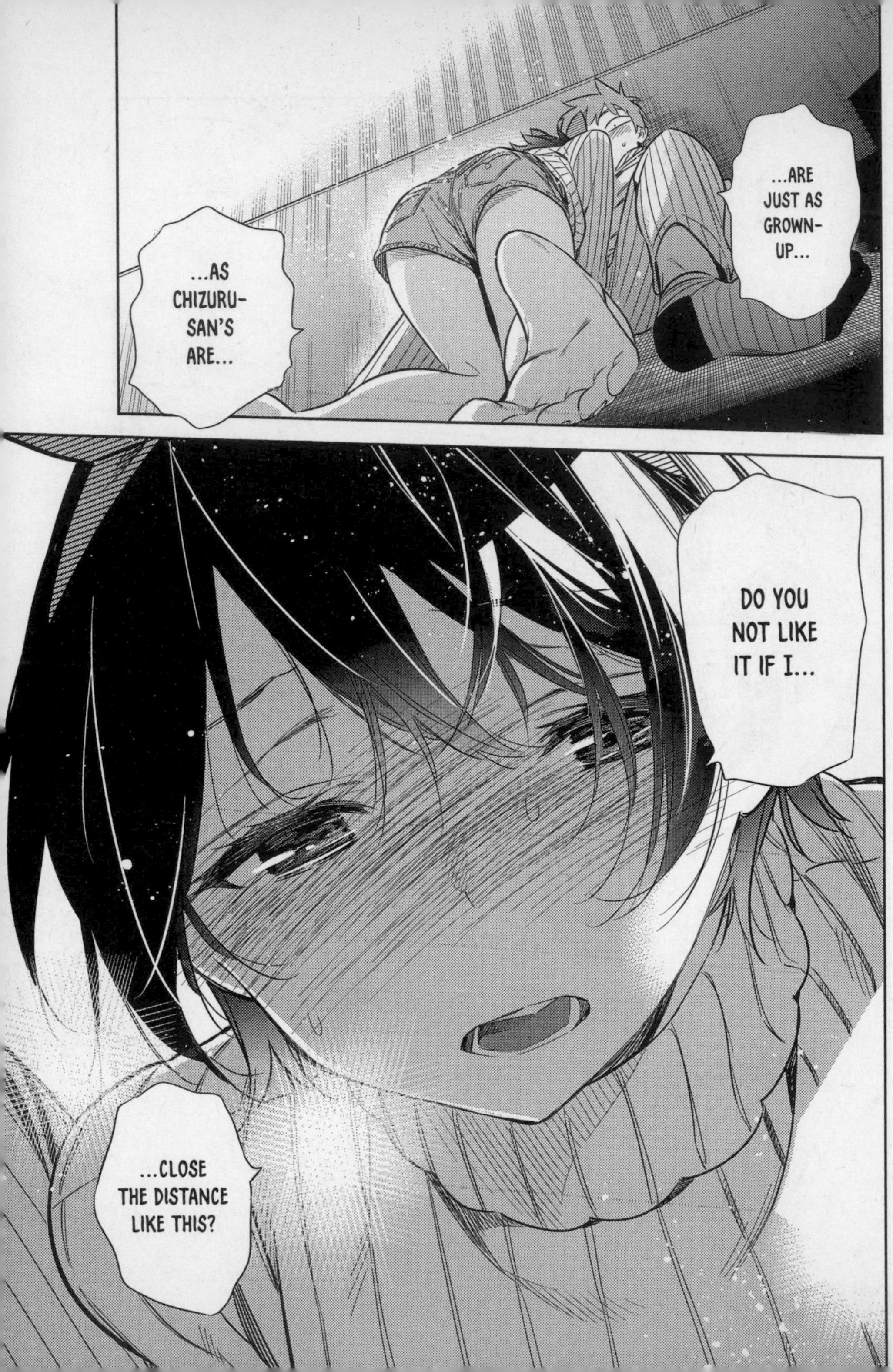
...ARE JUST AS GROWN-UP...
...AS CHIZURU-SAN'S ARE...
DO YOU NOT LIKE IT IF I...
...CLOSE THE DISTANCE LIKE THIS?

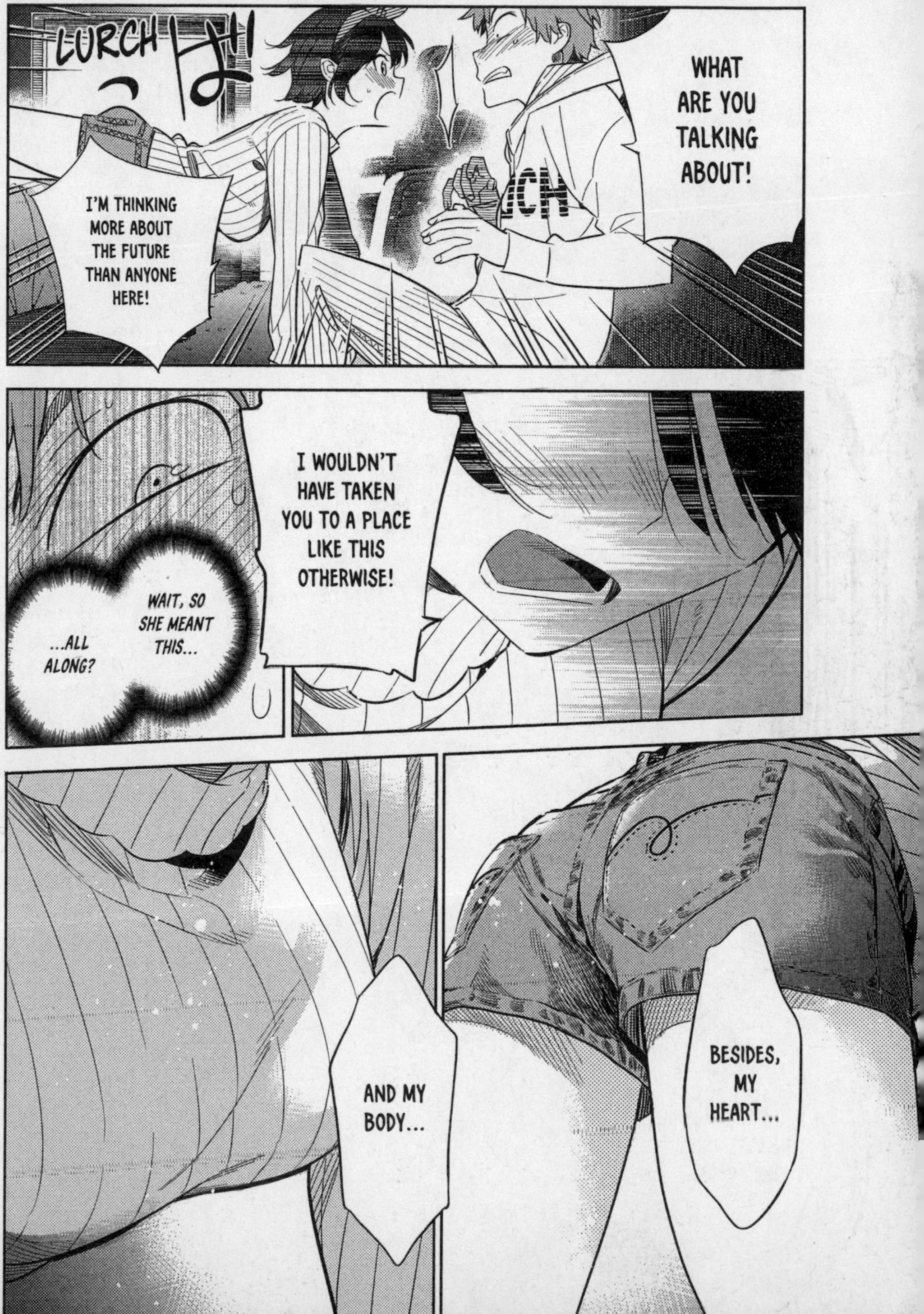
WHAT ARE YOU TALKING ABOUT!
LURCH
I'M THINKING MORE ABOUT THE FUTURE THAN ANYONE HERE!
I WOULDN'T HAVE TAKEN YOU TO A PLACE LIKE THIS OTHERWISE!
WAIT, SO SHE MEANT THIS...
...ALL ALONG?
BESIDES, MY HEART...
AND MY BODY...

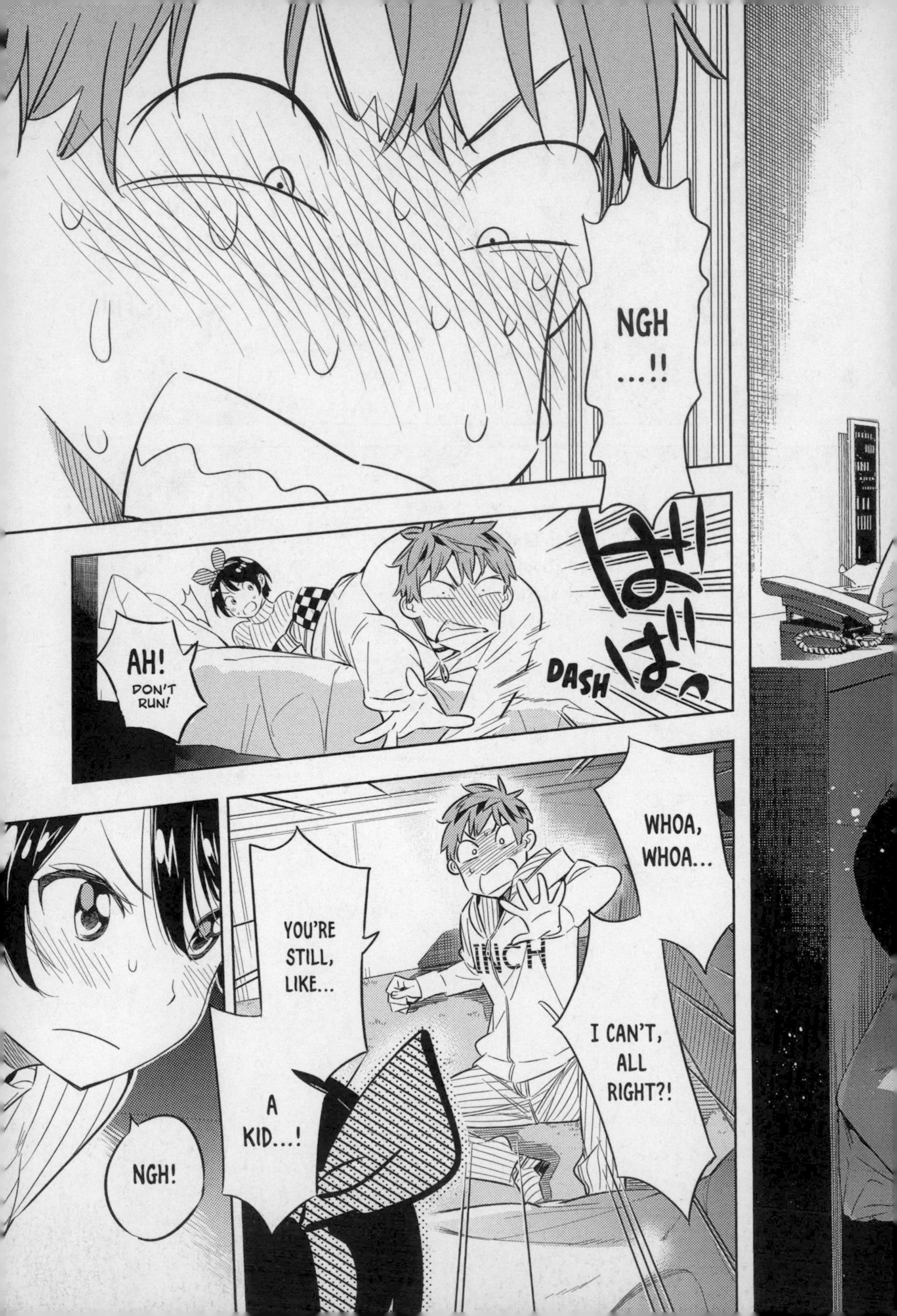
NGH ...!!
ばばっ
DASH
AH! DON'T RUN!
WHOA, WHOA...
I CAN'T, ALL RIGHT?!
YOU'RE STILL, LIKE...
A KID...!
NGH!

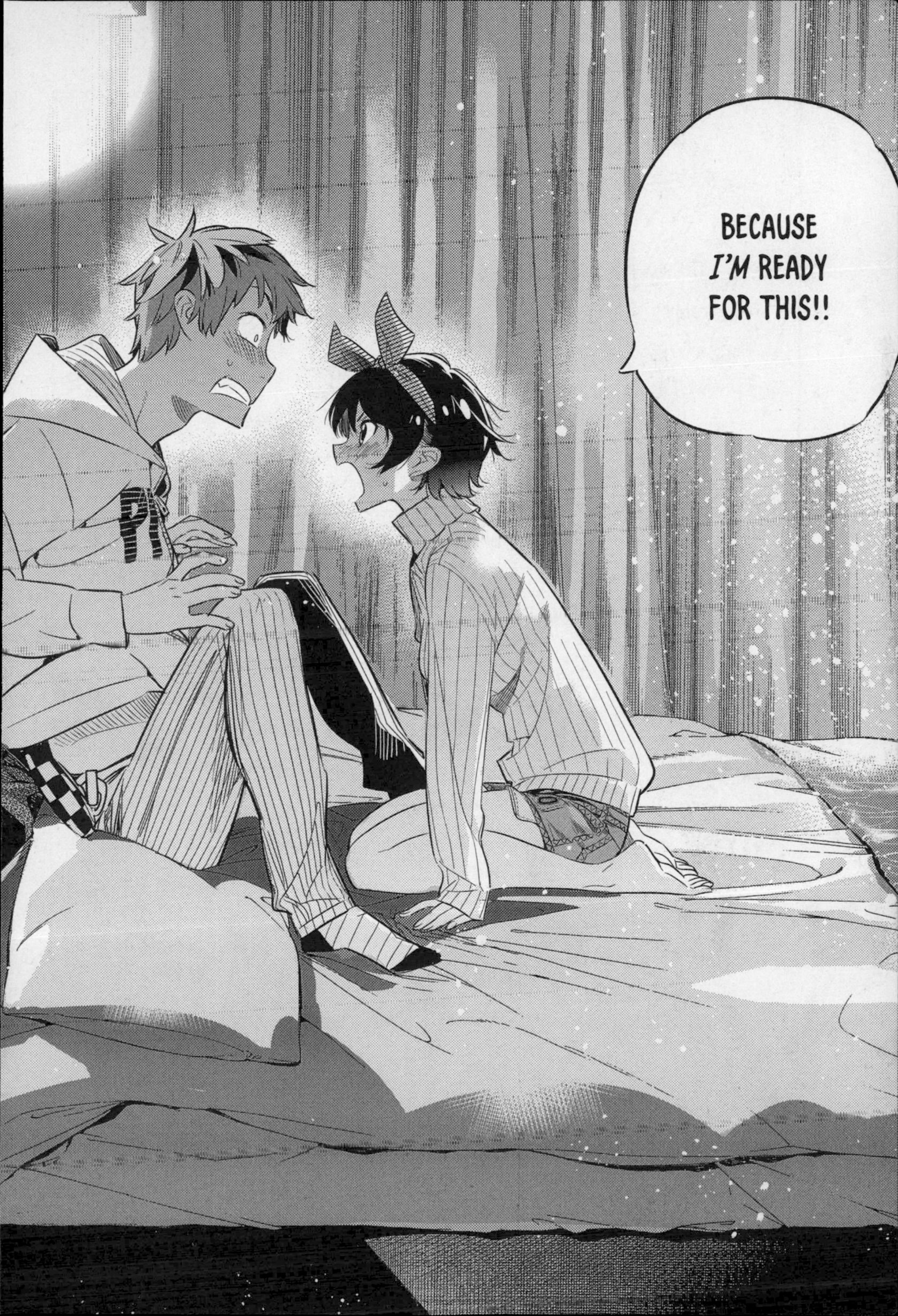
BECAUSE *I'M* READY FOR THIS!!

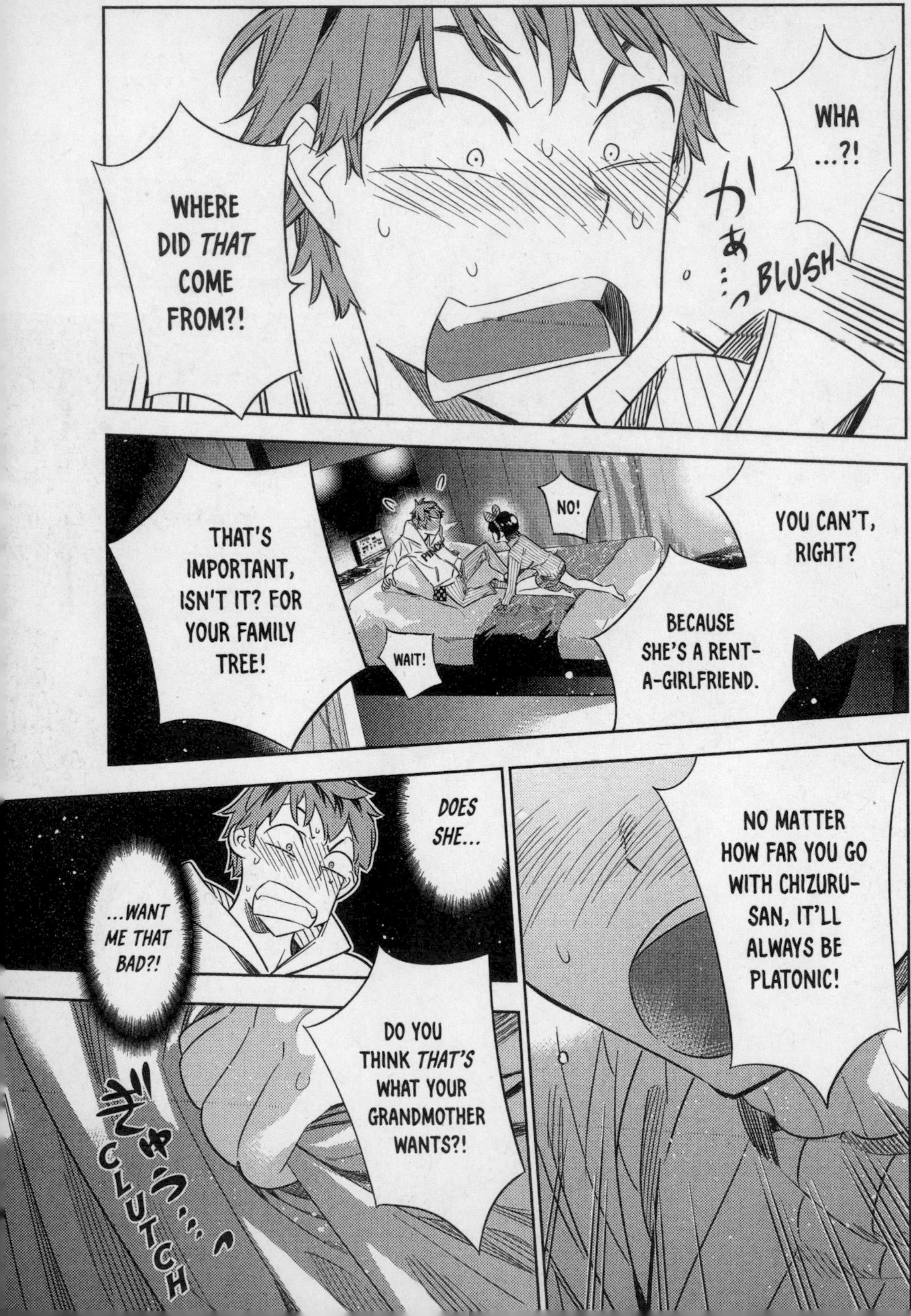
WHA ...?!
かぁ…っ
BLUSH
WHERE DID THAT COME FROM?!
YOU CAN'T, RIGHT?
NO!
BECAUSE SHE'S A RENT-A-GIRLFRIEND.
PINCH
THAT'S IMPORTANT, ISN'T IT? FOR YOUR FAMILY TREE!
WAIT!
NO MATTER HOW FAR YOU GO WITH CHIZURU-SAN, IT'LL ALWAYS BE PLATONIC!
DOES SHE...
...WANT ME THAT BAD?!
DO YOU THINK THAT'S WHAT YOUR GRANDMOTHER WANTS?!
ぎゅう…
CLUTCH

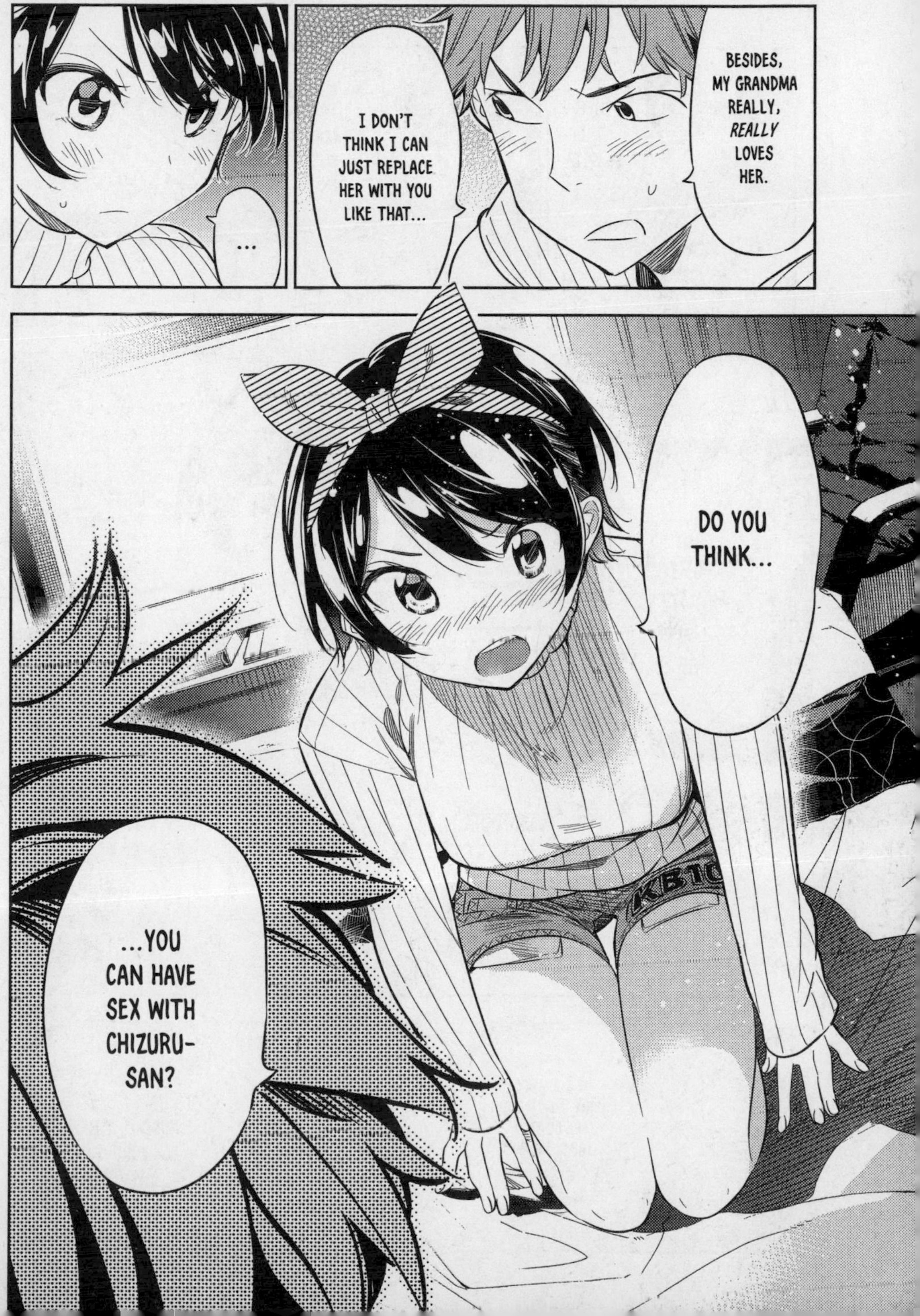
BESIDES, MY GRANDMA REALLY, *REALLY* LOVES HER.
I DON'T THINK I CAN JUST REPLACE HER WITH YOU LIKE THAT...
...
DO YOU THINK...
...YOU CAN HAVE SEX WITH CHIZURU-SAN?

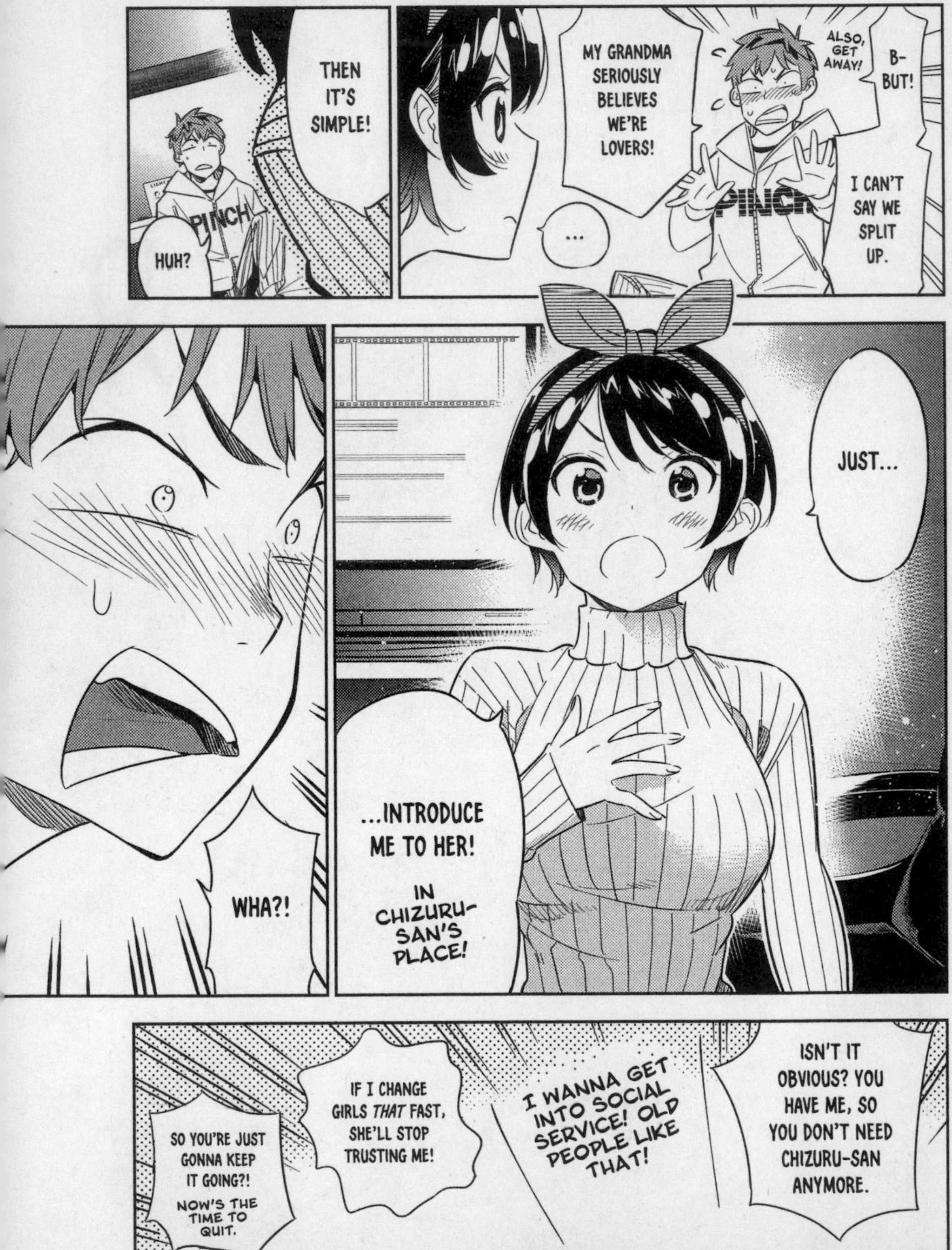
B-BUT!
ALSO, GET AWAY!
I CAN'T SAY WE SPLIT UP.
MY GRANDMA SERIOUSLY BELIEVES WE'RE LOVERS!
...
THEN IT'S SIMPLE!
HUH?
JUST...
...INTRODUCE ME TO HER!
IN CHIZURU-SAN'S PLACE!
WHA?!
ISN'T IT OBVIOUS? YOU HAVE ME, SO YOU DON'T NEED CHIZURU-SAN ANYMORE.
I WANNA GET INTO SOCIAL SERVICE! OLD PEOPLE LIKE THAT!
IF I CHANGE GIRLS *THAT* FAST, SHE'LL STOP TRUSTING ME!
SO YOU'RE JUST GONNA KEEP IT GOING?!
NOW'S THE TIME TO QUIT.

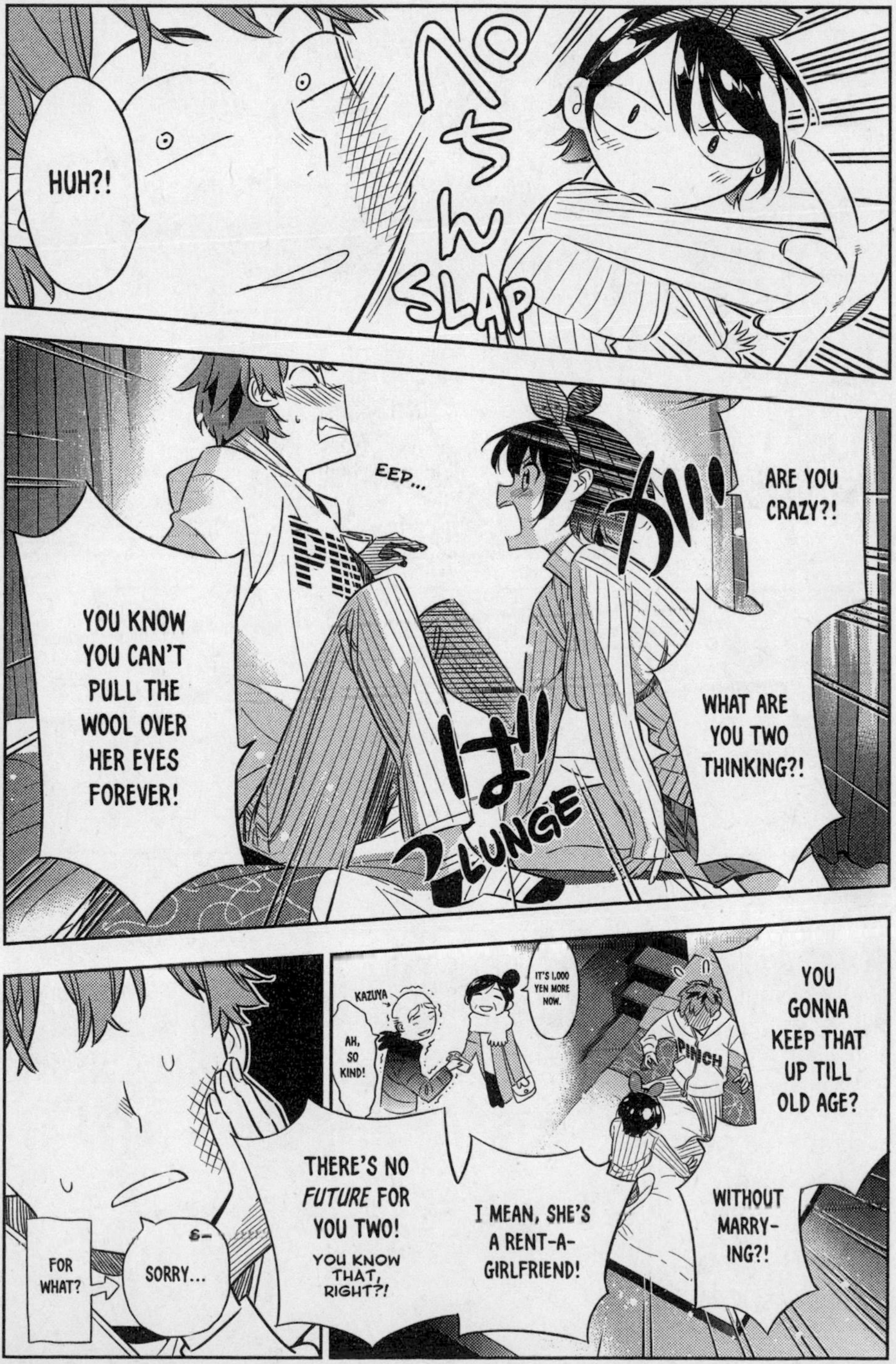
へちん
SLAP
HUH?!
ARE YOU CRAZY?!
EEP...
WHAT ARE YOU TWO THINKING?!
ばっ
LUNGE
YOU KNOW YOU CAN'T PULL THE WOOL OVER HER EYES FOREVER!
YOU GONNA KEEP THAT UP TILL OLD AGE?
WITHOUT MARRY-ING?!
I MEAN, SHE'S A RENT-A-GIRLFRIEND!
IT'S 1,000 YEN MORE NOW.
KAZUYA
AH, SO KIND!
THERE'S NO *FUTURE* FOR YOU TWO!
YOU KNOW THAT, RIGHT?!
S-
SORRY...
FOR WHAT?

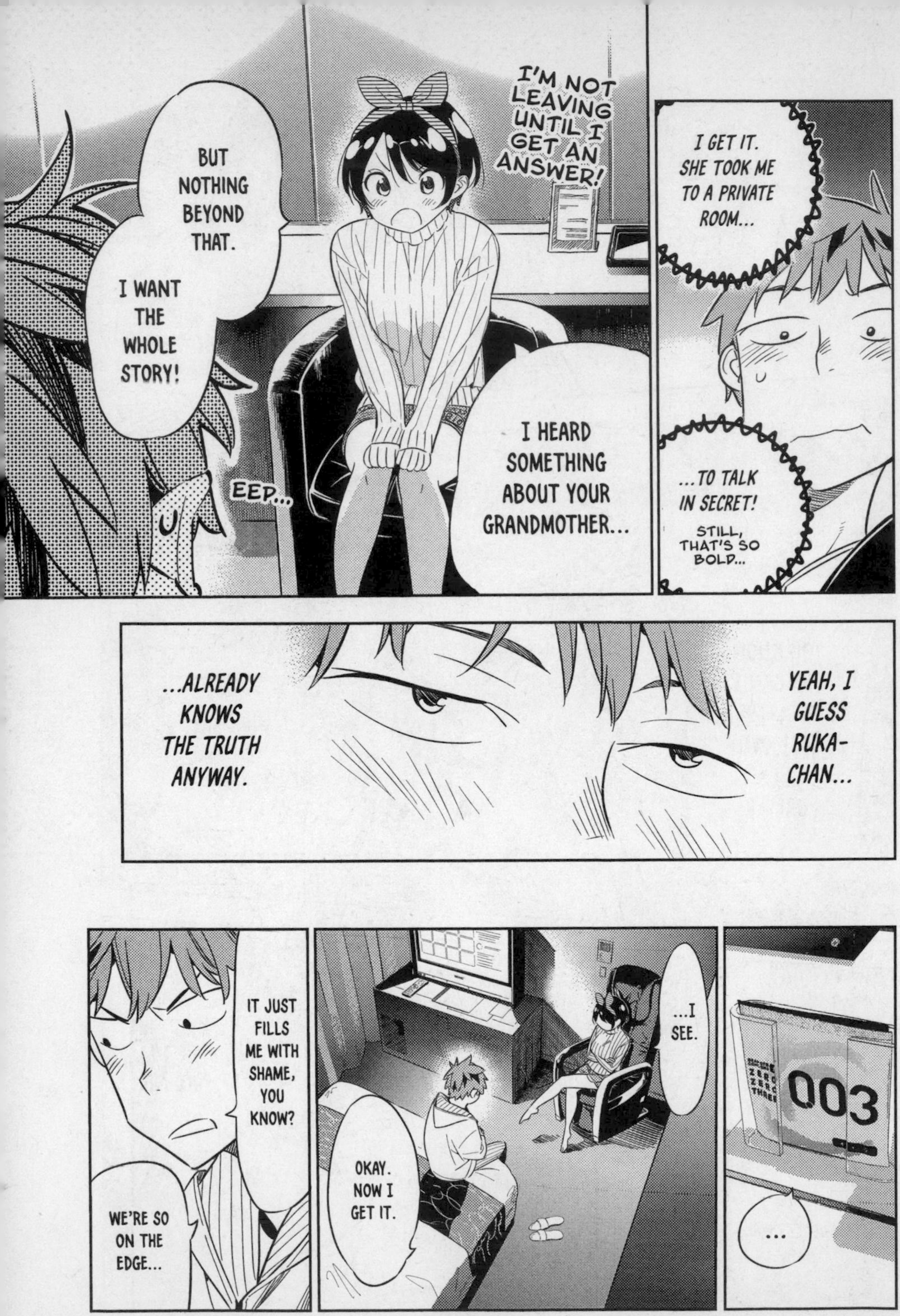
I GET IT. SHE TOOK ME TO A PRIVATE ROOM...
...TO TALK IN SECRET!
STILL, THAT'S SO BOLD...
I'M NOT LEAVING UNTIL I GET AN ANSWER!
I HEARD SOMETHING ABOUT YOUR GRANDMOTHER...
BUT NOTHING BEYOND THAT.
I WANT THE WHOLE STORY!
EEP...
YEAH, I GUESS RUKA-CHAN...
...ALREADY KNOWS THE TRUTH ANYWAY.
003
...
...I SEE.
OKAY. NOW I GET IT.
IT JUST FILLS ME WITH SHAME, YOU KNOW?
WE'RE SO ON THE EDGE...

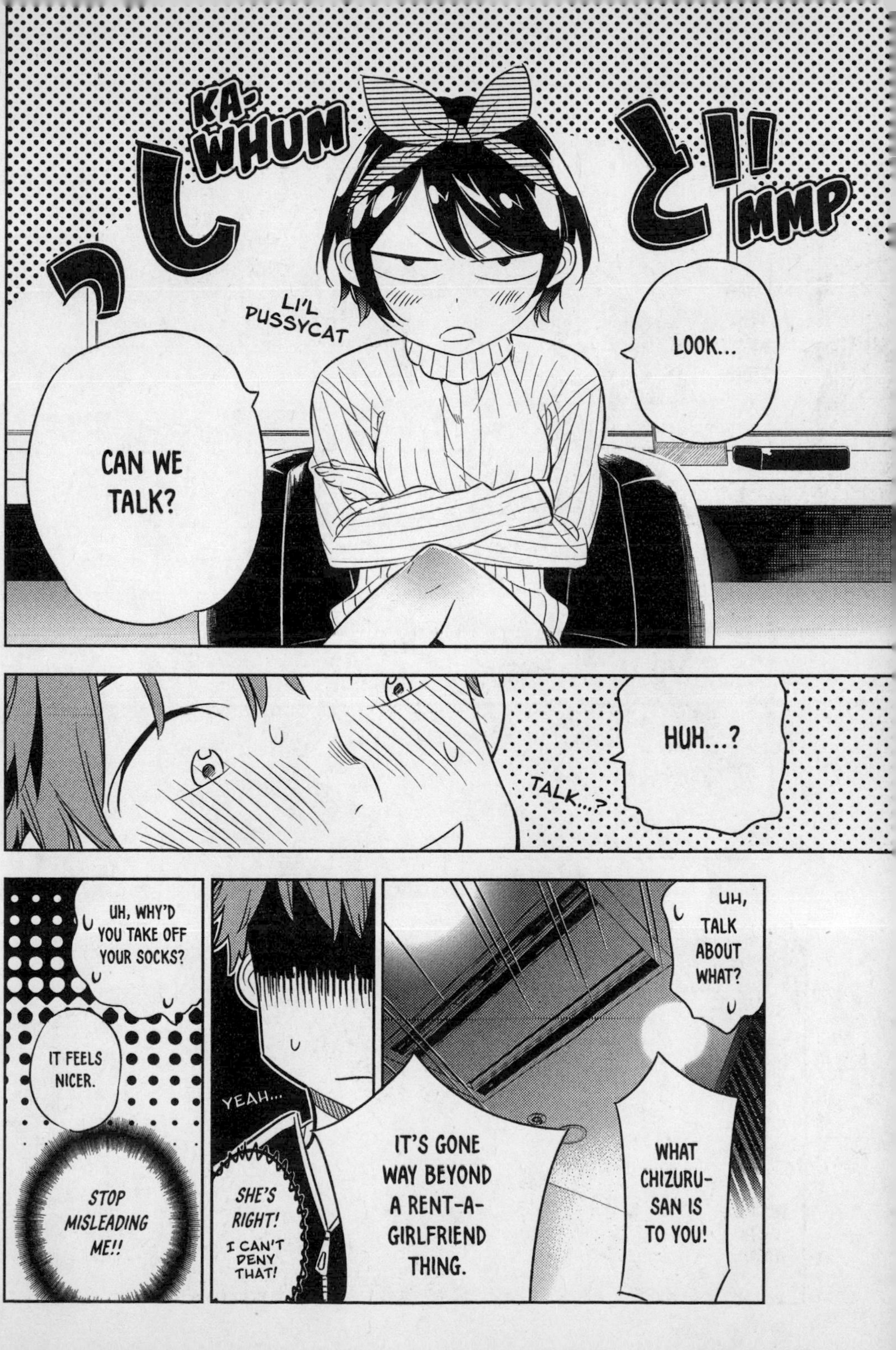
KA-WHUM
MMP
LOOK...
LI'L PUSSYCAT
CAN WE TALK?
HUH...?
TALK...?
UH, TALK ABOUT WHAT?
WHAT CHIZURU-SAN IS TO YOU!
IT'S GONE WAY BEYOND A RENT-A-GIRLFRIEND THING.
YEAH...
SHE'S RIGHT!
I CAN'T DENY THAT!
UH, WHY'D YOU TAKE OFF YOUR SOCKS?
IT FEELS NICER.
STOP MISLEADING ME!!

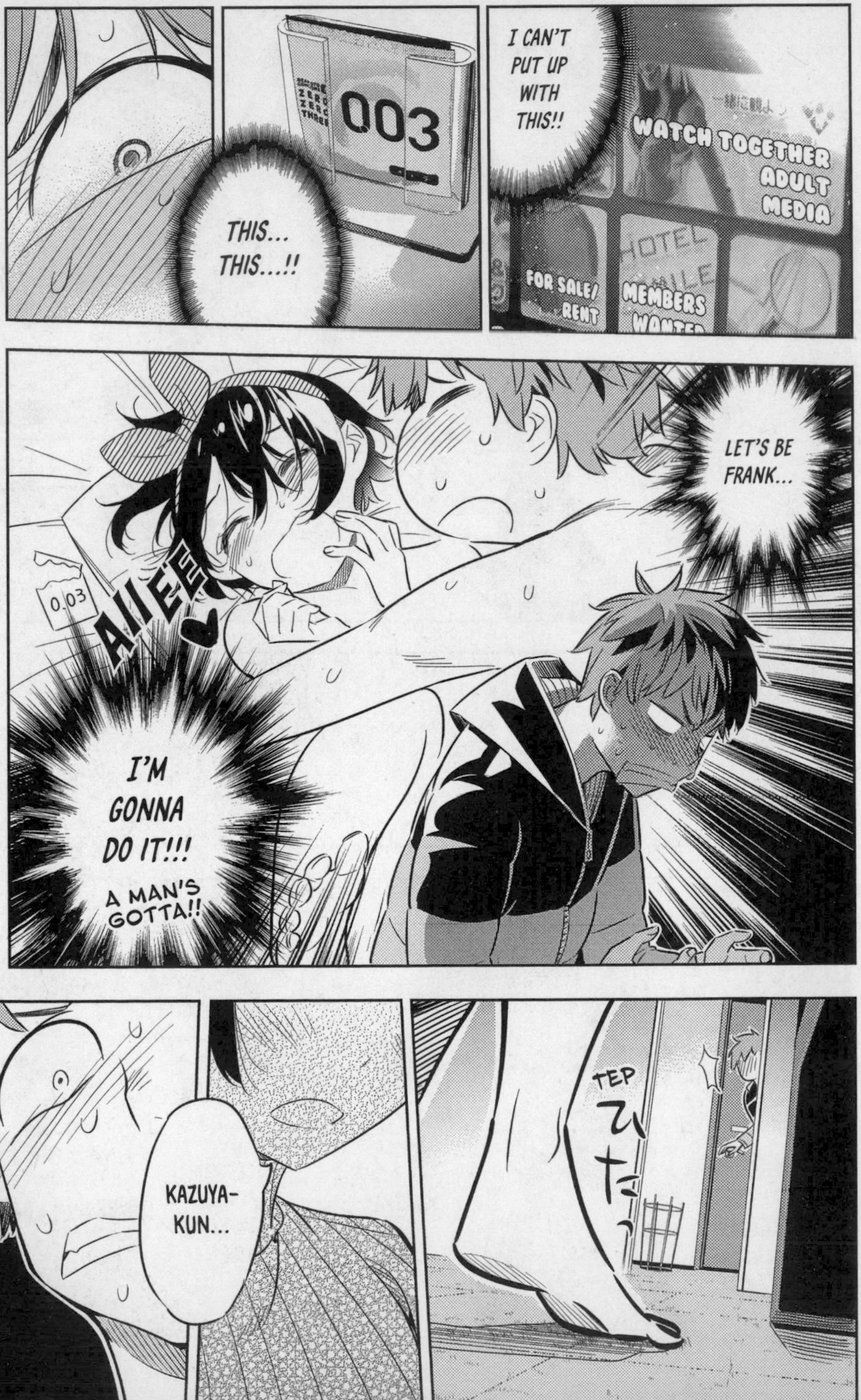
I CAN'T PUT UP WITH THIS!!
WATCH TOGETHER ADULT MEDIA
FOR SALE/ RENT
MEMBERS WANTED
003
THIS... THIS...!!
LET'S BE FRANK...
0.03
AIIEE
I'M GONNA DO IT!!!
A MAN'S GOTTA!!
TEP
ひたっ
KAZUYA-KUN...

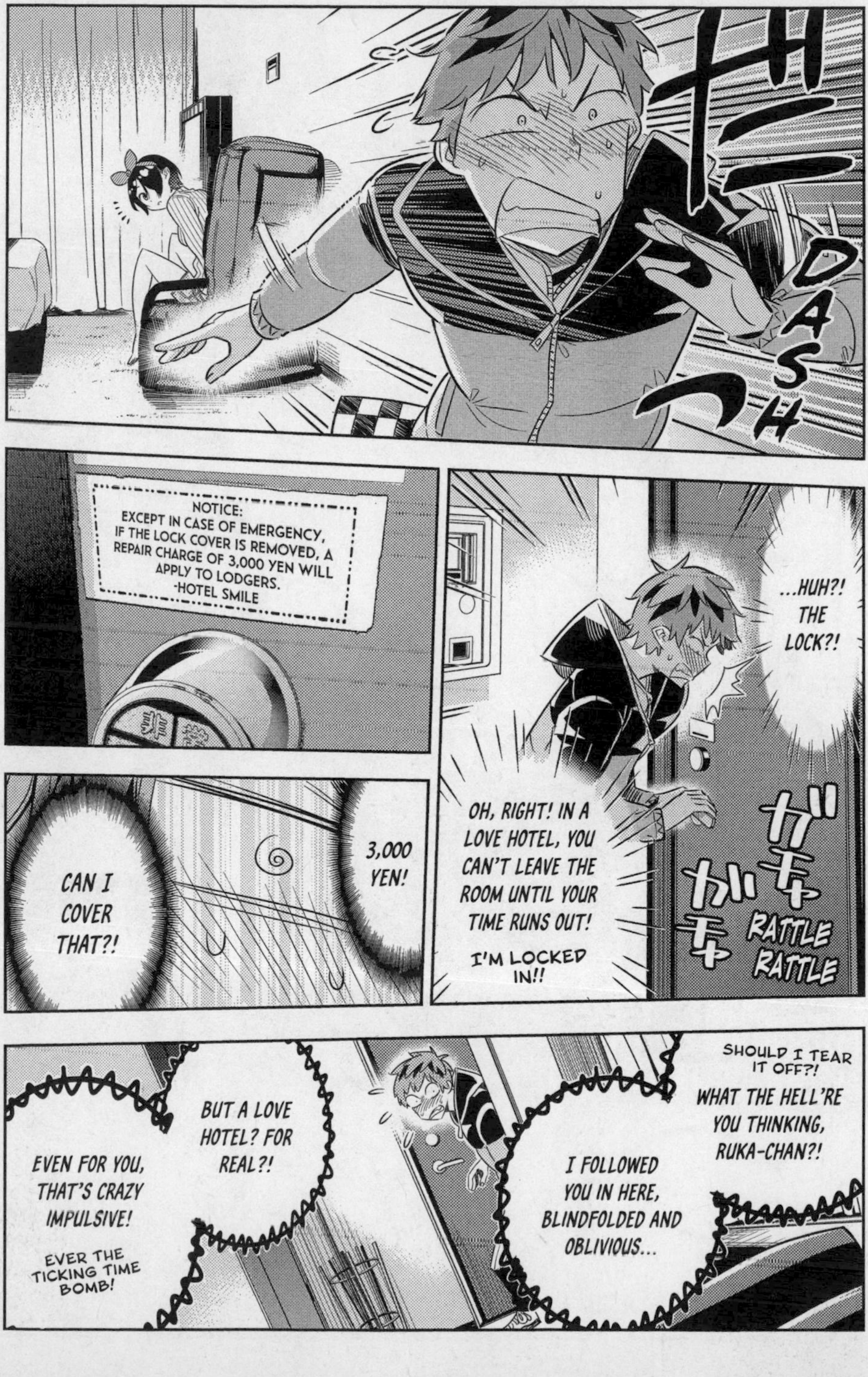
DASH
...HUH?! THE LOCK?!
OH, RIGHT! IN A LOVE HOTEL, YOU CAN'T LEAVE THE ROOM UNTIL YOUR TIME RUNS OUT!
I'M LOCKED IN!!
RATTLE RATTLE
NOTICE: EXCEPT IN CASE OF EMERGENCY, IF THE LOCK COVER IS REMOVED, A REPAIR CHARGE OF 3,000 YEN WILL APPLY TO LODGERS. -HOTEL SMILE
3,000 YEN!
CAN I COVER THAT?!
SHOULD I TEAR IT OFF?!
WHAT THE HELL'RE YOU THINKING, RUKA-CHAN?!
I FOLLOWED YOU IN HERE, BLINDFOLDED AND OBLIVIOUS...
BUT A LOVE HOTEL? FOR REAL?!
EVEN FOR YOU, THAT'S CRAZY IMPULSIVE!
EVER THE TICKING TIME BOMB!

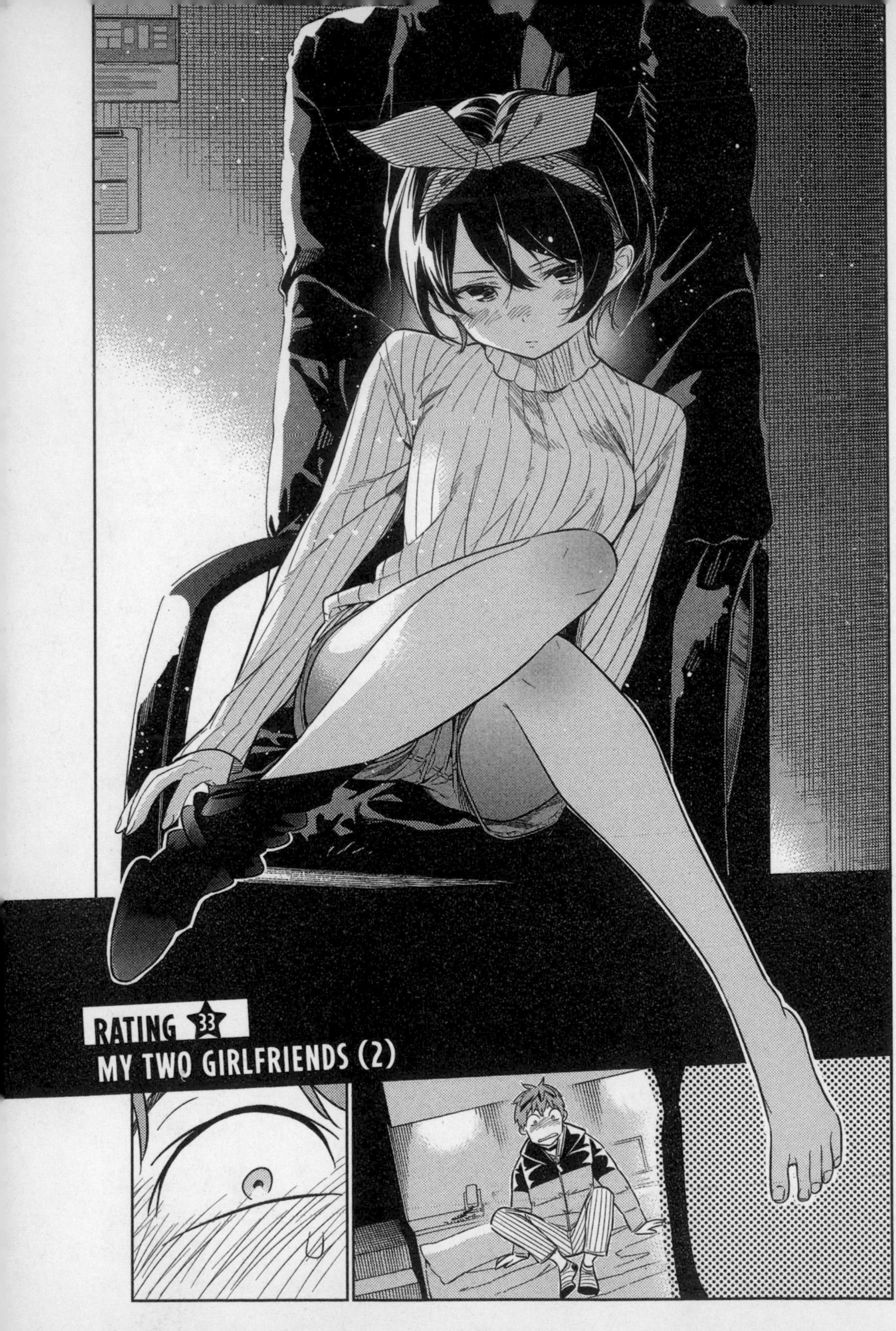
RATING 33
MY TWO GIRLFRIENDS (2)